COMBAT TEAM

The Captains' War: An Interactive Exercise in
Company-Level Command in Battle

John F. Antal

★
PRESIDIO

This book is dedicated to the tankers, infantrymen, artillerymen, engineers,
medics, mechanics, administrators, and supporters of the Dragon Force,
TF 2-72 Armor, 2d Infantry Division, Camp Casey, Korea
You help keep the peace!
Dragon Force! Second to none!

Copyright © 1998 John F. Antal

Published by Presidio Press
505 B San Marin Drive, Suite 300
Novato, CA 94945-1340

Library of Congress Cataloging-in-Publication Data

Antal, John F., 1955–
    Combat team : the captains' war : an interactive exercise in company-level command in battle / John F. Antal.
            p.   cm.
    ISBN 0-89141-635-8
    1. War games. 2. Command of troops. I. Title.
    U310.A5724   1998
    355.4'8—dc21   98-9324
                                                        CIP

Printed in the United States of America

Contents

Acknowledgments

Writing a book is a difficult undertaking; writing an interactive fiction is particularly challenging. This book could not have been written without the help of many people who deserve to be mentioned. First, special thanks to Lt. Gen. Tommy Franks for taking time out of his demanding schedule to write the foreword to this book. Great thanks to Capt. Ken Webb and S.Sgt. Steve Krivitsky for reviewing the manuscript and playing devil's advocate with the sections. Next a great debt of gratitude to Bob Kane, Richard Kane, and E. J. McCarthy of Presidio Press for their encouragement, insight, and patience.

Most importantly, I want to thank my darling wife, Uncha, for her love, patience, and inspiration. Only with her help and constant encouragement was this effort possible. Last but not least, thanks to my parents, Mr. John L. Antal and Dr. Francis Antal, for giving me the opportunity to learn how to make decisions and the chance to lead.

Foreword

Everything in war is very simple, but the simplest thing is difficult. The difficulties accumulate and end by producing a kind of friction that is inconceivable unless one has experienced war.

—Carl von Clausewitz

The peace today is still threatened by war and rumors of war. Warfare, therefore, is still required study if we are to learn how to avoid conflict and master conflict termination. Lieutenant Colonel John Antal's latest book, *Combat Team*, provides vivid insights to the company level—the level where war is personal—the level where survival or ruin, victory or defeat depend on the skill, determination, and luck of the leader. With this in mind, *Combat Team* should be read by those who wish to know what it means to be a leader in combat where there is no "honorable mention" for second place.

There is just one definition of winning in war—to accomplish the mission in minimum time and at least cost to soldiers. Battle command—the art of battle decision making, leading, and motivating soldiers and their organizations into action to win in combat—begins with the training of leaders. Trained leaders, ready to take decisions, and exploit opportunities as they arise, are fundamental to success on the field of battle.

In war, a leader must arrive at a decision and devise a plan of action in minimum time. As the nature of war evolves in the next century, and as reaction time in combat continues to narrow due to advances in weaponry, competent and rapid decision making becomes a priority task. We must ensure that our speed of decision making overmatches that of our potential enemies.

Today, war is too important to be prosecuted by the unprepared. Leaders must be capable of visualizing the current state and desired future states and then deciding how to get from one to the other at least cost to the force. They must make their decisions rapidly, in the face of apparently overwhelming friction, and they must decide correctly.

Foreword

Military education is more than the application of checklists, the learning of skills or the acquisition of facts. To be thoroughly grounded in the art of war, leaders must practice decision making under stress. Friction is the medium of combat. Hundreds of distracters and impediments impact simultaneously on the junior leader during combat operations. Our leaders must be brought face-to-face with this reality early in their training. The nurturing of the ability to think under time pressure, in the face of friction must be a fundamental objective of training in decision making.

Lieutenant Colonel John Antal's *Combat Team* is an excellent exercise in small unit tactics and decision making. The reader is thrust into challenging situations which demand an immediate answer by the combat commander. Hesitation results in defeat. Decisive action is required. This book sets the basis for discussions that will enhance the planning, preparation, and execution of tactical operations because it forces the reader to think and act.

Combat Team is a remarkable work. Educational and entertaining, it brings to life the world of the soldier and soldier-leader who go in harm's way. We owe a debt of gratitude to John Antal and to all soldiers who "go there."

TOMMY R. FRANKS
Lieutenant General, U.S. Army

Introduction

Potential adversaries may recognize U.S. shortcomings and devise asymmetrical responses that negate U.S. technological superiority. Thus the United States must retain flexible and adaptive forces that can be effective across the range of military operations.
—Maj. Gen. Joseph Garrett, November 1996

The Next War

What if the unthinkable happened and a war erupted in Northeast Asia? Do you have what it takes to lead American soldiers in battle?

In *Combat Team* you are an active participant in a future battle. In this book you are in command. Unlike the usual novel, this book is an interactive fiction—a form of tactical decision game. *Combat Team* offers the reader the opportunity to experience the complexities of modern, armored combat and make decisions to determine the outcome of the battle. You are the commander of Team Steel. You decide the fate of the U.S. Army tankers, mechanized infantrymen, and engineers as you combat a determined and fanatical enemy in a desperate battle in Northeast Asia.

To military readers, the book offers an opportunity to enhance their military education. To the general reader, it offers a unique insight into the difficult and deadly world of the combat soldier. This book will challenge your leadership skill and decision-making abilities; it will test your tactical savvy. Your skill, tactical knowledge, and luck will determine victory or defeat, life or death. You do not need military experience to win, but the more you understand military operations, the more informed your decision making will be. A good place to start is to read my books *Armor Attacks* (Presidio Press, 1991) and *Infantry Combat* (Presidio Press, 1995).

The Scenario

Fearing the imminent collapse of their political, social, and economic structures, a renegade Northeast Asian country launched a surprise attack on its neighbor—a country where U.S. forces are de-

Introduction

ployed to protect the peace. The U.S. forces in-country were bloodied in the enemy's surprise attack and are regrouping to counterattack. America's usual trump card—airpower—is temporarily negated by enemy commando attacks, improved enemy air defense weapon systems, and extremely bad weather. Significant U.S. ground reinforcements will take weeks to arrive.

The enemy has planned a short-war campaign. Having created a window of vulnerability, he is driving hard to end the war quickly and force a negotiated settlement on his terms. He intends to grab as much territory as possible, threaten to use weapons of mass destruction, and demand a cease-fire. From a position of strength he intends to negotiate the withdrawal of U.S. forces and arrange a power sharing situation with the country he has invaded.

To accomplish his goals the enemy needs one big victory against the United States—a battle where he can clearly be seen as having defeated U.S. forces in the field.

The Challenge

You are Capt. Thomas Nathan Casey, a twenty-nine-year-old tank officer who has just graduated from the Armor Officer Advanced Course at Fort Knox, Kentucky. You arrived in-country just before the war started. Now you are trying to get to your unit.

Leadership in tough situations is never easy. In *Combat Team* you will immediately be thrown into a desperate leadership situation. It won't be fair. You will have to make decisions without having a full picture of the situation—as you would in real life. You will lead soldiers who are thinking human beings, not robots. Men who are wet, cold, hungry, tired, and fearing death are in an emotional vice grip. Tensions are exacerbated in such situations. Good leadership, sound decision making, a deep understanding of human nature, and trust will be demanded if you expect to win.

Scrambled Text

Combat Team is a scrambled text. At the end of each section you will be required to make a decision. You will jump from one section to the next, as directed by your choice of options or your luck. You will hop around the pages of this book, following the path of your decisions. The sections are scrambled on purpose. Decision making in the confused dynamic of modern combat is never linear. You may, however, find it useful to list the sections in the order that you choose them to assist in the exploration of alternate paths to the decisions offered in the book.

If in some scenario you feel that you have been tricked into making a wrong decision, don't feel like the lone ranger; that's what it's like to be a leader. You have to assess the situation, use the resources at hand, and take a decision. Remember, as Gen. George S. Patton was fond of saying, "Don't take counsel of your fears."

No decision maker makes the best decisions every time. Good combat commanders *take* decisions, adapt, improvise, fight through, and overcome. Each decision you make will influence the future course of the battle. Chance and the friction of war will also play their part against you. If you select a section where you are eventually killed or captured, you start over from previous decision points and can use the knowledge of your past mistakes to earn victory.

Combat Team has many endings that offer many degrees of success or failure. Several paths lead to marginal victories. Only one path leads to decisive victory. Choose well!

Are You Ready?
In this tactical decision game you will have an opportunity to test your tactical prowess and leadership. Your modern, combined-arms company team—Team Steel—will be given a desperate mission. Victory will require agile thinking and effective leadership. Are you prepared to use the technological and training overmatch of U.S. forces to their maximum advantage in the rugged, mountainous terrain?

Your challenge is to survive and accomplish your mission. What tactics, techniques, and procedures will you apply to conduct decisive tactical operations in restricted terrain?

You are now in a shooting war. You are outnumbered. You will have to make up for your lack of numbers and firepower through superior leadership and expert tactical decision making. Besides, if this situation was easy, then the army wouldn't need captains.

Time is of the essence. What are you waiting for? Don't just stand there—get going!

Map Symbols - U.S. Forces
Team Steel
Leaders, their Vehicles and Radio Call Signs

 Company Team Commander - M1A2
(Capt. Tom Casey, Steel Six)

 Company Team XO - M1A2
(First Lieutenant Stonevitch, Steel Five)

 Fire Support Team - FIST-V
(Second Lieutenant Keeley, Steel Guns)

1 **M1 A2 Tank Platoon - 1st Platoon**
(Second Lieutenant Andrews, Red One)

2 **M1 A2 Tank Platoon - 2d Platoon**
(Sergeant First Class Scott, White One)

3 **M2 Bradley Platoon - 3d Platoon**
(Second Lieutenant McDaniel, Blue One)

4 **M2 Bradley Platoon - 4th Platoon**
(Second Lieutenant Pender, Green One)

 Engineer Platoon - M113
(Sergeant First Class Tremain, Sapper One)

 Company Trains - M113
(First Sergeant Washington, Steel Seven)

 Rifle Company - (1-12th Infantry, Bayonet)

Map Symbols - Enemy Forces

 T-62 Tank Platoon

 T-72 Tank Company

 VTT-323 Mechanized Infantry Company

 Rifle Company

 Self-Propelled Artillery Battery

 S-300 Air Defense System

 ZSU 23-4 Self-Propelled Antiaircraft System

 Antitank Minefield

RADIO CALL SIGNS

STEEL SIX — Captain Casey [Commander] (M1A2 - *Cossack*)

STEEL FIVE — 1st Lieutenant Stonevitch [XO] (M1A2 - *Crom*)

STEEL SEVEN — 1SG Washington (M113)

STEEL ADA — SSG Sellers [Bradley Stinger Fighting Vehicle Commander]

STEEL GUNS — 2LT Keeley (FIST-V)

SAPPER ONE — SFC Tremain [Engineer Platoon]

RED ONE — 2d LT Andrews [1st Platoon (M1A2)]

WHITE ONE — SFC Scott [2d Platoon (M1A2)]

BLUE ONE — 2LT McDaniel [3d Platoon (M2)]

GREEN ONE — 2LT Pender [4th Platoon (M2)]

Wolverine One — SGT Jacobs [Heavy Assault Bridge Section Leader]

[Note: Vehicles in each platoon are numbered as follows: Blue One = Platoon Leader / Blue Two / Blue Three / Blue Four = Platoon Sergeant]

Team Steel
Order of Battle

 Commander and
XO 2 M1A2s

 1st Platoon
4 M1A2s

 4 engineer
squads

 2d Platoon
4 M1A2s

 1 M9 armored
combat engineer
vehicle

 3d Platoon
4 M2A2s

 1 combat
engineer
vehicle

 4th Platoon
3 M2A2s

2 Wolverine heavy assault bridges

 1 Bradley
Stinger fighting
vehicle

 2 M113
ambulances

 1 fire support
team vehicle

 13 M113 armored
personnel carriers

 1 HEMMT
2500 gallon
fuel truck

 1 M88 tank
recovery
vehicle

Section I

The rain started again.

Cold, wet, and tired, the captain wished for just one hour of sleep in a warm bed.

Hell, he thought. I'd be happy just to crawl into a corner of my Humvee and pull a poncho over my head.

He knew that this wish was impossible. America was at war again—a deadly, desperate war that had surprised everyone except the fanatical aggressor. A thin green line of American soldiers was preparing to turn the tide of battle. Right now, the enemy had the initiative. The captain knew that the U.S. Army would change that. There would be time for rest after the fighting was over.

The Humvee bounced slowly across the narrow mountain road, second in a column of four vehicles. Two big green five-ton trucks followed closely behind in a single-file column. The second truck brandished a .50-caliber machine gun, manned by a drenched soldier standing in the small circular hole in the roof of the truck's cab.

The rain plopped in misty droplets against the Humvee's mud-splashed windshield. The windshield wipers kept time in a slow, dull cadence, adding to the noise of the high-pitched hum of the vehicle's engine. The mesmerizing effect of the windshield wipers made the captain drowsy. Two hours ago the rain had poured down in sheets. Now at least it was only falling at a drizzle. He fought off the urge to close his eyes.

To his left, Corporal Kim stood grim-faced in the open hatch of the hard-topped Humvee manning the MK19 (Mark 19) automatic grenade launcher. Water streamed down his green camouflage Gor-tex pants and jacket into the cab of the truck. Everything was wet. There was no escaping the rain, even inside the cab. The roof leaked like a ship's badly battened cabin in a squall.

Captain Thomas Nathan Casey leaned over to look up at the gunner manning the grenade launcher and tugged at his poncho.

"Okay, sir," Corporal Kim replied, looking down between the grenade launcher and the roof of the cab. "Ready for anything."

Casey nodded, then quietly returned his gaze to the winding mountain road. The vehicle leading the column was a military police Humvee. All columns, no matter how small, were being escorted. Casey was in the second vehicle in line. His M-16 rifle was clamped to the right side of the dashboard.

"God, what I wouldn't give for a sunny sky," the driver said. "I've never seen so much rain."

The lead vehicle turned around a sharp bend in the road. Without knowing why, Casey suddenly felt uneasy. He reached for his rifle and unclasped the weapon from its holder. "Sometimes the rain lasts for two to three weeks," he announced as he placed the M-16 between his legs. "Don't worry, you'll get used to it."

The driver, Pvt. Jimmy O'Sullivan, shook his head. "No, sir. Give me sunny California any day."

Wham! The ground quaked as a terrible explosion erupted directly in front of the lead vehicle. Rocks and dirt burst up from the two-lane, concrete road in a shower of smoke and flame. The lead Humvee flipped over on its roof and smashed against the rocks on the right side of the route.

"Ambush!" O'Sullivan cried as he slammed on the brakes.

The Humvee skidded on the rain-soaked pavement. Casey braced himself as the vehicle slid, leaning with the motion of the truck against the right side door.

The deadly efficient rattle of a machine gun reverberated in the hills. Bullets ripped into the exposed belly of the overturned vehicle.

The enemy is on the ridge to the right, Casey thought, even though he couldn't see them. Casey felt the nervous quickening of his blood as the adrenaline of fear shot through his body. Events unfolded in slow motion as he moved. He heard Kim curse as the corporal pulled back the charging handle of his MK19 automatic grenade launcher and fired a burst of grenades into the wood line.

There was no room to maneuver. Casey's mind raced to find an answer to the disaster cascading before him. He quickly searched the road. It was bordered by high, rocky ground to the right and a sheer dropoff to the left.

"Sir, I see them. They're up there, to our right," Kim shouted, looking down at the captain.

"Keep firing," Casey bellowed as he kicked open the door of the Humvee and shot a burst of 5.56mm rounds toward the wood line.

Casey knew that he had to act quickly if they were going to survive. *Thunk! Thunk! Thunk!* The grenade launcher hurtled a string of 40mm grenades toward the ridge. Casey watched as the grenades slowly arced toward the wood line. A string of explosions detonated along the hill.

Casey shot a glance at the upside-down Humvee. A wounded MP staggered from the wreckage of the overturned vehicle. At the same time an enemy machine gun targeted the wounded American. In a frenzy of bullets, the MP fell, face down, in the muddy road.

Casey saw the flash of the enemy light machine gun and fired the rest of his magazine in the direction of the fire. Out of ammunition, he crouched next to the open door of the Humvee and quickly reloaded. Glancing to the right, he saw a group of soldiers cringing beside the closest five-ton truck. The soldiers seemed stunned. None of them was firing at the enemy.

Casey knew that in an ambush every gun must be turned on the ambushers. Furious at his soldiers' lack of action, he screamed: "Fire at that goddamned ridge!"

Thunk! Thunk! Thunk! Casey's gunner was the only one shooting. Kim scattered the grenades in a wild pattern all over the hillside. Few of the rounds were landing close to the enemy.

Angry rounds from a machine gun on the hill shot back, kicking up spires of water and mud in the road directly in front of Casey's Humvee. With a loud, splintering sound, bullets destroyed the supposedly bulletproof windshield and riddled the top of the Humvee.

Casey ducked to the ground as the windshield shattered, the bullets missing him by inches. So far his luck was holding; he prayed that it would continue. Unfortunately, Kim wasn't as lucky. The corporal slumped in the top hatch. O'Sullivan, to Kim's left, flew back in his seat. A stream of thick blood covered the right shoulder of his Gortex jacket.

"I'm shot!" O'Sullivan screamed in shock.

Casey jumped back inside the Humvee. He had to get to the

grenade launcher. He pulled on Corporal Kim. A gooey red pulp lined Casey's hands as he struggled to bring Kim inside the protection of the Kevlar-lined cab. He placed the corporal on his back, then saw the bloody cavity where the soldier's face had been.

"Oh, my God," O'Sullivan screamed as he saw Kim's head. "They blew his fucking face off!"

Casey didn't answer. He quickly turned and moved into the hatch to man the grenade launcher. As he stood in the open hatch, the enemy machine gun targeted the Humvee in front of him. Bullets tore into the exposed undercarriage of the overturned vehicle, igniting the vehicle's fuel tank in a powerful explosion. Casey cringed as the shock wave swept over him. Thick black smoke blanketed the narrow mountain road.

Behind him Casey could hear the crack of half a dozen M-16 rifles. The enemy machine gun stopped for a moment.

Casey's grenade launcher steamed as the rain hit the hot barrel. He charged the handle but realized that the grenade launcher was out of ammunition. In a flash he ducked down and grabbed the loose end of a belt of 40mm ammunition. Bullets ricocheted off the rocks and peppered the top of the Humvee. Casey shot up into the hatch, frantically struggling with the wet bandolier. He popped open the feed tray of the grenade launcher, fumbled with the heavy ammunition, and loaded the 40mm grenade belt into the tray.

The enemy machine gun opened up again, firing long, deadly bursts. Then the fire suddenly dwindled. Casey heard a whistle blow and saw the enemy rise out of the trench, blazing away at the soldiers taking refuge behind a five-ton truck.

Standing in the opening of the Humvee, Casey charged the weapon, aimed at the attacking riflemen, and fired.

Thunk! Thunk! Thunk! The slow-flying grenades sliced through the air, arced through the thin branches of short, stubby trees, and plopped in front of the advancing enemy soldiers. Small puffs of black smoke dotted the hillside as the grenades exploded.

Thunk! Thunk! Thunk! The grenade launcher rocked the Humvee with the energy of each shot. The grenades plopped through the sparse vegetation, consuming the ridge where the enemy had been.

Casey stopped firing to save his last few rounds. The smoke

cleared as the rain picked up, and the captain searched for more targets. The enemy was no longer in sight. They have gone to ground, he thought. They must be waiting in the trench.

A strange silence engulfed the battlefield, interrupted only by the distinct crackling sound of the burning overturned Humvee and the ringing in his ears. The rain rolled down his face. Casey glowered at the ridge through the sights of the grenade launcher. "Sergeant Jacobs! You okay?"

"Roger, Captain!"

"Move up that hill and flank them. I'll cover you. Move now!"

"Wilco!" Jacobs yelled.

There was a pause. "Damnit, you heard the man," Jacobs cursed to the soldiers cowering in the ditch next to the truck. "Let's move!"

Thunk! Thunk! Thunk! Casey peppered the trench again with a quick burst of grenades. The 40mm high-explosive shells landed in a line right along the enemy's trench. Casey shot a quick glance at the body of an enemy soldier, cut in half by a grenade, as the corpse rolled down the hill and stopped a few feet away from Casey's Humvee.

Sergeant Jacobs and six soldiers quickly climbed the steep, rocky slope. Casey held his fire as Jacobs's men entered the right side of the trench. The grenade launcher's butterfly triggers felt slippery and wet in his hands. His hunter's eye scanned the ragged hillside for the enemy. Where were the bastards? How many were there? Did I get them all?

Casey aimed the MK19 at the smoking trench as tense seconds ticked by. A few short bursts of fire rang out as the Americans entered the trench line. Casey flinched but held his fire. A few more shots rang out. Then there was silence.

Casey strained to see what was happening. "Jacobs. Report!"

"We're okay, Captain." Casey saw the tall, thin figure of Sergeant Jacobs standing near the left end of the trench. "You got 'em all—all six of 'em."

Casey sighed in relief, glad to be alive. He scanned the hill, then yelled: "Check out the entire trench. Search them, disable their weapons, and let's get the hell out of here."

"Wilco, sir!" Jacobs yelled from the side of the hill.

The overturned Humvee smoldered. The wet air carried the acrid smell of cordite, flaming rubber, and smoke. The popping of bursting oil cans, the cracking of burning gear, and the ringing in his ears filled Casey's senses.

He looked at the bloody upper torso of the enemy soldier who had rolled down the hill. The man held a stick grenade in a death grip in his right hand. Casey suddenly realized how close he had come to death. If his aim had been off . . .

O'Sullivan moaned in pain.

"Hold on, Sully, I'm coming," Casey announced as he slithered past Kim's body. He checked the corporal's neck for a pulse. Kim was dead. The captain carefully pushed him to the backseat, then reached for O'Sullivan, who was slumped against the wheel. Casey gently pulled him back. Blood rushed from the back of O'Sullivan's shoulder.

Casey placed his hand over the exit wound, applying direct pressure to the hole. The driver jerked forward in pain.

"Damn! It feels like a hot poker is digging into my shoulder," O'Sullivan mumbled. He turned his head to the body of the man lying by his side. "Is Kim dead?"

"Yes," Casey said, nodding his head. "He's dead, but you're going to make it. Hang in there."

"Damnit, I should have seen it coming," O'Sullivan said.

With his left hand, Casey removed a first-aid dressing from the wounded man's suspender pouch. He bit open the green plastic package and pulled the bandage out of its wrapper, then he quickly removed his hand and surveyed the damage. The bullet had entered the top of the driver's right shoulder.

He's lucky, Casey thought as he placed the field dressing on the entrance wound. "This will probably get you sent home as soon as we get to battalion. Can you move your arm?"

"I don't know," O'Sullivan answered feebly. The young man tried to move, grimaced, and blinked in and out of consciousness. "I'm so tired."

"Sully, pay attention," Casey ordered firmly, trying to get the soldier to remain awake. "Press down on this dressing while I get some tape from the first-aid kit."

Corporal Kim lay sprawled out on the center section of the Humvee, his feet near the windshield and his head toward the rear. Blood was oozing onto the floor of the Humvee. O'Sullivan looked over at Kim's lifeless feet. His friend had been alive only a few seconds ago. O'Sullivan closed his eyes again and mumbled, "It's my fault. I should have moved quicker. It's my fault."

"No way, Sully," Casey replied slowly, pacing the words with a tempo that showed both compassion and strength. He'd seen enough death in the last week to understand that people die in war—and sometimes there's not much you can do about it. "It's nobody's fault. You did your best. We all die. At least Kim died trying to save us. He died a soldier."

Casey reached for the green first-aid box that was at the bottom of the left backseat. He popped open the box; extracted an additional dressing, a pair of scissors, and some white medical tape; and cut pieces long enough to hold down the driver's bandage. He rapidly placed a dressing on the entrance wound and used the tape to hold the dressing in place.

"Press down on this bandage, O'Sullivan. Keep the pressure up even though there's tape on it."

Private O'Sullivan nodded, wide eyed. He began to shiver.

He's going into shock, Casey thought.

Sergeant Jacobs stood by the open right door as Casey was bandaging his driver. "We searched the bodies, or at least what was left of them. We didn't find anything on 'em—no rank, patches, maps, or frequencies—nothing. They didn't even have a radio. Two of them were wearing allied army uniforms. They look like they're all special forces troops—well fed, in good shape, and well equipped. They're probably from a sniper battalion."

"I'm not taking any more chances," Casey answered, staring at the dead enemy soldier near his Humvee. "I don't care what they said at headquarters. This road isn't secure."

"What do you want to do?" Jacobs asked.

"I've been here before. I know this area. We'll stay off the main roads. I know a trail at the bottom of this hill that will lead us to the battalion assembly area."

Jacobs grunted in agreement. "I'll collect our dead and wounded and get ready to move out. We lost three MPs in the lead Hummer and your gunner. Your driver and one other man are the only wounded, but I think they'll both be okay."

Casey nodded. "Put the wounded and the rest of the replacements in the first truck. Put the dead in the second truck with the supplies. I don't want the replacements in the back of the truck with our dead."

"Roger, sir. I'll see to it."

"We'll have to hurry," Casey said, looking at his watch, "if we expect to make the assembly area before 0730."

"What happens at 0730?" the sergeant asked as he cradled his M-16 rifle against his side.

Casey unzipped the top of his Nomex uniform and extracted a brown envelope. He wagged it in front of the sergeant. "Important orders for battalion."

"Anything interesting?" the sergeant asked.

"Just your typical suicide mission," Casey said cynically, the strain of combat and the guilt of losing four men coloring his words. "I can only pray that the poor bastard who gets this mission will have better luck than we did today."

The sergeant nodded as if he understood. "By the way, sir, that was some damn good shooting. You saved our ass."

"Maybe . . . or you might say that I led us into an ambush."

Jacobs shook his head, a look of gratitude expressed on his sweat-stained, unshaven face. "We could all be dead right now, with the enemy rummaging through our pockets. Believe me, you saved us."

Casey ignored the compliment. Sometimes it was luck, and sometimes you made your own luck. He stared at the five-ton truck and pointed to the .50-caliber machine gun on the roof. "What happened to the machine gun on the five ton?"

"Jammed," Jacobs replied. "I'm serious, Captain. If you hadn't hit them with the grenade launcher, we'd all be dead right now. That's a fact."

Casey closed his eyes for a moment. He considered that Private Kim and the three soldiers in the lead Humvee might argue that point—if they could argue. Command. Responsibility. He felt the weight of the responsibility for the lives of the soldiers he led, and the ones he'd lost. It weighed on him like a heavy stone.

"Captain . . . you okay?"

"Yeah," Casey said with a shrug and a slight smile. "Get that damn gun working, Sergeant. Then let's get the hell out of here."

"Roger." Jacobs saluted—a quick, jerking gesture that ended the conversation and demanded no response from Casey—and then walked away. Casey turned back to look after his driver as Sergeant Jacobs bellowed out orders to the detachment of replacements.

A new driver, named Basilone, took O'Sullivan's place as Casey's driver. In a few minutes the column was ready to roll again.

Thunder crackled in the heavens. Casey flinched automatically as a bolt of lightning arced across the gloomy sky. It took a moment before the captain relaxed, thankful that the noise was thunder and not the crash of artillery fire. Casey gave Private Basilone the order, and the Humvee moved out with the two five-ton trucks following close behind.

A few seconds later the clouds opened up and the rain descended as if a giant was pouring water from a huge pitcher. As the Humvee bounced along the rocky trail, Casey unzipped the side pants pocket of his Nomex uniform and pulled out the orders he was carrying. Careful to shield the paper from the drops falling from the roof of the Humvee, he scanned the cover sheet stapled to the operations order that bore the division commander's signature. Pulling back the first page he examined the order with incredulous eyes. The mission of Task Force 2-72 was desperate: to plan, prepare, and execute a company team–sized raid deep into enemy territory.

Go to Section 112.

Section 2

In the development of a commander, nothing is more important than the outlook with which he approaches his problems.
                                                              —B. H. Liddell Hart

The Humvee pulled into the fog-covered assembly area. The rain had stopped. Casey's first impression of the area was that the unit had been hit hard during the first week of bloody, desperate combat. Broken armored vehicles, parked haphazardly among short fir trees, lay in various states of repair.

"Stop here," Casey ordered.

The Humvee halted inside the patchwork of tanks and armored personnel carriers. The leading five-ton truck stopped inches behind the Humvee. Sergeant Jacobs exited the right door of the truck's cab.

A wounded tank, sporting an ugly black scar on the flank of the hull, stood as grim testimony to the fierceness of the first week's struggle. A fist-sized hole marked the spot where an enemy tank round had punched through the M1A2's flank armor. Casey folded the map on his lap and exited the cab of his Humvee. He walked over to the damaged M1A2 and inspected the hole in its side.

Casey looked up from the M1A2 and spotted an M577 command post vehicle that was decorated with a red cross painted on its dark green side. He slung his M-16 rifle over his shoulder, pointing the barrel toward the ground. He walked through the mud to the back of the truck. Jacobs followed.

"Okay, Sergeant Jacobs. Dismount the men. The aid station's over there," Casey said, pointing to the M577.

"Wilco, sir," Jacobs replied. He turned and walked back to the truck, yelling, "Everybody out. Move the wounded to the medics. Wallace, you and Lewis help me with the second truck."

The soldiers inside the truck stood up, shifted to the opening, and started throwing duffel bags of personal gear out of the truck. A young private first class moved patiently to the end of the truck. He stood on the edge and slung a heavy duffel bag over the side, losing his balance at the same time. As the young man's feet touched the soggy ground, Casey's steady hand caught the private's shoulder, preventing him from landing on his face.

"Easy, soldier. We need every man we can get."

"Uh, yes, sir," the young soldier replied, looking at the captain with awe. "Thanks, sir."

The captain nodded as the hint of a smile flashed across his face. "Give O'Sullivan a hand with his IV bottle."

Two men helped Private O'Sullivan out of the back of the truck, gently easing the wounded man to the ground. O'Sullivan held his IV bottle with his left arm. The plastic tube trailed off to his right arm. One soldier helped hold the IV bag over O'Sullivan's head.

"You'll be okay, O'Sullivan," Casey said, quickly checking the soldier's wound. "Thanks for driving for me."

O'Sullivan nodded and managed a faint grin as the two soldiers helped him to the medics.

"Sir, I guess this is it," Sergeant Jacobs replied. "I just hope they assign me to your company."

"Well, don't wish for anything too hard, Jacobs. You just might get it. Take care of the men. I'll find out where they're supposed to go."

"Sir, I mean it. If you can get me in your company, I'd be honored to serve with you."

"What's your MOS?"

"I'm a 12B," Jacobs replied proudly. "My specialty is the new Wolverine heavy assault bridge. There's not a ditch, bridge, or stream that I can't span to keep the big boys rolling."

"A bridge layer, huh?" Casey smiled, the vision of a column of "big boys"—the engineer's nickname for tanks—crossing the twenty-four-meter armored bridge. "You handled yourself like a pro during the ambush. Thanks. If I ever get an engineer platoon assigned to my outfit, I'll ask for you."

"You do that, sir." Jacobs grinned. "I'll come a-runnin'."

"Captain Casey," a loud, emotionless voice shouted from near the front of the truck.

"That's me."

"I'm Sergeant Danlier. The CO sent me for you. Follow me and I'll take you to Major Cutter."

Casey grabbed his duffel bag and headed through the thick morning fog. He was surprised to hear that Major Cutter was in command. This information meant that the lieutenant colonel who commanded the tank battalion was either dead or wounded. Things must be pretty rough, Casey thought.

The sergeant led Casey through a maze of parked armored vehicles. Sleek-looking M1A2 Abrams tanks, deadly M2 Bradley fighting vehicles, and boxy M113 armored personnel carriers dotted the fallow rice paddies and the ragged wood line. Parts boxes, oil cans, ammo boxes, and crates of rations littered the spaces between the vehicles. The entire area was a beehive of activity—a unit licking its wounds and getting ready to go back to war.

The task force assembly area was nestled in a secluded valley. About 800 men and 230 vehicles were crammed into the tight, one-by two-kilometer tract of land. The mist-shrouded valley was surrounded by high, rocky mountains that protected the Americans from enemy observation and artillery fire.

The artillery fire during the first few days of the war had been hell; it caused most of the U.S. casualties. Against this enemy, Casey knew, it was their artillery that killed you. You could handle their tanks, which were mostly museum pieces. The enemy infantry was tough, but they lacked the latest antitank weapons. The enemy artillery, however, would blast you to hell like the hammer of the red god of war.

Casey struggled with his duffel bag, which was balanced over his right shoulder. The air smelled of rain, oil, diesel, and human urine. The telltale, high-pitched whine of an M1A2 tank's turbine engine filled the moist air and mixed with other muffled noises of hammers, tanker's bars, and slamming hatches. Soldiers moved about, completing the necessary tasks of feeding, fixing, and maintaining their armored combat vehicles.

One tank crew and two mechanics struggled to lift a heavy engine into the blackened hull of an M1A2 tank. The men cursed. Their Nomex tanker's coveralls were covered with the grease and mud of five hard days of fighting. The M88 tank recovery vehicle hoist dangled a shiny new tank engine over the open hull of the M1A2. The old engine sat on the ground, leaking oil, as a swarm of mechanics stripped it of its vital parts.

Modern war feeds on itself, Casey thought as he watched the men work.

The new tank engine suddenly clanged against a metal grill plate that had been left upright.

"Damnit, McGreger! You knucklehead. I told you to drop the engine plates!" bellowed a sergeant, standing with his hands on his hips and his eyes full of fire, to a young tanker standing on the back deck of the tank.

"Got it, Sarge," the man replied as the heavy engine dangling in the air was jammed against the engine plate. McGreger pushed the engine back with both arms and forced the heavy plate down with his foot. The plate slammed against the hull with a loud, metallic ring.

"I'll have you on guard duty for the rest of the war if that cover is broken!" the sergeant growled. He turned to the tank retriever crew, which was manning the hoist that held the heavy engine in the air. "All right, damnit. Ease the friggin' engine down."

Casey turned away and saw that Sergeant Danlier had left him behind. Casey walked around the M88, then picked his way over the dank ground through the densely packed armored vehicles. He saw Danlier standing by the entrance to the battalion command post. A tank—with bumper markings HQ-66 and the name *Firebreather* painted on the gun tube's bore evacuator—sat next to the command post. *Firebreather's* crew was busy loading heavy 120mm tank ammunition through the loader's hatch on the turret's top.

"In here, sir," the sergeant said as he pulled open the flap on the tent extension of the tactical operations center—TOC in army jargon—of the armored heavy task force. "Major Cutter's inside."

Casey passed through the water-slicked olive green vestibule and entered the TOC. The shelter connected to four M577 armored command post vehicles. Each of the M577s had their big ramps down, opening into a central officelike area. The TOC was humming with activity as radios blared status reports and NCOs swarmed about map boards and telephones.

13

Casey dropped his duffel bag in the corner of the TOC and looked around.

The major sat at a field table positioned in the center of the TOC. With their ramps down, the M577s looked like large shoe boxes with one short side open, offering easy access to the bank of radios that lined the walls of each M577. A sergeant handed the major a report, then ducked back inside an M577.

Casey stood in front of the major's table. "At least you're out of the rain in here."

Cutter glanced up. The vexed look on his face swiftly transformed into a wide smile. "Tom. Tom Casey! Man, am I glad to see you! You've arrived just in time."

"Major Cutter, sir! We picked a fine time for a reunion," Casey said with a crisp salute. "I heard you guys might need a captain up here."

Cutter returned the salute, then stood up, grabbed the younger man by the arm and shoulder, and shook his hand. "God, it's good to see you. It's been . . . what . . . almost two years since we were together in the OPFOR at the National Training Center."

"Yes, sir. Seems like a lifetime ago. I understand you're in command here."

"Yeah, at least for the time being," Cutter said as he stared off into the distance and remembered the events of the last four days. "We had a hell of a fight yesterday. Casualties have been heavy, especially among the key leaders. We lost the old man on the third day. To make matters worse, the C Company commander was killed last night."

"I'm sorry. What happened?"

"Tom, it's been a bloody nightmare. The enemy hit us without any warning. One day we were at peace and the next day it was high-intensity conflict."

"Hell, sir, if they're shooting at you, it's always high-intensity conflict."

Cutter offered a weak grin, then got serious again. "A lot of good men died in the chaos of the first few days—just because we underestimated the bastards. We won't underestimate them again."

Casey nodded. He sensed that the mood inside the TOC was somewhere between desperation and rage. He took the envelope that he was carrying and handed it to the major. "Here, this is for you. I'm afraid it's not good news."

Cutter grasped the envelope, opened it, and took a few moments to read the instructions. "I was expecting this. Have you read the orders?"

"Yes," Casey replied, getting the same uneasy feeling in the pit of his stomach that he used to get back at school before his final exams. He studied Cutter's face and saw the fatigue in his eyes. "I thought I was tired. When was the last time you slept?"

"Sleep? What the hell is that?" the major replied with a weary grin, then motioned for the captain to sit down. The two men plopped down on folding metal chairs that bordered a rectangular map table. The table was topped with a plastic-covered 1:50,000-scale map of the battle area.

"As I said, I lost Captain Jeff Buford last night. Buford was our best company commander. He was going to command this raid and had worked out the details with brigade. He went to the brigade TOC last night to get the final order. On his way back to us he was killed in an ambush—maybe the same bastards who tried to get you. Now I need a commander to replace him."

Casey's eyes narrowed. He knew Cutter—respected him. He heard the desperation in his voice. Like a condemned prisoner waiting for the hangman to pull the trapdoor of the gallows, Casey suddenly realized what was coming next.

"I'll cut to the quick," said Cutter. "The enemy knows he has to fight a short war to win. He wants to smash those poor grunts and push us as far south as possible before trying to negotiate a cease-fire. We're running out of time."

Casey grew pensive, waiting.

"You will take command of Team Steel. I want you to lead the mission to break through to the infantry." The major paused as he saw the disbelief on Casey's face. "They didn't tell you at brigade?"

"Hell, no," Casey replied, looking as though he was in shock. "I guess they were saving the honors for you."

Cutter shook his head, then rubbed his cheek with his right hand. The strain of command reflected in his tired face. "Buford's XO is getting Team Steel ready, but he doesn't have the tactical plan or any of the details of the operation. Hell, things have been happening so fast, I told him only four hours ago that Buford was killed."

"Is Team Steel ready to go back into the fight so soon?" Casey asked, his face shaped with concern. "Especially after losing their commander?"

"No choice. I just got off the MSE phone with the brigade commander and the commanding general. Colonel Woods told me that you were coming as a replacement. I told him that you were the best man for the job. It's a stroke of luck that you arrived when you did."

"That's me," Casey said with a smirk. "One very lucky son of a bitch."

"The 1-12 Infantry won't last without help," Cutter said seriously. "They're seven kilometers behind enemy lines surrounded by enemy thicker than fleas on an old dog. We can't get any air support to them in this blasted fog, and we can't pull them out by helicopter. The task force will attack tomorrow at 2000. Until then, Team Steel is their only chance."

Casey stared straight ahead, his mind racing. He looked at the map, and then glanced up at the major. "So, Team Steel punches through enemy lines, links up with the infantry, and defends until the remainder of the task force arrives. Why do this piecemeal? Why not send in the entire task force right now?"

"Good question. The bottom line is we're not ready," Cutter answered. "You've seen the orders. The timing of the corps' counterattack is very precise. The division commander had to promise his firstborn to the corps commander just to get a company team released. You attack tonight at 0045. I'll attack with the rest of the task force twenty hours later. You have to reach the infantry, link up with them, and defend there until we arrive."

"You sure you want an outsider to lead this? I've just arrived. Team Steel won't know me from Adam."

"You're the best man for the job," Cutter insisted. "Quit bellyaching. I know your quality. You know how to fight an M1A2 team better than anyone I know. You were brilliant at the NTC. You've been here before and you have experience in this terrain. But most of all, I know you can do it."

Casey looked at the map, then back at the major. He smiled. "Well, then, I guess I accept."

"You never had a choice," Cutter said with a tired, determined grin. "I'm giving you all the combat power I can spare. Team Steel is a damn good company team. Your XO is an independent sort, but he's the best in the battalion. Your first sergeant is superb and a great team player."

"Any chance of helicopter support?" Casey asked.

"Probably not. As you know, during the first hours of the war the enemy's special forces, missiles, and saboteurs hit airfields and helicopter bases hard. Casualties were heavy, and they knocked out a lot of our stuff on the ground. Most of the airfields were also cratered. The stuff that survived the first attacks flew to the south. In addition our air force took heavy losses from the enemy's air defense system. The enemy has radically improved his mobile air defenses. They have moved dozens of these new super S-300 air defense systems forward to defend their attacking columns. The S-300 is similar to our Patriot air defense system, only newer and more accurate. The S-300s can destroy targets as low as ten meters above the ground and as far away as a hundred fifty kilometers. If you see any of these damn things, destroy them; they're high-priority targets."

"So, no air support or intelligence information?"

"Air support is being reserved for the corps attack. The corps commander wants to hit them with one massive punch. As far as the enemy situation goes, I don't know much more than what's in the order. The division's UAV checked out the bridges last night. Both bridges are still up. They also reported a couple of dismounted platoons and some VTT-323 APCs on Highway Seventeen. They didn't see any obstacles that would block the route. As I get more information, particularly electronic warfare reports, I'll send you a digital message update."

Casey paused, soaking up the information and wondering if the UAV (an unmanned aerial vehicle, a reconnaissance drone equipped with sophisticated cameras and thermal sights) could have missed a major enemy force in the misty defiles.

"What will I do for fuel? I can refuel just before crossing lines, but that will give me only ten hours—fifteen if we stretch it using our auxiliary power units—before I have to refuel. If you want me to stay out there for twenty-four hours . . ."

"The Bradleys and M113s will make it without refueling. You'll have one twenty-five-hundred-gallon HEMMT fuel truck. To hedge your bets I gathered thirteen M113 APCs with drivers, in addition to the four in your engineer platoon and the two APCs in C Company. These extra APCs will carry food, water, and ammo for you and the 1-12th. We've also scrounged twenty-five Flexcel fifty-five-gallon cylindrical bladders. They were designed to hang on the bustle rack of the tanks, but I've ordered that they be placed inside the M113s. The HEMMT and the banana blivets will give you a total of three thousand eight hundred seventy-five gallons—enough to fill seven empty M1A2 tanks."

"Armored resupply." Casey grinned. "A unique solution. Trucks would never make it."

"Right. Just guard that damn HEMMT. It's a tempting target for the enemy."

"What about artillery support?" Casey asked.

"You'll have all the artillery battalions in range for support—three battalions of 155mm and one MLRS battery. The MLRS will fire a prep for you just north of the LD on Highways Seventeen and Twenty-one. They'll move after that and set up to fire one more volley for you, on call, about two hours after you cross the LD."

Casey nodded, appreciating the devastation that even one multiple launched rocket system could provide. Each MLRS could fire twelve rockets to a range in excess of thirty kilometers, saturating an area the size of a football field with eight thousand grenade-sized submunitions. The MLRS fire might punch a hole through the initial crust of the enemy's lines, or at least stun the defenders long enough to give Casey's team an early advantage.

"Communications with the artillery will be the biggest challenge," Cutter continued. "We've lost most of our radio retrans units. I don't have to tell you how these friggin' mountains inhibit line-of-sight radio transmissions."

"Can you spare a TACSAT?"

"Not a one," Cutter answered, shaking his head. Casey wished that the tactical satellite systems were available. "I don't even have one in the battalion. Besides, from what I've heard, most of our satellites aren't working right now."

"You got any other good news, sir?"

"We have a window of opportunity for the next twenty-four hours. The enemy ran out of steam yesterday. The G2 says that the bad guys won't be able to continue the attack for another forty-eight hours. Our electronic warfare teams have developed a false picture for this sector, portraying all U.S. forces far to the south. Bottom line—you have a good chance to take them by surprise."

"What's this about the new enemy tank?" Casey said. "I saw an M1A2 in the assembly area here with a baseball-sized hole in the flank armor. I thought their tanks couldn't penetrate our armor."

"Yeah, well, the enemy has some surprises of his own," Cutter replied, handing Casey a one-page intelligence report from the stack of papers on his field desk. "They're not new tanks. It's some kind of new, improved hypervelocity titanium ammo that the enemy has purchased from one of our 'allies.' Apparently, their T-72s carry a few rounds of this new ammo, so watch out for the T-72s. These 125mm rounds can take out an Abrams from the flank and rear. Lucky for us they still can't penetrate the M1A2's front or turret."

"Isn't it nice to have 'allies' in a world made safe for capitalism?" Casey joked. "What about their older T-62 tanks? Can they fire this new ammo?"

"No. The new stuff is only in 125mm, so the T-62s with their 115mm gun can't use it. The enemy's RPGs, AT-4 antitank rockets, and T-62 tank cannon rounds still can't penetrate the frontal *or* flank armor of our tanks. That's one of the reasons we think you can break through to the 1-12th."

"What's another reason?"

"We don't have any other options," Cutter replied, looking directly into Casey's eyes. "You've got to do it."

Casey scanned the 1:50,000-scale map with the plastic operations overlay taped to it. The overlay displayed the boundaries, objectives, and enemy positions. A circle of red lines encompassed the blue positions that represented the 1-12th Infantry Battalion.

A thousand questions raced through Casey's mind. Bold graphics on the map, he knew, must eventually translate into a rifle squad or a tank crew taking the fight forward into a prepared enemy position. He knew that young men for whom he would be responsible would now have to move forward and endure the gut-wrenching fear of death or disfigurement, and attack and kill the guy on the other side of the hill.

"What's the latest on the 1-12th?" Casey asked.

"They're seven kilometers from the line of departure, surrounded by enemy tanks, APCs, and infantry," Major Cutter said, pointing at the map with his right index finger. "They can't break out and they're down to their last few antitank missiles."

Casey stared at the map. Seven kilometers isn't much in the desert, where there are wide, open fields of fire. But in this restricted, mountainous terrain, seven kilometers might as well be a hundred miles.

"I wish I could give you a better picture," Cutter added. "I won't tell you how to fight this. Buford worked out the plan. Use what he started with and adapt it to fit your needs. It's your call."

Casey smiled. Cutter hadn't changed, even under the pressure of combat. It had always been the particular mark of Cutter's leadership to grant a wide scope of independent judgment to his subordinate leaders—to tell them the task and purpose and leave the method of execution to their discretion. At the NTC, Cutter never prescribed the way missions should be carried out. He trusted his commanders to think.

An NCO interrupted the conversation as he thrust a message in front of Major Cutter. The major read the message quickly as the NCO stood silently staring at Captain Casey.

"This message confirms that the lead units are worn out from six days of fighting," Cutter said. "Second- and third-echelon forces are slowly moving forward to replace the lead enemy elements now. It appears that our window of opportunity for saving the 1-12th is closing. In addition, the rains have swollen the Gang River to seven or eight feet. Your tanks can ford only four feet of water. You'll have to seize a bridge to make this work."

"Any recommendations?" Casey prodded.

"Consider Highway Seventeen as your main axis of attack. It will offer you the best fields of fire and is the most maneuverable. There are two bridges across the Gang River. The one that crosses Highway Twenty-one is probably forty tons. The bridge across the Gang on Highway Seventeen is a seventy-ton steel-reinforced structure. It's well built and won't be easy for the enemy to destroy. I intend to use Highway Seventeen as my main direction of attack for the task force when we cross the LD to relieve you at 2000 on 3 October."

The hairs on the back of Casey's neck tingled. "What if the enemy destroys the bridges?"

"Unlikely. They're reinforcing their lead units to continue the attack, so the bridges are important to them. Just in case, I've given you two heavy assault bridges. The Gang is too wide to span with HABs, but you may be able to find a way to use them near one of the fixed bridges, especially if they are only partially destroyed."

Casey looked at Cutter and nodded. Cutter handed him a written task force order outlining the actions that would support Casey's raid.

"When do I cross the LD?"

"Tonight at 0045. The rest is in the brigade operations order. You'll have to plan the rest yourself."

"Sir," the NCO interjected. "The brigade commander wants you to meet him at Checkpoint Quebec in thirty minutes."

Cutter nodded and looked at his watch. "Tom, I've got to get going. I'll tell the old man that it's on for tonight. If you *can't* break through and link up before 0800 tomorrow, we won't get another chance."

"Have you told the XO I'm taking command?" Casey asked.

"No, I wanted to make sure you made it here first," Cutter replied. "Now that I have to meet the brigade commander, you'll have to tell him on your own. You're in command. I'll back you with any decision you need to make."

The two officers looked at each other in silence for a few seconds. Casey wondered if this was the last time he would see his old friend.

"It's a big risk, but we wouldn't try this if so many lives weren't in the balance," Cutter said, pulling a cigar out of his pocket and hand-

ing it to his young friend. "This is my last cigar. Smoke it when your
mission is over and we link up with you at Objective Dragon."

"I'll do that." Casey smiled, putting the brown plastic cigar tube
in his Nomex pants pocket. "Don't worry, Major. You just be sure to
make it to us on time. We'll do our part."

"That's a promise," Cutter replied.

Go to Section 111.

Section 3

> *The combat value of every unit depends on the quality of its offi-
> cers. An average-trained unit, which has its weak points, can still
> give a good performance if it has a good commander.*
>
> *In the same manner, a well-trained and experienced unit may fail
> under a mediocre commander. The value of good leadership is proved
> by the confidence of the troops in their leaders, the improvement of
> their fighting qualities and finally by success in combat.*
>
> —Generalfeldmarschall Albert Kesselring

He who hesitates is lost, Casey reminded himself. He quickly glanced
at his watch. He didn't have time for this. It was time to act. He
needed an XO who would support him, not argue with his every
move.

"Lieutenant Stonevitch," Casey announced in a strong, steady
voice. "You are relieved. Gather your gear and report to Major Cutter at the task force TOC immediately."

Stonevitch blinked hard. "What? You're kidding. You can't relieve
me!"

"Lieutenant, I can, and I just have. This conversation is over," Casey answered. He looked at Stonevitch, then turned and left the dazed officer standing at the rear of the tank. Casey quickly tramped back to the front of the tank. "Who's the next ranking lieutenant?" The platoon leaders looked at Casey in stone-cold silence. Each of them understood what had happened, just as a man at sea understands when a sinking ship finally dips beneath the waves.

"I guess I am," Lieutenant Andrews answered. "McDaniel and I have the same date of rank, but I beat him out alphabetically."

Casey shifted his stance, an uneasy gesture as he struggled to announce his decision. "Lieutenant Stonevitch is relieved as the XO. Andrews will replace him. We will attack tomorrow morning at 0045 to penetrate enemy lines and link up with the 1-12th Infantry. The 1-12th is surrounded by the enemy and fighting for their lives. The rest of the task force will link up with us the next day. Our direction of attack is up Highway Seventeen, which is now designated as Direction of Attack Viper."

"You got anything we can tell our men now?" McDaniel asked, then added, almost as an afterthought, "sir."

"I intend to attack with 2d Platoon leading, followed by 3d, my command group, the engineers, 1st Platoon, the trains, and 4th Platoon," Casey replied, pointing to Viper on the map laid out on the front slope of the tank. "We know that the enemy needs the bridges, but we have to assume that he has rigged them for demolition and will destroy them if we get close."

The officers mumbled among themselves.

Casey pointed to the map and continued. "If we blow a hole through their lines with the MLRS, and race like hell to the Highway Seventeen bridge over the Gang, maybe—just maybe—we can take it before they blow it up."

The officers stared at the map. Each seemed lost in his own thoughts.

"I'll issue the operations order in one hour," Casey added.

"You're going to lead with tanks?" McDaniel snapped.

"That's right," Casey answered, ignoring the lieutenant's tone. "Sergeant Scott's tanks will fight a running battle down Viper. We'll follow in his wake, like a convoy of ships following an icebreaker. His firepower, and the surprise of our attack, will force us through. Are there any more questions?"

No one moved or gave the hint of offering a suggestion or any opposition. The only dissension Casey noticed came from Lieutenant McDaniel, the thin infantry officer who led the 3d Platoon. The lieutenant's glare said more than any words.

"All right, then. I need each of you to support me one hundred percent. Brief your troops on what I've told you. I'll visit each platoon after the OPORD and ask them questions about the mission, so don't waste a minute."

Casey paused as his orders sank in. He thought through the possibilities and wondered if he needed to say anything more.

As if to punctuate the finality of his decision, thunder roared in the heavens. The rain began to fall in large droplets. Lieutenant Stonevitch, looking tired and forlorn, walked slowly past the group toward his tank. Casey's eyes followed Stonevitch until the lieutenant moved out of view behind one of McDaniel's Bradleys.

"Okay, that's it. I want the XO and FIST with me," Casey ordered, regaining the men's attention. He searched their faces. Most looked away. Only McDaniel's unfriendly gaze met his eyes. Casey stared back, afraid to back down now that the die was cast. "Gentlemen, this mission is crucial. Keep a clear focus on what is required; our lives depend on it. Meet me at my tank to receive the completed operations order in one hour—1115. Dismissed."

Go to Section 110.

Section 4

The captain squared off and faced his XO behind the muddy grill doors of the tank. Stonevitch glared back in fierce resentment.

For a moment the world stood still.

Casey smiled, then rubbed his forehead, trying to relieve the tension that was pressing down on him. He realized that his first mistake was not talking to Stonevitch in private, before addressing the platoon leaders. After all, Casey reasoned, Stonevitch was the acting company commander. The men looked to him for leadership. The tall, hawk-eyed lieutenant had helped command the unit for a week of tough, bitter fighting. Even Major Cutter, whom Casey held in the highest esteem, regarded Stonevitch as the best XO in the battalion.

What had Cutter called Stonevitch—independent? He certainly was that, Casey thought.

The cold, hard fact was that Casey needed Stonevitch, even if Casey resented his fractious attitude. It was obvious that Stonevitch was a fighter. Casey needed an executive officer with spirit—a man with the confidence to make decisions. A green second lieutenant wouldn't do. Casey wanted Stonevitch on his team.

"Okay. I'm willing to listen to your case, but you have to work with me. We can plan the attack up Highway Twenty-one, Cobra, as our base plan. We can designate Highway Seventeen as Viper and make it the branch plan."

"I'm telling you, Casey, Viper won't work."

"Stonevitch, hear me out," Casey replied sternly, standing his ground. "It's important that we work together. In a few hours,

whether you like it or not, I will lead Team Steel into battle. I'd like
to have you as my second in command. You know the men, the equipment, and the terrain. I need your experience and leadership. I can't
make it without you. Can I count on you or not?"

The two men locked gazes again, for a long, desperate minute.

"It matters less how we attack and a lot more that we attack as a
team," Casey added.

Stonevitch shifted his stance and looked down. "It's been a tough
week. All I care about is these men—Team Steel. These guys are my
responsibility. We've been through a lot together."

"I can see that. That's why I need you. Nobody can do the job better." Casey smiled and extended his hand.

Stonevitch looked up, gave a boyish smirk, and took Casey's hand.

"Then it's a deal?" Casey asked.

"Yes, sir," Stonevitch nodded as he clasped Casey's hand tight. "My
friends call me Stoney."

"Okay, Stoney. Tell me about Team Steel."

"Here's our status," Stonevitch answered, pulling his hand away
but keeping his eyes focused on Casey's. Stonevitch unfastened his
Kevlar helmet and placed it between his right arm and his chest.
"The 1st Platoon has four M1A2 tanks and is led by Second Lieutenant David Andrews. He's dependable—fought well in the two battles we've been in. He lost one soldier in the last fight—Private First
Class Brannigan from Tank One-Two. Other than that he's sometimes short on initiative but long on determination.

"The 2d Platoon is led by Sergeant First Class Scott. He took over
when Lieutenant Shriver was killed. Scott's solid and very aggressive.
You can count on him. Buford couldn't say enough about the man."

"I'm sorry about Buford," Casey said solemnly. "I never met him,
but I've heard that he was one hell of a commander."

"The absolute very best," Stonevitch answered, looking off into the
distance as if he could see Buford walking toward him. "I served with
him for almost ten months. I've never met a finer soldier. There's
nothing the men wouldn't do for Captain Buford."

"What about our two infantry platoons?"

"Lieutenant McDaniel is very good. He has four Bradleys in 3d Platoon. He's been a platoon leader for a while, knows the terrain, and

is at his best when he's leading his infantry on foot," Stonevitch continued. "Lieutenant Pender, on the other hand, is new. I don't know him. His platoon, which you designated as the 4th Platoon, has only three Bradleys. He lost one the other day in our fight on Highway Seventeen. Both platoons carry only four or five infantrymen in the back of their Bradleys—eighteen dismounts in the 3d Platoon and thirteen in the 4th."

Casey nodded. As usual, the infantry was understrength, due to undermanning and not casualties. A Bradley had a crew of three and was supposed to carry seven infantrymen in the back. Most mechanized infantry units in peacetime considered themselves lucky to field three or four riflemen per Bradley.

"The engineer platoon leader is Sergeant First Class Tremain. I don't know him either. He joined us last night."

"How about the first sergeant?" Casey asked.

"First Sergeant Jefferson George Washington. He's one of the best. He and Buford were like a hand and a glove. There was nothing the two of them couldn't do."

Casey took off his helmet and rubbed his forehead with his left hand. "What's our total combat power?"

"Ten-seven-one," Stonevitch fired off as if he were a machine reporting stock prices. "Ten M1A2s, seven Bradley infantry fighting vehicles—four in 3d Platoon and three in 4th Platoon—and one Bradley stinger fighting vehicle. In addition we have the engineer platoon; Lieutenant Keeley, our FIST; two heavy assault bridges; one M88 tank recovery vehicle; a fuel HEMMT; and seventeen M113 APCs—one for the first sergeant, one for the mechanic team, two medic APCs, and thirteen in this makeshift resupply group that Major Cutter saddled us with."

Stonevitch handed a three-by-five card to Captain Casey that displayed the combat power of their company team.

"What's this?" Casey asked.

"This is how we report combat power. Whenever I have a chance I'll hand you one of these cards or send you a digital report by the IVIS. I'll always report tanks, then Bradleys, then engineers, as shown. Normally I'll send you a combat power total that just shows the bottom row. Captain Buford used these all the time."

TM C Unit	M1A2 Tank	M2 IFV	BSFV [ADA]	FISTV	Engr M113	CEV	ACE	HAB Bridge	Medic M113	M88 [Rec]	FUEL HEMMT	M113 APCs
1 Plt	4											
2 Plt	4											
3 Plt		4										
4 Plt		3			4							
Engr						1	1	2				
HQ	2		1	1								
Mech												1
1SG									2	1	1	1
M113s												13
Total	10	7	1	1	4	1	1	2	2	1	1	15

"Thanks, this will come in handy," Casey said with a smile. He unzipped the top left pocket on his Nomex tanker's coveralls and placed the combat power card inside. He looked up at the darkening sky. "We need to take advantage of every available minute. What are your recommendations?"

"You and I should put together the plan while First Sergeant Washington gets things organized and the platoon leaders get their units ready."

Casey nodded.

"Uh-hmmm," a young, dark-haired lieutenant coughed, interrupting the conversation. "Captain, I'm Lieutenant George Keeley, your fire support officer. I've just received the latest intelligence info from brigade. I thought you'd want to see it right away."

"Okay, Lieutenant," Casey replied as he took the brown envelope from the lieutenant's hand. "Let's see what you have here."

Go to Section 104.

Section 5

> *But in very mountainous country, where there are ordinarily but one or two principal routes into which other valleys open, even from the direction of the enemy, the concentration of forces becomes more difficult, since serious inconveniences may result if even one of these important valleys be not observed.*
>
> —Antonne Henri Jomini, *The Art of War*

"Okay, let's say we choose Cobra. Do we lead with tanks or infantry?" Casey asked.

"Infantry," Lieutenant Stonevitch answered without hesitation. "Jim McDaniel is your man. He can move forward, firing with his 25mms, then dismount when he senses trouble. His dismounts will keep us from running into an ambush. He knows that defile and can lead us there in the dark."

"I hope so," Casey replied, "because that's exactly what he's going to have to do."

Stonevitch nodded. Lieutenant Keeley, the fire support officer, was standing by as Casey and Stonevitch discussed the operation. The young artilleryman looked as if this was the first time he had participated in a company team decision process.

"Because Cobra is so narrow, we'll want tight control on the engineers," Stonevitch continued. "If they place a deep enough minefield in the defile, the enemy might stop us from breaking through. I recommend that you put me with the engineers. First Sergeant Washington can coordinate the passage of lines."

Casey nodded in approval. "We'll attack up Cobra. McDaniel's infantry will lead. You take charge of the engineers."

Lieutenant Stonevitch smiled as he unfolded his arms. "Excellent. I'll get the platoon leaders organized and give them a warning order while you complete the plan. George can assist you with the coordination of artillery fires."

"Right," Casey replied. "Have my tank crew attach a tarp to the side of my tank and I'll work there."

Stonevitch nodded in acknowledgment. "I'll get *Cossack* set up right away. I'll tell the first sergeant to drop by to see you after he has the ammo and fuel situation in hand."

Casey smiled, happy to see the team coming together. Stonevitch snapped to attention and saluted. Casey returned the salute.

I believe that I have won the first battle, Casey deliberated silently, the battle for the respect of my men. We're working as a team now. That's always the first step to success.

Casey looked up at the cloudy sky. The cold rain fell in a fine, persistent drizzle against his face. Now, all *we* have to do, he thought, is penetrate a heavily defended enemy front, race behind enemy lines, link up with a surrounded infantry battalion, defend for about twenty-four hours, and wait until the rest of the task force links up with us. What could be simpler?

"Okay, Keeley," Casey said to his artillery officer. "Tell me what you think the artillery can do for me today."

Go to Section 8.

Section 6

The tank is the primary offensive weapon.

Its firepower, protection from enemy fire, and speed create the shock effect necessary to disrupt or defeat the enemy. Tanks can destroy enemy armored vehicles, infantry units, and antitank guided missile units. Tanks can break through suppressed defenses, exploit the success of an attack by striking deep into the enemy's rear areas, and pursue defeated enemy forces.

—U.S. Army Field Manual 100-5, *Operations*, 1996

Casey opened his map and placed it on the rain-drenched side of the heavy assault bridge. "If we take Coral, then attack west to Viper, we can take the Highway Seventeen bridge from the flank."

Stonevitch looked at the map, then at Casey and nodded. "That's my read too. After I saw the enemy laying mines in front of Cobra and Viper, I became a believer. They'll be ready for us on Cobra and Viper. Better to hit them where they ain't. Coral to Viper is our best bet."

"Any problem with artillery support if we take Coral?" Casey asked, looking at his artillery officer.

"No problem with range," Lieutenant Keeley responded. "The guns will be in range no matter which way we attack."

"Then it's agreed," Casey replied, the finality in his voice clearly ending further discussion. "It's Coral to Viper. Sergeant Jacobs, good thinking—your idea with the underwater bridges was innovative but just too risky. Your heavy assault bridges, however, may still make the difference if the enemy tries to damage the bridge along Viper."

Jacobs nodded, disappointed at the rejection of his idea.

"We still have to get to the river," Stonevitch announced, pointing at the narrow trail. "Coral looks pretty narrow as it passes through the mountains. We'll have to attack through that area in column."

"That's right," Casey answered. "Attack in column, lead with tanks with mine plows, and don't stop for anything."

Stonevitch nodded. "I recommend that we attach a section of engineers with 2d and 3d Platoons. This way each platoon will have a self-contained mobility team. I can keep the assault bridges, CEV, and ACE with me. Washington can ride herd on the APCs and the HEMMT."

"Good idea," Casey replied. "Speed is essential. If we run into a minefield along Coral, we need to plow it aside with the tanks or blow a single lane through with the MICLICs. The engineers can help breach any minefields we can't plow through."

"It may just work," Stonevitch said.

"Get the platoon leaders organized and issue them a warning order while Keeley and I complete the plan. Our order of march will be 2d Platoon, command group, 3d Platoon, you with bridges, CEV, ACE, then 1st Platoon, team trains, and 4th Platoon."

"Wilco. I'll get your tank crew to set up a tarp on the side of your tank to give you a place to work."

Casey nodded, feeling the bond of respect that was developing between them. "Excellent."

Stonevitch snapped to attention and saluted, a gesture of respect that was a product of Casey's leadership. Casey returned the salute, caught the gleam in Stonevitch's eye, and smiled. The XO departed.

Casey looked up at the cloudy sky. The cold rain fell against his tired face. The team was coming together. He had a plan and the XO was working with him. His patience was paying off, but a surge of new doubts suddenly filled his mind. What if the enemy defended Coral in strength? What if they were waiting to trap Team Steel there? What if Team Steel couldn't fight through?

Do not take counsel of your fears, he thought. He turned toward the young, eager artillery officer who was waiting patiently for Casey to complete the artillery fire plan. "Keeley, let's look over the artillery plan."

Captain Tom Casey remembered the first lesson that his platoon sergeant, Sgt. Harry Stipes, had taught him when he was a young second lieutenant straight out of West Point: "A tank commander's responsibility is to fight his tank. A platoon leader's responsibility is to fight his platoon. A company team commander's responsibility is to fight his company team. Focus on your job. Let the NCOs do the rest." Casey felt that he had prepared well for the attack. Good old Sergeant Stipes would have been proud of him. Now all Casey had to do was execute.

The gloom was thickening fast as the fog rolled in like a heavy cotton blanket. The M1A2s and Bradleys from Team Steel moved to the side of the road and lined up next to a row of big, eight-wheeled fuel trucks. Soldiers on the ground—men from the battalion support platoon, identified only by the glow of tiny chemical light sticks—guided each armored vehicle into position. The men quickly handed fuel hoses to the tank crews. Loaders and gunners jumped from hatches, grabbed the metal-tipped fuel nozzles, and quickly refueled their armored vehicles.

Cossack, Casey's M1A2 tank, carefully moved next to a 2,500-gallon HEMMT fuel truck. Sergeant Charles Graham and Specialist Andy Kriel—Casey's gunner and loader—refueled *Cossack* as Casey thought over his moves.

The sound of the fuel pumps whirred noisily in the damp night air, mixing with the whine of ten M1A2 tank engines and the rumble of seven Bradley fighting vehicles.

Casey waited patiently. Refueling at night is a dangerous but vital operation, he mused. The M1A2s drink fuel at an startling rate. Even with its 2,500-gallon fuel tank, the M1A2 could run only ten hours before refueling.

Ten hours of fuel was enough to get them to the 1-12th Infantry, Casey calculated. Once he linked up with the infantry, the tanks could use their auxiliary power units, or APUs. The APU was a small diesel generator that could run the tank's electronic systems when the engine was off. The APUs saved rivers of fuel. As insurance, Team Steel would have the 2,500-gallon fuel HEMMT and the forty-five small rubber fuel bladders carried inside most of the M113s.

The decision when and where to refuel would be a critical one. If Team Steel was under the enemy's guns once it broke inside the 1-12th's perimeter, it might not have a chance to refuel at all. You can't refuel under artillery fire. A tank without fuel is like a battleship stranded on a reef —vulnerable and dead in the water. The refueling operation, therefore, would take careful timing.

Artillery fire detonated to the north, masking most of the sounds of Team Steel's preparations to cross the line of departure and begin the attack. These sounds also masked Casey's concerns. In a few minutes, Casey knew that he would lead Team Steel into battle. Had he done everything to make the team ready for the attack? Would fuel be their biggest problem?

The fog rolled off, offering a clear view of the ground for the first time this night. Casey checked his watch, pressing the light button to illuminate the digits. On schedule, the night air filled with the sound of artillery shells arcing through the dark sky. The shells, detonating in a terrible rumble, blasted unseen targets along axes Cobra, Viper, and Coral. The earth trembled from the explosions.

"Jesus," Sgt. Charlie Graham exclaimed as he stood on *Cossack*'s rain-slick back deck. "Our artillery is clobbering them. As my old drill sergeant used to say, 'If at first you don't succeed, call for artillery.'" Casey placed his CVC helmet on his head. "I've got a feeling that we'll be needing some good tank gunnery before the night's out."

"Well, sir, *Cossack*'s the best shooting tank in the company," Graham answered proudly. "We're ready."

"I've always believed that the gunner is the most important member of the crew, Sergeant," Casey answered, his words punctuated by the sound of explosions falling along Direction of Attack Coral. "You fight the tank, I'll fight Team Steel."

"Yes, sir," Graham answered as he handed the fuel nozzle to a soldier on the ground. "You can count on me."

Somehow, Casey knew that Graham meant what he said. Graham was the kind of noncom that immediately instilled confidence. His thick southern drawl and his fondness for old drill sergeant aphorisms put Casey at ease. Casey felt lucky to be heading into combat with such a man.

The tank in front of *Cossack* finished refueling, revved its engine, and moved forward. Graham locked down the fuel cap and climbed back into *Cossack* through the loader's hatch. Specialist Kriel followed close behind his sergeant.

Cossack crawled forward at five miles an hour, following the engineer APCs that trailed the last tank in Sergeant Scott's 2d Platoon. Keeley's FIST-V and Sergeant Sellers's Bradley Stinger fighting vehicle followed *Cossack*.

"Steel Six, this is Steel Seven," First Sergeant Washington reported to Casey over the company team command radio frequency.

"Steel Seven, this is Six. Send it," Casey replied.

"I've just linked up with the allied unit at the contact point south of Phase Line Audi on Coral. They're ready for us to cross at 0045. They've marked the lane with the thermal and infrared chem lights that I gave them. Drivers will be able to see the passage lane with their thermal viewers or their AN/PVS-7 night vision goggles."

"Roger. Good job, Steel Seven. Anything further?"

"Affirmative. The unit we will pass through reports that the enemy is digging in north of Phase Line Audi on Cobra and Viper. They report enemy infantry in the village of Masan. Over."

Casey thought about this new information. He hadn't expected enemy in Masan. Why did he always receive a clearer picture of the enemy after he issued his plans?

"Roger. I was hoping that we would find Masan empty. Did they say how many enemy they saw?"

"They identified one antitank platoon, with AT-4 antitank missiles, and some mortars," First Sergeant Washington radioed.

"Steel Six, this is Steel Five," Stonevitch interrupted. "I've been monitoring. I'm sending you a sketch on IVIS now."

Casey scanned his IVIS screen.

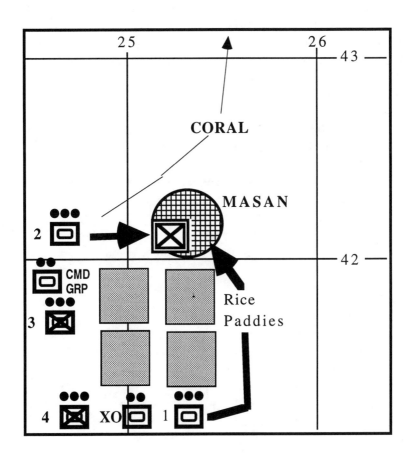

Section 6

"It sounds as if the enemy is trying to block Coral with forces inside Masan," Stonevitch continued. "We could run into trouble if we bypass an enemy strongpoint there—especially if they can hit us as we go by with AT-4 missiles."

Casey thought about this new information. He had hoped that he could bypass Masan without a fight. It seems that the enemy had a mind of his own and were not playing by his plan.

"Roger. Do we know what size enemy force is in Masan?" Casey asked over the radio.

"I have a partial report of one antitank missile platoon—probably AT-4s—and some mortars," Stonevitch answered. "If there are mortars, there could be at least a company."

"Roger Steel Five, stand by," Casey radioed, as he glanced at Stonevitch's plan on the IVIS screen.

The AT-4 antitank missiles has a range of four thousand meters. The mortars were probably 82mms. Since the enemy didn't have a very robust night vision equipment capability, the mortars might be there to provide illumination for the antitank platoon to fire in the dark.

Casey considered the options: bypass Masan and leave an enemy force in his rear or clear Masan. Decide!

**If Casey decides to bypass the enemy in Masan,
go to Section 10.**

**If Casey decides to clear the enemy from Masan,
go to Section 23.**

Section 7

The West also needs to consider the fact that the Third World is rapidly changing its military capabilities, and gunboating in any form is not a substitute for combined arms.
—Anthony H. Cordesman and Abram R. Wagner,
The Lessons of Modern War

Time was pressing. Casey looked at his watch, then at Stonevitch. "Perfect may be the enemy of good enough, but the best plan usually provides for flexibility. If we attack up Cobra, we'll be committed from the beginning. The mountains hem us in and deny us the Viper or Coral approach."

"So what do you want to do?" Stonevitch's voice cut in sharply.

"First, I need your experience, Stonevitch," Casey replied, forcing another smile. "You and I will make the decision together. But once we decide, we execute as a team. Agreed?"

"Agreed," Stonevitch answered. "Go on."

"Second, I want to move up to the line of departure and see the ground for myself. One of my rules is to never make a decision on a course of action without making a reconnaissance."

"I wouldn't bet on seeing much in this fog," the XO offered.

"It doesn't pay to bet when you're betting on your life," Casey replied. "We won't see anything if we stay here. Time spent in reconnaissance is seldom wasted, especially in restricted terrain."

"Okay," Stonevitch agreed, checking his watch. "We must issue the operations order by 1530 if we expect to brief our people and conduct rehearsals."

Casey nodded again. "I like the way you think, XO. Tell me, who has the best tank platoon in the company?"

"Sergeant First Class Scott, without a doubt," Stonevitch replied. "He leads from the front and keeps cool when things get hot."

"Who's the senior second lieutenant?"

"Lieutenant Andrews and Lieutenant McDaniel have the same

date of rank," Stonevitch answered. "If you're looking for the next to command in an emergency, then McDaniel's your choice. He's the tall, thin grunt who leads 3d Platoon. His platoon has four Bradleys."

"How many riflemen can he put on the ground?" Casey asked.

"Only eighteen."

Casey shook his head. Both of his Bradley mechanized infantry platoons were understrength. Instead of the standard thirty-six men in a platoon—twelve crewmen for four Bradleys and six infantrymen in the back of each Bradley, for a total of twenty-four dismounted riflemen—McDaniel's platoon was six men short. "I want you and the platoon leaders to go with me on the reconnaissance. We'll use my tank and two APCs to carry the recon group."

"If I go, who will supervise the resupply and get the company ready for tonight?" Stonevitch protested, his brow wrinkled in concern.

"From what you've already told me, it sounds like First Sergeant Washington can handle it," Casey answered. I want to meet with him before we leave. Have him meet us here while I talk to the officers."

"Yes, sir," Stonevitch replied.

"Now, I want to talk to the platoon leaders."

The two men returned to the front of the tank. Casey faced the platoon leaders, and Stonevitch stood by Casey's side. Casey unfolded the map for all to see. The platoon leaders looked at the dark blue arrows that designated Cobra, Viper, and Coral.

Casey took off his helmet and rubbed his forehead with his left hand. "We don't have time to get acquainted. I know your quality. I also have a pretty good idea of how rough the past few days have been. I'm asking you to put that behind us and take a leap of faith. I will do my best. I will expect the same from you."

The officers and NCOs looked on intently, listening to Casey and glancing at Stonevitch.

"Platoon leaders will leave with me in twenty minutes to conduct the reconnaissance. Have your platoon sergeants get your platoons ready for tonight's mission. We'll take my tank as security and two APCs as transport."

Stonevitch nodded.

"First Sergeant Washington will be in command until I return," Casey continued. "I'll issue the order here at 1500. I want every combat vehicle fully loaded and fueled, and I want the crews briefed on our general mission and the three possible directions of attack by then. Any questions?"

Lieutenant Keeley offered a brown envelope to Casey. Casey took the packet, reviewed the contents with eager eyes, then looked up. "Gentlemen, you have your orders. Stonevitch, call battalion and clear it for us to go forward and check out Highways Seventeen and Twenty-one from here to the line of departure."

"Wilco, sir," Stonevitch answered.

"Okay, let's get cracking."

If decisions were a choice between alternatives, decisions would come easy.
Decision is the selection and formulation of alternative.
                                                        —Kenneth Burke

---

Go to Section 108.

Section 8

Ground in which the army survives only if it fights with the courage of desperation is called "death.". . . In death ground I would make it evident that there is no chance of survival. For it is the nature of soldiers to resist when surrounded; to fight to the death when there is no alternative, and when desperate to follow commands implicitly.
                                                —Sun Tzu, *The Art of War*

The night was pitch dark. The last hint of a moon had disappeared behind the low black clouds. As the clouds darkened the heavens, a wave of fog rolled into the valley, masking the area in a thick and menacing veil. The fog swept in and out, taking turns with the rain. One minute, visibility was three to five hundred meters; the next minute, the fog rolled in and restricted vision to only a few feet. Even with the M1A2's driver's thermal viewers, a new and welcome upgrade to the formidable tank, Casey's driver could see only to the next vehicle.

The M1A2s and Bradleys of Team Steel moved quickly to the side of the road and lined up next to the big, eight-wheeled HEMMT 2,500-gallon fuel trucks. Loaders jumped from hatches as men on the ground handed the tired tankers the metal-tipped fuel nozzles. Within minutes the fuel was flowing into the thirsty tanks.

The high-pitched whine of the powerful 1,500-horsepower engines of Team Steel's M1A2s filled the night air. The refueling was executed in total darkness: the tanks and soldiers on the ground used only night vision goggles and passive and thermal night-driving viewers. Small chemical light sticks identified the fuel trucks and the soldiers on the ground. The men of the battalion support platoon, the unsung heroes of modern armored warfare, were the men responsible for refueling and rearming the task force's 234 vehicles. The well-drilled support platoon soldiers guided the tanks, Bradleys, and APCs to predesignated positions on both sides of the road.

Captain Tom Casey stood in the commander's station of his M1A2 and watched as his loader and gunner refueled the tank. Each tank took five hundred gallons, but he needed only a three-minute shot to fill his vehicle's fuel tanks. Refueling just before crossing the line of departure was a routine operation. With a consumption rate of about fifty gallons an hour, an M1A2 tank could run for only ten hours without refueling. Fuel, he knew, would be one of his biggest concerns.

Beads of sweat fell from the brow pad of Casey's CVC, his combat vehicle communications helmet, as he silently reviewed the mission. He worried about the fog. He worried about keeping his force together. Placing the XO with the engineers would help keep that critical unit in tow. Putting the first sergeant at the contact point for the passage of lines would keep him informed. So far, so good, he thought.

Cossack's engine rumbled quietly as Casey took off his CVC and listened to the sound of a unit preparing to attack. His thoughts wandered as the refueling continued. He thought about the name of his tank, christened *Cossack* by the late Captain Buford. All the tanks in C Company were given names starting with *C.* He could understand why Stonevitch might call his tank *Cossack;* instead, Stonevitch's tank had the name *Crom* emblazoned on the bore evacuator of the 120mm gun tube. Why was Buford's tank named *Cossack?* There must be an inside joke that Casey didn't know yet.

The light of the IVIS display and other instruments in the tank commander's station gave the turret a soft green glow. Casey's gunner, Sergeant Graham, and Specialist Kriel, the loader, crouched on the back deck of the tank and placed the fuel hoses that extended from the huge HEMMT fuel trucks that lined the road. Every vehicle in Team Steel was refueling at almost the same time.

The fog rolled off, offering a clear view of the ground for the first time this night. Casey checked his watch pensively.

A roar that sounded like a runaway freight train drowned out the noise of *Cossack's* turbine engine. The artillery prep had started. The 155mm shells tore through the dark sky, then roared in rippled waves of thunderous explosions, targeting selected points along axes Cobra, Viper, and Coral. The detonations rumbled ominously in the dark, damp air.

War has its own peculiar sounds, Casey thought, looking to the north; the whine of the M1A2 tank engine and the clatter of its tracks as it moves across a paved road; the scream of a shell whistling through the air; the clang of a Bradley starting its engine; the staccato crack of a machine gun. Each sound contained its own special fierceness borne of danger and death.

"Jesus," Sgt. Charlie Graham exclaimed as he stood on *Cossack's* back deck. The earth trembled with the blast of successive explosions. "Our artillery is clobbering them. Maybe this won't be so hard after all. No one can withstand that much steel."

Casey didn't answer. He placed his CVC helmet on his head.

The vehicles in front of Casey raced their engines. The 3d Platoon, composed of four Bradley infantry fighting vehicles led by the able

Lieutenant McDaniel, finished refueling and moved off to the SP (start point). Graham finished refueling and climbed back into *Cossack* through the loader's hatch. Specialist Kriel followed close behind his sergeant.

"Steel Six, this is Steel Seven," First Sergeant Washington reported to Casey over the company team command radio frequency.

"Steel Seven, this is Six. Send it," Casey replied.

"We're all set for 0045. I've coordinated the passage of lines. They're ready for us. They've marked the lane with stakes. Drivers will be able to see the passage lane with their thermal viewers or their AN/PVS-7 night vision goggles. The allied unit we're passing through has laid several antitank minefields to the sides of the passage lanes. Tell everyone to keep in the marked lane."

"Roger, Seven. Anything else?"

"Our allies report that the enemy is digging in all along Phase Line Audi. Their listening posts can hear the shovels working. They haven't, however, identified any exact locations. The fog is too thick. That's all I've got. Over."

"Understood. See you on the other side. Out." Casey pushed the light button on his digital watch. In five minutes, at 2400, his company team would move into battle. He had timed the route from the AA (assembly area) to the LD (line of departure). It would take exactly forty-five minutes. "All Steel elements, this is Steel Six. Finish refueling. We move out in five minutes."

The thick fog rolled back, hiding the column and reducing normal vision to less than fifty meters.

A flurry of radio traffic followed. Casey ordered his driver, Private First Class Weaver, to move out and follow the Bradleys in front of him. Casey turned around in his open turret to see if his FIST (fire support team leader), Lieutenant Keeley, was following him. Casey knew that he would have to keep a close eye on Keeley's location. The FIST-V, an upgraded M113 APC modified with a special "hammerhead" turret that permitted the FIST officer to laze to targets, was slow and would have trouble keeping up with Casey's fast-moving M1A2.

The army should have bought a new FIST vehicle years ago, Casey complained silently.

Casey could barely see Keeley's FIST-V trailing close behind in the dense fog. Casey couldn't see McDaniel's Bradleys. Reports on the radio told him that all of his vehicles were rolling.

The whine of *Cossack*'s engine and the chatter of the command radio kept Casey busy as his driver followed the marked trail that led through friendly lines. At the start of the lane, First Sergeant Washington would pass each vehicle and then report when the last vehicle was in line.

The fog grew thicker. Drivers slowed down to avoid losing their way. The column soon crawled at a snail's pace.

"Weaver, keep in the lane," Graham said. "We don't want our allies shooting us."

"We're friendlies, why would they shoot at us?" Weaver questioned.

"As my old drill sergeant used to say, 'The only thing more accurate than incoming enemy fire is incoming friendly fire,'" Graham replied. "Just make sure you stay in the lane."

"Clear the intercom," Casey announced. The thick fog worried him. He ducked inside the turret and checked his IVIS display. The IVIS automatically registered the location of his armored vehicles on the map screen. These locations were accurate and were automatically updated by the POS/NAV satellite system on each armored vehicle.

Unfortunately only twenty-one of forty-five vehicles in Team Steel were equipped to send this digital information. Team Steel was a mixed force of digitally equipped and nondigital vehicles. The M1A2s, Bradleys, FIST-V, BSFV, and Wolverines had POS/NAV systems that interfaced with *Cossack*'s IVIS. The M113s, engineers, and HEMMT, however, had to determine their location in the old-fashioned way, with PLGRs (pronounced "pluggers"), maps, and night vision devices. Digitization was expensive and could be afforded only for combat vehicles.

Casey looked at his watch. It was 0045. He scanned his IVIS screen and saw that he was just a few meters short of the passage lane.

"Steel Six, this is Blue One. LD now. Zero and Four. No contact," Lieutenant McDaniel reported.

"Roger, Blue One. Continue mission. Out," Casey replied, happy that things were going as planned in spite of the fog.

Section 8

The terrible background music of modern war, the sound of artillery, continued to crash in the distance. Right on schedule the howitzers shifted their fire to targets along Team Steel's direction of attack.

Cossack passed lines and carefully followed the markers designating the passage lane, which followed a narrow dirt trail. Some of the lane markers were very difficult to see. Weaver was able to make them out only in his driver's thermal viewer. Casey closely followed the readings on his POS/NAV system, guiding Weaver through the predesignated course.

After what seemed like a lifetime, *Cossack* exited the passage lane. Casey looked through his CITV and saw the Bradley platoon to his front, moving cautiously forward to the valley to their left front. He turned the viewer around to look behind him and saw the FIST-V, the Bradley Stinger fighting vehicle, and the four tanks of Lieutenant Andrews's 1st Platoon.

Casey scanned to the rear to view 1st Platoon. The CITV screen showed Lieutenant Andrews's tanks in column, moving steadily through the passage lane.

"Steel Six, this is Steel Five. We've got a break in contact," Stonevitch radioed Casey. "Sapper Six, do you have all your engineers?"

There was an ominous silence on the radio, then a harried response. Casey waited nervously for the response while he switched to his IVIS screen.

"I'm not sure, Steel Five," Sergeant Tremain answered weakly. "I'm right behind you and I can't see a thing in this fog."

"Steel Five, this is White One. I'm following one of the HABs," Sergeant First Class Scott reported. "Have we changed passage lanes?"

"Negative, White One!" Casey shouted, taking over the conversation. "Stop where you are, White, and get control over the Sapper elements. Steel Five, wait on the north side of the passage lane and collect all our elements before you move forward."

"Wilco, Steel Six," Stonevitch's voice replied, obviously exasperated over the unraveling of the plan.

"Steel Six, this is Green One. I've got my elements and a bunch of APCs right behind White."

"Damn!" Casey cursed. In a panic he turned to his IVIS screen as the icons that depicted the four M1A2 tanks in Sergeant First Class Scott's platoon moved east of the passage lane rather than through it.

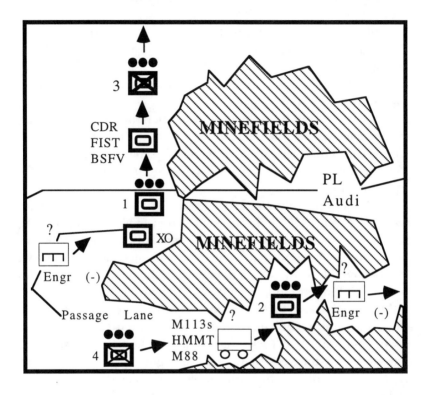

Casey looked at his watch. It was 0100. He could feel the rumble of the artillery as it rolled north, as planned. Half of his force had missed the passage lane and was headed in the wrong direction. Even in the age of high-tech navigation systems, navigation on a foggy, rainy night was an art form.

A northwesterly breeze picked up and the fog rolled off as the team tried to get through friendly lines. Miraculously, the drizzle stopped, but the low-hanging clouds promised the possibility of more rain. Through the M1A2's thermal sights, Casey could see as far as seven hundred meters.

Cossack rumbled forward, following the trail Bradley in McDaniel's 3d Platoon. Casey scanned the northern edge of the battlefield with his CITV.

Artillery flares suddenly fell through the clouds and illuminated the sky above the hill at CS218413. The flares burned brightly, lighting the wooded area near the 3d Platoon. Casey looked up at the flares as they floated downward, dangling back and forth in the moist breeze from their tiny parachutes.

Casey saw flashes from the northwest, then saw green tracer bullets fly diagonally across the battlefield toward McDaniel's column. The Bradleys increased speed and raced up Highway 21.

"Steel Six, this is Blue One. Contact. Enemy infantry at CS210418. Engaging now!"

McDaniel's Bradleys fired a wild volley of 25mm cannon fire toward the enemy. The shells sparkled as they exploded in twinkling bursts. The fire seemed to wake up the enemy. In seconds a full wave of return fire from two more machine guns sliced at the Bradleys.

Casey could see the splash of enemy fire bouncing off the flanks of the trail Bradley. Additional flares ignited overhead.

McDaniel's Bradleys charged ahead, firing at their attackers while they rolled north. Graham slewed the turret toward the enemy.

An enemy antitank rocket flashed across the field and smashed harmlessly into the trees, shattering in a bright explosion to the right rear of the Bradleys. The warhead blew up in a shower of orange-red sparks. The Bradleys directed their fire at the missile launch site, plastering a wide area with high-explosive shells.

"Steel Six, do you want me to assault?" McDaniel's excited voice shouted over the radio.

Casey knew that he had to decide. His force was engaging the enemy too soon. Should he commit to a fight while half of his company team was still south of the passage lane?

He immediately saw two options: reorganize, or continue to press the attack. If he fell back, reorganized,and then attacked with his full force, he would have more firepower. If he attacked with what he had with him north of the passage lane, he could develop the situation while the rest of his units moved north to join him.

Decide!

If Casey decides to fall back south of the passage lane and reorganize, go to Section 13.

If Casey decides to attack with what he has north of the passage lane, go to Section 14.

Section 9

> *Risk then represents the possibility that this predicted chance of success will be degraded by lack of information. Luck stands for the possibility of the chance of success being either enhanced (good luck) or degraded (bad luck) by some event that is unpredictable and completely outside either side's control.*
> —Richard E. Simpkin, *Race to the Swift*

Casey didn't have much time to react. Rather than close his hatch, he turned the gun toward the site of the missile launch. "Graham!"

"Identified," Graham screamed.

"Fire!" Casey yelled as he reached back to close the hatch. The rest of 2d Platoon blasted away in a rippling volley of 120mm fire at the missile launch sites located southeast of the bridge.

Cossack raced forward, jinking left and right to evade incoming missiles. Casey glanced through the opening in his hatch and saw the missiles coming straight for *Cossack*. Unable to react in time, he braced himself for the impact.

Two AT-4 antitank missiles struck *Cossack* at the same time. The first hit the turret on the left side, blinding Casey and throwing him against the rear wall of his tank commander's station. The second missile flew high and dived onto the top of *Cossack*'s turret, exploding in a terrible splash of fire and molten steel against the .50-caliber machine gun.

Casey died in that same instant, torn to pieces by the force of the blast.

You have fought hard but lost.
Go back to Section 42 and roll the dice again.

Section 10

> *The most important requirements in a maneuver are speed and quick execution.*
> —Col. I. N. Vorob'yev, "Fires, Assault, Maneuver,"
> *Krasnaya Zvezda*

Team Steel was on the move, rolling slowly northeast just short of the passage lane. The blasts of mortar and artillery shells muffled the squeaking tank tracks and the whine of the gas turbine engines.

Casey paused as he thought over the possibilities. Clearing Masan would take time, too much time. The enemy usually protected his infantry strongpoints with mobile tank reserves. They might use the time it took to deploy against Masan to maneuver tanks to counterattack his team. Every delay would make the chance of linking up with the 1-12th more difficult.

On the other hand, leaving the enemy in Masan could cut off Coral as a route of withdrawal if something went wrong. Casey guessed that this was what worried Stonevitch.

The focus of Casey's entire career in the army had been the motivation of soldiers—the ability to switch on their energy to realize their full potential and accomplish the mission. He knew that all the leaders of Team Steel were listening to his discussion with Stonevitch. He was asking his soldiers to do two difficult tasks: to put themselves in mortal danger and to kill other human beings while remaining a focused, disciplined force.

Casey knew that he couldn't inspire his soldiers to fight without first winning their hearts. He knew that soldiers, no matter how disciplined, do not go forward just because a faceless voice over a radio receiver tells them to. He would have to lead by example.

Casey checked his watch. It was time to decide.

"Steel Five, this is Steel Six," Casey radioed to his executive officer. "If we clear out every enemy position between the line of departure and Objective Dragon, we'll never reach the 1-12th. Our mission is to break through enemy lines and reach the infantry. The 1-12th is counting on us. We must bypass the enemy at Masan."

There was a long pause, then Stonevitch radioed his reply. "How will the APCs and HEMMT fueler make it past the town if the enemy has antitank weapons in Masan? What if something goes wrong on Coral and we have to return this way? There is no way out of Coral once we enter it."

"Speed is what is important," Casey replied. "Forget everything else. We have to reach the infantry. We don't abandon our own to the enemy."

"Wilco," Stonevitch said grimly. "I'll contact battalion and see if they can get us some radio-jamming support. Maybe the enemy hasn't had a chance to run commo wire back to his headquarters yet."

"Good idea," Casey offered, knowing that the risk of bypassed enemy infantry was the price of admission to this contest. "We'll plaster Masan with artillery fire and smoke, move fast, and fire on the move as we bypass the northwest flank of the town. No one enters Masan. It would take us hours to clear the town of enemy infantry."

"Steel Six, this is Steel Seven," First Sergeant Washington interrupted. "The surest way to take casualties is to be too careful. Hell, let's get in the ring and box."

"My thoughts exactly," Casey replied. There wasn't time for further discussion. He keyed the radio mike again. "Steel Guns, I want the densest smoke screen you've ever seen on Masan as we pass. Over."

"Roger, Steel Six. You'll get it," Keeley's eager voice answered. "I'll start the fire as soon as our lead element crosses the forty-two grid line. Then it will be continuous until the last element crosses the forty-three grid line."

"Good job," Casey replied, happy that Keeley was anticipating battle requirements. That was a key trait in any officer but particularly important in an artilleryman. Casey checked his watch again. "All Steel elements. The enemy has antitank teams in Masan. Shoot and destroy them as you pass, but don't stop. Out."

Cossack rumbled forward at five miles an hour. Casey looked out into the gloomy fog, using his night vision goggles to see the trail and help guide Weaver. Weaver, using his AN/VAS-3 DTV (driver's thermal viewer) and his POS/NAV aids, moved with a precision that amazed Casey. The DTV produced a TV-like image by sensing variations in temperature between objects and their backgrounds; it was not dependent on visible light as were the older-generation passive viewers.

Casey's tension eased as he scanned his IVIS and saw superimposed on a map the exact locations of the IVIS-equipped vehicles in his team. The IVIS reported the exact six-digit location of the M1A2s, Bradleys, and Wolverine heavy assault bridges. At the push of a button Casey knew exactly where his forces were during a battle. In addition, as soon as any of his vehicles lazed on an enemy target, the system registered the exact location of the enemy. This information could be flashed to all of the combat vehicles in the team. Casey felt that this marriage of excellent technology and well-trained soldiers would be a decisive advantage.

The whine of *Cossack*'s engine seemed to grow louder as the fog grew thicker. The passage lane followed a narrow dirt trail, marked on both sides by thermal and infrared chem lights. Weaver slowed down as the visibility decreased to avoid missing turns in the passage lane. Casey looked at his watch. It was 0045. He scanned his IVIS screen and saw that they would be out of the passage lane and able to maneuver in just a few more meters.

"Steel Six, this is White One. LD now. Combat power is four tanks and two engineer APCs. No contact," Sergeant Scott reported.

The fog rolled away to the south as *Cossack* dashed behind the 2d Platoon trail vehicle. Visibility improved dramatically. Casey locked his hatch in the open-protected position and peered out into the dark with his night vision goggles (NVGs).

"Roger, White One. Pick up the pace," Casey ordered. He checked his IVIS screen and saw Team Steel stretched out for twelve hundred meters. As 2d Platoon crossed Phase Line Audi, the line of departure, the trail element was still twelve minutes away. Getting caught in the passage lane by the enemy's artillery was Casey's worst fear.

The sounds of artillery buffeted the night air. The enemy's guns didn't reply. After several tense minutes, *Cossack* exited the passage lane. Casey looked through his CITV and saw the 2d Platoon to his front, moving swiftly along Coral toward Masan. *Cossack* picked up speed. So far, so good, Casey thought.

"Steel Six, this is Steel Five. Battalion confirms jamming on enemy command and artillery nets vicinity Masan."

"Roger," Casey answered, happy that the enemy would not be able to immediately radio in his position. "Good job."

Cossack rolled forward at twelve miles an hour as 2d Platoon accelerated to the north. The tank bounced across the rocky trail that served as the center of Direction of Attack Coral. Casey checked his IVIS screen as 2d Platoon reached coordinates CS245420.

"Steel Six, firing the prep on Masan. Over," Keeley's voice beamed over the command frequency. "Battalion TOT."

The sharp crack of dozens of artillery shells exploded in a tremendous fire strike over Masan. A battalion of 155mm howitzers fired a "time on target" attack on the town. White-hot explosions detonated over Masan. The town was engulfed in a firestorm of DPICM bomblets. Secondary explosions lit the town on fire. The ground trembled from the intense hammering.

Casey scanned the northern edge of the battlefield through his CITV as *Cossack* rolled forward. Although Masan was on fire, the wind was blowing the smoke to the south, so there was a clear view of the western edge of the town. Sergeant Scott's four M1A2s led, racing in column across a trail that crisscrossed an abandoned ginseng field. As the tanks moved northeast, the artillery smashed into Masan with increasing fury.

"Steel Six, this is White One. Contact! Enemy infantry at CS253423. They're in the west side of the town. Engaging now!"

"Roger, take them out but don't stop. Continue on Coral," Casey ordered as he scanned his IVIS screen. Scott's tanks raced forward, firing on the move. "Steel Guns, I need that smoke screen at Masan. The wind is blowing the smoke south."

Mortar flares suddenly ignited overhead.

Casey stared up at the flares through the crack in his turret hatch. The four tanks of 2d Platoon suddenly opened fire on targets in Masan, adding to the brilliant light that was transforming the dark night into day.

"Missile launch!" Scott shouted over the radio.

Before Casey saw what Scott's tanks were shooting at, the enemy fired a volley of AT-4 antitank missiles.

Roll the dice.

If you roll 2-3, go to Section 54.

If you roll 4-12, go to Section 85.

Section 11

The enemy antitank missile struck *Cossack* in the right side, smashing into its fast-turning tracks. In a screech of broken metal, *Cossack* pivoted abruptly to the right.

At the same time a flurry of machine-gun fire tore at *Cossack*'s side.

"Back up, Weaver. Don't give them a sitting target to shoot at!" Casey yelled as he reached for the button to fire the grenade launchers. "Grenades!"

Cossack surged backward, pivoting in a circle, then jammed onto a rock. The tank ground to a halt. The engine howled and the right track tore at the rocky earth, but the tank wouldn't budge. Weaver had driven *Cossack* onto a big rock; the tank was like a battleship run aground.

Casey looked out his vision blocks. The sky was light with the bright glare of mortar flares. He saw a cloud of white smoke enveloping the tank. In a panic he realized that the turret pointed north, away from the enemy.

Before he could jerk the turret toward the enemy and place the heavy armor toward the threat, another missile struck the tank. This time the missile hit the rear of the turret.

The turret jerked forward as the on-board ammunition in the rear of the turret exploded. In a powerful shudder, the explosion threw Casey and Kriel to the bottom of the tank. The 120mm tank ammunition exploded straight up from its compartment, sending the heavily armored blow-out panels high into the half-lit sky. The metal

53

ammunition door protected the crew from catastrophe. As the fire raged, the door glowed red hot.

The engine stopped and the turret went black as the tank lost electrical power.

Casey tried to think what to do. They couldn't escape the tank from the loader's or tank commander's hatch; the fire shooting out of the turret was too hot. They couldn't wait for the fire to die down; they might not survive another missile strike.

The sound inside the turret was horrific as the 120mm rounds exploded. Casey looked at the turret. He suddenly realized that it was over the side of the tank. With the turret in this position it was possible to climb out through the driver's compartment.

"Weaver, are you okay?" Casey yelled as the ammunition exploded in the compartment only a few feet from him.

There was no response. Casey reached down and felt for Weaver. He saw that the driver had already abandoned the tank and that the hatch was open.

Casey shook Graham. He seemed stunned but alive. Kriel was out cold from the concussion of the blast.

"Get out through the driver's hatch," Casey ordered Graham. "I'll take care of Kriel."

Graham obeyed and carefully slithered through the tiny space in the turret basket. Casey pulled at Kriel. He crawled backward into the driver's compartment, pulling Kriel by his Nomex rescue strap.

The heat inside the turret intensified. Casey's ears rang from the loud explosions of the detonation of the 120mm ammunition. Beads of sweat poured from his face as he struggled through the tiny opening, hoping to escape.

Finally he made it to the top of the driver's hatch. Casey pulled Kriel forward as far as he could, then crawled out, planning to reach back inside to pull him up.

More flares burst overhead. Casey felt as though he was in the center of a maelstrom that was crushing in all around him.

The fresh air was an instant relief. With his heart pounding, Casey reached inside the driver's compartment just as an enemy machine gun opened up. Dozens of bullets sparked against *Cossack*'s flank and front. Casey fell off the side of the tank, mortally wounded.

A tank roared past about fifteen feet away. Casey lay on his back as the sparks shot skyward. A cold breeze passed over him like a silent dream. He felt his life escaping and he couldn't stop it.

You have been killed in action.
Go back to Section 108 and try again.

Section 12

> Seventy percent (70%) of the deliberate attacks and seventy-six percent (76%) of the defend in sector missions resulted in commander losses. . . . Commanders who actively engaged the enemy with their weapon systems were three times more likely to be killed than those who fought their unit and only fired as a last resort.
>
> —Command and Continuity of the AirLand Battlefield, *Lessons Learned*

A 120mm projectile exploded in a sizzling flash against the enemy tank's turret. The tank flew apart at the seams, its turret flipping end over end from the force of the explosion. Burning pieces of the mangled turret showered to the ground.

Casey sighed in relief and rested his head against the gunner's primary sight (GPS) extension. He was alive, but what about Team Steel? He tried the radio, but without electrical power in the turret the radios were useless.

Casey thought about the inevitable mistakes that occur in the chaos of war. He thought about his men. He knew the human face of war—the energy and the depletion. He was tired.

A flare burned brightly overhead, falling slowly in the southerly breeze. Tank cannon boomed to the north. Casey looked forward and saw the flickering lights of burning vehicles. A 1st Platoon tank raced past *Cossack,* blasting away to the north with its main gun as it charged forward. Standing in *Cossack*'s turret, Casey waved at the 1st Platoon tank, but it drove on.

Casey looked to his rear and saw more M1A2 tanks racing north, their guns blasting away as they moved. The few remaining enemy tanks abandoned their attack and tried to flee to the west. Team Steel's tanks ran them down like hunters shooting wild boar.

Casey watched the tank attack to the northwest, helpless to influence the outcome of the battle. Modern-day commanders are tied to their electronics, he thought. Without them, command is impossible.

He had to get to a radio.

The firing diminished. Casey scanned the battlefield. In seconds the battle was over. Casey assumed that the M1A2s had won the day against the older, less capable enemy tanks. The valley was scattered with their burning, mangled hulls.

"I'm headed outside," Casey shouted as he bent down inside the turret. "Graham, get up here with Kriel and man the machine guns. Cover me, just in case."

Casey muscled out of his hatch, his 9mm pistol cocked and ready to fire. The battlefield was ominously quiet except for the rumble of Team Steel's tanks as they moved west. Carefully Casey climbed down the tank.

As he touched the ground a dazed enemy soldier suddenly staggered in front of *Cossack.* Surprised, the enemy hesitated for a second, then fired his weapon.

Casey took three rounds in the chest before he could fire. The last thing he saw was the tracers of Kriel's machine gun cutting the dazed enemy soldier in two.

You have fought and failed.
Return to Section 104, make another decision, and fight again!

Section 13

> *Some time ago, a group of scholars had an opportunity to look at defeat from the standpoint of soldiers and junior officers who had been through the experience. . . . Thirty factors were listed as crucial by one group or the other. . . . One category of factor was cited in almost every operation: tactics.*
>
> —Col. Trevor N. Dupuy, *Understanding Defeat: How to Recover from Loss in Battle to Gain Victory in War*

More flares popped overhead. Seconds later a few scattered artillery shells slammed into the ground near 3d Platoon.

Enemy artillery, Casey thought. They're finding their range now. In a few minutes all hell could break loose.

"Observing artillery," McDaniel reported. The sound of his 25mm cannon firing at the enemy echoed in the background of the radio transmission. "I think I can take the sons of bitches if I move north, then flank them from east to west. Over."

Casey scanned the battlefield with his CITV. Things were happening so fast that he didn't have a clear picture of the situation. He had no idea how big an enemy force he was up against. He wasn't sure what McDaniel would attack into if he let him loose. And the enemy's artillery was reacting faster than he anticipated.

Casey took a deep breath, then keyed his radio. "Blue One, this is Steel Six. I won't risk a piecemeal attack. Disengage immediately. Move back to Contact Point Alpha. Over."

Thungkt! Thungkt! Thungkt! Casey heard the distinctive sound of the Bradley's 25mm cannons firing. He shot a glance outside his turret to the north and saw the flash of McDaniel's Bradleys.

"We're decisively engaged now, Steel Six," McDaniel screamed over the radio, the roar of his firing echoing in the transmission. "We can't pull back. Over."

Casey shook his head. He didn't want to make his way through an enemy force with only one platoon. He needed the rest of Team Steel. He quickly scanned his IVIS screen.

Section 13

"Steel Six, this is Steel Five," Lieutenant Stonevitch interjected, his voice sounding strained over the radio. "McDaniel is right. If we pull back now we won't get this attack going till daylight. Over."

"Damnit!" Casey cursed over the radio. "End of discussion. Pull back, *now!* That's an order. Steel Guns, get me an artillery smoke screen in front of Blue. I want smoke and immediate suppression to assist his disengagement."

"Wilco, Steel Six," the voice of Lieutenant Keeley replied over the command net. "Blue One, I'll fire once you send me a grid."

"Steel, this is Steel Six. All units will assemble five hundred meters south of Contact Point Alpha. Steel Seven, you organize units in an assembly area as they arrive."

"Wilco, Steel Six," First Sergeant Washington answered.

An artillery flare popped directly above *Cossack*. The flare burned brightly, illuminating Team Steel's command group. Casey looked up at the flare as it dangled toward him, floating in the wet breeze by its tiny parachute.

Cossack slowed to a halt, then pivot-steered and turned around.

"Steel Guns, Steel ADA, let's turn around!" Casey shouted over the radio to the vehicles in his command group.

Karrummp! Artillery churned up the ground two hundred meters left of *Cossack*.

"Driver, get us out of here!" Casey yelled over the tank's intercom as he stood up in the turret and reached to pull the hatch closed.

Roll the dice.

If you roll 2-7, go to Section 19.

If you roll 8-12, go to Section 79.

Section 14

Thungkt! Thungkt! Thungkt! Even with his CVC helmet on, Casey could hear the distinctive sound of 25mm cannons firing to the north. He saw McDaniel's Bradleys flashing fire as they maneuvered off the highway and echeloned to the northeast.

"Engaging troops, Steel Six," McDaniel screamed over the radio, the roar of his firing echoing in the transmission. "They're dug in thicker than Arkansas ticks. Looks like company strength. Enemy machine gun at CS210418."

Casey scanned the battlefield with his CITV. Things were happening so fast that he didn't have a clear picture of the situation. He had no idea how big an enemy force he was up against. He wasn't sure what McDaniel would attack into if he let him loose. And the enemy's artillery was reacting faster than he anticipated. Casey remembered something that Gen. George S. Patton had once said: "Execution to plan is as 5 to 1—don't take counsel of your fears."

"Driver halt, face left front," Casey ordered on his tank intercom. *Cossack* came to a gentle stop on the slick concrete pavement of Highway 21. Casey keyed his radio as he watched the Bradleys return fire to the northwest. "Blue One, this is Steel Six. Report. Over."

More flares popped overhead. Seconds later a few scattered artillery shells slammed into the ground near 3d Platoon.

Enemy artillery, Casey thought. They're finding their range now. In a few minutes all hell could break loose.

"Observing artillery," McDaniel added. The sound of his 25mm cannon firing at the enemy echoed in the background of the radio transmission. "I think I can take the sons of bitches if I move north, then flank them from east to west. Over."

"Blue One, get off the road and continue the attack. You have priority of fires. Steel Guns, get him all the artillery he needs. Break. Red One, pull up to my location ASAP and support Blue's assault. I want you to Blue's left, between them and the enemy. Over."

"Roger, Steel Six," an anxious Lieutenant Andrews answered. "Increasing speed. We're still in the passage lane."

"Get here as fast as you can," said Casey. "Break. White One, get the Sapper element in front of you turned around and get through the passage lane ASAP. The lane is marked by thermal chem lights. Stay on the damned trail. I don't want you wandering into a friendly minefield."

"Wilco," Sergeant First Class Scott answered. "Executing now. White One. Out."

"Green One, you're at the end of White's column. Don't worry about the order of march. Go directly to the passage lane and get your three Bradleys over here to support our attack!"

"Roger, Steel Six. Turning around now," Lieutenant Pender replied.

"Immediate suppression on the way, Steel Six," the voice of Lieutenant Keeley replied over the command net. "Splash. Over."

"Splash. Out," Casey replied as he observed three high-explosive and white phosphorus shells billow in puffs of white electronic haze on his CITV screen.

"You're right on target, Steel Guns," Lieutenant McDaniel replied. "Repeat. Fire for effect."

Casey scanned his IVIS and checked the POS/NAV grid location of the enemy minefield reported to be a kilometer north of Phase Line Audi. "Blue One, this is Steel Six. Be careful to check your POS/NAV for the minefield reported on the west side of the valley."

"Roger that, Steel Six. We're moving east of that position, hugging the tree line to the left of the highway."

Cossack dashed to a position south of the minefield to support 3d Platoon. Casey stood up in his open hatch and surveyed the area. In the light of the artillery flares, he saw Keeley's FIST-V and Sellers's Bradley stop to his left.

Cossack was the only tank ready to fire. Lieutenant Andrews's 2d Platoon was still moving forward. Casey quickly jumped down to his

CITV, acquired the enemy machine gun, and, with the press of a button, swung *Cossack*'s 120mm cannon on target.

"Gunner, HEAT, enemy machine-gun nest!"

"Identified!" Sergeant Graham screamed over the intercom, eager to get into the fight.

"Up," Specialist Kriel, the loader, shouted.

"Fire and adjust!"

Time stood still for an instant. Casey braced himself for the report of the gun, then *Cossack*'s cannon roared. The tank jerked back slightly as the fast-flying, 120mm, tank-piercing round exited the smoothbore cannon, the gun recoiling in its carriage.

"Target!" Casey exclaimed as his sights registered the destruction of the enemy position. With his eyes still glued to his CITV screen, he searched for more targets. He saw little round hot spots popping up just above the ground near the smashed machine-gun position. "Troops!"

"On the way!" With the flip of a switch, Sergeant Graham changed the weapon system from main gun to the coaxially mounted 7.62mm machine gun. The range was only seven hundred meters, and the enemy, crouching in a trench line in the pitch darkness, was clearly visible in Graham's thermal sight.

Cossack's machine gun hummed like a brand-new lawnmower as Graham moved the turret back and forth, spraying the enemy position with bullets. The 3d Platoon moved forward at a crawl, taking short halts to scan, acquire targets, and fire their 25mm cannons. Sergeant Sellers's Bradley Stinger fighting vehicle opened up in concert with *Cossack* and punched the enemy line with high-explosive 25mm rounds.

"Red One, this is Steel Six. Get up here fast!" Casey demanded, feeling as if he was fighting the battle all by himself.

"I'm with you now, Steel Six. I'm moving just to your right flank."

"Roger, Red One," Casey replied, swinging his CITV to scan the right side of the battlefield. He observed 1st Platoon's tanks traveling in column. "Form a firing line between the enemy and the Bradleys. Orient north-northwest. Support by fire."

"Roger, Steel Six," Andrews answered coolly. "We see the enemy. Engaging now."

More artillery flares popped overhead, lighting up the night. Two more enemy artillery shells smashed into the muddy ground. The enemy's artillery would be close behind those flares, Casey thought. There wasn't a moment to lose.

Andrews's tanks raced northwest, slowing as they climbed over the rice paddy dikes that covered the fields in a checkerboard fashion. The tanks crossed the highway, tearing through a flimsy corrugated steel highway fence, firing as they moved. Flashes from their cannon fire lit the valley for brief, surrealistic moments. The four M1A2s moved over the paved road and across the broken ground.

The enemy line exploded with return fire. Small arms, machine guns, and antitank grenades lit up the area to the northwest with their fire. Andrews's tanks used only this to identify their targets and quickly plastered the enemy's positions with fire.

After moving to within six hundred meters of the enemy trench line, the four tanks stopped and blasted away. The sound of battle rose as the tank platoon fired 120mm cannon and machine gun. The tank fire silenced the enemy.

Casey scanned the battlefield with his CITV; he was now confident in Team Steel's power to defeat the enemy. He switched from his CITV to his IVIS screen to check the battlefield. McDaniel's Bradleys were moving along the wood line, flanking the enemy position from the east. Andrews's tanks were delivering support fire as the Bradleys advanced. Pender's Bradleys were now in the passage lane, slowly inching forward. Sergeant First Class Scott's 2d Platoon was moving just south of the lane's entrance.

So far, so good, Casey thought. Now, at least, Team Steel was moving in the right direction.

"Steel Six, this is Blue One. I'm turning to the west, following the wood line," Lieutenant McDaniel reported, his voice resounding with confidence. "I'm ready to cut across the open area and assault the trench with my infantry."

Everything seemed in place, but Casey hesitated. More than half of Team Steel was still south of the passage point. He still didn't know how big an enemy force he was fighting. Was this enemy company an isolated position in the enemy's security zone, or was it part of a battalion defense? He glanced down at his IVIS screen and checked his combat power:

TM C Unit	M1A2 Tank	M2 IFV	BSFV [ADA]	FISTV	Engr M113	CEV	ACE	HAB Bridge	Medic M113	M88 [Rec]	M113 APCs
North of PP	5	4	1	1							
South of PP	5	3			4	1	1	2	2	1	15
Total	**10**	**7**	**1**	**1**	**4**	**1**	**1**	**2**	**2**	**1**	**15**

Casey must decide. He saw three options. Should he order McDaniel to assault, dismount, and clear the enemy trench? Should he tell McDaniel to bypass the enemy and continue the attack? Or should he order McDaniel to wait and support by fire as Andrews's 1st Platoon continues the attack?

There is never a situation in combat where you have perfect information. Decide now!

If Casey orders Second Lieutenant McDaniel's 3d Platoon to assault the enemy position and clear the trench while the tanks of 1st Platoon support by fire, go to Section 20.

If Casey orders Second Lieutenant McDaniel's 3d Platoon to bypass the enemy infantry and continue the attack, go to Section 21.

If Casey orders Second Lieutenant McDaniel's 3d Platoon to hold and orders Second Lieutenant Andrews to continue the attack, go to Section 38.

Section 15

We cannot allow the infantry and armor close battle to be a fair fight. Eye-to-eye combat is not a boxing match or a football game. Conflict with both sides evenly matched in firepower will only prolong the horror and cause needless friendly casualties.
—Maj. Gen. Robert H. Scales, *Firepower in Limited War*

"Dismount your infantry and clear the bridge," Casey ordered over the radio. "The enemy detonated a cratering charge in the southern lane. I don't know if a tank or Bradley can cross. Get to the other side. I'll support you with fire."

"Roger, dismounting now," McDaniel answered.

All four Bradleys raced toward the bridge and dropped their ramps. A dozen infantrymen, led by McDaniel, inched their way cautiously across the bridge.

"You're right, Steel Six," McDaniel reported over his dismounted radio. "An M1 tank would never make it past this crater. There's not enough room. You'd fall into the hole and then you'd block the route. We'll need an assault bridge up here to fix this."

"Roger, Blue One. Get to the other side first and we'll place the bridge."

"Wilco," McDaniel replied. His platoon moved forward, crouching on both sides of the concrete bridge. A squad automatic weapons team lay prone on the left side of the bridge, ready to fire cover support if needed.

Casey held his breath as McDaniel's platoon slowly moved across the bridge. The enemy remained quiet. Casey scanned the far bank of the Gang River with his CITV. "Graham, do you see any enemy? Anything at all?"

"Scanning," Graham said as the turret jerked back and forth. "There. I see men on the far side."

"Blue One, this is Steel Six. We see enemy on the far—"

Before Casey could finish his sentence, a series of explosions detonated along the north side of the bridge. Towers of flame shot skyward. The blasts rocked the bridge.

"Blue One!" Casey screamed, worried that McDaniel's men had been caught in the explosions. "Blue One, this is Steel Six. Report!"

"We're okay, Steel Six," McDaniel's shaky voice responded. "I'm moving forward to survey the damage."

The squad automatic weapons team opened fire along with a dozen M16 rifles. Casey watched in apprehension as the tracers bounced against the concrete on the far side of the bridge.

"No dice, Steel Six. They've cratered both sides of the bridge. I've got four big holes in the highway floor. Infantry can cross, but you'll never get the tanks or Bradleys across, even with the heavy assault bridges."

Casey shook his head in disgust. They'd come all this way—they were only two and a half kilometers from the surrounded 1-12th Infantry—only to be stopped at the bridge.

Casey stood in *Cossack*'s open hatch and considered his options. He knew that the enemy knew where he was. There is no better target reference point than a seventy-ton concrete bridge. Casey had to face the facts. There was no way to cross the Gang. The longer he waited in this vulnerable spot, the more chance he had of being hit by the enemy's artillery.

He had to make a decision. He still had a chance if he tried to stack the heavy assault bridges at the ford site. It was risky, but it was his only option.

"Blue One, get back here ASAP. All Steel elements, move back to Coral."

Before he could close his hatch, the sky erupted in fire. An enemy multiple rocket launcher (MRL) strike landed on the south side of the bridge in a furious blast, like a power hammer smashing a glass bottle. Casey was torn apart by the explosion and died instantly.

You have fought hard and failed.
Go to Section 29 and make a different decision.

Section 16

A cavalry general should be a master of practical science, know the value of seconds, despise life and not trust to chance.

—Napoleon

Casey grabbed his pistol. Before he could pull the trigger, the enemy soldier launched his RPG.

The grenade soared with a trail of sparks right into the rear end of the Wolverine. The bridge launcher jerked to the right and froze in a half-deployed position. Its engine caught fire. Sergeant Jacobs and his driver jumped from the burning bridge launcher as the fuel from the engine ignited in billowing flames.

Casey fired rapidly, hitting the enemy gunner in the head, shoulders, and torso. The man crumpled dead to the paved road.

"Damnit!" Casey cursed. He pushed the radio transmission switch forward. "Steel Five, this is Steel Six. The assault bridge has been hit. I'm going to try to pull it out of the way with my tank. Get the M88 up here and the second assault bridge!"

"Wilco," Stonevitch answered.

Casey opened his hatch and climbed down *Cossack*'s side to survey the damage. The engine fire raged like a blowtorch, lighting up the south side of the bridge. It would be a while, Casey guessed, before anyone could even get close enough to put it out. Pushing it forward was out of the question; that would only jam the assault bridge into the concrete bridge and clog the route even more.

Casey considered his options, then thought about blasting the Wolverine with HEAT rounds to put out the fire. Sergeant Jacobs, bruised and angry but uninjured, convinced Casey that only an M88 could winch the heavy assault bridge (HAB) and launcher out of the way and free up the entrance for the second HAB.

Precious time raced by as the Wolverine burned and Casey waited for the M88 recovery vehicle to maneuver to the bridge.

Suddenly the south side of the bridge erupted in a terrible wave of bursting rockets. The enemy's multiple rocket launcher strike engulfed everything near the bridge in fire. Casey and Jacobs were standing in the open, unprotected, when the huge 240mm rockets detonated in the air above their heads. Both men died instantly.

You have failed in your mission.
Go back to Section 59 and try again!

Section 17

Casey watched the enemy's artillery flares burst in the cloudy sky above the passage point. He knew that the enemy must have an observer nearby, directing the fire. He also knew that every minute was critical. If he didn't move fast, his men stuck in the passage lane would be the enemy's next artillery target.

"Steel Five, stop the column and sort it out!" Casey ordered over the radio. "Break. White One, report."

"Steel Six, this is White One. We're headed northeast, following Viper. I expect to make the turn to the north in a few minutes. The fog is thinning out. Artillery has shifted to the north. No contact. Over."

"Roger, White One. I want you and Blue to take up hasty defensive positions and hold where you are. I'll send my FIST and BSFV to your position. We've got half the force tangled in the passage lane. I'm heading south to fix it. Steel Six. Out."

A breeze suddenly picked up from the north and the fog began to lift. Visibility improved to a few hundred meters. "Weaver, turn around, fast! Head back through the passage lane," Casey shouted over *Cossack*'s intercom. There was only one thing to do: Casey had to go back to the passage lane and get his team unsnarled from the minefield before they were destroyed by the enemy's artillery. He switched his CVC to radio: "Steel Guns and Steel ADA, move forward to 3d Platoon and wait for me there."

"Wilco," Lieutenant Keeley replied. "Hurry back. From the look of the enemy's artillery flares, he knows where we are."

Weaver pivot-steered the tank around as Casey opened his hatch and turned on his night vision goggles. Although the fog had thinned, the chance of missing a turn in the winding path through the minefields was too real to ignore. As Weaver peered through his thermal viewer to follow the path of the thermal chemical sticks, Casey used his night vision goggles to search for the infrared chem lights that marked the way.

Casey scanned to the southwest and saw the lights of two burning APCs. The fires flickered viciously in his green-tinted, light-intensification goggles. He wondered how many men he had lost.

Casey dropped back inside the turret and turned his CITV toward the south, hoping to get a glimpse of the forces stuck in the minefield as the visibility improved. He could feel the rumble of the artillery as it rolled north; it was on schedule. If he was going to take advantage of the artillery strikes, he had to move quickly.

"Steel Five, SITREP. Over," Casey demanded.

"Steel Six, this is Steel Five Delta," the voice of Andrews's driver replied. "The lieutenant is on the ground. Some of the engineers are wounded. The lieutenant is trying to organize a medevac by APC. Over."

"Roger," Casey answered as the sweat beaded up on his forehead. "I'm headed to your position. Have Andrews call me as soon as he returns."

The artillery fire along Cobra and Coral stopped. The fires were now all falling along Viper, several kilometers to the north.

"Steel Six, this is Steel Five," an out-of-breath Lieutenant Andrews reported. "We've lost nine men, all engineers. I've got six critically wounded. We're backing up from the minefield, one step at a time."

"I'll be there in five minutes," Casey answered. "Get as many vehicles back on the lane as you can. I'll guide them north as soon as I reach your position. Over."

"Wilco, Steel Six."

Suddenly a burst of artillery fire detonated near one of the burning APCs. The enemy shell was followed by two, then six, then twelve more.

"Weaver, move faster!" Casey shouted as he reached for the lever to close the tank commander's hatch.

Roll the dice.

If you roll 2-5, go to Section 22.

If you roll 6-9, go to Section 72.

If you roll 10-12, go to Section 88.

Section 18

> *Many badly conceived enterprises have had the luck to be successful because the enemy has shown an even smaller degree of intelligence.*
>
> —Thucydides

Casey slewed the turret and fired from the tank commander's position. "On the way!"

The big, ugly 152mm howitzer fired at the same moment. The high-explosive shell shot over *Cossack's* turret, barely missing the tank. At the same instant, Casey's SABOT round hit the self-propelled howitzer and smashed through its thin armor like a shotgun blasting a pheasant at close range.

"Damn, that was close!" Graham shouted joyfully. "Good shooting!"

Casey didn't reply; he was breathing too fast to speak.

The M1A2s pushed forward relentlessly, firing on the dazed enemy artillery group. As the column turned northwest toward Objective Dragon, two VTT-323s fired antitank missiles at the lead tanks. Both rockets missed their intended targets and burst harmlessly south of the trail. In a quick rotation of turrets, Team Steel's tanks seemed to turn on their attackers en masse; they pulverized the enemy APCs with half a dozen hits before the enemy gunners could reload to fire another volley.

Casey watched the VTTs burn brightly as *Cossack* turned the corner to the west. The American tanks fired at everything in range, adding more fire to the scene of burning trucks and exploding ammunition haulers. Five hundred meters to the east of the burning APCs, a huge explosion burst skyward in a bright shower of sparks and flame. Fire shot out from several artillery ammunition carriers as if they were Roman candles on the Fourth of July.

Enemy howitzers, APCs, and ammunition carriers exploded in fiery eruptions of high explosive. Thick clouds of oily black smoke filled the sky. Three enemy guns frantically reoriented south to oppose the American tanks. McDaniel's Bradleys punctured the enemy howitzers with their 25mm cannons, killing the hapless enemy crews. The Bradleys raced past the dead vehicles, then dashed to the main highway and turned west.

The battle area became a field of brilliant flashes, tearing metal, and billowing black smoke. In the confusion, Team Steel cut through the enemy artillery as if it wasn't even there. Resistance became futile. The tanks and Bradleys were moving too fast and shooting too accurately to be stopped or slowed.

A battery of enemy artillery in the northeast tried to escape the ever-widening arc of destruction. Gunners frantically scurried about as they struggled to hook up their guns to waiting trucks. The trucks and support vehicles were easy targets, massed as they were in hasty, unorganized clumps. Several M1A2 tanks and Bradleys zeroed in on these unlucky souls and slammed them with fire. Panicked truck drivers raced about trying to avoid the 25mm shells and 120mm rounds. In seconds all eighteen trucks were burning, disintegrated wrecks.

Team Steel destroyed every vehicle in range of their guns. The enemy artillery dissolved under this withering deluge of steel and bursting high explosive. The valley, filled with spires of black smoke, was so clogged with burning and exploding vehicles that the surviving enemy artillerymen couldn't find an avenue of escape. The enemy stopped fighting back, dropped their weapons, and ran from the fire. Ragged groups of stragglers fled to the northeast.

Casey felt the adrenaline run through his veins as *Cossack* dashed forward. The path along Direction of Attack Asp burned brightly with the shattered remains of the enemy's artillery group.

What had once been a powerful enemy artillery group was now a slaughter pen. Casey almost felt sorry for his enemy—almost.

Now we've got you, you bastards, he thought.

"Steel Six, this is Steel Guns," Lieutenant Keeley radioed. "That's it for our artillery. If they follow the plan, we'll have another barrage landing here in forty minutes."

"Roger," Casey acknowledged over the radio as *Cossack* turned west toward Highway 17 and Objective Dragon. Casey changed radio frequencies to the one designated for the 1-12th Infantry. He pushed forward on his CVC transmitter. "Bayonet Four, this is Steel Six. We'll be arriving in your perimeter in a few minutes. Hold your fire."

Go to Section 48.

Section 19

> L'audace toujours l'audace *must be the motto of every advanced guard or forward body, whether of a large force or a platoon, in the attack, and when it makes contact with an enemy resistance it must be imbued with a determination to press on and overcome the resistance.*
>
> —B. H. Liddell Hart

Several artillery shells fell to *Cossack*'s left flank. The tank churned the ground, pivot-steering around in a circle to reverse direction and return through the passage lane. Casey locked his hatch in the open-protected position, shielding himself from the shrapnel that whizzed over the tank.

Section 19

Cossack's engine growled as the tank surged forward and headed south. Casey brought his night vision goggles to his eyes. He stared through the narrow slit of the hatch into the darkness. The fog had rolled out. Visibility was improving.

"Where's the damn fog when you need it!" Casey cursed. He pushed the lever on his CVC helmet to transmit over the radio. "Steel Guns, is *our* artillery firing smoke for Blue One?"

"Not yet. It's on the way," Lieutenant Keeley answered. "They had to cease fire on their planned targets and redirect the guns."

Casey swiveled his CITV to the right rear and viewed the area where McDaniel's platoon was withdrawing from the battlefield. Suddenly Casey's thermal sight registered a white-hot object in the center of the screen. A Bradley had been hit and exploded.

"Damnit!" Casey swore to himself. "No, no!"

"Steel Six, this is Blue Four. We just lost Blue One. There are RPGs all over the place!"

"Get out of there, Blue Four!" Casey screamed over the radio. "Steel Guns, where is my smoke?"

More flares ignited overhead. In the bright light, Casey saw the FIST-V and Bradley Stinger fighting vehicle racing south ahead of *Cossack,* negotiating the winding passage lane that bypassed friendly minefields.

Karrummp! Karrummp! Two more 152mm rounds smashed into the ground, this time to *Cossack*'s right flank. They've bracketed us, Casey thought.

Karrummp! Karrummp!

A tremendous violet and yellow explosion erupted in front of *Cossack,* and the seventy-ton M1A2 jerked to an abrupt halt. Red-hot sparks gushed skyward where the FIST-V had once been. For one brief moment there was a loud, echoing silence.

Casey looked through the narrow slit between the top of his turret and the bottom of the tank commander's hatch. In the light of the enemy's artillery flares, Casey saw the burning hulk of the FIST-V. The vehicle had been blown apart, right down to its tracks, like a cardboard box stepped on by a giant. No one could have survived.

"Driver, move around the wreckage," Casey ordered, shaking in anger, grief, and regret.

Roll the dice.

If you roll 2-7, go to Section 27.

If you roll 8-12, go to Section 72.

Section 20

> *The principal problem in almost every attack on every battlefield is to maintain momentum.*
> —Max Hastings, *Overlord, D-Day and the Battle for Normandy*

A desultory fire, aimed at the Bradleys of 3d Platoon, erupted from the enemy positions. An enemy antitank rocket fired at the Bradleys but missed. The rocket exploded in a crash of sparks as it slammed into the ground. Bradleys plastered the area where the rocket was launched. The target area sparkled with the devastating twinkle of high-explosive 25mm shells.

"Blue One, dismount and assault to clear the trench. Red One will support by fire," Casey ordered.

"Wilco," McDaniel replied. "Moving now."

Casey watched through his CITV as the Bradleys moved on-line to assault the enemy trench. Andrews's tanks aimed rapid fire against the trench line. The enemy fire stopped. The massive firepower of Andrews's tanks suppressed even the bravest enemy soldier from raising his head above ground level.

Suddenly the far right Bradley burst into flame as a powerful explosion ripped through its right flank and exited out the other side.

"Damnit!" Casey swore to himself. "No!"

"Steel Six, this is Blue Four. We just lost Blue One. Enemy anti-tank missiles are firing at me from the northeast."

"Get out of there, Blue Four!" Casey screamed over the radio. "Steel Guns, I need some smoke!"

More flares ignited overhead. Casey stood in his open hatch and watched the three remaining Bradleys in 3d Platoon taking fire from an unseen enemy to the northeast. Suddenly Casey realized his mistake. The enemy infantry they were attacking was the left company of a battalion-sized engagement area. He had sent the 3d Platoon in a flank march across the center of the enemy's fire sack to attack the far left position. In the bright light of the flares, Casey saw three Bradleys firing furiously to the right.

Kaboom! Another Bradley was enveloped in fire as an enemy missile struck its flank.

"Blue Four, this is Steel Six. Get out of there! Move back to me. Over."

Blue Four didn't reply. Casey stood in his turret and watched another Bradley explode.

Karrummp! Karrummp! Two more 152mm rounds smashed into the ground, this time to *Cossack*'s right flank.

"Observing heavy artillery fire," Lieutenant Andrews reported. "Those last few artillery shells were too close. We've got to move out of here!"

They've bracketed us, Casey thought. They know exactly where we are. They're trying to kill us with artillery fire.

Karrummp! Karrummp!

A tremendous violet and yellow explosion erupted to *Cossack*'s left as one of the seventy-ton M1A2s was struck by a 152mm artillery shell. A terrible metal-on-metal clang echoed in the valley as the tank jerked to an abrupt halt. Red-hot sparks gushed skyward as the shell smashed into the M1A2's engine compartment. For one terrible moment a loud blast signified that the tank's engine had exploded.

Casey looked through the open slit between the top of his turret and the bottom of the tank commander's hatch. In the light of the enemy's artillery flares, Casey saw the crew bailing out of their stricken tank and rushing to the safety of their wingman.

Casey had lost the 3d Platoon and one tank from the 1st Platoon.

"Steel Six, this is Steel Seven. One of the heavy assault bridges drove off the trail near the passage point and is blocking the passage lane. We can't get around it because of the friendly minefields. It's going to take me a while to get the M88 in there and clear the lane."

Casey didn't answer. He remembered a passage he had once read: "Everything in war is very simple, but the simplest thing is difficult. The difficulties accumulate and end by producing a kind of friction that is inconceivable unless one has experienced war."

"Sir, Top is calling you," Casey's gunner, Sergeant Graham, announced over the intercom.

Casey still didn't answer; he just stared at his IVIS screen.

"Go ahead, Steel Seven," Graham cut in. "Six hears you."

"I'll rally the rest of the company at CS218397 while I work on clearing the lane. It'll take quite a while to get organized. The bridge layer is on its side. The driver's banged up but okay. We probably won't be ready to move until after sunrise."

"Roger, Steel Seven. We copy," Graham answered.

An artillery flare popped directly above *Cossack*. The flare burned brightly, illuminating Casey's command group. Casey looked up at the flare as it dangled toward him, floating in the wet breeze by its tiny parachute.

Karrummp! A volley of artillery slammed into the ground near *Cossack*.

"All Steel elements, this is Steel Six. Return to the new rally point at CS218397," Casey yelled in vain as he reached to pull the hatch closed.

Roll the dice.

If you roll 2-3, go to Section 37.

If you roll 4-12, go to Section 79.

Section 21

Armor must and can operate effectively in all types of terrain. The assumption that terrain, and terrain alone, can stop tanks is entirely false. At its worst, terrain can only limit the use of armor; it cannot stop its use entirely. This would seem basic, but it was ignored in 1940 in the Ardennes and again in 1950 in Korea.

—U.S. Army Armor School, *Employment of Armor in Korea. The First Year*

A flurry of 7.62mm and 14.5mm machine-gun fire splattered the Bradleys of 3d Platoon. An enemy antitank rocket sliced through the dark, narrowly missing one of the American armored infantry fighting vehicles. The antitank missile smashed into the ground, exploding in a shower of sparks and flame. The Bradleys returned the fire, plastering the area of the missile launch with devastating 25mm high-explosive shells.

Casey remembered that his mission was to break through to the beleaguered 1-12th Infantry, not to mop up every enemy rifle squad that he came across. "Blue One, disregard the enemy in the trench. Red One will attack them by fire. Continue the attack and secure the entrance to the defile at CS216427," Casey ordered.

"Wilco," McDaniel replied. "Moving now."

Through his CITV, Casey saw the Bradleys move forward and bypass the enemy trench. Andrews's tanks fired a devastating, rapid fire against the trench line. The enemy' fire slackened as the massive firepower of four 7.62mm co-ax machine guns, sighted by gunners using thermal sights, drilled any enemy soldier who raised his head above the trench.

Andrews is earning his pay, Casey thought as he watched the machine-gun tracers dance over the enemy's trenches.

The far right Bradley burst into flame. A powerful explosion ripped through its right flank and a huge ball of flame exited the other side. Suddenly Casey's attention was riveted back to the infantry.

"Damnit!" Casey swore. He watched in sad disbelief as the Bradley burned. He couldn't tell if anyone escaped from the wreckage.

"Steel Six, this is Blue Four. We just lost Blue One. I've got AT-4s firing at me from the north and east."

"Go to ground, Blue Four!" Casey screamed over the radio. "Steel Guns, I need smoke on CS215420, ASAP!"

"Roger, Steel Six," an exasperated Lieutenant Keeley answered. "It will take a few minutes to get artillery; they're firing on scheduled targets."

"Get me mortars. Anything!" Casey screamed. "Stay here and control those fires. Red One, follow me. We're attacking north, up Cobra."

"Roger, Steel Six," Lieutenant Andrews answered, the excitement ringing in the young officer's voice.

"Driver, move out, right front," Casey commanded over his intercom. He looked to the front, in the eerie light of flares and explosions, and saw that another Bradley had been hit by enemy fire. The Bradley was burning fiercely.

"Blue Four, SITREP. Over," Casey shouted over the command frequency.

"I've had to dismount my infantry. Lost Blue One and my Three-Two track. They're all over us!"

"Steel Five, bring up the rest of the team," Casey ordered. "I need help."

"I'm moving now with what's with me," Stonevitch answered.

"Steel Six, this is Steel Seven. One of the HABs is blocking the passage lane. We can't get around it because of minefields."

"Handle it, Steel Seven, I'm busy. Hang on, Blue Four, I'm on my way," Casey replied.

Cossack dashed forward. Casey glanced to his left as he cut across the line of fire of Andrews's 1st Platoon. He looked over his shoulder and saw Sergeant Sellers's Bradley following close behind.

"Move it, Red One," Casey ordered over the radio. "Follow me."

"Moving now," Andrews replied.

Casey looked to his front, stood up in the turret, and charged his .50-caliber machine gun.

"Load HEAT," Casey shouted over his intercom. "At my command."

"Up," the loader cried, signifying that the cannon was ready to fire. Another Bradley disintegrated in fire as an enemy missile slammed into its flank.

"Blue Four, this is Steel Six. Over."

Blue Four didn't reply. Casey stood in his turret and watched the last Bradley go up in flames as an enemy missile smashed against its thin armor. *Cossack* sprinted forward, hugging the tree line to the right and moving to the right of the burning Bradleys.

Karrump! Karrump! Mortar shells fell in the opening of the defile eight hundred meters to *Cossack*'s right front. *Cossack* cleared the woods, then all hell broke loose. A fusillade of machine-gun fire engulfed *Cossack* as it turned the corner and found itself in the center of an enemy infantry company position.

Roll the dice.

If you roll 2-8, go to Section 26.

If you roll 9-12, go to Section 46.

Section 22

> *The finest theories and most minute plans often crumble. Complex systems fall by the wayside. . . . The raw truth is before us.*
> —Maj. Gen. Charles W. O'Daniel

Artillery shells burst all around *Cossack*. Brilliant flashes and smoke bathed the night battlefield.

"Shit!" Casey shouted. There was only one thing to do. He had to get Team Steel moving again, before they were chopped up piecemeal and destroyed. "Weaver, move through the passage lane."

Without answering Weaver shoved *Cossack* into high gear and headed south.

"Graham, scan for our vehicles in the minefield," Casey ordered. "Weaver, follow the markers and the old tracks, if you can see them. I don't want to end up like the engineers."

Graham moved the turret back and forth to the south, scanning for friendly forces. "I see four burning vehicles. Looks like two APCs and both heavy assault bridges."

Casey disregarded the report and switched his transmitter to radio. "Steel Five, this is Steel Six. Report."

No answer. Casey checked his IVIS screen and saw that Steel Five was registering as a mobility kill, possibly having lost one of its tracks to a mine.

"Missile launch!" Graham yelled. "We're taking fire from the south!"

Casey froze. Missiles from the south? He reached for the grenade launchers, wondering what had gone wrong. Then he remembered the allied unit and Andrews's report that they were nervous about enemy tanks.

Two powerful Javelin top-attack antitank missiles hit *Cossack* at almost the same time. Tearing through the thin top armor of the tank, the missiles killed Casey and his crew.

During Operation Desert Storm twenty-eight cases of fratricide were reported. Nine were air-to-ground engagements. Eleven Americans died and fifteen were wounded from these attacks. Sixteen of these were ground-to-ground engagements.

Twenty-four Americans died from these attacks and fifty-seven were wounded. The biggest killer of the Desert War, therefore, was ground-to-ground fratricide.

—Ian Kemp, "DOD Lists 'Friendly Fire' Casualties" in *Jane's Defense Weekly*, 24 August 1991

You have failed in your mission.
Go back to Section 111 and make a different decision.

Section 23

"Steel Five, this is Steel Six. You're right. If we don't clear Masan now, we'll have to fight through them later. We'll execute the plan you have sketched out. Over."

"Wilco, Steel Six," Stonevitch's voice beamed back over *Cossack*'s radio speakers.

"I want you to set an attack-by-fire position on the southeast side," Casey explained over the command radio frequency. "I'll attack by fire with 2d and 3d Platoons from the west. Once we've knocked out the enemy on the western edge of the town, I'll enter in the west and drive them out. You support me and catch them if they run east."

"Roger, Steel Six. Let's get 'em."

"All Steel elements, this is Steel Six. We're going to clear Masan. Digital sketch follows. Move out in sequence. Acknowledge upon receipt."

Casey scanned his IVIS screen as the battle plan was sent to each platoon leader. In return, the platoon leaders acknowledged that they had received the plan and understood their instructions.

The thick fog rolled back in as Team Steel passed from friendly lines into enemy territory. The visibility was less than fifty meters. Casey turned around in his turret and, with his NVGs, saw that Sergeant Sellers's Bradley Stinger fighting vehicle was following *Cossack*. Reassured, Casey struggled to see behind the FIST-V.

Casey saw Lieutenant Keeley, Team Steel's FIST (fire support team leader), rolling slowly behind the Bradley. Keeley was barely visible in the dense fog. Casey couldn't see McDaniel's Bradleys which were following the FIST, but a quick glance at his IVIS screen showed that they were moving as planned.

Casey loved the M1A2 tank. He took great satisfaction in knowing that the information that the tank could organize was a tactical commander's dream. Information is power. The CITV gave him the

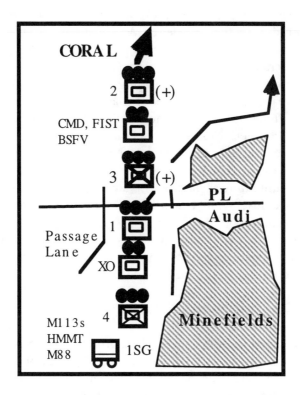

power to see independent of the gunner. He could use the CITV in a hunter-killer role, designating targets for his gunner, or to enhance his command and control. His IVIS screen gave him the power to command Team Steel beyond what he could see or hear. The IVIS screen became his battlefield vision. It registered the exact six-digit location of all his M1A2s, Bradleys, and Wolverine heavy assault bridges. This gave him the incredible advantage of knowing exactly where his forces were. In addition, as soon as any vehicle lazed on an enemy target, he could read the exact location of the enemy. He knew that this information advantage, if wedded to a well-trained unit, would be decisive.

The whine of *Cossack*'s engine seemed to grow louder as the fog grew thicker. The passage lane followed a narrow dirt trail, marked on both sides by thermal and infrared chem lights. Some of the markers were very difficult to see; Weaver was able to make them out only in his driver's thermal viewer. Weaver slowed down as the visibility decreased to avoid missing a turn in the passage lane. Team Steel soon crawled along at a snail's pace.

Casey closely followed the readings on his POS/NAV system, guiding Weaver through the predesignated course. Casey looked at his watch. It was 0045. He scanned his IVIS screen and saw that he had just a few meters more to go before they would be out of the passage lane and able to maneuver. The unit icons moved slowly across his computer screen. Team Steel's double envelopment of Masan was unfolding as planned. So far, so good, he thought.

"Steel Six, this is White One. LD now. Zero and Four. No contact," Sergeant Scott reported.

"Roger, White One," Casey answered. He shot a quick glance at his IVIS screen and took pleasure in the fact that things were going as planned in spite of the fog. "Steel Guns, fire the prep on Masan. Over."

"Executing now, Steel Six," Keeley answered. "Rounds on the way!"

In the dense fog Casey could feel the ground rumble as the American 155mm howitzers shifted their fire to targets on the suspected enemy defenses at Masan. So far, he had been able to orchestrate the combined effect of artillery and maneuver to prepare the battlefield. He hoped that the battle to clear Masan would be an easy one.

After several tense minutes, *Cossack* exited the passage lane. The fog suddenly thinned. Casey glanced through his CITV and scanned the battle area. He saw the 2d Platoon to his front, moving swiftly along Coral toward Masan.

The noise of the artillery increased. He looked at his watch. It was 0100. He could feel the ground tremble as the artillery shells struck to the northeast. Casey smiled. So far, no enemy contact. Maybe, just maybe this one time, he thought, the artillery has done the job.

Cossack picked up speed as the visibility improved.

Through his CITV Casey could see out to nine hundred meters. Masan was on fire. The artillery strike had to be thorough, he reminded himself, if Team Steel was to clear the town without major losses. He didn't want to send his platoons into a town crisscrossed with enemy antitank ambushes.

The drizzle stopped. A breeze suddenly picked up and blew the last vestiges of fog to the south. The battlefield north of Phase Line Audi suddenly cleared. Casey popped his hatch to the open-protected position to scan the area with his night vision goggles. The heavy metal hatch protected him from projectiles falling from above. If *Cossack* took direct fire, he could button up completely and rely on his vision blocks to direct the tank. Casey looked where the tank was going and jumped down to check the CITV.

Casey scanned the town with the CITV as *Cossack* rolled forward. Sergeant Scott's four M1A2s led, maneuvering in a tightly packed wedge formation across the trails that crisscrossed the abandoned ginseng fields near the town. As the M1A2s rolled east, the artillery fire increased.

"Steel Six, this is White One. Contact! Enemy infantry at CS253423—west side of the town. Engaging now!"

"Roger," Casey replied as he scrutinized the IVIS screen and watched the computer icons that represented Scott's tanks deploy into a jagged *W* shape about eight hundred meters southwest of the town. The tanks started firing. At the same time, Casey saw that Stonevitch's force was moving east but was still not in position to support. "Steel Guns, repeat the artillery on Masan."

"On the way," Keeley responded.

Artillery flares suddenly exploded high above Scott's tanks.

Casey glimpsed up at the flares through the crack in his turret hatch. The four 2d Platoon tanks blasted targets in Masan, adding to the brilliant fireworks that were transforming the dark night into day. *Cossack* darted to the right of the southernmost tank. The tank's shadow was cast against the ground by the light of the artillery flares. Before Casey could see the targets in Masan, a volley of AT-4 anti-tank rockets shot from the town toward the Americans.

Roll the dice.

If you roll 2-10, go to Section 52.

If you roll 11-12, go to Section 54.

Section 24

Casey listened for 2d Platoon. He could hear their machine guns and the occasional boom of 120mm cannon fire to the east of the highway. He concluded that the unit must be no more than four hundred meters away, on the other side of the road.

"Do you think we can make it over to the other side of the highway?" Casey asked his crew.

"Hell, Sir, do we have a choice?" Graham answered. "If we stay here, it's only a matter of time until the enemy's artillery finds us."

Weaver looked at Casey with wide eyes. Kriel pointed his rifle to the ground, tapped the magazine tightly into the receiver, and chambered a round. "I'm game."

A third burst of machine-gun fire smashed into *Cossack*'s left flank. The men instinctively ducked closer to *Cossack*'s right side for protection.

Casey looked at the highway to his east in the light of the flares. Highway 17, like many of the roads in this country, had long built-up stretches to avoid washouts from heavy rains. This section of the highway had been built on a ridge of dirt that was six to seven feet higher than the ground on both sides. That was why Casey couldn't see 2d Platoon. He would have to get his crew to the highway embankment and over it to reach the eastern side.

"We'll never make it unless we draw their fire," Casey said. "If I can get up to the fifty, I can give you three some covering fire as you run southeast and cross the highway."

"Sir, I'll do it," Kriel answered. "I'm a good shot with a fifty."

Casey looked at Kriel and smiled. Here was a soldier, Casey

thought, but no loader is good with the .50 caliber. "No, it's my job. I got us into this mess. Wait until I tell you to run, then sprint like hell to the southeast."

"Yes, sir," Sergeant Graham replied. "Once we get to the 2d Platoon, we'll come back for you. Then we'll finish off these bastards."

"Right," Casey answered. He listened to the sound of artillery fire falling to the east. The 2d Platoon's fire had dwindled. Maybe they were moving to him now. "Okay, I'll see you on the other side."

Casey reached for the metal bar of *Cossack*'s bustle rack and muscled up to the back deck. He crawled on the top and jumped into the tank commander's station. Working quickly, he slid the .50-caliber machine gun toward the enemy.

Casey flicked off the safety. Aiming through the machine gun's iron sight, he fired. A long burst of tracers flew at the hill. Sparks danced against the rocky slope as the heavy, .50-caliber, armor-piercing rounds struck the enemy trenches.

The enemy returned fire. A line of tracer bullets smashed against *Cossack*. Casey now saw exactly where the enemy machine guns were. He readjusted the machine gun and fired, marching the line of red tracers toward the enemy and sweeping the position from left to right.

"Go now!" Casey ordered as he fired. He didn't look back to see if his men obeyed. He fired short, fifteen-round bursts. Every time an enemy weapon returned fire, that point of light got the full attention of Casey's .50 caliber.

Bullets shattered against *Cossack*'s flat left flank. A splinter of lead from the fusillade hit Casey in the left shoulder, knocking him sideways. He stopped firing, reached for his left shoulder with his right hand, and felt the blood. Enraged, he fired again, screaming obscenities at the top of his lungs. The turret was filled with smoke. He fired again.

A dozen artillery flares ignited in a cascading fountain of light. Casey used the illumination to aim his .50 caliber; then he plastered his antagonists with armor-piercing bullets. A storm of return fire engulfed *Cossack*. Casey ducked down inside the turret.

A smothering cloud of smoke swirled about him, but the breeze blew it away and Casey kept firing. He bore down on the .50 caliber and fired until the ammunition ran out. Suddenly there was a brief silence.

A flurry of bullets struck the tank as the enemy opened up with weapons from several directions. Casey ducked down into the smoky turret and worked his way over to the loader's station. The loader's hatch was open. He stretched up and took a deep breath from the opening, like a submerged man gasping for air from a hole in an ice-covered lake. Then he saw the loader's machine gun.

Bullets ricocheted overhead as machine-gun bullets struck the turret. Casey waited for the firing to stop, gasping for breath from the open hatch. Finally the enemy firing stopped.

"They must think they got me," he said out loud. "Well, now I'll give the bastards an education on how to fight."

Casey edged up to the hatch and peeked over the top of the turret. Through a rift in the smoke he saw a group of black shadows moving toward him from his left. Ten or eleven enemy soldiers were in a ditch only thirty feet away, getting ready to rush the tank. Another wave of smoke engulfed Casey. Patiently he waited for it to clear, holding his breath so as not to inhale the noxious fumes.

Suddenly the smoke cleared and the enemy group was only fifteen meters from *Cossack*, moving forward at a run. Casey jumped up in the loader's hatch and charged the 7.62mm M240 loader's machine gun. He swung the barrel toward the enemy and fired, letting off a long, searing burst. A cluster of enemy soldiers fell like dominos in a column before they could reach the tank.

Suddenly a force hit Casey in the shoulder. He hesitated, dazed and confused. His shoulder stung as if he had been bitten by a snake. The armor vest he wore had helped slow the sliver of lead, but it had still cut through the Kevlar and penetrated his collarbone. His left arm went numb. The only thing he could think about was his crew and their chances of crossing the road to safety.

The enemy's fire picked up again. It seemed that every enemy gun fired at *Cossack* at the same time. In the next moment Casey was hit again by a full burst of fire. Mortally wounded in the face and chest, he fell inside the turret. Alone, amid the choking smoke and dark of *Cossack*'s turret, Casey died.

"Yes, sir, that's how I see it," Sergeant Graham answered. "If Captain Casey hadn't stayed to cover our withdrawal, none of us would be alive today."

"That's right, Major," Specialist Kriel added. Kriel's arm, bloody and bandaged, hung in front of his chest in a cravat tied around his neck. "He saved us. He's a hero. I hope he's okay."

Cutter nodded silently. "I hope so too. All right, that's it. Sergeant Graham, take your crew back to the aid station and get those wounds looked at."

Cutter looked at the map. Casey's raid had been an abysmal failure. Losses had been heavy: two M1A2 tanks, Casey's and Andrews's; three M2 Bradleys; the FIST-V; two heavy assault bridges; three engineer APCs; and most of the squads they carried. Unable to pass lines effectively, Casey had attacked piecemeal into the heart of the enemy's defenses and failed to get much farther than the mouth of the defile along Direction of Attack Cobra. Sergeant Scott and one Bradley from McDaniel's platoon were all that returned from the group north of Phase Line Audi.

"I know I'm handing you a mess, Lieutenant Stonevitch, but I've got no choice. The pressure is on. I want you to take command of Team Steel and get ready for tomorrow's attack."

"Don't worry, sir, we'll be ready," Lieutenant Stonevitch replied. "I only wish the poor son of a bitch had listened to me. Maybe he and a lot of other good soldiers would still be alive."

Go back to Section 111 and try again!

Section 25

Casey turned to the rear to close the hatch to the tank commander's station. He fumbled with the hatch as a 152mm artillery shell detonated directly above his tank.

Death came in that instant. The force of the explosion pulverized him against the hard metal of *Cossack*'s turret.

**Go back to Section 111,
make a different decision, and try again!**

Section 26

A blast of enemy machine-gun fire glanced off *Cossack*'s side and spilled over the top to rake the turret. Before Casey could react, he felt a burning sensation as hot metal slivers hit him in the face and shoulder. He jerked back violently, struggling to keep his balance in the commander's weapon station. He lost his footing and slumped down into the turret.

"Jesus Christ, the captain's hit!" Specialist Kriel screamed.

"Clear him away from the gun and fight the tank!" Graham yelled.

Kriel pushed the captain to the right side of the turret, away from the gun. "Up!"

At the same second, Sergeant Graham fired the main gun.

Bleeding profusely, Casey felt his life draining away. The last thing Casey heard before he died was the roar of *Cossack*'s cannon.

**Go back to a previous section,
make a different decision, and try again.**

Section 27

> *How can there be a science of war in which, as in every practical matter, nothing can be definite, and everything depends on countless conditions, the influence of which becomes manifest all in a moment, and no one can know when that moment is coming?*
> —Prince Andrea in Leo Tolstoy's *War and Peace*

The three surviving Bradleys of the 3d Platoon raced to return through the lines. Artillery shells detonated left and right of the Bradleys as they made their way through the winding passage lane.

More flares popped above the Bradleys. The retreating Americans were clearly silhouetted in the artificial, bright light of the flares.

A barrage of enemy artillery fire suddenly consumed the trail Bradley. Casey watched from the south side of the passage lane. The explosion buffeted the vehicle. In his CITV he saw sparks shooting out of the hatches. Then he witnessed the explosion of the Bradley's ammunition. None of the crew escaped the burning vehicle. He closed his eyes and shook his head.

Battles are lost by waiting, he thought. It's all a furious cycle of action, reaction, and counteraction. Once committed I should have forced the fight before the cycle swung against me.

"Steel Six, this is Steel Seven. There's no good place to assemble here. I'll have to move everyone farther south."

Casey didn't answer.

"Sir, Top is calling you," Casey's gunner, Sergeant Graham, announced over the intercom.

Casey still didn't answer; he just stared at his IVIS screen.

"Go ahead, Steel Seven," Graham cut in. "Six hears you."

"New coordinates to rally the company are CS218397. It'll take quite a while to get organized. One of the HABs drove off a narrow trail and fell on its side. The driver is banged up but he'll live. The biggest problem is that his damn Wolverine heavy assault bridge is blocking the road! We probably won't be able to move until after sunrise."

"Roger, Steel Seven. We copy," Graham answered.

Go to Section 37.

Section 28

> *In battle, there are not more than two methods of attack—the direct and the indirect; yet these two in combination give rise to an endless series of maneuvers. The direct and the indirect lead on to each other in turn. It is like moving in a circle—you never come to an end. Who can exhaust the possibilities of their combination?*
>
> —Sun Tzu, *The Art of War*

Swiftly, Casey grabbed the hatch release, pulled back the heavy, protective hatch, and buttoned up.

He was just in time. Seconds after closing his hatch, a huge explosion and wave of shell splinters pummeled the top of his tank.

The shock wave from the enemy explosions rocked the tank like a ship being tossed by the sea.

Casey looked through the narrow vision blocks that circled his tank commander's station. The artillery fell like fiery rain all around *Cossack*, exploding in huge geysers of dirt. One shell smashed onto the top of the turret of a 1st Platoon tank. Red-hot sparks burst skyward from the M1A2, then a tremendous orange and yellow flame shot fifteen feet in the air as the tank's fuel ignited.

Casey watched the tank burn. He realized that he had to act if he was to protect his force. He must get Team Steel moving or they would all die to the enemy's massed artillery fires.

"Red One, move now! Bypass Position A and take B. Blue One, support by fire."

"Roger, Steel Six," Lieutenant Andrews replied over the radio, his voice registering his anxiety as artillery shells fell near his tank. "I've lost One-Three. Combat power is three. I say again, I have three tanks."

"Attack now! I'll follow on your left flank," Casey screamed. He knew that he had no choice now but to commit every tank that he had. In a situation like this, even the company team commander was expendable. "Weaver, get us out of here. Head to your left front."

One-Three burned brightly. The dying tank showed no signs of life. *Cossack* rolled past the stricken M1A2 and moved north through the artillery fire. Flares illuminated the night sky. The three tanks of 1st Platoon sprinted forward in an uneven wedge. The tanks moved at fifteen miles an hour. *Cossack* followed, flanked on the left by Sellers's Bradley and Keeley's FIST-V. The vehicles moved closely packed—only ten to fifteen meters apart.

Casey popped his hatch to the open-protected position to get a better view of the battlefield. He needed to see forward to direct Weaver. The CITV is excellent for seeing targets that are far from the tank, but it is almost useless in helping the tank commander guide the driver across rough terrain at night. Casey peered out of his hatch with the night vision goggles to his eyes and braced himself as the tank bounced across the rough field.

As the tanks closed the distance on the defenders, enemy machine-gun tracers and antitank missiles shot out from Position B like sparks from a metal grinder. At the same time the survivors of Position A opened up with RPG fire from Casey's left flank. The enemy tried to adjust artillery and 120mm mortar fire on the advancing armor. Their effort was in vain. The enemy's shells fell far behind Casey's four tanks, exploding in bright, futile flashes.

A flurry of antitank missiles shot toward the 1st Platoon, but each one missed. In a fit of desperation the enemy fired machine guns and grenades, but they didn't slow the heavily armored M1A2s for a second. The American tanks replied with a devastating volley of cannon fire and plastered the defenders of Position A to the ground.

Cossack and the Bradley Stinger fighting vehicle aimed support fire while Andrews's tanks assaulted Position B. Andrews's tanks fired on the move, blasting the enemy with 120mm cannon fire. When the M1A2s closed to four hundred meters, the tanks switched to machine guns; the defenders could stand no more. A ragged line of soldiers suddenly jumped up from the trench and ran. The act was futile. The tanks mowed them down before the enemy soldiers could flee more than twenty meters from the trench.

A brilliant explosion suddenly flashed to *Cossack*'s right. Casey looked through his vision blocks and saw another M1A2 stagger to an abrupt halt. Casey quickly checked his IVIS screen and saw that the tank that had stopped was Lieutenant Andrews's.

"Red One, this is Steel Six. Report!"

"We're hit but okay, Steel Six. We must have run over an antitank mine. Our left track is off. We can still shoot. I'll have to support you by fire from here."

"Damn!" Casey cursed. He raced through the options. Another tank lost. If he didn't support McDaniel in time, the enemy infantry would eat him alive. With only three fully operational M1A2s and five M2s north of the passage lane, Casey's options were narrowing fast.

"Steel ADA, stay here and help defend Red One. The rest of us will head for Position B. Everyone, keep moving. Forget about the mines; you can't see them anyway. Just keep going!"

Roll the dice.

If you roll 2-10, go to Section 39.

If you roll 11-12, go to Section 72.

Section 29

A white-hot glow in *Cossack*'s thermal sight designated the location of the enemy missile launcher. In a half second, a dozen guns in Team Steel had acquired the heat signature and were plastering the area with fire. A heavy concentration of 120mm and 25mm shells pulverized the western edge of Masan. Casey watched the incoming wire-guided missile, which had to be guided to the target by the gunner, fly wildly into the air. Losing guidance control, the missile smashed harmlessly onto empty ground. Team Steel's quick, accurate fire had either killed or suppressed the enemy antitank crew.

The lesson to the enemy was clear: fire at the charging tanks and die. No more fire came from Masan.

Cossack's turret pointed away from Masan as the tank pushed northeast of the town along Direction of Attack Coral. Casey turned his CITV to the south for a quick glance at the town. Masan glowed with flame and smoke. No more missiles attempted to challenge Team Steel. A combination of artillery, direct fire, and aggressive movement had killed the enemy or caused them to hide from the searching guns. In either case, Casey thought, it didn't matter. His mission was to get to the 1-12th Infantry, not to clear Masan of all enemy opposition. Team Steel rolled on.

The night air grew chilly. The fog thinned as the temperature dropped. The cloud cover was still low, and the night was pitch dark, but the visibility improved as Team Steel moved north.

"Steel Six, this is White One," Sergeant Scott's confident voice echoed over the command frequency. "I've entered the defile at

CS255430. My plow tank is in the lead. Combat power is four tanks and two engineer APCs. Continuing mission. Over."

"Roger, White One. Keep moving. Forget the flanks. Just go!"

Smoke billowed from Masan as the artillery barrage peppered the town with smoke shells and shrapnel. The armored column bolted on. Many of the tanks and Bradleys and even some of the APCs fired at Masan as they sped by. This drive-by shooting, and Keeley's constant artillery attack, pinned down whatever enemy was left in Masan.

Casey popped his hatch to the full-open position and looked behind him. The burning town, punctuated by the brilliant light tracers and exploding shells, provided an eerie scene. *Cossack* dashed forward, following the engineer APCs that were the trail elements of 2d Platoon, and entered the defile.

Casey turned to the front and surveyed the Coral defile with his passive night vision goggles. This portion of Coral was very narrow— a gravel trail that was more creek bed than road. Casey hadn't appreciated from his map reconnaissance how narrow the defile was. The defile's ominous nature was magnified by the green-tinted, two-dimensional view from his night vision goggles. One well-placed minefield, he worried, could bottle up Team Steel for hours or block his advance altogether. As far as Casey could tell, Coral was no place for an armored column. His one chance for success, he mused, was his intuition that the enemy probably felt the same way.

Hell, he thought. What's the use of having intuition if you don't use it?

Soon every vehicle in Team Steel was inside the Coral defile, heading north. Casey checked the time. It was 0200. So far, he hadn't taken any losses. His bold race around Masan was paying off. He was only four kilometers away from his objective—the 1-12th Infantry on Objective Dragon. A quick check of his IVIS screen showed that almost all of his vehicles were north of the 43 grid line.

"Steel Six, this is Steel Guns," Keeley reported in a casual manner that seemed more apt for an exercise than actual combat. "Artillery has ceased fire on Masan. The guns will move to a new firing position, then shift their fires to the bridge on Viper. Over."

"Roger, Steel Guns. Good work. Steel Six. Out."

The column churned on through the dark, narrow defile. The turrets of the lead tank platoon moved back and forth. The tank gun-

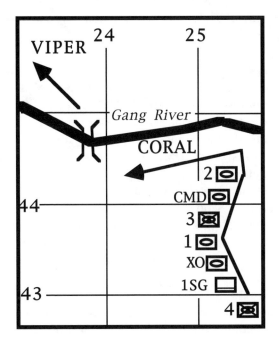

ners searched the nooks and crannies of the narrow mountain pass with their thermal sights for any signs of the enemy. If an enemy antitank crew was waiting in ambush for the lead tanks, the M1A2s would have only a fraction of a second to locate and fire on their attackers.

Casey tried to radio the 1-12th Infantry, but the high mountains that flanked Coral interrupted the FM radio line of sight. He was well aware that poor communications was another characteristic of fighting in restricted terrain. Right now he could talk to most of Team Steel directly and could relay through the XO and first sergeant to talk to all elements, but he could not reach battalion headquarters on the radio. When he exited the north side of the defile, just south of the Gang River, he hoped that he would be able to radio the 1-12th Infantry.

"Steel Six, this is Steel Guns," Keeley reported. "I've lost radio contact with the artillery."

"Roger, Steel Guns," Casey answered, anticipating the loss of communications. "The mountains are blocking our transmissions. Try again after we exit and get near the river."

"Steel Six, this is White One," Sergeant Scott's excited voice boomed over the command frequency, interrupting Casey's transmission to Keeley. I've got a vehicle with blackout lights headed right for me coming down Coral. We're still moving at fifteen miles an hour. Do you want me to take them out or capture them? Over."

Casey's curiosity was piqued. "A lone vehicle? Over."

"Roger. Looks like a BRDM. They'll see me in a few seconds. What do you want me to do?"

Casey has to decide. He recognized two immediate courses of action: tell Sergeant Scott to destroy the armored vehicle or tell him to try to capture it. If the enemy finds out that Team Steel is on Coral, there could be hell to pay. What if the enemy saw the column and radioed for help? Can Casey afford to take the chance of giving away his location?

If Casey orders Sergeant Scott to destroy the enemy vehicle and continue the mission, go to Section 42.

If Casey orders Sergeant Scott to capture the BRDM, go to Section 57.

Section 30

The sterner the challenge to men, the finer the response.
—Arnold Joseph Toynbee

Casey scanned the highway embankment to his east in the light of the flares. Like most of the roads in this country, Highway 17 had long stretches built up to avoid washouts from heavy rains. This section of the highway was built on a ridge of dirt that was six to seven feet higher than the ground on both sides. This was why Casey couldn't see 2d Platoon. If he abandoned the protection of *Cossack*, his crew would have to cross open ground, climb the embankment, and run across the highway to reach the protection of the eastern side.

"We'll never make it across the highway," Casey announced to his crew.

"Hell, sir, do we have a choice?" Graham answered. "If we stay here, it's only a matter of time until they call artillery on us."

Casey held his hand up to his ear, silencing Graham for a moment. He could hear the distinctive sound of .50-caliber machine guns and the occasional boom of 120mm cannon fire from 2d Platoon.

"The 2d Platoon must be just east of the highway, no more than four hundred meters away," Casey replied. "They'll work their way to us, I'm sure of it. Our best bet is to wait here."

Weaver looked at Casey with wide eyes. Kriel pointed his M-16 rifle to the ground, tapped the magazine tightly into the receiver, and chambered a round.

A third burst of machine-gun fire smashed into *Cossack*'s left flank. The men instinctively ducked closer to *Cossack*'s right side for protection.

A dozen artillery shells smashed into the ground to the east of the road. The ground trembled with each explosion, as if a huge hammer was striking the earth. More flares lit the night sky, most falling to the east. Occasionally a machine gun would fire on *Cossack*, as if to make sure that the horrible beast was dead.

Casey and his crew hugged the wet, muddy ground next to *Cossack* as the artillery fire intensified. Safe on their side of the road, Casey knew that the enemy was attempting to drive off 2d Platoon. After ten minutes of terrifying, earthshaking fire, the battlefield grew ominously quiet.

"Sir, 2d Platoon isn't coming for us," Graham announced. "I can't even hear their engines."

"We'd hear their engines if they were close," Weaver added.

A string of flares popped overhead, lighting up the battlefield on the west side of the highway. Casey heard a whistle blow.

"Shit, they're coming out to get us!" Graham announced.

Section 30

Casey shot Graham a quick glance and motioned for him to crawl to *Cossack*'s front and take a look. Casey crouched next to the rear of the tanks and looked north and northwest. In the fading light of the flares, he saw figures bounding toward him.

"Shit, they're coming on this side," Graham whispered. "Looks like a platoon or more."

Casey returned to Kriel and Weaver. "They're coming on the left too. We're going to have to make a stand here and hold out."

"Maybe we should surrender," Weaver suggested.

"These guys don't take prisoners," Graham replied cynically as he pulled out his 9mm pistol and chambered a round. "As my old drill sergeant used to say, 'Always honor a threat.'"

Casey nodded. He had seen the reports of Americans, shot on the side of the road, with their hands tied behind their backs. The enemy wasn't willing to slow down his drive south. A quick pistol shot to the head had been the reward for anyone who raised their hands. No, this would be a fight to the death.

"We're better off fighting from the tank," Casey announced. "I'll man the fifty. Kriel, you man the loader's machine gun. Graham, do you think you can fire the main gun manually in that smoke?"

"I'll have to traverse manually and fire using the manual blaster," Graham replied. "But with all that smoke in there, how will we breathe?"

"Most of the smoke has gone. It's our only chance. Maybe 2d Platoon will see or hear the firing and know we're still alive. Maybe the enemy will think we're fully functional and run back. Maybe, if we're lucky, we will still nail some of the bastards."

"It's worth a try. Shit, as my old drill sergeant used to say, 'When in doubt, empty your magazine.'"

"Okay. Graham, as soon as we climb in, load HEAT. Leave the hatches open; we'll need the air. Weaver, you stay out here and use this M-16 if they come up the sides."

Kriel handed the M-16 to Weaver. The young soldier took the weapon, nodded, and said, "Let's do it."

"Okay. Hurry. They're not far away."

The three men quickly climbed up onto *Cossack*'s back deck. The hatches were open. Graham slid into the commander's weapon

98

hatch as Kriel entered the loader's hatch. Casey crawled into the tank commander's station as Graham disappeared inside the turret.

The smoke was bad but bearable. Casey connected his CVC helmet as Kriel manually forced open the ammunition doors and loaded a HEAT round into the gun.

"Up!" Kriel yelled, signifying that the gun was loaded and ready to fire.

"Hold it, don't fire until I tell you," Casey ordered in a hushed voice. He slid the TC's machine-gun ring toward the right and charged the .50—ready to fire. Kriel popped up in the loader's hatch and pointed his M240 machine gun to the left.

Casey saw a group of enemy to the left front of the tank. "Fire!" he yelled.

Graham hand-cranked the turret as fast as he could, moving to the left in several seconds. The gun exploded in the half-lit night, blowing away a group of five or six enemy soldiers in the surprise blast. The men simply disintegrated in the force of the explosion. The HEAT round sailed through the air and struck the enemy's trench line six hundred meters to the north.

Graham suddenly switched from main gun to co-ax machine gun and let out a long stream of 7.62mm bullets to the north.

A volley of small-arms fire erupted against *Cossack*. Kriel fired his 7.62mm machine gun as Casey plastered the right side with .50-caliber fire. Enemy infantry suddenly appeared all around, much closer than Casey had expected. In a furious surge of fire, the tank machine guns cut down the enemy soldiers like broken rag dolls.

Working their way behind *Cossack*, three enemy soldiers charged the tank at close range. Kriel saw them and yelled to Casey. The captain swung the heavy weapon around and dropped the attackers.

Flares popped overhead and tracers whizzed past, splattering off the tank's armor in a splash of sparks. Suddenly Casey was thrown against the back of his hatch, struck in the shoulder by an AK-47 round. He lost his balance and crumpled into the TC's hatch.

"I'm hit," Casey mumbled, barely able to force the words from his mouth. Graham turned in his gunner's seat and pulled the tank commander down onto the turret floor. Casey felt the hot brass from Kriel's gun fall on him from above.

Events suddenly played out in slow motion. In seconds that seemed like minutes, Graham fired the .50 caliber until it ran out of ammunition. He then fired his pistol, jumped up, and fired several more times. Suddenly Kriel stopped firing and slumped in the loader's hatch, his feet dangling in the air above Casey's head.

Casey struggled to breathe at the bottom of the dark, smoky turret. He gagged in the acrid air. He tried to grab his own pistol but his arms wouldn't move. Graham closed the commander's weapon hatch and screamed that he was out of ammo. Casey tried to reach for his pistol, but he couldn't unbutton the snap. The stark reality of the turret started to fade. The last thing Casey felt was the enemy stick grenade that fell through the loader's hatch and landed right next to him.

You have fought and died.
Return to Section 110 and make a different decision!

Section 31

> There are circumstances in war when many cannot attack few, and others when the weak can master the strong. One able to manipulate such circumstances will be victorious.
> —Sun Tzu, *The Art of War*

In one quick move Casey jerked the hatch from an open-protected position to completely closed. In the next second one of the enemy's antitank missiles detonated with a loud roar against the side of *Cossack's* turret. A brilliant sheet of light covered the top of the tank, illuminating the inside of the turret.

Cossack's special armor protected the crew from the missile strike. The heavily armored M1 tank kept rolling forward, as if hit by nothing more than a large baseball bat.

Another missile struck just to the left of *Cossack,* hitting one of 2d Platoon's tanks. Casey looked out of his vision blocks and saw the tank stagger to a halt.

"Identified the bastard!" Graham screamed.

"Fire!" Casey yelled.

Cossack jerked as the round fired toward the enemy. The tank raced forward as Private Weaver jinked to evade the incoming missiles. The three surviving tanks of 2d Platoon fired in a rippling volley of 120mm fire at the missile launch sites located to the southeast of the bridge.

Casey pushed the transmission forward as adrenaline surged through his body "White One, report!"

"Steel Six. Contact. Enemy antitank missiles at CS239445. Engaging now!"

A volley of 120mm rounds proved Scott's report. The 120mm, high-explosive antitank rounds detonated just south of the bridge.

"Steel Guns, this is Steel Six. I need that artillery back!"

"Working it. No contact," Keeley's voice replied.

"Steel Six, this is White One. I've lost my One-Three tank. The missile hit their left track. The crew is okay, but it'll take time to fix."

"Roger. Continue to attack; we're committed," Casey ordered.

More missiles launched from the southern edge of the bridge. Several enemy machine guns added their fury to the fight. Apparently the enemy was well dug in and ready to defend the bridge. Casey had hoped to catch the enemy unprepared for a direct assault from the east. Now he was charging into a prepared defense.

"Missile launch! Due west!" Graham shouted over the intercom.

Weaver jerked *Cossack* to the left, raced a few meters, then jerked her back to the right. Zigzagging to avoid the enemy's fire, *Cossack* raced west along the south bank of the Gang River.

Roll the dice.

If you roll 2-5, go to Section 50.

If you roll 6-10, go to Section 70.

If you roll 11-12, go to Section 72.

Section 32

Graham fired again. The enemy tank, less than three hundred meters away, lurched backward as it snapped in two. The explosion of Graham's HEAT shoved the T-62's turret several feet to the rear of the hull. The hatches opened. Black smoke billowed from the loader's and tank commander's hatches. One member of the crew staggered out of the smoldering vehicle and fell to the ground.

Another enemy tank swerved into view. Graham switched to this target. Firing rapidly, he incinerated the T-62. Burning like an acetylene torch, the shattered T-62 spun to the left and blocked the path of the tanks that were following Graham.

The enemy kept firing at *Cossack*, trying desperately to drive it out of the company position. Enemy infantry rushed the tank from all sides, moving in groups of ones and twos, to fire RPGs or toss grenades. Three artillery flares illuminated the wet, dark night sky.

Casey's crew sprung into action like a bear cornered by hunting dogs. *Cossack*'s cannon struck as each attacker came into view. The actions of the crew were automatic. Kriel reloaded rounds into the massive breech of the 120mm cannon. Graham, now in control of the gun, aimed with a vengeance and killed everything he shot at. The men stopped counting how many infantrymen they had killed.

As Casey struggled with his .50 caliber, enemy infantry opened fire on him with machine guns from behind the burning T-62s. Casey scanned to his right and saw enemy infantry running on his right flank.

"Enemy infantry left front!" Weaver shouted, alerting the crew to what he saw from his driver's thermal viewer.

"Troops!" Casey screamed as he stood in the turret and saw men running everywhere. He gripped the butterfly triggers of the .50-caliber machine gun and swung the gun in the direction of the enemy. "Fire and adjust!"

Casey fired his .50-caliber machine gun, plastering the area with deadly bullets. Graham jerked the turret back and forth, slicing enemy soldiers in half and driving others to cover. *Cossack*'s 7.62mm machine gun hummed like a well-oiled sewing machine, cutting down the enemy as they attacked the lone tank.

A cold fist tightened around Casey's heart as he expended the last round of ammunition from the box. He reached to the right to grab another box of ammunition from *Cossack*'s right-side sponson box. At the same moment he saw an RPG team launch a rocket-propelled grenade from forty feet away. Casey ducked inside the turret.

"Weaver, back up!" Casey screamed frantically over the intercom. A brilliant explosion engulfed *Cossack* before the driver could register the order. The RPG rocket detonated against *Cossack*'s right side. Another explosion slammed against the left side.

Casey grabbed the .50 caliber and fired a wild, unaimed shot in the direction of the enemy as the tank spun around in a half circle. In the superbright light of the magnesium flares, Casey saw *Cossack*'s left track roll off the support rollers. The last RPG had hit the track and broken it in two. Weaver, not knowing that the left track was gone, jerked the tank to the right, driving it in a semicircle.

Cossack's rear grill doors were now facing the enemy. The turret swung wildly around as Graham tried to get a bearing on the next target.

Two men rushed out of the shadows toward the tank and fired more RPGs. One grenade detonated against the gun mantle of the tank, lifted Casey out of the turret, and flung him through the air. He felt as if he had been sucked out by a tremendous wind. He landed with a thud on his back about ten feet behind the tank.

The world went black. Suddenly, Casey regained consciousness. The ringing in his ears faded slightly, and he was suddenly aware of the sounds of the battle. Explosions echoed all around him. Men were running and screaming as machine-gun bullets kicked up the ground. Casey struggled to reach for his 9mm pistol, which was strapped in a shoulder holster to his side, but he couldn't move.

Dazed, he opened his eyes and looked up at the brightly burning artillery flare as it dangled toward him, floating in the wet breeze by its tiny parachute.

Casey looked toward his tank. Somehow he managed to raise his head enough to see that *Cossack* was on fire. He felt the heat from the blazing inferno that was shooting out of the top of its turret. Saddened, he lowered his head.

An enemy soldier abruptly appeared, staring down at him. Casey tried to scream. He kicked his legs but struck only air. The last thing Casey saw was the opponent's look of triumph as he thrust a bayonet into Casey's chest.

Return to Section 14 and try again.

Section 33

> *Military tactics are like unto water; for water in its natural course runs away from high places and hastens downwards. So in war, the way is to avoid what is strong and to strike at what is weak. Water shapes its course according to the nature of the ground over which it flows; the soldier works out his victory in relation to the foe whom he is facing.*
>
> —Sun Tzu, *The Art of War*

Graham immediately fired as *Cossack*'s cannon cleared the ridge and blasted the last enemy tank. The turret of the T-72 sailed into the air, sparking black smoke and flame. Eager for a kill, Casey ruthlessly turned the cannon toward the nearest enemy APC.

Two VTT-323 APCs lumbered forward, four hundred meters in front of *Cossack*. The VTT-323 was a lightly armored APC, built off the old Chinese design. Its puny 14.5mm machine gun wouldn't even scratch the depleted-uranium armor of an M1A2.

"Gunner, HEAT, two APCs, left PC," Casey ordered.

"Identified," Graham answered coolly.

As Sergeant Graham lazed to the target, Casey sent a digital contact report over his IVIS system to the rest of the platoon and the company at the push of a button.

"Up," cried Kriel as he pushed the mechanical safety lever to the fire position.

"Fire!" Casey shouted over the radio.

As the first HEAT round exited the muzzle of the tank's gun, the inside of the turret echoed the fury of the shot. The gun breech recoiled and ejected the base cap of the combustible projectile. This aft cap bounced on the floor of the turret.

"Target, right PC!" Casey shouted over the intercom, his right eye glued to his thermal sight.

With lightning speed Kriel loaded the gun, stood clear of the breech, pushed the safety handle to fire, and yelled, "Up!"

The 120mm tank cannon roared. Direct hit. Casey grinned as he looked through his CITV and saw that both enemy APCs were flaming wrecks. In this smoky battle, the M1A2s had the decisive advantage. The enemy never knew what hit them.

The survivors of Team Steel plastered the remaining enemy VTT-323s with cannon fire and gunned down the enemy infantry as they staggered out of their burning APCs. The fast-firing M1A2s and the remaining Bradleys drilled the VTT-323s to pieces before they could get very far. Soon there was nothing but burning wreckage and dead bodies on the eastern edge of Dragon.

Casey took stock of the situation. They had beaten off a powerful enemy attack and destroyed the better part of a reinforced tank battalion. The losses, however, had been high. Andrews was dead and his tank disabled. McDaniel had lost two Bradleys. Casey's force was low on ammunition. To make matters worse, the 1-12th Infantry was out of antitank missiles.

Casey resolved to gather up everyone—orders be damned—and fight his way south. But before he could issue the order, a new wave of explosions rocked the ground. Casey quickly closed his hatch to avoid the zinging steel. Shaking with the rocking of the tank, he steadied himself against the tank commander's sight extension and observed through his commander's station vision blocks. The artillery picked up in intensity; it seemed to crush in all around *Cossack*.

Roll the dice.

If you roll 2-4, go to Section 87.

If you roll 5-12, go to Section 91.

Section 34

It seems to be a law inflexible and inexorable that he who will not risk cannot win.

—John Paul Jones, from a letter to
Vice Admiral Kersaint, 1791

Suddenly everything stopped, instantly, as if *Cossack* was slapped by a giant hand. The noise was deafening. Casey blacked out for a moment, then regained consciousness. *Cossack*'s turret was filling with smoke.

Casey struggled to open the hatch. All power in the turret was out.

"Systems out, sir. No power. I can't move the turret," Graham shouted, coughing in the smoke.

"Try the APU," Casey ordered.

"Nothing!" Graham screamed.

"Weaver, report!" Casey yelled as *Cossack* was raked by machine-gun fire. "Crank her up!"

Weaver didn't answer. The smoke consumed the air inside the turret.

Casey waited a few seconds, then gave the order. "Bail out, abandon the tank!"

Kriel opened his hatch. The fresh air rushed in and he stood up to jump out, only to fall inside the turret, bleeding from the face. Bullets ricocheted off the top of the tank. Casey, driven down into the turret by the enemy fire, fumbled in the smoky fighting compartment to help Kriel.

The T-72s rolled through the storm of fire, finding other targets to shoot at. Casey could feel the vibrations of their tracks as they tore across the wet, rocky ground. When he felt that it was safe, he reached for Kriel. Tugging on the evacuation strap in the back of Kriel's Nomex uniform, Casey pulled the wounded man out of the turret. Graham followed right behind, coughing and fighting for air.

The three men lay on the ground in front of their tank. A T-72 churned up the ground as it headed right for them, firing its machine guns. Casey hugged the ground. Tracers flew wildly everywhere, ricocheting off *Cossack*. Casey was sure this was it.

The enemy tank moved closer. Casey heard a howling sound and saw a bright flash. He looked up just in time to see a Javelin explode against the top of the turret of the T-72. The surging monster immediately shuddered to a stop fifty feet in front of Casey. The driver's hatch on the front slope of the vehicle shot open, filled with searing flames. Thick, greasy smoke leaked out of every joint and opening of the dying tank. The top hatches opened as thick smoke billowed from inside the turret. Suddenly the turret blew apart in a bright explosion, scattering fragments of burning metal across the ground.

Casey heard shouts nearby. He pulled his 9mm pistol from his holster and chambered a round.

"Kriel's dead," Graham shouted above the noise of battle.

Another T-72 clanked into view only fifty meters away. This tank was immobilized by a well-placed antitank mine. The tank's track rolled off its road wheels. As smoke poured out of the hatches, dark figures emerged and jumped from the smoldering beast to the ground. Casey aimed his pistol and fired. The stunned enemy tankers fell before they had moved five paces from their tank.

The last Javelin rounds were shot. Two more enemy tanks went up in flames, but the enemy assault didn't waver. More tanks, followed by bunches of infantry, forced their way into the defensive position.

The sound of the battle echoed in muffled explosions in the hills. Short bursts of machine-gun fire from the few remaining defenders lashed out at the attacking enemy tanks. Unimpressed, the T-72 tanks blasted these points of resistance with cannon fire.

Casey grabbed Kriel's pistol in his left hand. He and Graham crouched in the ditch, waiting for the next attacker to come up the hill. Casey looked over the sheer gap between the living and the dead and he saw that there was no escape. Somehow, that no longer seemed to matter.

A fresh wave of enemy infantry surged forward. Casey and Graham fought. Firing a 9mm pistol in each hand, Casey dropped six of the attackers before he met his fate.

You have lost, but you died fighting.
Go back to Section 111, make a different decision, and fight again!

Section 35

> *Defenses in mountainous terrain also have their vulnerable spots. Their localized nature and the large gaps between strongpoints enable the attacking subunits to infiltrate to the rear of the defensively deployed enemy.*
>
> —Maj. Gen. V. G. Reznichenko, *Tactics*

Casey stood in the open hatch of his commander's weapon station. He looked anxiously at his watch. This was taking too long, he thought. He remembered something that he had learned from his previous studies of his enemy: it took about twenty minutes for them to call for fire and deliver a fire strike with one battalion of artillery.

In a terrible, agonizing shriek, the sky exploded. A 120mm rocket detonated directly above *Cossack*. The rocket burst in a tremendous ball of orange and red flames. Dozens of hot, burning metal fragments smashed into Casey's body before he knew what hit him. He died in the same instant.

You have fought hard but failed.
Go back to Section 111 and try again.

Section 36

> *Take your charts back and figure again on the basis of half that marching speed and twice the time length on your columns. . . . Night movement is filled with the unforeseen: troops that missed the proper road, bridges blown up, and columns mixed up with each other because one wasn't on time at the starting place.*
> —Maj. Gen. E. N. Harmon, *Combat Commander*

In a panic Casey turned to his IVIS screen as the icons that depicted the four M1A2 tanks in 1st Platoon moved east, missing the passage lane. He instantly knew what had happened: Pender had followed the engineers right into a friendly minefield. The rest of the column had veered off behind him like ducks in a row.

"Stop where you are, Steel Five, and get control over the damn Sapper elements," ordered Casey. "I'm already north of the passage lane. You'll have to take charge of that situation."

There was a long pause on the radio before Andrews answered. "I'm bumper to bumper with the last of Pender's Bradleys, Steel Six. I can't do a thing."

"Weaver, stop the damn tank!" Casey ordered, exasperated that he had lost an assault bridge and two engineer squads in a friendly minefield.

Weaver slammed on the brakes, throwing Casey against the front of his TC's station. Annoyed but too concerned over the loss of his engineers to take time to yell at Weaver, Casey opened his hatch and peered to the south. His force was now effectively cut in half. Without an experienced XO to take charge of the mess near the passage lane, Casey's choices seemed narrowed to two: hold the lead elements north of the passage lane while he returned south to unsnarl the mistake, or leave half of the company team in Andrews's hands and continue the attack.

The fog began to lift and visibility improved a few hundred meters. Casey looked at his watch. It was 0100. *Cossack* sat just north of the LD, on Viper, at CS240406. Casey could feel the rumble of the artillery shake the ground as the detonations rolled north. He was losing valuable time—time that could not be made up.

Artillery flares suddenly popped high above the hill at CS240410. The flares burned brightly, illuminating the passage lane. Casey looked up at the flares as they dangled downward, floating in the wet breeze by their tiny parachutes.

Casey had to decide!

If Casey decides to move south to get his snarled force through the passage lane, go to Section 17.

If Casey decides to continue to attack with what he has north of the passage lane, go to Section 67.

Section 37

> *Raids into the enemy rear have become an important and indispensable part of modern battle as demonstrated by the raid of a small group of Israeli tanks into the rear of the Third Egyptian Field Army in October 1973. This raid unhinged and threatened to defeat the entire Third Army.*
>
> —Col. Bogdan Swita

"Steel Six, this is Dragon Six," the voice of Major Cutter re-sounded in Casey's CVC earphones.

The rain fell in a constant drizzle over the gloomy company team assembly area. Casey had lost too many vehicles and men too early in the mission to continue the attack. By the time he had reorganized the company team to continue the mission, planned the artillery fire through the 4th Platoon's forward observer, and coordinated with the battalion, it was 1005.

Casey was tired, bruised from being flung back and forth in the turret, and dejected at the loss of his men and the failure of his mission. He pushed the microphone switch forward on the side of his CVC helmet. He was afraid to hear Cutter's orders, but he had no choice but to reply. "This is Steel Six. Go ahead, Dragon Six."

"Brigade has lost contact with the 1-12th Infantry. We believe that they have been overrun. If there are any of them left alive, they are on their own. Your mission is canceled."

Captain Thomas Nathan Casey closed his eyes and bit his lip. He thought about the men he had led in the chaos of the night. He thought about the good men he had lost, all in vain. He thought about the poor, bloody infantrymen of the 1-12th, surrounded and overwhelmed by an unmerciful enemy.

"Roger, Dragon Six. What are your orders?" Casey asked.

"Move Team Steel back to the assembly area. I'm putting Lieu-tenant Stonevitch in charge of what's left of Team Steel. Report back to my headquarters as soon as you arrive. You will be reassigned to brigade headquarters this afternoon. Out."

After-action Review

> *With many calculations one can win; with few one cannot. How much less the chance for victory has one who makes none at all!*
> —Sun Tzu, *The Art of War*

Time pervades all decision making in war. It defines the possible and the impossible. Time orders the sequence and tempo of military operations. Gaining a time advantage has been crucial to success at every level of warfare and in every age. Sun Tzu, the ancient sage of war, understood this and argued that good commanders gain advantage from making as many prudent calculations prior to battle as possible.

If combat decision making is a contest for time—a race to increase situation awareness to make good decisions in minimum time—then military commanders and staffs must be experts at decision making. The first step is to understand the types of decisions that commanders must make.

All military decisions can be categorized into three distinct types: organizational, informational, and operational.

Organizational decisions are usually made prior to combat. Organizational decisions concern the manning, equipping, supplying, and maintaining of military units. They also determine the role of the chain of command, the degree of independence associated with each unit, and the degree of centralization or decentralization allowed in the exercise of command. The German army of World War II, for instance, organized and equipped its units according to new concepts of mobility and firepower. The decentralized command doctrine of the Wehrmacht matched the requirements of organization and technology. The Wehrmacht, therefore, allocated a high degree of decentralized responsibility to their junior leaders and gained a tremendous combat multiplying effect from their efforts. The French army of 1940, on the other hand, organized and equipped their forces for combat according to the lessons of World War I; it severely restricted the organizational independence of its tactical formations. The French tried to bring certainty to the chaos of battle by applying a rigid equation of firepower and strict control. This organizational decision was a major reason for the total defeat of the French army to the more agile-thinking German army.

The French army of 1940, therefore, could not have executed a blitzkrieg because the organizational decisions made prior to the war precluded it from thinking in terms of decisive maneuver. This organizational decision framed every subsequent informational and operational decision made by the French.

Informational decisions specify the type of data required for decision making. Informational decisions also relate to the flow of essential elements of information: who talks to whom and how important information is passed. The Cold War–era Soviet army, for example, strongly believed in the need to scientifically justify every decision. Soviet officers required a high degree of intelligence and reconnaissance data before their informational needs were met to make decisions. Without this information, any decision they made would be unjustified and could result in serious personal repercussions. In World War II, for instance, Soviet officers who made decisions without appropriate justification *and failed* were often executed. The requirement for scientific certainty often led to decision-making paralysis.

Operational decisions are those decisions made during the fight (as opposed to the more specific military meaning of operational as a description of the levels of warfare—strategic, operational, and tactical). Operational decisions involve the movement of forces on the battlefield. Operational decisions are the easiest to critique after the fact. Many armchair commanders have criticized this or that famous general for not winning a battle based on operational decisions. "If Napoleon had only attacked to the right at Waterloo, then he would have . . ." Most of these operational decisions, observed years after the fact and supported by detailed information of the situation of both sides of a battle, seem obvious to the reader. The situation at the time of the fight, however, was often clouded in the fog, fear, and confusion of war. It is one thing to make a decision in the safe, pleasant confines of one's study and another thing to face the gut-wrenching ordeal of making one deadly decision after another when you are afraid, tired, cold, wet, and hungry.

Decision making is central to the commander's ability to command and control forces in battle. There are no magic formulas for success. Almost anything can happen in a battle, and it usually does. The commander, therefore, must control the things that he can control and minimize his mistakes. Simple mistakes, such as getting fouled up leaving the assembly area, misinterpreting orders, and being unprepared for battle, have doomed more operations to failure than the commander's lack of tactical prowess.

Team leadership is the oil that reduces friction in combat. Company team commanders can increase their ability to minimize mistakes by organizing their key leaders to accomplish specific tasks. Key leaders should be placed in charge of actions or areas that will help to reduce the number of mistakes that can occur prior to battle. Key leaders must feel free to, and should be expected to, make decisions on the spot to correct problems and inform the commander of the situation. Considering the lack of direct contact with the commander, these leaders should be expected to make decisions to accomplish the mission and secure the commander's intent.

Organizational and informational decisions support the commander's operational decisions in battle. At the cutting edge of battle, a company team commander has limited means of gathering information. His information assets are usually limited to what he can see or hear or what is reported. At the same time, a company team commander is completely immersed in an environment that requires rapid decision making. He must decide how to employ his forces rapidly and decide how to act and respond to quickly changing events of which he has very limited information.

Those who believe that technology will lift the fog of war and offer a situation where commanders will have *near total certainty* are living in a fantasy. A company team commander, therefore, balances the need for certainty (information, usually presented in the form of radio reports and reconnaissance) and the requirement to keep ahead of the situation and act faster than his opponent.

You have failed in your mission. Similar situations in which attacks have failed to get off to a good start have occurred countless times in the history of battle. Consider the organizational, informational, and operational decisions that you could have made to change the outcome of this engagement.

> *The god of war hates those who hesitate.*
> —Euripides, 425 B.C.

**Return to Section 111,
reconsider your options, and try again.**

Section 38

> *The advance through a defended defile or valley requires practice in fire and movement. Elements advancing without cover must not lack fire support. While the lead tanks work forward, the trail tanks and Bradleys suppress the enemy to both flanks of the defile. Mortar fire must suppress directly ahead of the lead tanks all suspected key-hole positions—artillery fire does the same farther up the defile. It is always a question of gaining local fire superiority and maintaining a rapid advance to avoid the enemy's artillery fire traps. Elements unable to advance seek cover and call for smoke and mortar fire for protection. Every opportunity is used to advance the combat power of the lead platoon and combat team.*
>
> —S.Sgt. Steve Krivitsky, U.S. Army, "The Three to Six Second Advantage," *Armor Magazine*

That was too easy, Casey thought. He quickly assessed the situation, checking his IVIS screen. His combat power was still at 100 percent:

TM C Unit	M1A2 Tank	M2 IFV	BSFV [ADA]	FISTV	Engr M113	CEV	ACE	HAB Bridge	Medic M113	M88 [Rec]	M113 APCs
North of PP	5	4	1	1							
South of PP	5	3			4	1	1	2	2	1	15
Total	10	7	1	1	4	1	1	2	2	1	15

He reminded himself that warfare is a two-sided affair. Everything in war is based on the enemy. He thought about what he knew of his opponent. In the security zone the enemy defends with company-sized combat outposts forward of battalion-sized strongpoints. If this was a battalion defense reinforced with tanks, he'd need to bring up the rest of the company team fast in order to punch through. Counterattack was the central theme of the enemy's defense doctrine.

If I was the enemy, he thought, defending with a battalion here, I'd have two companies up and one back. That means his engagement area is centered on the area near CS215420. I already know that a T-62 platoon was reported in the vicinity of Tongak. That could be part of the combined-arms reserve, centrally located in sector. I don't want to take the chance, he thought, that the enemy might counterattack with tanks from the east.

In spite of all the talk that Casey had heard about information warfare and America's high-tech advantage, the lives of his soldiers depended on how well he read the situation—a situation that he had to piece together in his mind. The greatest weapon on the battlefield, even in the information age, was a capable commander who could make decisions faster than the enemy could react.

Time was slipping by. It was already 0138, fifty-three minutes since Casey had crossed the LD.

As if to confirm Casey's hunch, a line of machine-gun and missile fire erupted from the north, near the mouth of the defile at CS216424. The enemy fire landed on 1st Platoon, some rounds sparking off the sides of the heavily armored tanks. Casey quickly moved to his IVIS and scrolled the orders on his screen to send to the tank platoon leaders.

Andrews's tanks were already returning fire. The boom from their cannons echoed in the wet, dark valley like a huge hammer pounding steel on a forge.

"Blue One, this is Steel Six. The enemy's center company is located due north, in the mouth of the defile, blocking Cobra. Hold where you are. Don't expose your right flank to the open ground to the east. I suspect he has another company there to take you in the flank as you pass. Form a firing line vicinity CS212415, orient north."

"Wilco, Steel Six," Lieutenant McDaniel answered confidently. "We identify the enemy to the north-northeast. Looks like dug-in PCs. We can only see a few. We'll keep the bastards pinned down."

PCs were enemy personnel carriers. Casey now knew that he was up against a unit with mechanized infantry support, which meant heavier antitank weapons than most enemy light infantry units carried. There was probably a company there, around the bend as the valley flowed northeast, but the enemy seldom defended with only one company.

Casey saw the red tracers from 3d Platoon's four Bradleys fly due north and strike the enemy positions at the mouth of the defile. In the dark the Bradleys, with their excellent thermal sights, held the advantage over the enemy infantry crouching in the darkness of their trench.

"Red One, this is Steel Six," Casey called for Lieutenant Andrews. "On order, I want you to assault north, bypass the enemy at CS210418, and hug the northwest valley wall until you get to the opening of the defile at CS215428. I've transmitted you the graphics. Do you understand?"

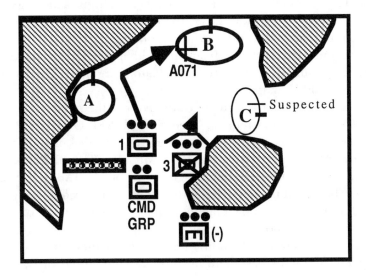

"Steel Six, this is Red One. Roger. I've got the graphics and I understand. I will execute on your order."

Artillery flares burst overhead, lighting up the valley.

"Affirmative. I've labeled the positions A, B, and C from left to right starting in the northwest," Casey said, hoping that he transmitted a clear picture to his lieutenant. "I'm not sure if the enemy's at C, but I don't want McDaniel rushing into a possible enemy fire sack."

"Steel Six, this is Blue One. I agree," Lieutenant McDaniel chimed in. "We're making out more hot spots on Position B. It looks like the enemy's dug in there. I can support Red's attack from here with 25mm and TOWs."

"Roger. Do that. Break. Steel Guns, where is my mortar fire? I need smoke and HE on target A071, ASAP," Casey ordered.

"Working it, Steel Six,"Lieutenant Keeley replied over the radio. "I've had trouble getting our allies to fire their mortars, but I worked through it."

Casey waited as the minutes ticked by. He stood in his open hatch and peered through the darkness with his night vision goggles. Tracers crisscrossed the sky as Andrews's tanks exchanged fire with the enemy on Position B. The enemy's antitank fire increased. Several missiles detonated near the 1st Platoon tanks. Hitting a moving tank at night takes great skill. Casey thanked his luck as each missile missed its mark and exploded in the soft, muddy fields.

Casey needed the rest of Team Steel with him before he made the assault. He didn't want to send 1st Platoon in alone. How much longer could he wait?

"Shot on the mortars," Keeley shouted over the radio.

"Shot. Out," Casey replied. "Steel Five, SITREP. Over."

"Steel Six, this is Steel Five. I'm just north of Phase Line Audi with all four APC engineer squads and two MICLICs. The 4th Platoon is in the passage lane now, but somehow one of the HABs is in front of it. The rest of the engineers—the other assault bridge, armored earth mover, and combat engineer vehicle—are still south of Audi following 2d Platoon."

"Roger. Keep 4th Platoon with you when they cross," Casey replied. He listened as bright bursts of 120mm mortar fire landed near Position B. The frustration caused by a missed turn was evident in the tone of his reply. The tanks he needed were now near the end of a long line of vehicles struggling to get through the passage lane. "I need tanks to assault the enemy at the mouth of the defile. As soon as 2d Platoon gets through the lane, we'll push forward."

An enemy machine gun in the northwest fired on McDaniel's Bradleys.

"Steel Six. Contact, enemy troops, CS214415. Blue One. Out." The echo of a 25mm cannon blasted in the background of McDaniel's quick message.

A flare ignited high overhead. Casey watched as the Bradleys in 3d Platoon took small-arms fire from the wood line. The noise of the battle rose in intensity. Abruptly Casey realized his mistake. He'd waited too long to attack.

Karrummp! Karrummp! Two 152mm rounds smashed into the ground only two hundred meters to *Cossack*'s right flank.

More flares. The dark sky lit up.

Karrummp! Karrummp! Two enemy artillery shells landed to Casey's left flank, detonating nearby in a shower of stringy, bright white phosphorus.

They've bracketed us, Casey thought. We'd better move out of here.

With an earsplitting crash, as if a huge freight train was roaring right at him down an invisible track, the enemy artillery shells shattered the earth surrounding his position. Casey pulled the lever in a frantic effort to close his hatch.

Roll the dice.

If you roll 2-7, go to Section 28.

If you roll 8-12, go to Section 79.

Section 39

Greatness lies in the freedom of the intellect and spirit at moments of pressure and crisis, and in the willingness to take risks.
—Hans Delbruck, *History of the Art of War*

Casey quickly turned his CITV toward Position B. He was amazed at how many enemy soldiers rushed out of their trenches. The enemy piled out of the position like termites from a rotten log. His tanks hadn't killed as many as he thought.

"Troops!" Casey screamed with a vengeance into his intercom mouthpiece. "Fire!"

Casey watched the result of his orders as if the action was played in slow motion. His heart was racing, but the minutes seemed suspended as he orchestrated the enemy's destruction.

Through his thermal sight he saw a wave of murderous machine-gun bullets tear into the enemy infantry running to the west. The enemy seemed unaware of its visibility to the searching thermal eyes of the M1A2 tanks closing on their trenches. Unable to run fast enough or hide, they died in bunches as they tried to escape in the dark.

At the same time mortar fire fell on the enemy positions, adding to the slaughter. The enemy infantry, caught on the horns of a dilemma between the machine guns and the mortars, ran out of options. Lieutenant Keeley is earning his pay, Casey thought as he watched the 120mm mortar rounds explode on Positions A and B.

The three M1A2s charged toward Position B. The FIST-V followed as closely as it could, moving frantically to keep up with Steel Six. Sergeant Sellers's Bradley Stinger fighting vehicle peeled off and took up a position near Lieutenant Andrews's stranded tank. Within seconds Sellers had acquired an enemy infantry position on B and was blasting away at it with his 25mm cannon.

Casey held on tight as *Cossack* jolted across the rough ground. Casey shot a quick glance at his IVIS screen:

TM C Unit	M1A2 Tank	M2 IFV	BSFV [ADA]	FISTV	Engr M113	CEV	ACE	HAB Bridge	Medic M113	M88 [Rec]	M113 APCs
North of PP	3 [C11]	4	1	1							
South of PP	5	3			4	1	1	2	2	1	15
Total	8	7	1	1	4	1	1	2	2	1	15

"Steel Six, this is Blue One," Lieutenant McDaniel screamed over the command frequency. "Enemy tanks directly in front of my position. Engaging now!"

Scanning in the direction of 3d Platoon's position, Casey saw the flashes of enemy tank fire. A chill ran down his spine. The enemy had launched a tank counterattack against his thin-skinned Bradleys. "Weaver, stop!" Casey ordered. "Graham, fire and adjust."

Casey turned his CITV in the direction of 3d Platoon. He saw at least two enemy tanks just north of McDaniel's position. A huge burst of light erupted from the lead enemy tank.

"Scratch one T-62, Steel Six," a jubilant Lieutenant McDaniel shouted over the radio. "Engaging with TOWs."

Casey watched as the T-62s swung in line against their nearest threat, the Bradleys of McDaniel's platoon. Two Bradleys fired furiously at the enemy armor, peppering the old Russian-made tanks with 25mm rounds as the tanks turned south into view. While these two Bradleys suppressed the enemy tanks, the other two Bradleys killed them with TOWs. Three more enemy tanks erupted in fire, hit by TOW missiles. The fourth enemy tank, moving aggressively around his burning comrades, got through this gauntlet, leveled its 115mm cannon at the Bradley farthest to the west, and fired.

The 115mm round struck the Bradley in the turret. Never designed to stand up against tank fire, the Bradley's turret separated from its hull in an angry cloud of red and yellow sparks.

"Steel Six, this is Blue One. They keep coming. We need help! Over."

"Hold on, Blue One!" Casey answered over the radio. "Red elements, SABOT, enemy tanks, due east of our position, frontal, fire!" The two remaining M1A2s of 1st Platoon seemed to move as one, swinging their guns toward the tanks attacking McDaniel's Bradleys.

"Weaver, move out. Follow 1st Platoon," Casey ordered. He turned his head just in time to see the telltale flash of an enemy antitank missile launched from Position B.

Roll the dice.

If you roll 2-8, go to Section 47.

If you roll 9-12, go to Section 54.

121

Section 40

> *The combined arms concept will remain with us but, with military technology ever advancing, the battlefield is becoming a more and more complicated place. This means that commanders at all levels, from section upwards, are going to need much greater breadth of thinking, a deeper understanding of the strengths and limitations of the weapons systems under their command, and an increasing ability to think and react even more quickly.*
>
> —C. R. M. Messenger

The area near the burning APCs exploded in fire and smoke. In shock, Casey watched as his force caught in the minefield died from the enemy's artillery. The enemy's accurate artillery fire blanketed an area that covered most of the force in the passage lane.

Through the thinning fog and the billowing smoke, Casey saw dozens of explosions erupting in the area where Lieutenant Andrews was desperately trying to redirect Team Steel. Suddenly, Casey knew what was coming next.

"Shit, here it comes!" Casey screamed as he forced *Cossack*'s hatch down and locked it. "Everybody button up!"

The night flickered through the tank's vision blocks as balls of orange flame exploded outside. The earth shook under the thunder of the enemy's barrage. Zinging metal, dirt, and rocks showered *Cossack*. Smoke filled the air.

Casey gasped for breath as each new round seemed to suck the air right from his lungs. Is the enemy using gas? he wondered. "My God, I can't breathe!" said Casey.

The crew immediately put on their gas masks. A strike of this magnitude could easily be a chemical weapons strike or could have chemical gas shells mixed with the high-explosive shells. Without orders Weaver kicked on the tank's overpressure system. The crew breathed easier as they hooked up their protective mask hoses to the tank's forced-air chemical protection system.

Casey's worst fears were coming true. The enemy had observed his force stranded in the minefield when the fog cleared. The burning APCs became the enemy's artillery reference points.

A massive fire strike hit Casey's position. The devastating shock of the exploding artillery shells crushed in around *Cossack*.

"Sir, what are we going to do?" Weaver shouted over the intercom.

An explosion erupted from the FIST-V as an enemy shell found its mark.

"They've hit the FIST-V!" Graham screamed. "We'd better get out of here."

Casey's head throbbed. His ears were ringing. It was difficult to think in the intense noise. The fire scraped against the tank, striking the outside with shards of flying steel and the dull whack of lead plastering against its hard sides. The rumble of the explosions filled Casey's senses. He felt as if he was being crushed.

Casey looked at the glowing remains of the FIST-V through his vision blocks. Suddenly the burning FIST-V exploded. The blast hurled jagged pieces of metal in all directions as the aluminum armored artillery vehicle exploded once more. With a loud clang, a large chunk of smoldering aluminum crashed against *Cossack*'s side.

Casey ducked as the sparks flew. He felt sick. His plans were collapsing in front of him like a house of cards on a windy day. He knew that he had to do something. He saw three courses of action: wait for the artillery fire to stop, move back to help Lieutenant Andrews, or move forward to 2d Platoon and continue the attack.

If Casey decides to move back to help Lieutenant Andrews out of the minefield, go to Section 22.

If Casey decides to go forward and join 2d and 3d Platoons, go to Section 76.

If Casey decides to wait for the artillery to stop, go to Section 88.

Section 41

I have found again and again that in encounter actions, the day goes to the side that is the first to plaster its opponents with fire. The man who lies low and awaits developments usually comes off second best.

—Erwin Rommel

Three 115mm high-explosive antitank rounds detonated to *Cossack*'s right, splashing in a brilliant fireball against the rocky ground. A fourth explosion erupted only a few meters in front of *Cossack*, bursting in a swirl of smoke.

"Weaver, move forward, hard left!" Casey yelled. "Let's get them. Move straight toward them. . . . Move!"

Cossack plunged through the smoke and jerked hard left. The BSFV and the FIST-V followed close behind.

A dozen enemy tanks rolled around the northern edge of the forest, firing at 2d Platoon. *Cossack* swung northeast, heading straight for them, firing on the move. Enemy tanks were advancing in a staggered column, firing from short halts. The night air flashed with explosions and burning vehicles as the distance between the T-62s and *Cossack* narrowed.

Graham fired at the first T-62 in view. The depleted-uranium SABOT round tore through the enemy tank as if it was made of paper. Sellers's BSFV opened fire at the same time, pelting the enemy tanks with high-explosive 25mm rounds. The 25mm burst distracted the enemy tanks as Graham began picking them off one by one.

Enemy tanks swarmed toward them. The lead enemy tank was a hundred meters away. An explosion pounded against *Cossack*'s flank armor, but the tank kept rolling. Sure of his armored protection, Casey played chicken and charged straight toward the enemy.

Cossack was moving very fast, too fast for the rough terrain. In the confusion of the assault, Weaver turned the tank violently to the left, in a last-second attempt to avoid crashing into a three-foot paddy dike. Missing the dike by inches, Weaver slammed the tank over the dike and into a deep ditch. The tank pitched forward, throwing the crew against the turret walls.

"Back up!" Casey cried as his head banged against the wall of his tank commander's station. *Cossack* shuddered. The tank shook back and forth as Weaver tried to move out of the ditch. Sergeant Sellers's Bradley lunged next to *Cossack,* trying to protect Casey from attack.

"We have to get out of here!" Sellers screamed over the radio. "They keep on coming!"

Casey heard Sellers but didn't have time to answer. Looking through his vision blocks, he saw the Bradley take a direct hit from an enemy tank cannon. The top of the turret of the Bradley absorbed the 115mm round, then erupted in a terrible stream of sparks and flame as the Bradley's 25mm ammunition exploded.

"Damn!" Casey shouted at the top of his lungs as he slew the gun onto Sellers's killer. "Get the bastard. . . . Get him!"

"Identified!" Graham yelled.

"Fire!"

"On the way!" Graham barked.

Casey watched with grim satisfaction as the 120mm projectile tore into another enemy tank. Clouds of smoke hung low over the battlefield, now bathed in the flickering light of torched armored vehicles.

"Weaver, can you back us up?" Casey asked.

"She won't budge, sir."

"Graham, keep firing! Get the bastards!" Casey yelled to his gunner.

Flares ignited overhead, lighting up the battle area. Casey looked out of his vision blocks and saw Keeley's FIST-V race for the cover of a rice paddy dike as *Cossack*'s tank cannon boomed at the enemy.

The battlefield became a confused maelstrom of flashes, explosions, and charging tanks. Graham fired another round, blasting another enemy tank. Then, as if swatted by a giant hand, *Cossack*'s turret jerked to the right. The hard armor of the M1A2 absorbed the blow, but the electrical system failed and the lights inside the tank went dark. A 115mm round struck *Cossack* on the left side of the turret.

Casey opened the hatch as bullets ricocheted off the top of the tank. He ducked down and looked through his right vision block just in time to see two enemy soldiers running toward his tank, carrying a large satchel. With *Cossack* jammed against the ditch, Casey couldn't swing the .50-caliber machine gun far enough to reach the enemy. Thinking quickly, he looked for an alternative.

Casey drew the 9mm pistol from his shoulder holster. In one fast move he stood up in the turret, aimed, and fired a magazine of 9mm slugs at the two enemy soldiers. Quickly he ducked down and slammed the hatch closed.

His heart racing, he looked through his vision blocks. The two enemy soldiers lay dead, fifteen feet from *Cossack*'s right flank.

Casey felt the ground shake as the enemy satchel charge exploded. Rocks and debris banged against the tank, reinforcing the lethality of the moment. He reached for a new magazine for his pistol and quickly reloaded.

"We're with you now," the jubilant voice of Stonevitch sounded over Casey's earphones.

"Action front! There's a tank right in front of us!" Weaver screamed.

Roll the dice.

If you roll 2-7, go to Section 12.

If you roll 8-12, go to Section 89.

Section 42

The rarest quality is the courage of the improviser, who, despite the most unexpected events, retains his force of mind, of judgment, and of decision.

—Napoleon

"Destroy it ASAP, White One, before he tells everyone we're here!" Casey ordered.

"Wilco," Sergeant Scott replied. A brilliant blast, followed by an almost instantaneous secondary explosion, lit the defile for a moment. "One BRDM is toast! Continuing mission."

Team Steel bulled ahead, pushing the shattered remains of the burning BRDM to the west side of the trail. Casey gazed down from the top of his tank to inspect the wreckage as *Cossack* drove by. The BRDM had almost disintegrated from the blast. No one could have survived long enough to make a radio call.

Casey turned the knob on his radio selector to battalion and pushed the transmission switch forward on his CVC. "Dragon Six or Dragon TOC, this is Steel Six. Over."

Nothing.

"Dragon TOC, this is Steel Six. Over."

Again, no response.

"Steel Seven, this is Steel Six. You're far back in the column. Can you reach Dragon TOC?"

"Stand by, Steel Six, let me try," First Sergeant Washington replied.

Several moments passed as Casey waited. The sound of artillery falling to the west, presumably near the bridge on Viper, reassured Casey that the plan was still in effect even if he couldn't reach battalion headquarters.

"Negative contact with any Dragon station, Steel Six," Washington responded. "My guess is that these hills are too steep."

"Roger, Steel Seven," Casey answered, annoyed that the line of sight for FM communications was restricting his ability to coordinate with battalion. "Continue mission."

The armored column clanked through the dank night at fifteen miles an hour, maneuvering along the winding trail with high rock walls on both sides. Casey worried that an ambush might strike his lead platoon at any moment. He dreaded the thought of an enemy infantry company, armed with antitank weapons and backed up by preregistered artillery, waiting for him up ahead. Tense with apprehension, he feared for the worst but pressed on. If the enemy ambushed him in Coral, he thought, the only orders he could give would be to charge forward and fight like hell.

"Steel Six, this is White One," Scott's voice shot out over the radio in a tone of mixed elation and relief. "We're at the northern opening of the defile. I can see the Gang River. No enemy contact."

Casey breathed a deep sigh of relief. "Good job, White. Turn west and head for the bridge. Let's take the bitch before they have a chance to blow it."

"Affirmative, Steel Six. We'll take it for you!" Scott answered exuberantly.

Casey saw the opening of the defile and saw the last engineer APC attached to Scott's platoon turn to the left. He looked behind him. In the dust he saw a long line of armored vehicles in the green tint of his night vision goggles. The vehicles were jammed close together, twenty to thirty meters apart, as far as he could see. He turned the corner and saw the rushing water of the Gang River.

Even through his night vision goggles, he saw that the water looked deep and fast flowing; he noticed a tree that was bent at an angle by the current. Casey determined that the river near the ford must have swollen to twice its normal width.

He wondered if he could have placed the HABs to cross the ford, then he shook off the idea. It was already 0245. It would be light around 0500, only two hours and fifteen minutes away. He didn't want to be crossing the river in the daylight.

The 2d Platoon moved quickly toward the bridge, deploying into a wedge in the open ground between the river and the mountain. Scott's engineer APCs followed behind the tanks in the center of the formation. To the west Casey saw the artillery falling on the bridge on Viper. The visibility was the best it had been all night, with no trace of fog.

Suddenly the artillery stopped. The battlefield was quiet except for the grinding of steel road wheels against metal tank tracks and the sound of the engines of the tanks and Bradleys.

"Steel Guns, keep the artillery firing," Casey ordered.

"I'm trying to reestablish contact," an exasperated Lieutenant Keeley answered over the radio. "I can't reach them!"

"Keep trying, I need that fire," Casey growled.

"You know what my old drill sergeant used to say," Graham interjected over the intercom. "'Commo will always fail as soon as you need fire support.'"

"Shut up, Graham," Casey ordered, shaking his head at his gunner's attempt to relieve the tension. "Scan for the enemy. As soon as you see them, take them out."

Cossack surged ahead. Casey knew that he needed all the available combat power forward if there was a fight for the bridge. He placed his tank on the far north of Scott's wedge, guarding his right flank. The FIST-V, followed by the BSFV, trailed *Cossack*. McDaniel's 3d Platoon, with its attached engineers, maneuvered out of the defile and raced to catch up with 2d Platoon.

So far so good, Casey thought. A grin replaced the worry on his face. This just might work.

Flares ignited high overhead. A burst of light to the west suddenly replaced his joy with dread. Casey snapped the hatch to the open-protected position.

"Missile launch! Due west!" Sergeant Scott's voice screamed over the radio.

Three missiles shot up from the west and flew in a staggered wave toward the right flank of 2d Platoon.

Roll the dice.

If you roll 2-4, go to Section 9.

If you roll 5-10, go to Section 31.

If you roll 11-12, go to Section 54.

Section 43

In war, audacity has often disproved calculations of what is possible.
—B. H. Liddell Hart

Section 43

"What did that sound like to you, Lieutenant?" Casey asked.

The weight of the world suddenly fell on Second Lieutenant Keeley's shoulders. He realized that his answer might decide the fate of Team Steel and the 1-12th Infantry. Keeley cleared his throat. "Sir, I heard them say that we are to stick to the original plan. We're being ordered to stay here and fight it out."

Casey nodded. "That's right. While the commander and his operations officer are away, the officers in the TOC are afraid to make a decision. So be it. We're staying."

Casey tried to consider his next move, but he couldn't concentrate. Mind-splitting rage filled him. His head throbbed with an unrelenting pain at the thought of what was to come. The captain gave the hand mike to Keeley, then turned to walk back to *Cossack*.

A series of shots rang out. Several Americans in the perimeter fell. Casey crouched and spun to the left.

"Snipers! Northern ridge!" Graham yelled from *Cossack*'s tank commander's hatch. The sergeant pulled back the bolt on the .50-caliber machine gun and sprayed a burst to the north.

It was too late. Another shot rang out. The snipers had been looking for commanders. A lucky shot hit Casey in the neck. He jerked sideways, then fell forcefully against the ramp of the FIST-V.

Keeley crawled over the ramp and yanked his mortally wounded commander inside the protection of the FIST-V. Graham plastered the ridge with machine-gun fire. Several other tanks and Bradleys in the perimeter also opened fire on the snipers.

"Hang on, sir!" Keeley said as he held his hand against Casey's gushing neck wound. The young lieutenant's efforts were in vain.

Seconds later, Casey died.

In the next three hours, so did the rest of Team Steel and the 1st Battalion, 12th Infantry.

Go back to Section 29 and try again!

Section 44

The outcome of a battle . . . is the result of one instant, one thought: one approaches with various combinations, one mixes it up. One fights for a while, the decisive moment presents itself, a mental spark tells one so; the smallest reserve wins the battle. War is composed altogether of accidents. . . . A great commander never loses sight of what he can do to profit by these accidents.

—Napoleon

Cossack was parked in a clump of trees near the northern opening of the defile on Coral. Sergeant Scott's platoon had deployed in an arc to the northwest. McDaniel's 3d Platoon had deployed in a similar arc to the northeast. To conserve fuel all the vehicles in the column had shut down, all except the engineers.

The two huge Wolverine heavy assault bridges passed *Cossack* and moved slowly into the fast-flowing Gang River.

Casey stood in the open turret, his plastic-covered map folded on top of the turret, as he watched the huge Wolverine assault bridges drive by.

Except for the sound of distant artillery fire falling to the west, the night was remarkably quiet. Casey was confident that the artillery he had requested to hit the bridge site on Viper was masking the noise that the Wolverines were making as they struggled in the Gang River.

The hardworking engineers were worth their weight in gold, he thought with a tired smile. The engineers worked in total darkness, using night vision goggles and infrared chem lights. The lights were almost invisible to the naked eye in the dark, damp night. Casey rubbed his tired eyes and through his night vision goggles watched the engineers lay the heavy assault bridge.

"Hey, sir," Graham's quiet voice asked in the Team Steel commander's earphones. "You know what my old drill sergeant would say at a time like this?"

"I'm afraid to ask," Casey answered his gunner over the intercom.

"'All battles are fought with an uncrossable river to your flank,'" Graham chided.

"Well, this one is in front of us," Casey said with a chuckle. "Let's just hope we can cross it."

Casey looked at his watch again. The tension mounted as he played "what if" with himself. *What if we can't cross here?* He turned on the map reading light on his night vision goggles and stared at Direction of Attack Asp and Objective Dragon.

So close, yet so far away!

"Wolverine One, this is Steel Six," Casey said, trying to hide his impatience. "Situation update."

"Steel Six, this is Wolverine One," Jacobs answered, very businesslike. "I'm almost set to lay the first bridge. I estimate another fifteen minutes until we're done. Don't worry, Steel Six, this will work!"

"Never doubted it," Casey replied. "Just call me when you're ready for us to cross."

The work in the river reached a critical stage. Casey watched as Jacobs laid the first bridge into the water, then drove the second Wolverine over the first bridge until the water level rose over the front blade of the bridge launcher. Slowly, Jacobs deployed the second bridge and laid it on the northern end of the first. Together, the two bridges spanned the thirty-eight-meter width of the Gang.

Stonevitch used the time to refuel the tanks. Casey watched as the engineers finished their job.

"Steel Six, this is Steel Five. Everyone has refueled except you. I've got just enough JP8 left to give you a three-minute shot, then we're dry. I'm sending them to you to fuel *Cossack* now."

"Understood," Casey replied, giving a nod to Kriel, who was listening to the radio conversation in the earphones of his CVC helmet. "I'll have my loader waiting by the trail."

Kriel hopped out of his open hatch and climbed down off the tank. In a few seconds the HEMMT fuel truck arrived. A soldier in the right side of the cab ran out and handed Kriel the fuel hose. Kriel opened the fuel cap and crammed the fuel nozzle into *Cossack*'s fuel intake.

"Steel Five, this is Steel Six. After I'm through refueling, I want you to stash the HEMMT in a narrow gully somewhere and camouflage it. Have the HEMMT crew ride in an armored personnel carrier. Sending an empty fuel truck forward of the Gang River is a needless risk."

"Wilco," Stonevitch replied. "That's just what I had in mind."

Casey smiled, then looked at his watch. It was already 0320. Dawn would break in a little over an hour and a half. If he expected to cut through to the 1-12th Infantry with minimal casualties, he had to attack at night and use the thermal sight advantage of his tanks and Bradleys.

The HEMMT pulled away from *Cossack* and headed south. Casey observed the river as Jacobs drove the second Wolverine launcher through the water to the north side. The bridges, hidden under the water, now raised the level of the ford high enough for tanks and Bradleys to cross. Jacobs moved slowly back to the south side of the Gang, then he placed metal poles into both sides of the Wolverine bridge. The poles, placed at five-meter intervals, marked the crossing site. Each pole had a thermal and an infrared chemical light taped to the top, to aid the drivers in keeping aligned on the bridges hidden under the dark water.

Jacobs's Wolverine launcher pulled up next to *Cossack*. Casey looked over at the engineer sergeant and grinned.

"They're all set, Captain," Jacobs said over the radio to Casey. "My engineers will guide the tanks up to the entrance and at the exit. All the drivers have to do is stay between the poles."

"Excellent!" Casey replied, the satisfaction at Jacobs's work ringing in his voice. "We'll cross 2d Platoon, 3d Platoon, the command group, 1st Platoon, the trains, and then 4th Platoon. You cross last and take down the poles so the enemy can't see the crossing site when the sun comes up. The 4th Platoon will wait for you on the north bank. As soon as you cross and the poles are down, you follow the trains. The 4th Platoon will cover your rear."

"Got it, sir."

Team Steel crossed the river without mishap. By 0415 all of Casey's vehicles were across the Gang. By 0430 Team Steel rolled north, following Direction of Attack Asp. If Casey's captured map was correct, Asp would bypass the enemy's tank and infantry defenses and pass along the southwestern edge of the enemy's artillery group. That ought to cause them some confusion, Casey thought.

It felt good to be moving again. Casey shifted in his open turret and looked to the rear of the column. Visibility was good. True to the capricious nature of the climate in this part of the world, the temperature had dropped and the fog that had covered his moves yesterday had vanished.

The ground along Asp rose in elevation as Team Steel pushed north, allowing Casey to look back and see most of his vehicles. As the lead tank platoon passed between the dark mountains to the left and a thick woods to the right, Casey contacted battalion headquarters. In a quick push of a button he sent a digital burst message to the tactical operations center that outlined the plan of attack and the schedule of artillery fires.

Casey shot a quick glance at the bottom of the IVIS screen. The message designator listed the message as sent and received. "Dragon TOC, this is Steel Six. My IVIS displays that you've received my digital message. Request voice confirmation. Do you understand what I am going to do? Over."

"Roger, Steel Six," the assistant operations officer responded. "Your transmission is breaking up. I do not have authority—" The transmission turned to static, then went silent. Casey waited anxiously for more information as *Cossack* surged ahead.

"Dragon TOC, this is Steel Six," Casey repeated. He checked his IVIS. They were no longer in communications range. "Break. Steel Seven, this is Steel Six. Try to reach Dragon TOC."

Steel Seven tried several times to reach the battalion headquarters by radio. "No luck, Steel Six. I'm close to where you talked to them. I can't reach them."

Casey tried again, received no answer, then slammed his palm against the side of the tank commander's station. Silently he cursed the equipment designers who gave him the finest tank in the world, a twenty-first-century command and control system, and then tied it all together with line-of-sight radio technology.

What did the operations officer mean when he said, "I don't have authority?" Casey remembered a lesson he had learned a long time ago from his first platoon sergeant. When you're in command, *com-*

mand. Sometimes you have to be smart enough to know when to disobey orders and stand by the consequences. Casey only hoped that the battalion would execute the artillery fires that he had requested. Team Steel raced north in a long, fast-moving column. It was 0455. The sky turned from dark to gray.

Suddenly a flash of fire in the north lit up the early-morning sky. The 2d Platoon was engaging targets. Casey shot a glance at his IVIS screen. The 2d Platoon was passing the woods at CS248468. The entire 2d Platoon was firing all at once at targets to the northeast.

"Steel Six, White One!" Scott's excited voice shouted. The sound of cannon fire echoed in the background of his transmission. "Contact. Self-propelled howitzers, APCs, and troops. CS254475. They're everywhere. Continuing to engage."

"Roger, White One. Don't stop. Just as we planned it, keep firing and moving. Kill what you can, but get to Dragon!"

Cossack leapt forward as Weaver accelerated. Casey lowered his hatch to the open-protected position. He looked to the northeast and saw the flat, wide-open ginseng fields full of enemy howitzers, APCs, support vehicles, and trucks. There wasn't an enemy tank in sight.

Right on schedule a burst of 155mm artillery erupted in the center of this large artillery group. The rounds could not be adjusted, but Casey didn't care; they added to the enemy's confusion.

Team Steel charged north, following Direction of Attack Asp. The tanks and Bradleys blasted away with cannons and machine guns, plastering their stunned opponents with a fierce wave of fire. Casey shot a quick glance at his IVIS screen:

"Get them, White One," Casey replied, his voice filled with ruthless tenacity. "Fire on the move. Don't let them stop you."

Through his CITV Casey could see at least three enemy artillery battalions. His tanks and Bradleys fired to their right and right front as the American armored column destroyed the enemy howitzers.

"Steel Six, this is White One," Scott reported. "We've surprised them. I see almost an entire enemy artillery group. The enemy guns are sitting in the open. My platoon is continuing to attack."

The enemy's return fire was minimal. The American tanks and Bradleys fired in rapid volleys. The firing increased as every tank and

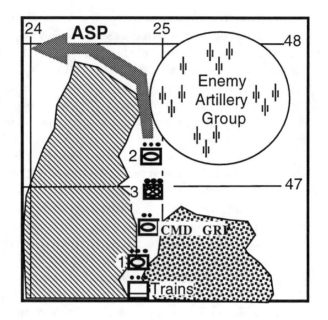

Bradley in Team Steel blasted at targets in the dense smoke. Fire, flying metal, and smoke filled the air as Team Steel's salvos smashed home. The tanks and Bradleys killed everything within the range of their guns.

At the same time, the American artillery hammered the enemy from above, forcing him onto the horns of a dilemma from which he could not escape. Enemy ammunition trucks exploded in terrible bright orange fireballs. Howitzers erupted in fire and smoke, blasting their hapless crews into instantaneous extinction. In less than ten minutes an entire enemy artillery group dissolved into a junkyard of burning wrecks and dying men.

"Steel Six, this is White One. I see enemy APCs coming at us."

Casey fixed his CITV to the northeast. What he saw was hard to believe, but the image in his thermal sight was true. The enemy was counterattacking his tanks with VTT-323s.

"Lovely, just lovely," Casey muttered to himself. He pushed the transmitter forward on his CVC helmet. "White One, take them out, then finish off as many of the self-propelled howitzers and the ammunition carriers as you can. Leave the trucks for later."

"Wilco," Scott replied. "Engaging now."

The American tanks engaged the lead platoon of VTT-323s that was bravely charging forward. This act of desperation by the enemy was completely futile. Scott's M1A2s chopped them to pieces. Huge clouds of black smoke billowed into the sky as 2d Platoon made short work of the thinly armored APCs.

Cossack bolted forward at twenty miles an hour, right behind McDaniel's platoon, shooting a six-foot sheet of flame of 7.62mm bullets from the co-ax machine gun. Enemy soldiers, confused and in a panic, ran all about. Graham fired his co-ax machine gun to the right flank, mowing down a group of dazed artillerymen.

Cossack drove by a shattered enemy artillery gun. As Casey looked through the slit in his hatch, he spied an RPG gunner. The enemy soldier calmly stood by the side of the burning howitzer, leveled his launcher, and fired.

The RPG missed *Cossack*'s turret by a few feet and detonated in the rice paddy to Casey's right.

"Gunner, troops!" Casey yelled as he turned the gun toward the RPG gunner.

A second RPG team fired from somewhere to *Cossack*'s right front. The grenade hit the engineer M113 just in front of *Cossack*. The APC, carrying an engineer squad attached to 3d Platoon, ruptured in a flash. The aluminum-armored carrier exploded in a huge fireball. Pieces of the five combat engineers who had ridden inside the APC were scattered all along the trail.

"Damn!" Casey cursed as Weaver jerked *Cossack* wildly to the left, barely missing the shattered remains of the burning vehicle. More RPGs exploded. Most hit the rice paddies, detonating in geysers of muck. Others hit the road embankment, exploding in spouts of dirt and rock. Tracers flew everywhere. The firing became chaotic.

The noise reached a crescendo that was loud even inside *Cossack*. Dozens of enemy infantrymen suddenly raced toward the road from the high ground to the right and left. "Identified!" the gunner shouted.

Casey couldn't believe his eyes. The fanatical enemy was making

Section 44

a last, desperate effort—like the Japanese banzai charges of World War II that he had read about. Nothing else was working, so they charged.

Casey shook his head. "Troops!"

Cossack blasted away at the enemy with its machine gun. The enemy fell in bunches. More tanks raced forward and added their weight to the battle. The tanks killed everything that moved, stood, or fired at them. Machine-gun fire from the advancing tanks tore into the rushing infantrymen, cutting them down like ripe corn at a fall harvest.

"Steel elements, keep moving, don't stop." Casey spat out the words, wondering how much longer the enemy could take the fury of Team Steel's attack. "Plaster them. Take out the bastards!"

Black smoke from burning howitzers wafted across the open field. The ground shook from explosions.

The tankers gunned down the RPG teams and kept killing them until there were none left standing. The tanks then butchered the remaining enemy infantry, but a small group of a dozen men made it to the road and readied their RPGs and grenades. Scott's M1A2s churned forward, running over the poor, stupid bastards who did not understand the power of seventy tons of steel moving at thirty-five miles an hour.

Cossack burst through the oily, thick black smoke that covered the road. Out of the corner of his hatch Casey suddenly saw a 152mm howitzer only a hundred meters from his right front. The big, 152mm gun was level and pointing directly at *Cossack*. In a panic, Casey quickly pulled the TC's override to slew *Cossack*'s cannon on target.

Roll the dice.

If you roll 2-7, go to Section 18.

If you roll 8-12, go to Section 69.

Section 45

A thick haze covered the battlefield as the enemy launched another wave of smoke shells to hide their advance. Graham quickly scanned east and northeast with his thermal sight. Casey searched the battlefield with his CITV.

The few remaining survivors of the 1-12th, about seventy men, quickly crawled out of their bunkers and occupied firing positions, ready to repulse another enemy assault.

Casey peered through the thick smoke with his thermal sight. He saw hot spots in his CITV. He saw the unmistakable, squat, ugly outline of T-72s as they maneuvered into view. The enemy tanks moved in paradelike fashion, rolling from column to platoon line formation. There were about ten T-72s moving toward Dragon—at least a company, with more probably on the way.

"Identified T-72s!" Graham shouted at the same instant. "Thirteen hundred meters and closing."

"Steel elements. Enemy tanks, northeast! Depth—tanks take the near targets, TOWs take out the far targets," Casey ordered over the radio. "At my command."

"Roger," Andrews's voice answered.

"Wilco," replied Lieutenant McDaniel.

Enemy machine guns opened up from the surrounding hills to support the attack. Plunging fire rained down on the Americans, striking several infantrymen. Enemy mortar fire slammed into the smoke, buffeting the defenders' positions with shrapnel.

"Sir, they're nine hundred meters and closing," Graham announced. "The lead platoon has turned the bend and is in the open."

"Steady," Casey replied with a voice so calm that it surprised him. "I see them. Wait for my command."

The lead enemy tank platoon fired a volley of rounds at the Americans. They fired on the move, and their 125mm rounds smashed into the ground, sending up big spires of dirt and rocks. A second T-72 platoon entered within range, then a third. In seconds an entire enemy tank company was packed into Casey's sights.

"Fire!" Casey commanded over the radio.

"On the way!" Graham yelled on the intercom.

Cossack jerked from the gun's recoil. The round screamed forward, hitting the leftmost enemy tank. The round sliced through the front of the tank at the driver's compartment, then stopped the low-silhouetted T-72 in its tracks. Undaunted, the nine remaining T-72s now raced toward Casey's position, moving fast.

"Target. Right tank," Casey yelled. He heard the sound of tank fire to his left. Looking through his vision blocks he saw Lieutenant Andrews's tank blasting away at the enemy tank formation.

A volley of antitank missiles arced toward the American lines. One of the missiles hit a Bradley in 3d Platoon. The T-72s and VTT-323s fired on the move as they conducted their all-arms assault.

Graham's round hit another T-72, sending another turret high into the air. The force from the strike tore apart the T-72.

With his heart racing, Casey watched the American SABOT rounds rip through the enemy tanks, clanging against their special reactive armor in a dazzling shower of bright sparks. Black mushroom-shaped clouds lifted skyward from the burning, turretless hulls as the M1A2s did their deadly work.

The lead wave of enemy tanks was gone. Nothing was left of them but burning wrecks. More enemy tanks charged forward.

As Graham smashed another T-72, Casey turned his CITV and identified a T-72 that had raced ahead and flanked *Cossack* on the extreme right. A 125mm round struck inches away from *Cossack*, showering the tank with rocks and dirt.

Roll the dice.

If you roll 2-4, go to Section 68.

If you roll 5-12, go to Section 90.

140

Section 46

> *It is my experience that bold decisions give the best promise of success. But one must differentiate between strategical or tactical boldness and military gamble. A bold operation is one in which success is not a certainty but which in case of failure leaves one with sufficient forces in hand to cope with whatever situation may arise. A gamble, on the other hand, is an operation which can lead either to victory or to the complete destruction of one's forces. Situations arise where even a gamble may be justified—as, for instance, when in the normal course of events defeat is merely a matter of time, when the gaining of time is therefore pointless and the only chance lies in an operation of great risk.*
>
> —Field Marshal Erwin Rommel

A blast of enemy machine-gun fire tore at *Cossack*'s side and bounced off the top of the tank. The bullets narrowly missed Casey as he ducked down into the turret.

"Fire!"

Before Casey could get the words out of his mouth, Sergeant Graham had already fired the M256 cannon at the nearest enemy threat. The HEAT round exploded in a shower of sparks only three hundred meters to *Cossack*'s front.

"Co-ax!" Casey screamed as he slew the turret to the left. An enemy RPG team was standing to the left, two hundred meters away.

Graham quickly switched the weapons select to machine gun and gunned down the exposed enemy crew. Enemy infantrymen, who were scattered in an arc in prepared defensive positions only two to three hundred meters to the front, ducked for cover.

Casey quickly checked his IVIS screen and listened to the battle chatter on the company radio net. The 1st Platoon had deployed in a ragged line to his left and was firing madly. He was the right flank of the company, or at least those elements of the company that were forward of the passage lane and had survived the enemy's fire. The battlefield became covered in smoke from mortar shells, adding an advantage to the Americans.

To the north an enemy APC jerked to a halt and prepared to launch a missile. Casey looked through his thermal sight and saw the clear outline of the driver of the VTT-323 APC close his hatch as the crew prepared to launch an AT-4 antitank missile. The VTT appeared as a white-hot silhouette in Casey's green CITV sight. Casey pushed the slew button to place the gun on target. The turret swung automatically onto the VTT-323. Casey didn't need to issue a fire command.

"On the way!" Graham screamed as another round fired from his deadly gun.

The shot struck the VTT-323 center of mass and instantly blew the VTT-323 apart. Burning, jagged metal flew in all directions.

"Target!" Casey announced, absorbed by the moment and feeling no remorse for his prey. There was no time for pity; the enemy was everywhere. Casey was fighting for the survival of his crew. To get out of this hornets' nest alive, Casey knew that his men had to kill every enemy soldier.

Casey slew the turret onto the next target with cold precision. "Left Vett, fire!"

"On the way!" Graham aimed at a VTT-323 to the left of the one he had just incinerated. At six hundred meters range he couldn't miss. The gun fired, recoiling in its carriage. The small metal stub of the expended 120mm round clanged to the floor.

Casey saw the second VTT-323 take the high-explosive round. The energy from the explosion flipped the crumpled hull front over back into its carefully prepared fighting hole. The shattered hull of the APC, now upside down, burst into flames.

A third VTT-323, hull down with only its small conical-shaped turret exposed, fired its 14.5mm machine gun at *Cossack*. The gun raked the front of the M1A2 in vain, making a futile pinging sound against the tank's superior armor. Graham fired another M830 120mm HEAT MP-T round. The M256 120mm cannon moved back in its carriage, efficiently exercising its familiar routine of death.

The tremendous power of the 120mm HEAT round obliterated the third VTT-323. The strike ripped it apart as if it were a tin can blasted by a shotgun at muzzle range.

"Got the mother!" Graham screamed with dark delight. In his thermal sight, the battle took on a surreal character. Casey saw the enemy APC's fuel ignite in a burst of white heat against the cold, dark background of his thermal sight. One of the crewmen of the burning vehicle was frantically trying to escape. Casey watched as the man, drenched in flames, danced a short dance of death and then fell to the ground.

An artillery flare popped directly above *Cossack*. The flare burned brightly, illuminating *Cossack* against the trees to the south.

"Captain! Tanks to our right!" Private Weaver shouted.

Four T-62s suddenly came out of the smoke to Casey's right—due east—and immediately engaged *Cossack* at point-blank range.

Roll the dice.

If you roll 2-8, go to Section 32.

If you roll 9-12, go to Section 89.

Section 47

> *Quality of art does not depend on size of canvas.*
> —B. H. Liddell Hart

An antitank rocket shot past *Cossack*'s turret and exploded harmlessly to the right of the tank. Thundering to the northeast at fifteen miles an hour, *Cossack* and the two remaining 1st Platoon tanks swung their gun tubes to the southeast.

"SABOT, left tank," Casey ordered over his intercom. "Weaver, keep moving toward Position B."

"Wilco," Weaver answered.

The tank pitched as it struggled over the rough terrain. The cannon, laid on the target and fixed by the M1A2's impressive stabilization system, remained as true on target as a compass needle facing north.

"Identified," Graham answered coolly.

"Fire!" Casey shouted over the command frequency. The turret echoed the fury of the shot as the first SABOT round exited the muzzle of the tank's cannon. The breech recoiled and ejected the base cap of the combustible projectile. Before the aft cap bounced on the floor of the turret, Kriel had loaded another round.

"Up!" Kriel shouted as he pushed the mechanical safety lever to the fire position.

"Target," Casey shouted over the intercom, his right eye glued to his CITV. "Right tank!"

The enemy obviously couldn't see Casey's tanks. The string of six T-62s—the remainder of the enemy tank company—attacked east with their cannons fixed on McDaniel's Bradleys. In rapid volleys the two tanks in front of *Cossack* fired a SABOT round every eight seconds.

As Sergeant Graham lazed to the targets, Captain Casey sent a digital contact report over his IVIS system to the rest of the company. This report traveled automatically to every M1A2 in Team Steel. The two M1A2s with Casey could scan their IVIS screens and see the exact location of the enemy.

"Fire!" Casey shouted over the intercom.

The gun roared again, turning another T-62 into an inferno of jagged junk. Out of the corner of his eye, Casey caught the actions of his loader. Kriel twisted to his right, activated the ammo doors knee switch, and opened the armored blast doors that protected the crew from the ammunition storage compartment. He hefted the heavy 120mm M829A2 SABOT round out of its retaining canister and released the knee switch to the ammo doors. They snapped shut. Twisting to his left, he inserted the round into the breech of the M256 cannon. Standing clear of the breech, Kriel pushed the safety handle to fire and yelled, "Up!"

Relentlessly, *Cossack* advanced toward Position B, bouncing across the rough terrain as its cannon fired again. The gun leapt back in its carriage with fifteen tons of force, ejecting another aft cap onto the turret floor. Kriel pushed the knee switch and opened the ammunition blast doors in drilled precision. In the blink of an eye, the young loader muscled another SABOT round into the open mouth of the tank's cannon.

Casey grinned as he looked through his CITV and saw the flaming wreckage of the enemy tanks. Direct hits. In a fast, confused fight such as this, his M1A2s had the decisive advantage. The enemy never knew what hit them.

Casey saw the outline of the last T-62, which had repositioned behind some scrub trees and bushes. The target stood out clearly as a white-hot silhouette on Casey's CITV screen. He pushed the slew button and placed the crosshairs on the enemy tank.

"Identified tank!" Graham screamed.

"Fire!" Casey ordered.

Cossack rolled to the north, its turret pointed to the east.

"On the way!" The gun fired. The SABOT round from *Cossack*'s cannon tore through the thinly armored enemy tank. The T-62's turret exploded.

Casey watched in grim fascination through the thermal sight of his CITV as the tank burned like a blowtorch. After several seconds the hull exploded, showering the roadway with sparks and fire as the on-board fuel and ammunition detonated. In less than a minute the Americans defeated the T-62 tank company counterattack and destroyed all ten enemy tanks.

"Poor bastards," Graham said as he watched the tank's soul flicker in the fog.

"It's them or us," Casey replied "I'd rather it be them."

"Steel Six, this is Steel Five," the hard voice of Lieutenant Stonevitch echoed over the Team Steel radio net. "All stray elements have closed on my position. I've got the Sappers and the rest of Team Steel. We're taking artillery fire but moving north."

At last, Casey thought, the rest of Team Steel is forward of the passage lane and has joined McDaniel's Bradleys. Now I must decide what to do next.

TM C Unit	M1A2 Tank	M2 IFV	BSFV [ADA]	FISTV	Engr M113	CEV	ACE	HAB Bridge	Medic M113	M88 [Rec]	FUEL HEMMT	M113 APCs
1 Plt	2											
2 Plt	4											
3 Plt		3										
4 Plt		3										
Engr. Plt					4	1	1	2				
HQTnk	2		1	1								
Mech												1
1SG									2	1	1	1
M113s												13
Total	**8**	**6**	**1**	**1**	**4**	**1**	**1**	**2**	**2**	**1**	**1**	**15**

Casey pulled up a complete combat power report on his IVIS screen to check his remaining combat power:

The two tanks of 1st Platoon suddenly opened fire on Position B. Before Casey could answer his XO, the enemy fired a volley of AT-4 antitank rockets at the three advancing American tanks.

Roll the dice.

If you roll 2-5, go to Section 54.

If you roll 6-10, go to Section 55.

If you roll 11-12, go to Section 56.

Section 48

Given mobility, an indirect advance is a better and more economic means of "fixing" the enemy than a direct advance.

—B. H. Liddell Hart

"We're glad to hear from you!" exclaimed Captain Broughton, the acting commander of the 1-12th Infantry. "Things are really bad here. Most of the officers are dead. I've got sergeants commanding companies and wounded all over the place. When will you get here?"

"We're coming in now," Casey replied.

"We see some T-62s to our northeast, on Highway Seventeen," Broughton explained, "so watch out for them. We'll hold our fire until you get all your elements inside our perimeter."

"Roger, hang tough! We're on our way," Casey promised.

Scott's 2d Platoon dashed toward the enemy, firing on the move. Four T-62 tanks were positioned near Highway 17. All were facing south. The T-62s never stood a chance. In seconds Sergeant Scott's platoon cut through them and overran an enemy infantry company that was with the tanks—defending from a blocking position that faced south—designed to keep the 1-12th Infantry bottled up in Dragon. The rest of Team Steel bulled through the shattered enemy infantry, crushing the enemy with their tracks as much as with their fire. Most of them ran away from the tanks and Bradleys. Those who didn't run were quickly shot down.

Cossack picked up speed and rolled into Objective Dragon in the wake of this destruction. Casey maneuvered his tank to a berm that offered protection and an excellent firing platform from which to shoot to the east. He opened his hatch and surveyed the scene.

The infantry occupied a position prepared for an allied artillery battalion. The bunkers in this position had saved the 1-12th and permitted their staunch defense. The defense, however, had been costly. The 1-12th's perimeter bore grim testimony to the fierceness of the struggle. Black charred holes outlined the scene of the most vicious fighting.

"Steel Six, this is Bayonet Four. Man, are we glad to see you."

"Roger, Bayonet Four," Casey radioed. "What's your situation?"

"We've been sniped at all night. Took heavy casualties yesterday. We repulsed two big infantry assaults this morning and we mauled them pretty bad. That taught 'em a lesson. They won't attack with just infantry again. Now they're moving up tanks and more artillery. I've only got about eighty riflemen left to man the defense, and I have more than a hundred wounded. When do we leave?"

Section 48

Casey knew that a critical point in the battle had been reached. He pushed the transmission switch forward on his CVC helmet. "Now, Bayonet Four. Load them up as fast as you can. We don't have much time."

Casey's force deployed to the center of Objective Dragon and took up positions only long enough to load up the 1-12th in every available armored vehicle. In twenty tense minutes the infantrymen were crammed into APCs, Bradleys, and the M88 recovery vehicle. Some of the infantry men rode on top of various vehicles, determined to help shoot their way out of the encirclement.

Lieutenant Keeley's FIST-V sat next to *Cossack*. Keeley's crew exited the FIST-V and rapidly erected a long OE254 antenna. Keeley sat inside, with the back ramp of his FIST-V open, listening to the battalion command radio.

Casey called several times, asking for instructions. He heard the battalion headquarters talking, but the signal was unreadable. He shot a glance at Keeley's big antenna, then jumped out of his hatch and climbed down *Cossack*'s side to the ground. He ran over to Keeley's FIST-V and stood on the back ramp.

Roll the dice.

If you roll 2-4, go to Section 43.

If you roll 5-12, go to Section 106.

Section 49

> *War is the realm of change. Man's will and nature's weather change; heroes occasionally cower, and cowards occasionally steel themselves to circumstances; overestimations and underestimations, miscommunications and misunderstandings, mistakes and misplaced intentions all abound; friends are seemingly immobile and often unreliable, while foes are seemingly relentless and usually unpredictable; friends rarely perform as well—or foes as poorly—as a commander could reasonably expect; and even when most men perform their duties, most commanders fail because war has few winners.*
> *All this and more is the "fog of war."*
> —Douglas Cohn, *Jackson's Valley Campaign*

"Weaver, stop the damn tank!" Casey ordered over the intercom, exasperated that he had lost a heavy assault bridge and two engineer squads in a friendly minefield.

Weaver slammed on the brakes, throwing Casey against the front of his commander's weapon station. The FIST-V and the BSFV staggered to a halt, inches from *Cossack*'s grill doors.

Casey opened his hatch and peered to the south. He couldn't see anything in the fog except the two vehicles idling right behind him. His force was cut in half. He wondered if young Lieutenant Andrews could straighten out the mess in the minefield. "Steel Five, stop the column and sort it out!" Casey ordered over the radio. "Break. White One, report."

"Steel Six, this is White One. We're headed northeast, following Viper. I expect to make the turn to the north in a few minutes. The fog is thinning out. Artillery has shifted to the north. No contact. Over."

"Roger, White One. I want you and Blue to take up hasty defensive positions and hold where you are. We've got half the force tangled in the passage lane. Steel Six. Out."

A breeze suddenly picked up from the north and the fog began to lift. Visibility improved to a few hundred meters. Finally, Casey thought, our luck is turning. Maybe Andrews will be able to back the column out of the minefield as the fog lifts.

Casey dropped back inside the turret and turned his CITV toward the south, hoping to get a glimpse of the forces stuck in the minefield as the visibility improved. He could feel the rumble of the artillery as it rolled north; they were on schedule. If he was going to take advantage of the artillery strikes, he had to move quickly.

"Steel Five, SITREP. Over," Casey demanded.

"Steel Six, this is Steel Five Delta," the voice of Andrews's driver replied. "The lieutenant is on the ground. Some of the engineers are wounded. He's trying to organize a medevac by APC. Over."

"Roger," Casey answered as the sweat beaded up on his forehead. "Have him call me as soon as he returns."

The artillery fire along Cobra and Coral stopped. The fires were now all falling along Viper, several kilometers to the north.

"Steel Six, this is Steel Five," an out-of-breath Lieutenant Andrews reported. "We've lost nine men, all engineers. I've got six critically wounded. We're backing up from the minefield, one step at a time."

"Steel Five, do everything you can to speed it up. Try to have the rest of the team bypass the stalled elements if necessary, but get things moving," ordered Casey.

"It's going to take a while, Steel Six, and I can't do much about it," Andrews replied, his voice tense with frustration. There was a short pause, then, finally, "Wilco."

The time raced by as Casey scanned his IVIS screen. Scott's platoon, followed closely by McDaniel's infantry, was holding just south of the ridge at CS241409, ready to charge north on his order.

Standing in the turret, Casey looked south, scanning the area with his night vision goggles. In the thinning fog he could make out the fires of two burning APCs. He looked at his watch. It was 0140. He had waited in position more than thirty minutes now.

Casey turned his view to the dark outline of the hill at CS236406, to his north. Through his night vision goggles he saw a pencillike beam of light shining to the south. He had seen this type of light many times before, at tank gunnery ranges. It could be seen only through the passive light-intensification capability of the night vision goggles. It was the telltale light of a laser.

We don't have any friendlies on that hill, Casey thought. Could the enemy have an artillery observer there with a laser designator or maybe a handheld laser range finder?

At the same time that these thoughts registered in his head, artillery flares suddenly popped high above him. More flares popped over the area where the APCs were burning. Casey looked up at the bright parachute flares as they fluttered earthward, sailing in the moist air around his tank. The flares burned brightly, illuminating *Cossack,* the FIST-V, and the Bradley.

Casey remembered something he had studied about the enemy's artillery capabilities: "The enemy uses artillery to kill tanks in predesignated artillery strike boxes. It normally takes no more than twenty minutes to coordinate massed fires." Helpless, he watched enemy artillery shells blast his force to pieces. He knew that his command group would be the next target.

Roll the dice.

If you roll 2, go to Section 25.

If you roll 3-8, go to Section 40.

If you roll 9-12, go to Section 88.

Section 50

> *War is the unfolding of miscalculations.*
> —Barbara Tuchman

Cossack jerked abruptly to the left to avoid the incoming missile. Casey struggled to see, balancing himself against the right side of the turret as the M1A2 jolted across the rocky ground. He looked through the vision blocks that surrounded his tank commander's station. His closed hatch protected him from enemy fire but limited his ability to direct the tank across the rough terrain.

Suddenly a huge splash to the right signaled the strike of the enemy warhead. The missile smashed into the ground twenty meters in front of *Cossack* in a bright orange and red plume of sparks.

Cossack jerked hard to the right as Weaver instinctively reacted to the blast of the enemy missile. Casey ducked down as *Cossack* hit a dip in the ground.

"My thermal's washed out!" Weaver shouted. "I can't see."

Casey shot a glance up through his vision blocks; it was too late. The tank charged to the right, went over a bank, and rolled into the Gang River.

Casey felt the sickening, out-of-control feeling of a seventy-ton tank rolling over. He slammed into the roof as the tank settled in the river, upside down. The electrical power flickered on and off as the engine whined. The tank's tracks whirled madly in midair.

"Move the gun. I can't open my hatch!" Weaver screamed.

Casey shook off the shock of his fall. Kriel was lying unconscious on the roof of the tank. Graham, tangled in his tanker's vest, was frantically trying to kick himself away from the gunner's seat.

Cold, muddy water seeped into the turret. Casey looked around in a panic. Tanks are not waterproof. If he couldn't find a way out . . .

Suddenly the power failed, and the inside of the turret turned black as death. Casey struggled at the hatch, but the tank was resting in the river on its roof, so it was impossible to escape. The designers of the M1 tank had not thought to put an escape hatch in its belly.

The last thing Casey heard was the cries of his tank crew as they slowly drowned in the cold waters of the Gang River.

You have been killed in action.
Go back to Section 29 and make another decision.

Section 51

Casey took a deep breath. The metal assault bridge creaked as the heavy, combat-loaded M1A2 Abrams tank moved over the metal treadway. Sergeant Scott's tank rolled slowly forward, one track pad at a time. The tank slowly inched across the bridge, spanning the gap. After several tense seconds, Scott's tank reached the other side.

Sporting a wide smile of relief, Scott waved to Casey from the far bank. The crossing was a "go!"

Casey radioed to Scott to send the rest of his platoon across. Casey glimpsed the time; he worried that every second he delayed at the bridge put his force in jeopardy. It was already 0830. He knew that he still had a full day of fighting ahead of him. As artillery smoke helped mask their crossing, Team Steel rumbled over the heavy assault bridge. Soon the entire force was on the north bank of the Gang River.

Eager to make contact with the 1-12th, Casey switched frequencies and radioed the unit. Captain Broughton, the latest in a succession of acting commanders due to casualties, answered the radio. Broughton explained that the battalion was down to less than a hundred men capable of fighting. He didn't know how many wounded he had. Although they still had small-arms and machine-gun ammunition, they had only three Javelin antitank missiles left.

"God, am I glad to hear from you!" Broughton's worried voice boomed in Casey's CVC helmet earphones. "Things are really bad here. Most of the officers are dead. I've got sergeants commanding companies and more wounded than I can handle. When will you get here?"

Casey pushed the transmit lever forward on the side of his CVC helmet. "In about fifteen minutes. Over."

"Outstanding! We see some T-62s to our south, on Highway Seventeen," Broughton continued, "so watch out for them. We'll hold our fire. Come on in!"

"Roger. Hang tough. We're on our way," Casey promised.

Team Steel sprinted forward and ran smack into the rear of an enemy infantry battalion at CS223460. The enemy infantry oriented north, staging to hit the 1-12th by attacking over the ridge.

Team Steel's lead tanks caught them in the open as they were assembling for their assault on Objective Dragon.

Team Steel slammed the enemy infantry between a rock and a hard place. Unable to flee, the enemy counterattacked across the open rice fields. Casey couldn't believe his eyes; it was like watching a Japanese banzai attack from World War II.

To support the infantry assault, five T-62s dashed southwest to challenge the American tanks. Scott's tanks fired a volley that destroyed three T-62s instantly. The two surviving T-62s fired a volley that hit the lead M1A2 tank. Both 115mm tank rounds hit the tank but bounced off its hard armor. Scott's tanks fired again, as if the enemy tank attack was merely an annoyance, and blasted the turrets off the last two T-62s.

The tanks and Bradleys fired as they moved. The armored column raced perpendicular to the enemy infantry, blasting away like the broadside of a line of dreadnoughts. The enemy infantry withered under this firepower, then panicked and ran back toward the ridge. A mob of soldiers tried to scurry up the steep slope of the ridge; others tried to hide behind the illusive protection of the hump-shaped rice paddy dikes. Neither option offered the slightest sanctuary.

"Sir, they're either very brave or very dumb," Graham said as he turned the turret onto a clump of enemy infantry. "We're slaughtering them."

"Shut up and fire!" Casey answered as he fired his .50 caliber at the enemy infantry. "If we don't kill them now, we'll just have to fight them later."

Cossack's 120mm cannon roared as Graham blasted the paddy dike with a high-explosive round, sending three enemy soldiers to oblivion.

By now the entire armored column was blasting away at the enemy to their flank. The tanks and Bradleys dropped the enemy on the ridge first, then picked off the others in the muck and mire of the rice paddy. Machine guns chewed up the rice paddies and scourged the ridgeline, cutting down the enemy like a scythe slicing wheat. In less than five minutes, Team Steel had ground them into dust.

Team Steel rolled on, unstoppable. The American infantrymen defending the battered perimeter of Objective Dragon cheered as Team Steel's lead platoon rolled in and occupied defensive firing positions along the perimeter.

Cossack took a winding dirt path through Objective Dragon, to a piece of dominating ground near the center of the perimeter. The M113s pulled up next to the bunkers and trenches, dropped their ramps, and unloaded ammunition, water, medical supplies, and rations to the beleaguered infantrymen.

For these battle-weary riflemen, the supplies that the tankers were dishing out were as welcome as Christmas presents.

Casey checked his map, then quickly surveyed the battle area. Objective Dragon was a prepared defensive strongpoint, created before the war as an allied artillery battalion firing position with predug trenches and bunkers constructed of sandbags, old tires, and dirt. Reinforced concrete bunkers, some big enough to hold fifty men, dotted the perimeter. Deep trenches with sides reinforced by old car tires and dirt linked the bunkers. These trenches and bunkers had saved the 1-12th Infantry. Without these fortifications, the unit would have been annihilated by the enemy's artillery.

Casey could also see that the staunch defense had been paid for in blood. The infantry hadn't had time to bury their dead. The perimeter was scattered with corpses, theirs and ours. Crumpled, blackened bunkers identified the locations of the most vicious fighting.

If the true value of a place is measured after you pay for it, Casey thought, Objective Dragon was now priceless.

Casey considered loading up the infantry and breaking out from the encirclement. Team Steel's attack on the enemy infantry to the south had opened a doorway through enemy lines. This door, however, would stay open only for a short time. If there ever was a chance to break out, this was it. Casey knew he would not get another chance.

His orders, however, were clear: "Link up and hold." Casey rejected the thought of breaking out. He would do his duty. Taking his map, he quickly sketched the fields of fire and prepared a company team fire plan to defend Objective Dragon.

"Steel Six, this is Bayonet Four. You guys are a sight for sore eyes. We'd thought the division had written us off," the commander of the 1-12th Infantry reported over the radio.

"We're happy to join your party, Bayonet Four," Casey radioed back. "What's your situation?"

"We've been attacked, mortared, and sniped at all night. The enemy tried to overwhelm us with infantry. They attacked by the hundreds and we killed them as fast as they came. They took very heavy casualties yesterday. We repulsed two attacks again around 0200. The enemy stopped hitting us just before you arrived. We think they are moving up tanks and heavy artillery for another assault. You got here just in time."

"What's your strength?" Casey asked.

"I think I have about eighty effectives and more than a hundred wounded," Bayonet Four answered. "If they come at us again, with a brigade-sized, combined-arms attack, I'm not sure we can stop them."

Casey sensed the desperation in the infantryman's voice. "Don't worry, we'll stop them. I've brought a dozen antitank missiles and plenty of small arms and grenades with me. My men are issuing them now to your guys. Over."

"Thanks," the weary infantrymen replied. "When does the rest of your force arrive?"

"Tomorrow morning. We have to hold until then."

There was a long silence on the radio. "Roger, Steel Six. My men still have a lot of fight left. Bayonet Four. Out."

Casey deployed 3d Platoon (three Bradleys) to the north, 2d Platoon (three M1A2s) in the center, and the M113s (thirteen) and engineers (one CEV and four M113 mounted squads) guarding the south. He coordinated the defense with the infantry. He positioned his command group in the center, on high ground that allowed him to fire northeast to southeast. The high ground he occupied allowed him to fire over the heads of the friendly troops. Keeley's FIST-V rolled next to *Cossack*.

Casey tried several times to contact battalion headquarters on the radio, but he couldn't reach anyone outside Objective Dragon. Ei-

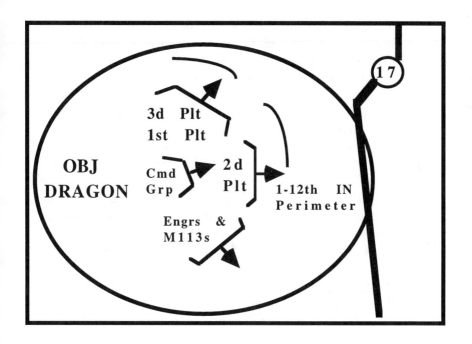

ther the mountains were blocking the transmissions or something had happened to the battalion and brigade radio retrans sites.

Suddenly an explosion blasted about eighty meters to *Cossack*'s left flank. Enemy mortar rounds began falling nearby, billowing in geysers of dust and smoke. Soon heavy-artillery shells smashed into the American perimeter, adding to the fury of the mortar bombs, as if in angry response to the surprise American attack on the southern edge of Objective Dragon. Shells blanketed the defenders. The Americans took each hammer blow in silence as the tankers cringed inside their turrets and the infantrymen of the 1-12th Infantry Battalion hugged the bottom of their bunkers.

After almost ten minutes, the pounding stopped. The quiet after the shelling echoed in Casey's soul, at a level as loud as the sound of the explosions. Suddenly he realized how tired he was. The need for sleep—just fifteen minutes would do—overwhelmed him. His eyes blinked, his mind wandered off to unconsciousness, then he jolted back to reality. The enemy was out there, ready to kill him. He waited in *Cossack*'s turret, searching through the narrow vision blocks of the TC's station, and prayed for night.

The enemy seemed determined to annihilate the defenders. The infantry reported hearing the sounds of enemy tanks. Casey cracked his hatch to the open-protected position and saw a thick blanket of white smoke covering the battlefield.

Standard procedure, he thought. The enemy struck first with artillery, then they smoked the battlefield. Even though they knew that the American tanks and Bradleys had thermal sights, the smoke would conceal the attackers from many of the defender's weapons. When the smoke was thick, the combined-arms assault would begin. It wouldn't be long now.

Casey put his CVC helmet on his head and keyed the intercom switch. "Can you see them?"

"Nothing yet, Captain," Graham answered calmly. "But I'll bet you a month's pay that they're coming."

"That's not a fair bet," Casey chided. "I get paid more than you do."

Graham laughed. Casey suddenly realized how important the human touch was in leading men in combat. Men are not machines, he thought. They don't follow orders, fight in desperate situations, and give their all because of regulations or fear of punishment. Maybe that kind of motivation worked for Frederick the Great's soldiers, but it wouldn't work in modern war. A touch of human nature gives men courage when things get tough. One human act can turn a cat into a lion.

The seconds shot by as Casey scanned the northeast for enemy tanks. He waited as the sweat rolled down his face. Hollywood makes war look pretty exciting, he thought. It's a different story when you're part of it.

"Identified T-72s!" Graham shouted, his voice filled with tension. "Look at the bastards. They must think we can't see them in the smoke. They're moving on-line to assault."

Casey looked through his thermal sight. He saw the big, ugly T-72s as they maneuvered on the open ground, in paradelike fashion, moving from column to platoon line formation. Nine or ten

T-72s were moving toward them; it was at least a company, with more probably following. The enemy commander was obviously an arrogant son of a bitch, or he had never fought M1A2s before.

"Steel elements, hold your fire," Casey announced over the radio. The battlefield was narrow. Restricted terrain doesn't offer the luxury of too many long-range shots. If Casey's tanks fired early, the enemy would lose its lead elements and might not enter the battle. Casey realized that he had to gamble that the enemy might not know what he was coming up against. Casey would have to let them get as close as possible before executing his firetrap.

Casey quickly turned to the northwest and searched the enemy formation. "Let them deploy. I want to get as many of them into the open as possible before we start shooting."

The enemy tanks moved in geometric precision. They rolled forward at five miles an hour, getting closer to the eastern edge of the 1-12th Infantry perimeter with each second.

The 1-12th Infantry opened fire all along the perimeter. Machine guns blazed in the direction of the advancing tanks, but they had little effect. Without thermal sights, except on their Javelin antitank systems, the American infantrymen could not see the advancing T-72s in the thick smoke. A wave of Javelins shot up from the defenders, pierced the smoke, and struck the advancing T-72s in a crushing wave of destruction.

The enemy assault picked up speed. A devastating volley of enemy artillery fire exploded in the western and southern portions of Dragon.

Casey scanned his IVIS again:

"Steel elements, main gun, and TOWs, enemy battalion, depth," Casey ordered over the radio. "Second Platoon, take the near targets. Third and 1st Platoon, take the far targets. At my command."

"Roger," Scott's voice answered. "Let's show them what some tanks can do!"

"Wilco," replied Scott's wingman.

Machine guns opened up from the surrounding hills. Enemy mortar fire slammed into the defenders' positions. The T-72s fired a wild volley of 125mm rounds through the smoke. The rounds tore into the ground near *Cossack*'s position.

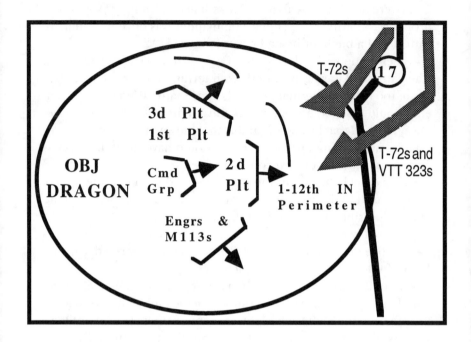

"They're nine hundred meters and closing," Graham reported. "If we let 'em get any closer, I'll be able to spit on 'em."

Casey didn't answer.

"Sir?" Graham pleaded. "They must see us."

Casey tracked the lead enemy element in his thermal sight, then switched to the far northeast to glimpse the trail element. He saw enemy APCs moving into line. He pushed the transmitter switch forward on his CVC helmet. "Fire!"

"On the way!" Graham yelled on the intercom, pulling the trigger a millisecond after the captain's command.

The tank jerked from the gun's recoil. The round screamed forward, hitting the leftmost enemy tank in the front at the driver's compartment and stopping it in its tracks. The SABOT round tore the T-72 apart.

Blazing and shattered enemy armored vehicles littered the battlefield. The enemy's courage and determination had not been enough to escape Team Steel's trap of fire. In the first few minutes of the fight, the combined firepower of Scott's and McDaniel's platoons devastated the enemy's formation. The lead combat reconnaissance patrol and a company-sized forward security element hit a wall of fire. The M1A2s chopped them up in quick order. Undeterred, the enemy's main force pushed faster into the melee, rushing into the smoke and debris without a sense of the trap that Casey was about to spring.

"Lovely, just lovely," Casey said to himself. The sound of hypervelocity armor-piercing rounds tearing through metal turrets punctuated his thoughts. He ducked down to view the battle through the thermal sight, wishing that his CITV was still functioning. He checked his digital display for losses. McDaniel's platoon lost one Bradley, dropping his strength to two M2A2s. Casey could also see three of his M113s burning.

The enemy turned south, away from the fire that was smashing them from inside the smoke. Several enemy tanks straddled the trench line and fired point-blank into the concrete bunkers. A quick wave of 120mm fire from 2d Platoon blasted the T-72s to pieces.

"Steel Six, this is White One," Sergeant Scott interjected. "We've destroyed at least two companies of tanks and a dozen Vetts, but they're still coming. They can't see us in this smoke."

"Steel Six, this is Bayonet Four," Captain Broughton interjected. "I lost eighteen men in that attack. We fired eight of the twelve Javelins you brought us. We'll hold if we have to use bayonets, but we won't be able to shoot tanks much longer."

The noise of battle increased to a fever pitch. Team Steel concentrated on destroying the enemy tanks first. The T-72s disintegrated to Team Steel's concentrated firepower. The enemy infantry jumped from their VTT-323 armored personnel carriers and dashed west across the rising ground. The M1A2 tank and Bradley machine guns cut them down in the thick smoke before the enemy infantry had a chance to engage. In seconds Team Steel blasted every VTT to oblivion. The enemy infantry that survived crawled for cover, ran east, or was cut down by machine-gun fire.

The firing continued for another minute or so, then it was over. An enemy combined-arms battalion lay broken and burning across the length of the eastern perimeter of Objective Dragon. Not a single enemy vehicle had escaped the killing touch of Team Steel. It had all happened in less than four minutes.

Casey pressed forward the radio switch on his helmet. "Blue One, this is Steel Six. Send me a SITREP. Over."

"This is Blue One. I've lost two Bradleys to enemy tanks," the infantry platoon leader reported with regret. "We killed them as fast as they came up. If they keep coming like this, I don't know how much longer we can hold them. I'm down to two rounds of TOW ammunition."

"Cross level ammunition, Blue," Casey answered sternly, wincing at the casualties that McDaniel reported. Casey scanned his IVIS screen and saw the disposition of his tanks superimposed over the 1:50,000 map. "We're staying here until relieved."

"Roger, Steel Six," the mechanized infantry platoon leader replied. "Don't worry. We will hold."

"I'm out of HEAT and also red on machine gun," Lieutenant Andrews, 1st Platoon's leader, answered, indicating that he was low—red—on 7.62mm ammunition.

Casey popped his hatch to survey the battlefield. The smoke thinned in areas and revealed the horror of the fight. It had looked so clean in his thermal sights. He reconsidered breaking out to the south but realized that the opportunity for that option had swung shut.

The enemy launched another furious artillery barrage. Shells rained down on the perimeter with a vengeance, striking the bunkers and plastering Casey's tanks and Bradleys. As soon as the artillery stopped, the enemy began sniping and mortaring the defenders. More artillery followed, then a furious combined-arms assault erupted in the southeast. The enemy overran two infantry bunkers before Team Steel and the 1-12th defeated the attack.

The battlefield was quiet for a moment. The 1-12th Infantry, now down to about sixty fighting men, crawled out of their bunkers and occupied their firing positions after the latest attack. Soldiers moved wounded men quickly to the medical bunker, which was now overflowing with wounded. Casey watched the determined infantrymen prepare for the next onslaught. He admired their courage and stoicism.

Casey knew, however, that courage was not enough. He reviewed the situation. The defenders' casualties were mounting. The shelling destroyed two more M113 APCs and killed seven infantrymen.

The seconds pressed down on Casey like a huge weight. He looked to the east and, just by chance, saw a green signal flare shoot up, high over the slope of the hill behind him. He slammed his hatch shut. How much longer could they hold out? He knew that he had to do something.

The artillery signaled the beginning of a new assault. Artillery shells fell all around, their smoke billowing in great white clouds. Things were happening too fast, Casey thought as he watched the enemy lay the artillery smoke screen on Dragon. They have the initiative as long as we sit here.

Casey keyed the radio mike and tried again to reach Major Cutter on the battalion's command frequency. He could not reach battalion. Casey reconsidered his mission. The purpose of the raid was to save the 1-12th Infantry. Could he do that if he stuck to the plan and defended from Objective Dragon? The defense was becoming increasingly untenable. The tanks were almost out of machine-gun ammo, and each tank was down to approximately twenty main-gun rounds per tank.

Casey reconsidered breaking out and attacking south. His ability to move the 1-12th was decreasing with each vehicle he lost. Casey knew that it wouldn't be long before the enemy launched another major assault. He had to decide!

**If you decide to follow orders and stay and defend,
go to Section 53.**

**If you decide to disobey orders and risk fighting your way south,
go to Section 100.**

Section 52

A brilliant flash and a wave of heat engulfed the top of the tank. An AT-4 antitank rocket hit the left front of *Cossack*'s turret before Casey could slew the turret toward the enemy fire coming from the town of Masan. Casey ducked as the force from the blast pushed him down into the turret.

"Shit! We've been hit!" Graham yelled. "Anyone hurt?"

Casey couldn't breathe. He opened his eyes and struggled for air. Suddenly his lungs began to work again and he gasped in a long breath.

"You okay, Captain?" Graham asked over the intercom.

"Yeah," Casey finally replied. "Just got the wind knocked out of me. Crew report!"

"Driver up," Weaver replied.

"Loader up," Kriel answered.

"Gunner up, and I identify three Vetts, direct front!"

Cossack moved forward and ducked behind a mound of dirt. The four tanks to *Cossack*'s left boomed as their cannons blasted at targets on the western edge of Masan.

Casey swung into action. He tried to swivel the CITV onto the enemy, but the device wouldn't move. He tried again, then realized that the blast had damaged it. His hatch was still in the open-protected position.

Casey peered through the opening in his hatch. More flares dotted the night sky. In the light he saw the western edge of the town. A dazzling display of fireworks erupted from the town as Sergeant Scott's tanks plastered the area. Through their thermal sights the M1A2s blasted away at suspected areas. The enemy missile fire stopped.

Tense minutes passed as 2d Platoon carried the fight against the enemy in Masan. McDaniel's 3d Platoon moved up to *Cossack*'s right flank.

"Steel Six, this is Steel Five. The 1st Platoon is moving into the support-by-fire position now. I don't see any enemy on this side. I can enter the town from the southeast and catch them before they know we're in Masan."

"Negative, Steel Five," Casey answered over the radio. He checked his IVIS screen and saw 1st Platoon at CS257413. "Attack by fire only. Enemy antitank systems have fired at us from the west side. I want you to direct support fire into the town. Level it from your end!"

"Wilco," Stonevitch answered.

"Steel Guns, this is Steel Six. Focus your artillery on the western edge of the town at CS253422. Over."

"Already on the way," Lieutenant Keeley answered. "DPICM in effect."

The western edge of Masan began to glow like the embers of a huge campfire. Casey scanned the fog-filled darkness with his night vision goggles. Without his CITV thermal sight he couldn't see very much of his company in the fog, but he could see their fire. Scattered artillery flares fell to the southeast. The light from the flares illuminated the western edge of Masan. Casey could see that the enemy antitank systems were either out of commission or had moved deeper within the protection of the town.

Successive volleys of 155mm DPICM rained on the town. Casey waited as the artillery did its work. The 2d Platoon continued to fire on the town from the west, aided now by the 25mm cannons of McDaniel's 3d Platoon Bradleys.

After several minutes more, Casey saw the flashes of Stonevitch's force as they fired at Masan from the southeast. Caught in this crossfire, Masan was quickly turning into a charnel house. Fires raged through the gutted houses as if they were made of paper and had been doused with gasoline.

More artillery flares popped overhead. Casey searched the western side of the town for antitank missiles but found none. Graham scanned the western edge of town with his thermal sight, ready to fire at the first indication of an enemy missile launch.

More shells exploded above the town, pulverizing the enemy with a vengeance. A tremendous orange-yellow flame shot skyward from the center of the town. The ground shook as if from the strike of an immense cudgel. Hot, burning sparks zigzagged across the dark sky.

Suddenly, a shower of sparks and flame covered the M1A2 to *Cossack*'s left. Another bright explosion erupted to *Cossack*'s right, ripping a Bradley in half.

"Action rear!" Sergeant Scott screamed over the command frequency. "Enemy tanks!"

Roll the dice.

If you roll 2-5, go to Section 41.

If you roll 6-9, go to Section 63.

If you roll 10-12, go to Section 71.

Section 53

> *Ground that is reached through narrow gorges, and from which we can only retire by tortuous paths, so that a small number of the enemy would suffice to crush a large body of our men: this is hemmed-in ground. . . . In hemmed-in ground, resort to stratagem.*
> —Sun Tzu, *The Art of War*

A dense pall of acrid black smoke lay over the battlefield. Objective Dragon was looking more and more like a cemetery. Casey considered his options and wondered if he was staring at his personal date with eternity.

We're following our orders, he thought. It's 1520. All we have to do is hold on for about nine hours. Nine hours, he argued with himself, might as well be a hundred years.

In thirty minutes the artillery started again, followed by a fresh wave of T-72s, VTT-323s, and infantry. This time the enemy supported his attack with AT-4 antitank missiles on the high ground to the northeast and southeast. Team Steel's casualties increased. The Americans defended stubbornly, making the enemy pay a heavy price for each meter of real estate given away. The perimeter tightened as the defenders dwindled. After four major assaults, the Americans were almost out of ammunition, but the enemy showed no signs of giving up.

Casey checked the ammunition remaining on *Cossack*. His .50-caliber machine gun was out of ammunition and the 7.62mm co-ax machine gun had less than a hundred rounds left. There were only four HEAT rounds and three SABOT rounds left in the ammunition storage compartments. The rest of Team Steel was in the same shape—running out of ammunition.

Casey shook his head. He regretted that none of the ammunition-carrying M113s had crossed the bridge. He shook his head as if to cast off these recriminations. You take the cards you are dealt and play accordingly, he thought.

He raised his binoculars to his eyes and scanned the battlefield. Burning vehicles lit the scene. The screams of anguish of the wounded wafted above the whine of *Cossack*'s turbine engine. Not all the cries were in English. The enemy casualties were tremendous, at least five times greater than those of the Americans. Enemy dead lay stacked like wood across the northern and southern ridges. The eastern edge of the perimeter was a charnel house. Casey took grim solace in the thought that he would make the score even higher before the day was over. He wondered how long the enemy could afford to pay this price.

The blast of artillery confirmed Casey's suspicions. He quickly closed his hatch to avoid the zinging steel. Shaking with the rocking of the tank, he steadied himself against the tank commander's sight extension. The artillery picked up in intensity; it seemed to crush in all around *Cossack*.

Casey looked through his tank's vision blocks and watched in disbelief as a number of the exploding shells discharged spires of yellow, wisping smoke.

Section 53

"Gas!" a suppressed, anonymous voice shouted over the command radio frequency.

"No," Casey muttered. "They can't be using gas."

Fear shot down Casey's spine like liquid fire. He grabbed for his protective mask and frantically forced it over his face. The rest of the crew did the same, executing a drill they had practiced hundreds of times in training but hoped they would never have to test in war.

"Crew report!" Casey ordered, the words flying from his mouth as he found himself almost out of breath. He knew that the over-pressure system of the M1A2 tank would keep out the enemy's chemical agents. He also knew that a tank is hardly an airtight vehicle. The rule is to mask whenever you anticipate chemical agents. Caution, in this case, needed no further incentive.

"Gunner up, scanning for targets," Graham shouted in anger over the intercom. "Bastards! I can't believe they slimed us!"

"Loader up," Kriel replied, his voice muffled by his gas mask microphone.

"Driver up!" Weaver reported, his voice tinged with fear. "Sir, don't you think we ought to get out of here?"

Casey didn't answer. Where could they go? Leaving the infantry was out of the question. God, Casey thought. The poor, bloody infantry. The wounded wouldn't last long in positions doused in chemical agent. Open wounds exposed to nerve agents meant certain death. Holes in chemical suits might register the same end, depending on the type of agent.

"Sir, we can't stay here!" Weaver continued.

"Shut up, Weaver," Graham ordered in a voice that sounded as strong as steel. Graham moved the turret back and forth, scanning for targets. "As my old drill sergeant used to say, 'It's ruin to run from a fight.' We're not running."

Casey surveyed the misty battlefield. A yellowish green gas floated across the area. More gas shells rained down on Dragon. Armageddon, Casey thought. The enemy had opted for total annihilation. This is the end, he thought.

More explosions blanketed the position as the enemy added a wave of high-explosive shells to the gas strike. Two explosions rocked *Cossack,* missing the tank by meters and hammering its sides with shrapnel, rocks, and debris. Casey's protective mask made it difficult to see the battlefield through his vision blocks. The high-pitched whine of the tank's chemical pressure system kicked in. Casey looked outside the tank and saw an American soldier climb out of a trench. The man wasn't wearing a protective mask. Gagging for air, he fell to the ground and started kicking madly, tearing at his throat and eyes. Casey watched, powerless to help, as the man died in agony.

Damn them, he cursed. Damn them to hell.

A brilliant flash erupted to *Cossack*'s left as a 152mm artillery shell slammed into Lieutenant Keeley's FIST-V. Keeley and his crew died instantly. The artillery tore apart the thin aluminum–armored track as if it was a cardboard box. Debris, twisted metal, and flesh shot out in a geyser; burning hunks of metal and diesel fuel were spread over a fifty-meter area.

Cossack shuddered with the impact of each artillery shell. The deadly shrapnel and gas flew over the battlefield like the grim reaper.

Just when Casey thought he could stand no more, the artillery fire slackened, then stopped.

"Kriel, get a Two-Five-Six kit started," Casey said, glancing at the loader. Kriel's eyes looked as big as silver dollars inside the eyepieces of the black protective mask. "Kriel, do you understand?"

Kriel nodded, then reached for a chemical detection card to check the type of chemical agent. Casey peered through his vision blocks. He heard the distinct crack of small-arms fire.

"Okay, lads, let's keep our cool," Casey calmly ordered over the intercom, as much for himself as his crew. "We're going to make it."

The sound of small-arms fire and tank machine guns erupted all across the perimeter. The intensity of the defenders' fire was much less than before. Casey knew that the chemical strike had done its deadly work.

"Here they come again," Graham's muffled voice announced as he turned the turret toward the enemy. "Identified. Troops. Northeastern ridge. They're wearing gas masks."

"We're down to less than three hundred 7.62mm rounds," Kriel reported.

"Roger. Save the machine-gun ammo for when they get closer. Fire HEAT," Casey ordered, forcing himself to speak slowly into the microphone of his protective mask.

"Switching to HEAT," Graham shouted.

"Two HEAT rounds left," Kriel yelled as he shoved forward the main gun firing safety lever. "Up!"

Casey looked through his sights at the enemy infantry as they crested the ridge. "Fire!"

"On the way," Graham yelled.

The 120mm cannon roared. The round split through the gas-filled air and hit the ridge. A dozen enemy soldiers fell from the blast. At this range, Casey thought, it was impossible to miss them. The ridge was filled with enemy infantry.

Cossack and Scott's tanks fired madly at their attackers, who were closing the range to the tanks in quick rushes. There were so many enemy soldiers rushing toward them that Casey realized that a fresh infantry brigade was attacking. The enemy infantry fired RPGs and hurled grenades in a fanatic, supreme effort to destroy the Americans. For every enemy killed, ten more seemed to appear from behind the ridge. The enemy dead were stacked up in mounds, but more soldiers climbed over the mounds and kept coming.

The enemy overran the infantry bunkers and surged forward to take on the tanks. The enemy attacked in bounds, dashing from one gully to another. As the enemy assault squads alternated forward, their support elements fired machine guns and RPGs on the American positions. Graham fired his co-ax machine gun, cutting down several waves of attackers.

Soon the enemy infantry were everywhere, like locust in a cornfield. The battle turned into a wild melee of individual battles—men against tanks and Bradleys. A dozen infantrymen popped up behind Casey's position. Suddenly there was a blinding flash that registered through the vision blocks.

"Troops, left front!" Weaver announced. "They've got RPGs."

"Where in the hell did they come from?"Graham shouted. He swung the turret into action and immediately ripped off a short burst of 7.62mm. The machine gun stopped.

"Out of ammo!" Graham shouted. "Load HEAT."

"Weaver!" Casey yelled. "Back us up."

Casey looked through his vision blocks to the right rear and saw men running all around *Cossack*. The tank suddenly sprung backward, grinding three enemy soldiers into the hard, rocky ground.

Kaboom! An RPG smashed against the turret.

"Misfire!" Graham screamed.

"Keep backing up!" Casey shouted to his driver over the intercom. "Hold your right track!"

The big M1A2 lurched backward, pivoting to face left. *Cossack* now pointed northwest as Graham continued to try to fire the main gun.

"Misfire!" Graham cried in desperation. "I can't get it to fire!"

"Weaver, move forward!" Casey yelled, ignoring his gunner. "Charge them . . . move. . . . Move!" *Cossack* raced up the rough, high ground, flattening another enemy soldier under its tracks.

Kaboom! Casey heard a huge bang and the agonizing sound of twisting metal. *Cossack* lurched to the left in a fierce, uncontrolled spin, then pitched to the side, throwing the crew against the turret walls. The tank cantered to its right flank and listed like a ship sinking at sea.

"Back up!" Casey cried as he struggled to see.

"We've lost a track!" Weaver yelled. The engine howled but the tank didn't roll. It jerked back and forth as the sole working track tore at the dirt. "She won't budge."

Boom! Another violent blast shoved the tank's turret to the right. Casey was hurled against the side of the TC's station. Kriel slammed against the breech block, then fell to the floor unconscious. Graham struggled to move the turret.

"Can't see anything. . . . The turret won't move!" the gunner shouted.

Cossack's engine screeched like a pressure cooker ready to burst. The tank shuddered back and forth as the left track twirled. It was a fruitless effort. The ditch had imprisoned the seventy-ton beast in a death grip.

"I see 'em, must be fifty or more," Weaver mumbled, his voice barely audible over the intercom. "They're all around us."

Casey's mind raced as he sought a way out of their predicament. The tank couldn't move, and none of the weapons inside the turret could fire. His options narrowed to one. He grabbed his 9mm pistol from his shoulder holster. "I'm going to try to get out and grab the loader's machine gun. You use your pistol and follow me."

Graham nodded, his heavy breathing in his protective mask coming over the intercom. He forced out an "okay."

Casey strained to hear signs of the enemy. He listened the way an animal at bay listens to a pack of wolves closing in for the kill. For several seconds he waited. He knew that he would have to act quickly. He grabbed the handle of his TC hatch, then hesitated. The sweat formed on his face. He could barely see through the face piece of his protective mask.

Hell, he thought, it's now or never. He grabbed the handle again and, with a mighty heave, forced the hatch open.

Two enemy soldiers stood only a few feet away. Casey fired his pistol, hitting one man with several shots before the second blasted him with a full magazine of Kalashnikov fire. Casey sank against the side of the TC's hatch and died as the enemy rifleman shoved a grenade past his limp body into the turret.

You have fought a hard and gallant fight but failed.
Return to Section 104, make another decision, and fight again!

Section 54

> *Combat experience, including that gained during recent local wars, demonstrates that success in offensives in mountainous terrain is vitally dependent on the timely preparation of subunits and the ability of personnel to operate boldly and with initiative.*
> —Maj. Gen. V. G. Reznichenko, Tactics

Casey saw the flash of the enemy missile out of the corner of his eye. He heard someone scream over Team Steel's command frequency. "Missile! Turn hard right!"

There was no time to react. The enemy antitank missile struck the side of *Cossack*'s turret. Flame and sparks splashed across the top of the turret like fiery water, gushing into the opening in the tank commander's hatch that was locked in the open-protected position.

Casey felt a wave of heat hit him in the face. He closed his eyes.

The explosion slammed him into the bottom of the turret. He tried to get up, then blacked out.

"Take it easy, Captain," a calm male voice reassured him in the darkness.

Why can't I see? Casey thought. Where am I? Where are my men?

Casey tried to scream but couldn't. His voice wouldn't work. He struggled with his hands. He couldn't feel his left arm. Someone suddenly grabbed his right arm and forced it down.

"Doctor, you'd better get over here," the male voice announced. "He's conscious."

Casey tried to get up but he couldn't move. The world smelled of alcohol and sickly clean antiseptics. The world outside was gone. He could hear. He was alive, he was sure, but where? Why?

"Take it easy, Captain," a different voice—it was female—replied, apparently talking to him from somewhere near his right side. "I'm Doctor Young. You are in a hospital in Japan. You have been seriously burned. Your head and shoulders are completely bandaged; that's why you can't see."

Casey forced his lungs to work and managed a squeaky whisper that hurt his throat. "Team Steel? My soldiers?"

"I don't know, Captain. All I know is that you and a few others were the only survivors of a battle about four days ago. We've pieced you together as best we could. You're very lucky to be alive. Apparently you were one of the few who survived."

Casey's heart sank. In the darkness, with bandages covering his eyes, he realized the enormity of his failure. How many men had he lost? What could he have done to make things turn out differently?

"I have to talk to my men. Where are they?"

"Don't try to talk now," the female voice interjected as gentle hands held him to the bed. "The war is over for you."

The time to cry over your soldiers is after the battle is won.
—Maj. Gen. Lucian Truscott

You have failed in your mission.
Go back to Section 111 and try again.

Section 55

Before Casey could place the gun on the enemy fire, a flash of fire and a tremendous crash signified the detonation of an antitank rocket on *Cossack*'s turret. Casey ducked instinctively.

An instantaneous flash and wave of heat engulfed the top of the tank. *Cossack* kept moving forward. Casey opened his eyes. He took a deep breath and realized that death had passed him by again.

"Everyone okay?" Graham yelled.

"Crew report!" Casey shouted into his intercom.

"Driver up," Weaver replied.

"Loader up," Kriel answered.

"Gunner up, and I identify three Vetts. Direct front!"

Cossack was now in the lead, driving through the center of Position B like an iron spear through a wooden shield. Casey swung into action. He tried to swivel the CITV onto the targets. It wouldn't budge; it had been hit in the last blast. He popped the TC's hatch to the open-protected position. Peering through the opening in his hatch, he saw the enemy trenches on Position B alight from the fire of machine guns and the brilliant splash of friendly artillery shells.

"Steel Six, this is Steel Guns," Lieutenant Keeley's voice sounded over Casey's CVC earphones. "I've got One-Five-Fives dropping Vee Tee on Position B now."

"Good work, Guns," Casey replied. The FIST had called for artillery support just as *Cossack* and the two tanks from 1st Platoon broke into Position B.

"Break. Steel Five, get everybody moving north. Link up with 3d Platoon. Then break through Position B. I'll link up with you in the defile vicinity CS217430."

"Roger, Steel Six," Stonevitch answered. "We're on our way."

The pounding sound of machine-gun bullets bouncing off the tank's armor echoed inside the turret. Graham started to fire *Cossack*'s co-ax machine gun without a fire command. *Cossack* was in the middle of Position B with infantry and APCs all around them. "Steel Guns, repeat artillery target AO71. Over!" Casey screamed into the transmitter.

"Roger, Steel Six, repeat!" Lieutenant Keeley parroted. "Repeat on the way."

Illumination flares popped overhead again as enemy gunners tried to range the rushing tanks. The light added to the eerie scene of exploding artillery, 120mm tank rounds, and machine-gun tracers.

Casey struggled to see. The CITV would not function. He peeked out of the slit of his hatch. Keeley kept the artillery falling, causing a rain of death that rocked the earth in a tumultuous barrage of exploding shells and zinging steel.

The tanks slowed down as they entered the enemy defensive position. Enemy infantrymen jumped up from concealed positions and fired RPGs at *Cossack* and the two tanks following close behind. In spite of the enemy's bravery, *Cossack* destroyed each target as the enemy came into view. The tanks behind *Cossack* swept the flanks of enemy soldiers who ventured out of the trenches.

Cossack surged forward, zigzagging through Position B to avoid shell craters. Graham swung the turret left and right, gunning down any enemy bold enough to expose himself within the range of his 7.62mm machine gun. Artillery burst twenty meters off the ground, nailing the enemy to the bottom of their trenches.

Cossack churned across the broken ground, straddling a trench and crushing an enemy soldier too slow to get out of the way.

Casey jumped up, opened the hatch, and fired his .50 caliber to the east. He knew that it would be sheer luck to hit a target when the tank was moving, but he hoped that the swarm of tracers belching from his .50 caliber would give the enemy something more to think about. All Casey wanted to do now was to break through to the other side.

"Tank in a keyhole position, left front!" the alert driver, Private Weaver, shouted.

Roll the dice.

If you roll 2-6, go to Section 32.

If you roll 6-11, go to Section 66.

If you roll 12, go to Section 72.

Section 56

> *Moreover, the opportunity is offered small units for independent, quick and bold conduct. Opportunities to deceive the enemy are numerous.*
> —Concerning mountain warfare in German Field Service Regulations, *Truppenfuhrung,* 1936

An antitank rocket hit the front of *Cossack*'s left side before Casey could slew the turret toward the enemy fire. Casey ducked instinctively.

A bright flash and a wave of heat engulfed the top of the tank. The blast forced Casey inside the turret like a huge hand pushing him down.

"Shit! We've been hit!" Graham yelled as *Cossack* dashed forward. "Is anyone hurt?"

Casey, momentarily dazed, opened his eyes. He found himself leaning against the laser range finder. He couldn't breathe. Struggling for air, his lungs suddenly kicked in. He gasped for breath, realizing that the blast had knocked the wind out of him.

"You okay, Captain?" Graham asked over the intercom.

"Yeah," Casey finally replied. "Crew report!"

"Driver up," Weaver replied.

"Loader up," Kriel answered.

"Gunner up, and I identify three Vetts, direct front!"

Visibility improved to seven hundred meters as the fog suddenly rolled south. Casey struggled with the CITV, but the blast had damaged it. His hatch was still in the open-protected position. He peeked out of the slit in the hatch. Flares dotted the night sky.

Cossack pushed on toward Position B. The enemy was only five hundred meters away. With his CITV inoperative, Casey had to fight with his hatch open. He peered through the opening in the hatch and saw the fire of machine guns and the dazzling splash of friendly artillery shells light up the enemy positions.

Casey quickly scanned his IVIS screen:

TM C Unit	M1A2 Tank	M2 IFV	BSFV [ADA]	FISTV	Engr M113	CEV	ACE	HAB Bridge	Medic M113	M88 [Rec]	Fuel HEMMT	M113 APCs
North of PP	3	3	1	1								
South of PP	5	3			4	1	1	2	2	1	1	15
Total	**10**	**6**	**1**	**1**	**4**	**1**	**1**	**2**	**2**	**1**	**1**	**15**

"Steel Six, this is Steel Guns," Lieutenant Keeley's voice sounded over Casey's CVC earphones. "I've got One-Five-Fives dropping Vee Tee on Position B now."

The artillery landed just as *Cossack* and the two tanks from 1st Platoon broke into Position B.

"Good work, Steel Guns," Casey replied. "Break. Steel Five, continue the attack. I'm sending you a map now."

"Wilco, Steel Six," Stonevitch answered, the eagerness to continue the fight evident in his voice. "Combat power eight tanks and six Brads."

Casey quickly scrawled the graphics of his attack on the IVIS screen.

Two bursts of bright light from Position B caught Casey's eye before he could answer his executive officer. Missile launches! The stationary tanks and the FIST-V, standing in the open and close to the enemy, were easy targets. Casey moved to react to the enemy missile launch.

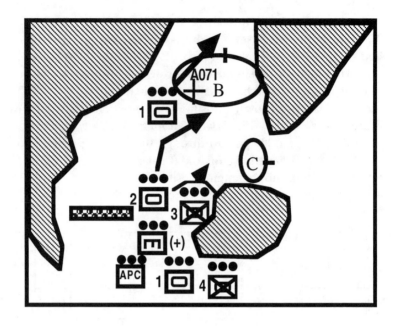

Roll the dice.

If you roll 2-4, go to Section 54.

If you roll 5-12, go to Section 102.

Section 57

> *In mountains superiority of leadership plays a dominant role.*
> —German Field Service Regulations,
> *Truppenfuhrung,* 1936

"White One, capture that vehicle," Casey ordered. "Do whatever you have to, but don't destroy it or let it get away."

"Wilco," Sergeant Scott responded.

Casey stood in his open hatch, straining to see ahead with his night vision goggles. The trail wound to the left and right. Because the vehicles were traveling only twenty to thirty meters apart, Casey was able to get an occasional glimpse of the front of the column.

A spatter of sparks and the sound of a machine gun echoing in the defile told Casey that Scott was attempting to obey his orders. Casey heard a loud crash, then the sound of grinding metal.

Scott's tank had rammed the BRDM. Casey saw the BRDM through his night vision goggles; it was knocked off to the left side of the road. The BRDM lay on its side with its wheels facing the road.

The clamor of another burst of machine-gun fire from Scott's lead tank shot out. *Cossack* jerked to a quick halt as the column stopped.

"Steel Six, this is White One. We've shot him up a bit and pushed him off the road. I'm dismounting with my loader to check it out."

"Roger, White One. Be careful," Casey replied. He waited, taut with apprehension, as the armored column lay still in the narrow gorge. He took off his CVC to listen to the action. The low rumble of diesel engines and the high whine of the tank turbines filled the air.

A pistol shot rang out. Casey waited.

"Steel Six, this is White One. We got ourselves a command car. I've captured an artillery colonel and all his maps, and I've copied his radio frequencies."

A wide grin of satisfaction lit up Casey's face as he answered the lead platoon leader. "Great job. Send those papers back to me. How many men did you capture?"

"Only the colonel," Scott radioed. "The driver died in the crash, and two others we had to shoot. The colonel isn't too cooperative either."

"Don't take any chances with him," Casey ordered. "Check him for weapons, tie him up, and guard him in an engineer APC. I want to start moving in five minutes."

"Wilco," Scott replied. "I'm sending my loader with the maps and frequencies to you now."

A young tanker in a Nomex uniform and carrying an M-16 rifle ran up to *Cossack*. Casey leaned over the right side of his turret and grabbed the maps as the soldier handed them up. Casey jumped back inside the turret, then studied the enemy information with the aid of his blue-filtered flashlight.

The column started to move again.

Casey pushed the transmitter switch forward on his CVC helmet as *Cossack* moved along the trail. "Steel Five, this is Steel Six. This map shows the disposition of the forces in our zone. It shows the enemy forces surrounding the 1-12th Infantry. It also shows the locations of the minefields and artillery fire boxes."

"Roger, Steel Six. Sounds like a gold mine. Do you believe it?"

"We'd be stupid not to," Casey answered. "You were right about the bridge on Viper. It's an ambush waiting to happen. They've laid mines and antitank positions all over. It's also covered by an MRL strike box."

"Well, I told you that Viper was bad," Stonevitch reflected. "So what do we do now?"

"We'll take Jacobs's idea and cross at the ford by stacking the heavy assault bridges. If we take Asp, we'll avoid the enemy's main strength, and we can chop up some of his artillery on the way."

"Roger. I'll radio Jacobs and Washington and work out the details."

"There's one more thing," Casey added.

"Send it," Stonevitch replied.

"If I read this map right, Objective Dragon is targeted for a nerve agent strike sometime soon."

There was a long silence on the radio, then Stonevitch answered. "The bastards haven't used chemical weapons yet. I guess they're desperate to kill as many Americans as they can. They must think that one big victory will force us to demand a negotiated end to the war."

"Roger, but we aren't going to give them the chance. We'll break into Dragon, load up the 1-12th as fast as we can, and fight our way back to friendly lines."

There was another long silence on the radio as Stonevitch contemplated his commander's fast-paced decisions. *Cossack* picked up speed as the column in front of Casey's tank accelerated.

"I agree," Stonevitch replied. "It's the only way now. But which way do we return?"

"We'll place the bridges on the ford at CS257447, cross Team Steel, knock down the poles that mark the crossing, move to Dragon along Asp, and return the same way we came."

"Roger," Stonevitch answered. "I'll sketch out the plan on my IVIS and send it to you for your approval."

"Affirmative. Steel Six. Out."

"Sounds like a wild ride, Captain," Graham snickered over *Cossack*'s intercom. "You know what my old drill sergeant used to say."

"No, but I'm sure you can't wait to tell me."

"'If your advance is going well,'" Graham repeated, saying the words slowly in his thick southern drawl for dramatic effect, "'you're walking into an ambush.'"

"That may be," Casey retorted. "Or you're hitting them where they're weak, which is one of the fundamentals of tactics."

"Think we can pull it off?" Graham pressed, his tone more serious this time.

"No battle plan ever survives contact with the enemy," Casey replied calmly. "This one is better than most. We'll just have to charge in and try."

Go to Section 44.

Section 58

> *Never draw fire. It irritates everyone around you.*
> —Anonymous

Casey jerked the hatch lever and ducked inside the turret. A 152mm HE shell burst directly next to *Cossack*, exploding in a dazzling sheet of flame. *Cossack* surged forward, undamaged. Casey had closed the hatch just in time.

More artillery shells fell outside; they scattered along the highway and on both sides of the road. The sky ignited in bright light as illumination rounds popped overhead.

"Identified tanks!" Graham shouted. "Six hundred meters!"

Section 58

The explosion engulfed *Cossack*. The tank slammed to the right and onto a large dirt mound. Casey smashed hard against the gunner's primary sight extension.

"Mine!" Weaver shouted, coughing out his report. "Right track's busted."

"I see 'em," Graham yelled as he jerked the turret to the left.

Kriel pushed forward the safety lever and yelled, "Up!"

Two more explosions crashed into *Cossack*. The first 115mm round smashed against the turret, rocking the tank backward but causing no other damage. The second round hit *Cossack* in the right side.

Casey shook off the shock of the strike. "Fire and adjust!"

"On the way!" Graham screamed. The big 120mm gun thundered, jerking the tank with its recoil.

Casey struggled to see through his CITV.

"Got him," Graham yelled with glee. "Identified left tank."

Kriel pushed forward the arming lever on the cannon. "Up!"

"On the way!" Graham fired again. Casey saw the T-62 explode in flames in his CITV screen. The burning hulks of the other T-62 bore testimony to Graham's quick thinking and excellent aim. Then Casey saw a third enemy tank.

Another 115mm round hit *Cossack,* this time striking the top of the turret. Undeterred, Graham shouted that he was firing again. Casey braced himself in the TC's station. The tank rocked from the blast as Graham fired a third round, destroying the T-62 tank that had hit them.

"Got the son of a bitch!" Graham shouted. "All three are smoking!"

"Crew report," Casey ordered as he recovered from the shock of being hit. His nose was bleeding. He quickly checked himself for other wounds. Nothing. He was fine.

"Gunner's all right," Graham reported, coughing as electrical connections sizzled from beneath the cannon. A wisp of smoke rose inside the turret from under the gun. "Something's burning. I'm checking our status."

Casey turned to his CITV to view the battlefield. The CITV didn't move, and the screen was dead. He ran a systems check. The green and red lights inside the turret suddenly flickered on and off.

"Driver okay," Weaver announced. "My alert lights are lit up like a Christmas tree. I'm getting an engine abort light."

"Loader up!" Kriel shouted.

The electrical components of the tank flickered off and on.

"Sir, I'd better shut down the engine," Weaver announced. "We must have taken some damage. She might burn up if we don't."

Before Casey could answer, the engine stopped and the tank suddenly blacked out. Smoke began seeping from the engine compartment into the turret. Casey checked his switches and fiddled with the radio. The tank was totally without electricity.

"I got total systems failure," Graham yelled, coughing. "No electrical power."

The turret slowly filled with acrid, choking smoke.

"I can't breathe down here!" Weaver yelled, gagging in the smoke.

Suddenly one of the Halon automatic fire extinguishers went off. Casey opened the TC's hatch. "Everybody out!"

Casey struggled out of the turret, patting his side to check that his 9mm pistol was still secure in his shoulder holster. He climbed onto the back deck and ducked low next to the turret. The exhaust gas from the Halon fire extinguisher poured out of the turret. Graham exited the TC's hatch and Kriel jumped out of the loader's hatch, carrying an M-16 rifle. The three men crouched on the flat back deck of the tank, next to the turret.

Artillery flares dangled in the dark, cloudy sky overhead. The bright, flickering light cast surreal shadows on the tank and the ground.

Casey surveyed the damage. *Cossack* pointed east. The tank's left flank faced north, offering the enemy a clear shot. The gun pointed over the left flank, aiming north. Casey saw that the CITV, which was cased in a cylindrical armored shield on top of the turret and forward of the loader, was smashed. The tank's right track lay flat on the ground, broken in half and off *Cossack*'s support rollers, in front of the idler wheel. The crew would never get *Cossack* moving again without help.

More illumination shells burst overhead. Casey saw the burning carcasses of three T-62 tanks to the north, in the mouth of the defile. The enemy had paid a heavy price to disable *Cossack*. He had improved his T-62s with add-on armor, laser range finders, passive night sights, and improved fire control systems, but it was still basically a product of 1960s technology. The T-62s were no match for Casey's M1A2s. If *Cossack* hadn't hit an antitank mine, it wouldn't even have slowed down.

Still, Casey thought, we're stranded here, in the enemy's fire sack, "unhorsed."

"Quick, off the side, get behind the tank," Casey ordered.

The men rapidly obeyed, each sliding down the south side of the tank, huddling beneath the overhang of the turret. Weaver crawled out of his driver's hatch and over to the right side of the tank to join the group. An enemy machine gun opened up, striking the flat flank of the tank in a splash of sparks.

There must be an enemy infantry company defending with the tanks, Casey guessed.

"Where's the FIST-V?" Weaver asked. "It was just to the left a few minutes ago."

Casey scanned the terrain. He looked to the southwest and saw the burning remains of the FIST-V, a mere one hundred meters behind them. Casey brought his night vision goggles to his eyes and looked carefully, but he saw no survivors.

"Damnit," Casey cursed, closing his eyes tightly for a moment. Keeley had been their chance to escape. He looked at the burning hunk of aluminum that had once been a FIST-V and then looked to the ground. "Those enemy tanks must have hit Keeley at about the same time we ran over the antitank mine."

"What are we going to do now, sir?" Graham asked desperately.

Casey saw two options: leave the tank and try to link up with 2d Platoon on the other side of the highway, or sit tight and hope that they came to him.

Another volley of machine-gun fire raked the left side of *Cossack.* The four dismounted tankers cringed under the cover of the tank's protection as the bullets splashed harmlessly against *Cossack*'s battle-scarred armor. Casey took stock of their equipment; each man wore his CVC helmet and the thin "chicken-plate" chest armor and carried protective masks and 9mm pistols. In addition, Kriel had thought enough to pull his M-16 rifle from the tank.

"What are your orders, Sir?" Kriel asked, the desperation of the moment ringing in his words.

If Casey decides to make a break for it to reach 2d Platoon, go to Section 24.

If Casey decides to stay with *Cossack* and wait for 2d Platoon to link up with him, go to Section 30.

Section 59

> *In mountainous terrain where only a single road net is available, the exploiting force must rely on detailed planning, close coordination and rapid aggressive movement, along this single route to secure its objective.*
>
> —Employment of Armor in Korea in the
> 2d Infantry Division, 1951

"Go now," Casey ordered over the radio. "Take your Bradleys and cross. Use the left lane. There's a crater in the right lane close to the entrance of the bridge. I don't know if a tank can cross, but I'm sure a Bradley will make it. Get to the other side. I'll support you with fire."

"Roger, moving now!" McDaniel answered.

All four Bradleys raced toward the bridge. McDaniel led, inching his Bradley past the crater.

"You're right, Steel Six," McDaniel reported. "You'd never make it in an M1. Your right track would just fall into the hole and then you'd block the route. We'll need an assault bridge up here to fix this."

"Roger, Blue One. Good report. Now get me to the other side of this damn bridge!"

"Wilco!" McDaniel replied. The rest of the M2s moved slowly past the crater and then raced north up the bridge, firing machine gun or cannon to the front and flanks.

Casey held his breath as McDaniel's platoon charged across, triggering no return fire from the enemy. Casey scanned the far bank with his CITV. "Graham, do you see any enemy movement? Anything at all?"

"Negative, Captain. Just hot spots from where 3d Platoon's tracers are landing."

Casey looked to his left and saw the gleam of tracers as 1st Platoon fired on positions on the north bank, east of McDaniel's advance. Turning back to the bridge, Casey saw the last of McDaniel's Bradleys exit the northern end. Suddenly they blasted away with their 25mm cannons.

"We've got the bridge!" McDaniel reported exuberantly. "They were trying to blow this end, but we got them first. A bunch are running to the northeast. We're knocking them down."

"Roger, Blue One. Great work," Casey said, breathing a sigh of relief. "Defend the north side. We'll be across soon."

"Don't take too long," McDaniel replied. "I've grown used to you tankers."

"Steel Six, this is Steel Five," Stonevitch interjected. "I've got Sergeant Jacobs coming up to lay the HAB over the southern crater in the bridge. He can be in position in fifteen minutes and have the bridge laid in half that time."

Casey smiled. "Roger, Steel Five, make it happen. In the meantime get 4th Platoon up here ASAP and start recovering the two tanks down in 2d Platoon."

"Already moving to do that, Steel Six. We've already fixed the M1A2 that lost a track to the minefield. I've got the recovery section working on short-tracking the one that was hit by antitank fire. Over."

"You'll be a great commander someday, Stonevitch," Casey announced.

Stonevitch looked at the ground. "We've got three killed and two wounded."

Casey suddenly felt very tired. A wave of guilt swept over him as he remembered Lieutenant Keeley. This wasn't a game; his people were dying. In the elation of taking the bridge, Casey had forgotten the cost of seizing the real estate.

Casey took off his CVC helmet and rubbed his dirty hand over his short-cropped hair. He quickly scanned his IVIS display and saw that his force was deploying as directed. He knew that his mission was far from over, but at least he had a bridge across the Gang River.

Casey popped open his hatch and watched with night vision goggles as Sergeant Jacobs moved the HAB toward the south side of the bridge. Jacobs deftly lowered the front blade of the Wolverine and prepared to extend the heavy assault bridge across the crater that the enemy had blown in the southern right lane of the bridge.

Casey stood in the turret of his tank, breathing in the cool night air as he watched the operation. Kriel was inside the turret, reloading the machine gun with Sergeant Graham.

Casey knew that time was essential. He had to get his entire force across the bridge before dawn. His mission was to link up with the 1-12th and defend until the rest of the task force attacked. He was determined to accomplish that mission.

Suddenly an enemy soldier popped up from a bunker, walked out to the road, and casually aimed an RPG at Jacob's Wolverine. Casey couldn't believe it. The enemy soldier was only twelve meters away, standing in the wide, open road. The captain abruptly reached for his shoulder holster.

Roll the dice.

If you roll 2-7, go to Section 16.

If you roll 8-12, go to Section 82.

Section 60

There was a brief, earsplitting whistle followed by a resounding crash. Suddenly the south side of the bridge erupted in a terrible wave of exploding rockets. Hundreds of tiny bomblets burst above the tanks of 2d Platoon and the Bradleys of 4th Platoon. The bridge was devastated.

My God, an enemy multiple rocket launcher strike, Casey thought mournfully. They must have targeted us from the first shots near the bridge.

Another wave of blasts rocked the air and ground. Casey closed the tank commander's hatch and braced himself as the tank rocked from the explosions. He realized that if he kept the 1st and 3d Platoons in position on the north side of the bridge, they would become the next targets. He pushed forward the transmitter switch of his CVC helmet.

"Steel elements north of the bridge. Move northwest on Viper now."

McDaniel and Andrews acknowledged their commander's orders and moved out rapidly toward Objective Dragon.

Cossack rumbled northwest as the rockets began falling farther to the north. Casey scanned his IVIS screen. It registered the two tanks of 2d Platoon and the three Bradleys of 4th Platoon as damaged. He had no way of knowing how badly. His decision to move had been correct, he thought as he looked back.

"Steel Five, this is Steel Six. SITREP. Over."

There was no answer. Casey bit his lip.

"Five, this is Six. Over."

"Six, this is Seven," the weary voice of First Sergeant Washington answered. "We've been hit bad. The XO is down. Lots of casualties. Most of the tanks are mobility kills. I can't tell if anyone is alive in 4th Platoon; they were crossing the bridge when the strike hit us."

"Can you cross the bridge and get to me?" Casey questioned, his fists knotted tightly as he thought about his losses.

"No way, and you can't get south. Bradleys are blocking the bridge. It will take hours to clear."

Casey braced himself as *Cossack* jolted across a rough piece of ground. He was following the tanks of 1st Platoon. McDaniel's Bradleys were following him. He was already committed.

"Steel Seven, do what you can. If you can't cross the bridge, head back the way we came and get back to friendly lines. I'm headed forward to Dragon. Over."

"Roger, Steel Six," Washington answered. His voice sounded as though he was saying a final farewell. "Good luck. Get them for us!"

What was left of Team Steel surged on. Casey finally reached the 1-12th Infantry Battalion on their battalion command net and told them that his force was two minutes out and to hold their fire. Casey's column rapidly moved northwest, fought through some startled enemy infantry, and rolled into the southeastern edge of Objective Dragon. Casey maneuvered his tank to a berm that offered protection and an excellent firing platform from which to shoot to the east.

Casey deployed his five tanks and five Bradleys in Objective Dragon. He set Andrews's four tanks in the northeast and McDaniel's four Bradleys in the southeast. He positioned his tank and Sergeant Sellers's Bradley in the center.

Dawn broke through the gloomy sky. Casey opened his hatch and surveyed the scene. The infantry occupied a prepared allied artillery battalion strongpoint. The allies had abandoned it after the second day of the war. The 1-12th Infantry had found the position as they fought their way south. These bunkers had saved the poor, battered infantry from the rain of enemy shells and mortar bombs.

Casey could see the grim signs of close combat: burned-out bunkers, blackened shell holes, and more bodies scattered about the perimeter than he cared to count. The fighting had been fierce, eye to eye, and, consequently, very bloody.

"Steel Six, this is Bayonet Four. Man, are we glad to see you."

"Roger, Bayonet Four," Casey radioed. "What's your situation?"

"We've been sniped at all night. Took heavy casualties yesterday and repulsed two attacks this morning. The enemy's stopped hitting us with just infantry. Now he's moving up tanks and more artillery. I've got about eighty effectives and more than a hundred wounded. When does the rest of your force arrive?"

"This is it, Bayonet Four. We're all that's coming until 1st Brigade attacks tomorrow morning."

There was a long silence on the radio. Casey switched frequencies and tried several times to reach the artillery, First Sergeant Washington, or Major Cutter, all with no success. Something had obviously happened to the battalion and brigade radio retrans sites. With the bridge on Viper down and radio communications inoperable, Casey was truly on his own.

Suddenly an explosion blasted about eighty meters to *Cossack*'s left flank. Enemy mortar rounds fell throughout the perimeter, billowing in geysers of dust and smoke. Soon heavy-artillery shells added to the din, smashing into the American perimeter with the force of an earthquake. The infantrymen hid inside their bunkers. Moving out in the open would be suicide.

The ground shook as a heavy 152mm shell fell a few feet from *Cossack*.

Roll the dice.

If you roll 2-7, go to Section 45.

If you roll 8-12, go to Section 87.

Section 61

> *Plans must be simple and flexible.*
> *Actually they only form a datum plane from which you build as*
> *necessity directs or opportunity offers. . . . The order itself will be short,*
> *accompanied by a sketch—it tells what to do, not how. It is really a*
> *memorandum and an assumption of responsibility by the issuing*
> *commander.*
>
> —Gen. George S. Patton Jr.

"George, what did that sound like to you?" Casey asked.

Keeley cleared his throat. He suddenly realized that his answer might decide the fate of Team Steel and the 1-12th Infantry. "Sir, I heard them say that we are to stick to the original plan. We're being ordered to stay here and fight it out."

Casey nodded. "That's right. While the commander and his operations officer are away, the officers in the TOC are afraid to make a decision."

Casey passed the hand mike back to Keeley.

"They don't know what we know. We've seen the enemy's plan. If we stay, we'll pay for it in useless casualties."

Keeley took the hand mike and looked solemnly at his commander. "Sir, are you going to disobey orders?"

"Lieutenant, orders are only guidelines for action. They keep the force going in the right direction. Orders, however, cannot cover every contingency. In the U.S. Army, an officer is expected to think and take decisions."

Keeley smiled.

"Hell, yes, I'm going to disobey orders," continued Casey. "Tell all Steel elements we move out in three minutes."

"Yes, sir!" Keeley replied with a huge grin.

Casey turned to walk back to *Cossack*. A series of shots rang out. Several Americans in the perimeter fell. Casey crouched and spun to the left.

"Snipers! Northern ridge!" Graham yelled from *Cossack*'s tank commander's hatch. The sergeant charged the bolt on the .50-caliber machine gun and sprayed a burst toward the north.

Another shot rang out, missing Casey by inches. Casey calmly walked to *Cossack*'s side.

"Damnit, Graham!" Casey snapped. "I don't have time for this shit. Take out those pissants and let's get moving."

Graham plastered the ridge with machine-gun fire. A figure jumped up seven hundred meters to *Cossack*'s left, trying to flee. The sniper ran in a low crouch to the east. Graham fired a long, steady burst and the figure tumbled out of sight.

"Well, I don't know if I got him, but he isn't shooting at us anymore," Graham announced.

Casey crawled up *Cossack*'s left front slope, climbed into the TC's hatch, and connected his CVC helmet.

Graham quickly slid down to his gunner's seat. "Sir, do you know what my old drill sergeant would say at a time like this?"

Casey keyed his intercom. "I can't imagine."

"He'd say that a good commander always knows when it's time to get out of Dodge."

"I'll agree with that," Casey replied. "Weaver, let's go. Head northeast."

"You know what he'd also say?" Graham continued.

"What?"

"That a good commander always knows *how* to get out of Dodge," Graham persisted. "Captain, are we headed back the same way we came?"

"Roger that. It's the only way."

"I'd hate to be in the middle of the river during a battle. Do you think we can cross the underwater bridge before they hit us?"

"There's only one way to find out."

In a few minutes, Team Steel was rolling north with every living member—178 men—of 1st Battalion, 12th Infantry.

Go to Section 105.

Section 62

Casey quickly turned the turret to the north. Graham immediately identified enemy infantry in position on the north side of the bridge. With fierce satisfaction, the well-trained gunner pasted the enemy on the north bank with machine-gun fire.

Casey swung his CITV to the west and searched the bridge. Men were moving on it. Casey feared that they might be trying to destroy it or crater it. He pushed forward the transmission key of his CVC helmet. "White One, this is Steel Six. Keep moving. Get to the bridge. Forget the mines!"

"Steel Six, this is Steel Guns," Lieutenant Keeley's voice interrupted. "I've got the artillery back. We'll have Vee Tee and smoke on the bridge in two minutes."

"Roger. Break. Blue One, move fast to the northwest. Follow my command group. I'm heading for the bridge."

"Roger, Steel Six," McDaniel answered. "I'm moving behind you now. I'll keep the bad guys to your right busy."

"Missile launch, northeast!" Graham screamed. "On the way!"

Cossack shuddered as Graham fired a 120mm HEAT round at the enemy missile launch site. Casey looked through his vision blocks and saw the flash of the missile as it struck behind *Cossack*.

"Holy shit!" Sergeant Sellers yelled on the radio. "They hit the FIST."

Casey looked forward, toward the bridge. "Steel ADA, stop and pick up the survivors."

Section 63

"No survivors" was Sellers's curt reply.

Casey's anger boiled inside him. Graham turned *Cossack*'s turret toward the bridge and fired at the enemy soldiers at the south entrance to the seventy-ton concrete bridge. With grim satisfaction, Casey watched in his thermal sight as the figures fell to Graham's accurate fire.

A few figures remained. Suddenly the reason for their presence was revealed. The south portion of the bridge suddenly erupted in a tall, bright geyser of fire. The enemy had detonated a demolitions charge on the bridge.

"Weaver, faster! Get to that bridge!" Casey yelled into the intercom. The sounds of battle and the roar of the tank's engine echoed in the earphones of his CVC helmet.

Roll the dice.

If you roll 2-5, go to Section 64.

If you roll 6-7, go to Section 72.

If you roll 8-12, go to Section 75.

Section 63

We've got no place in this outfit for good losers. We want tough hombres that will go in there and win!
—Adm. Jonas Ingram, 1926

Casey quickly grabbed the TC override and swung the turret over the back deck.

"Identified, tanks!" Graham shouted.

The sky lit up like daylight from the blast of explosions and artillery flares. At the same time that Scott's tank platoon engaged three enemy tanks to the north, another enemy tank company opened up on McDaniel's Bradleys from the woods to the southwest.

"Fire and adjust," Casey screamed.

"On the way!" Graham shouted.

Cossack's 120mm cannon roared. The three surviving tanks of Sergeant Scott's platoon joined in the fire.

"Target!" Casey yelled. He saw one of the T-62s burning like a blowtorch.

Sergeant Sellers's BSFV burst into flames as a 115mm tank round smashed into the Bradley's thinly armored turret. The turret disintegrated from the strike in a shower of white-hot sparks. The remaining three Bradleys of McDaniel's platoon immediately turned around and fired their 25mm cannons at the T-62 tanks firing at them from the wood line at CS245415. By the time *Cossack* turned to the southwest to fire at this new threat, another one of McDaniel's Bradleys had been hit.

"On the way!" Graham screamed as he fired another round. The cannon roared. Casey saw a splash of sparks as another enemy tank was turned into a burning mass of metal.

"Target!" Graham yelled with a vengeance. The crew executed their deadly drill in a frenzy of adrenaline and destroyed every enemy vehicle that opposed them. Kriel reloaded rounds into the massive breech of the 120mm cannon with drilled precision.

Desperately Casey searched his IVIS screen. His force was divided by the rice paddies. Two enemy tank companies were attacking him, one from north of the woods at CS245423 and another in the woods at CS246415. While Casey was busy drilling the town of Masan into ashes, the enemy had launched a tank-heavy counterattack at the rear of his western force. Casey knew he had to act quickly or he would lose everyone.

Burning Bradleys littered the battlefield behind the tanks, helping to illuminate the battlefield for the enemy. *Cossack* fired and destroyed a third T-62 just as *Cossack* was hit by three 115mm rounds. The first round hit the turret and smashed into a million brilliantly shining sparks, but the tank drove on. The second round, from a tank to the south, hit *Cossack* in the right track skirt, penetrated the skirt armor, and cut the track.

"Weaver, back up!" Casey ordered.

Cossack spun forcefully to the left, pivoting on its damaged track. Stalled and stuck, a third enemy round smashed against the *Cossack*'s 120mm cannon.

The impact of the third round flung Casey hard against the turret. The electrical components of the tank flickered off and on. The engine aborted and *Cossack* blacked out. The turret suddenly filled with acrid, choking smoke.

"Get out. Abandon tank!" Casey shouted as he forced open his hatch. Fresh air swirled into the turret as Casey muscled his way onto the canted roof of the tank. Graham struggled out a few seconds later.

Casey could hear the sound of 25mm cannon fire to his left and the boom of tank cannons to his right. The night air burst brightly again as more enemy flares popped overhead. Suddenly, Lieutenant Keeley's FIST-V, only fifty meters to *Cossack*'s left, blew apart in a tremendous explosion.

In a flurry of sparks, a fusillade of machine-gun bullets tore at *Cossack*'s roof. Casey fell from the tank as a dozen enemy machine-gun rounds cut into his body.

You have been killed in action.
Your mission has been a complete failure.
Return to Section 111 and make another decision.

Section 64

> *Loss of hope rather than loss of life is what decides the issues of war. But helplessness induces hopelessness.*
>
> —B. H. Liddell Hart

Weaver pulled ahead, increasing speed to reach the bridge before the enemy did more damage to it. *Cossack* jolted roughly across the rocky ground. Suddenly a large ditch appeared directly in front of *Cossack.*

Weaver jerked the tank violently to the right to avoid the enemy fighting position. Machine-gun tracers flew wildly through the air, bouncing off the tough sides of the M1A2 in a shower of sparks. At the same time, artillery shells landed on the bridge, bathing the area in the bright light of their explosions.

Casey struggled to see as Weaver dodged a line of enemy fighting positions. Enemy infantry seemed to be everywhere, like ants in an anthill that's been disturbed. Casey shot a worried glance up through his vision blocks; he wanted to make sure that Weaver was not moving too far to the north. His concern came too late. The tank bounded over a steep bank and rolled into the Gang River.

Casey felt a gut-wrenching, out-of-control feeling as the seventy-ton M1A2 tank turned on its side and then onto its roof. Although the action seemed in slow motion, Casey was unable to react in time and brace for the fall. With a heavy thud, Casey crashed onto the roof of the tank. He heard the bones in his neck crack and felt a numbing sensation run up his spine. Within seconds he blacked out and died.

You have been killed in action.
Go back to Section 62 and roll the dice again.

Section 65

> *Keep moving. Do everything fast. You're always heavily outnumbered; surprise and speed is what saves you.*
> —Robert Heinlein, *Starship Troopers*

"White One, this is Steel Six. Report," Casey shouted over the radio. Quickly he glanced at his IVIS screen as *Cossack* bounced over the rough terrain, racing northeast to escape the enemy's artillery fire sack.

"Negative contact. We're facing north, ready to move on order," Sergeant Scott answered. "Are you still going to continue the mission?"

"You're damned right I am," Casey said with a ruthless determination ringing in his voice. "All Steel elements. Steel Seven will reorganize the units south of the LD. Once he's got everyone together, he'll join us. Continue mission."

"Steel Six, this is White One. You want us to move north now?" Sergeant Scott asked incredulously.

"Affirmative, White One. Get it in gear. Move now!"

Casey looked at his IVIS screen and saw the icons that represented Scott's four M1A2 tanks moving north along Viper in a modified wedge, three up and one back. The Bradleys of McDaniel's 3d Platoon followed right behind.

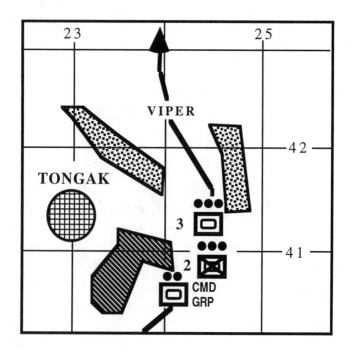

Cossack pulled up behind 3d Platoon. The attack force was moving through the dark at fifteen miles an hour, pushed by Casey to make up for lost time. The fog had thinned, increasing the visibility to about four hundred meters. With their thermals, Casey's tanks and Bradleys saw almost twice that far.

A series of bright flashes and booms erupted up front. Casey swung his CITV forward as he heard the thunder of tank fire from 2d Platoon.

"Steel Six, contact! Enemy tanks, CS246415. Engaging!"

Casey stared at his IVIS screen and saw the four tanks of 2d Platoon echelon right and fire, at almost point-blank range, at targets in the woods. In seconds an enemy tank platoon was reduced to burning junk by the power of Sergeant Scott's 120mm guns.

The enemy, however, anticipated Casey's move north. The sky lit up like daylight from the explosion of enemy illumination flares. At the same time that Scott's tank platoon was engaging three enemy tanks to the northeast, an entire enemy tank company opened up on McDaniel's Bradleys from the northwest.

One of the Bradleys burst into flames as a tank round hit its thinly armored turret. The turret exploded from the strike of the round, showering the ground around it with white-hot sparks. The other three Bradleys stopped and immediately fired their 25mm cannons at the enemy to the northwest. As they fired, they were struck by two enemy tank platoons firing from the west, hiding in the debris of the town of Tongak.

Before Casey or Scott could react, the remainder of McDaniel's M2s were struck by the 115mm guns of the six T-62s waiting in ambush at Tongak. The two enemy platoons fired in volley from prepared positions in Tongak. The T-62 platoon north of Tongak switched its fire to the exposed left flank of Scott's tanks. By the time *Cossack* turned to the left of 3d Platoon to engage the dug-in enemy tanks to the northwest, McDaniel's entire platoon had been destroyed and one of Scott's tanks was hit in the left track, making it a mobility kill.

"White One, enemy tanks, east and northeast. Orient toward Tongak!" Casey screamed over the radio as he swung the turret in the direction of the enemy fire. "Tanks! Fire and adjust."

Section 65

"Identified," Graham shouted. "On the way!"

Cossack's main gun fired as the tank quickly turned left toward Tongak. Casey observed that two T-62s in Tongak were billowing thick black smoke and fire from the accuracy of Sergeant Graham's gunnery. Sellers's BSFV fired, the 25mm rounds flying wildly through the air as the Bradley darted to *Cossack*'s left side. *Cossack* fired as fast as Kriel could load, then it bounded into the enemy's fire sack.

Unfortunately, Casey knew that it was not enough.

The enemy was delivering a one-two punch, sacrificing an entire platoon to trap the attacking force. The Americans' courage and determination had not been enough to escape the trap that the enemy had carefully constructed. In the first few minutes of the fight, the lead elements of Team Steel were devastated. Casey suddenly saw the gate of fate swing quickly open, showing a brief chance for survival, then slam shut once and for all.

Blazing and shattered, Team Steel's remaining armored vehicles turned toward the enemy's fire and charged. Burning Bradleys littered the battlefield behind the tanks, helping to illuminate the battlefield for the enemy. *Cossack* closed the range on the enemy to five hundred meters as Graham destroyed a third T-62. Three 115mm rounds hit *Cossack* as the tank sprinted forward. The first round hit the turret and smashed into a million brilliantly shining sparks, but the tank drove on. The second round, from a tank to the northeast, hit *Cossack* in the right track skirt, penetrated the skirt armor, and cut the track. *Cossack* spun forcefully to the left and into a ditch, listing to port like a ship in a gale. Stalled and stuck, the tank was hit by a third round, which smashed against the turret and the 120mm cannon.

Casey was flung hard against the side of the tank from the impact of the third round. The turret jerked to the left. The electrical components of the tank flickered off and on. Finally the engine aborted and all power was lost. The turret began filling with acrid, choking smoke.

"Bail out, abandon tank," Casey screamed as he popped open his hatch. The fresh outside air swirled into the turret as Casey muscled his way onto the canted roof of the tank. His left leg hung limply, apparently broken in the crash. Graham struggled out a few seconds later.

200

Casey could hear the sound of 25mm cannon fire to his left and the boom of tank cannons to his right. He fought against unconsciousness as a sudden gush of pain rushed throughout the left side of his body. "We've got to get Kriel out!"

"I'll get him," Graham answered, choking and coughing from the smoke.

The night air burst brightly again as more enemy flares popped overhead. Suddenly, Sergeant Sellers's Bradley, only fifty meters to *Cossack*'s left, blew apart in a tremendous explosion. Machine-gun bullets tore at *Cossack*'s roof. Graham's shadow fell from the tank as a dozen rounds cut into his body.

Casey lost consciousness for a moment as the pain overwhelmed him. He suddenly found himself surrounded by enemy soldiers. The men kicked him and knocked him off the top of the tank. Casey fell in the soft mud and heard the bone crack in his leg as he landed. Convulsed in pain, he struggled to turn over on his side. Before he could, an enemy soldier put a pistol to his head and pulled the trigger.

You have been killed in action. Your mission has been a complete failure. Return to Section 111 and make another decision.

Section 66

> *An armored force cannot claim immunity from the law contained in 2,000 years of historical experience—that only an indirect approach can hope for success, except against an enemy radically inferior or paralytically stupid.*
>
> —B. H. Liddell Hart

Instinctively Casey stooped down inside the safety of his armored turret. The enemy missile missed the tank by a few feet and detonated against the ground to *Cossack*'s right front. A tremendous violet-yellow geyser, spewing a stream of red-hot fire, shot into the air as the antitank missile exploded. Casey felt the heat wave from the detonation pass over the top of the tank. Sparks billowed into the air and fell on *Cossack*'s back deck as the tank raced forward.

"That was close!" Casey cried, relieved to be alive for another moment. "Let's get the son of a bitch who fired at us!"

"Roger, sir," Graham replied.

"Weaver, keep moving. Graham, shoot any target you identify. Load HEAT," Casey yelled into his intercom.

Cossack continued forward, jinking around foxholes and bunker positions that looked too dangerous to run over and plowing over others that Weaver felt confident the tank could handle. Keeley's FIST-V, armed only with a single 7.62mm machine gun, raced its engine to keep up with the more maneuverable M1.

More artillery flares burst high overhead, illuminating the heavy, dark night air. The enemy needed the flares to see their attackers. A wave of small-arms fire erupted from a trench near the northwest corner of the opening to the defile. Elsewhere on Position B, enemy soldiers ran about, trying to get away from the tanks.

"Left front! Troops!" Weaver shouted as he picked up another group of determined defenders coming toward *Cossack*. "They're all over the place!"

"Identified tank! On the way!" Graham yelled, ignoring the driver's less dangerous target.

Casey braced himself against the side of the TC's station. The tank jerked as the round fired and the big M256 cannon recoiled from the blast.

Graham's target, a T-62 tank, was less than three hundred meters away. The 120mm HEAT round burned through the turret ring of the enemy tank. The T-62 lurched backward as if snapped in two, its turret moving several feet to the rear of the hull. Black smoke billowed from the loader's and tank commander's hatches. Moving the turret in rapid searches to scan the battle area, Graham placed the gun onto a VTT-323 that was dug in to the northwest side of the hill, with only its small conical turret and AT-4 missile launcher showing.

"On the way!" Graham screamed.

The cannon roared. Casey saw a splash of sparks as the APC's turret disintegrated from the force of the explosion.

"Target!" exclaimed Graham with morbid glee. His eyes were glued to the cannon sight and he was in control of the gun. "Load HEAT."

The crew executed their deadly drill in a frenzy of adrenaline as they destroyed the enemy vehicles that opposed them. The defenders fought a futile fight, determined to repulse the tank attack. Kriel reloaded rounds into the massive breech of the 120mm cannon with drilled precision. Graham jerked the turret around back and forth, firing at targets as *Cossack* cut through the enemy defensive positions like an icebreaker splitting a thin Arctic crust.

Machine-gun bullets rattled against *Cossack*'s armor in a desperate attempt to drive the tank out of their defensive position. Enemy soldiers rushed the tank from all sides, moving in groups of ones and twos, to fire RPGs or toss grenades. In the light of the flares, Casey saw the shadowy figures darting up and down in the rough terrain. He looked through his vision blocks and saw an enemy machine gun sparking from behind one of the burning T-62s.

Casey jumped up to fire his .50-caliber machine gun. He sprayed a group of infantrymen to the right with a long burst of tracer bullets. The bullets flew wildly all over the area, lighting up the sky in a red trail of light.

A half-dozen artillery flares burst in a bright circle in the sky directly above *Cossack*. The huge M1A2 jerked to a sudden halt as Weaver searched for a way to span the wide ditch that appeared in front of him. Graham moved the turret to the left, firing down the trench in enfilade. Casey fired his .50 caliber in the other direction, the rounds striking down the long axis of the dark trench and flickering in a dazzling display of sparks as his large-caliber bullets hit rocks and metal.

Enemy riflemen suddenly poured out of the trench like ants in a colony that was just turned over with a shovel, but *Cossack*'s machine guns cut them down. Those able to avoid the enfilade fire were chopped up by the two tanks behind *Cossack*. A few enemy squads continued the assault with grenades and assault rifles, in spite of taking heavy casualties to the M1A2's overwhelming firepower. These enemy fell, and the counterattack melted away like snow on a warm winter day.

Casey stopped counting how many infantrymen he'd seen fall to *Cossack's* machine guns.

"Weaver, get us out of here. Go forward!" Casey ordered.

Cossack started to move again, dipping down into the trench and climbing up the other side. A separate group of enemy infantrymen appeared from the north and closed to within fifty feet of *Cossack* as the tank climbed the north bank of the ditch. A quick volley of small-arms fire and RPG rockets focused on *Cossack.*

Roll the dice.

If you roll 2-3, go to Section 26.

If you roll 4-5, go to Section 72.

If you roll 6-12, go to Section 74.

Section 67

> *For his own sake, and of those around him, a man must be pre-pared for the awful, shrieking moment of truth when he realizes he is all alone on a hill a thousand miles from home, and that he may be killed in the next second.*
>
> —T. R. Fehrenbach

The fog rolled away, offering a clear view of the ground for the first time this night. Casey opened his hatch and looked to the south. Peering through the darkness with his night vision goggles, he saw artillery flares burst above the passage point, illuminating his forces in the minefield to enemy artillery observers who might be on the hill to the north. He knew that every minute was critical. He had to buy time for Lieutenant Andrews to unsnarl the mess in the minefield. Casey had to give the enemy something more important to shoot at.

"Steel Five, stop the column and sort it out. Move north to me as fast as possible with whatever you can get out of the minefield," Casey ordered Lieutenant Andrews over Team Steel's command frequency. Casey switched his view to the north. He struggled to see through the thinning fog, then made out what appeared to be one of the Bradleys in McDaniel's platoon. "Break. White One, report."

"Steel Six, this is White One," Sergeant Scott responded. "We're headed northeast, moving at a crawl, following Viper. I expect to make the turn to the north in a few minutes. Visibility has improved. Our artillery has shifted to the north. No contact with the enemy. Over."

"Roger, White One. I want you and Blue to pick up the pace and continue north. I'm following right behind Blue. We've got half the force tangled in the passage lane. They'll have to catch up with us later. Over."

"Roger, Steel Six. Wait . . ."

Casey saw a series of flashes and heard the boom of tank cannon to the north. He quickly scanned his IVIS screen and saw that one of Sergeant Scott's tanks had engaged a target in the woods east of Tongak. Within seconds all four of Scott's tanks were banging away.

"Steel Six, White One. Engaging enemy tanks, CS243414. Out."

"I'm coming up on your left, White One. I see 'em," McDaniel's voice announced over the radio.

"Weaver, let's move!" Casey ordered. Casey looked nervously at his IVIS screen and glanced at the open area east of Tongak. A strange feeling of premonition came over him. He had learned not to ignore these flirts with intuition in the past. "Steel Guns, get me some immediate suppression on that target, and put some smoke in the open area just east of Tongak."

"Already sending immediate suppression based on Scott's digital call," Lieutenant Keeley proudly replied over the radio. "I'll get you smoke east of Tongak in three minutes."

The allied artillery preparation along Cobra and Coral trickled to a few last rounds, then ceased. All friendly artillery fires were now striking along Viper, several kilometers to the north of 2d Platoon.

Section 67

Cossack surged forward, followed by the FIST-V and Sergeant Sellers's BSFV. While Weaver negotiated the rough ground with the aid of his driver's thermal sight, Casey stood in his turret using his night vision goggles to help Weaver avoid the deep holes that pitted the battlefield.

"Steel Six, this is Steel Five," Lieutenant Andrews announced, sounding out of breath. "We've lost nine men in the minefield, all engineers. I've got six critically wounded. We're backing up from the minefield, one step at a time."

"Roger, Steel Five. Get here as fast as you can. Break. Steel Guns, where's my artillery?"

A huge flash of flame suddenly erupted in the north, to the left of the tanks blazing away with 120mm cannon at the wood line at CS243414.

"That's not artillery," Casey muttered to himself as he stood in the turret and looked to the north. *Cossack* rolled to and fro with the rough ground. With his right hand Casey held onto the .50-caliber machine gun as he placed the night vision goggles back up to his eyes. "Oh, no!"

Casey saw two more intense explosions follow the first as tracers zinged across the battlefield, coming from the northwest. The detonation of several rounds near his Bradley platoon confirmed his worst fears. He jumped down to his CITV and struggled to place the sight on the source of the blast.

A dozen artillery shells crashed into the woods to Casey's left front. *Cossack* charged forward, aiming at the dying Bradley that was spewing brilliant flames to the clouds.

"Shit, they're behind us!" Scott's voice shot out over the company command frequency. "Steel Six, I'm taking tank fire from the west! We've got three Bradleys down, burning. I've wasted three enemy tanks—they look like T-62s—in the woods. Don't know if there are any more there."

"Blue One, report!" Casey yelled, exasperated at the loss of his Bradleys as he confirmed the damage in his CITV. He switched to his intercom. "Weaver, move to the northwest of those burning Bradleys. Graham, scan for targets! Due west."

A string of artillery flares suddenly burst directly above *Cossack*. The flares burned brightly, illuminating *Cossack*, Keeley's FIST-V, and

206

Sergeant Sellers's BSFV. At the same time, smoke began to fall just east of Tongak.

"Splash on the smoke," Keeley replied. "I'll repeat until you tell me to stop."

Casey didn't have time to answer.

"Identified tank!" Graham yelled.

"Up!" Kriel shouted loud enough to be heard without the intercom system.

Cossack pitched to one side as Weaver drove with his left track over the edge of the rising embankment of Highway 17.

"Fire and adjust," Casey ordered.

Cossack raced forward, now the left flank of Team Steel.

"On the way!"

Graham fired. The target, a T-62 tank, was less than six hundred meters away. The 120mm SABOT round tore right through the turret ring of the T-62 like a nail driving through Styrofoam. The T-62 snapped in two; the turret broke from the hull in a dazzling shower of sparks and fire.

"Left tank."

"Up."

Graham fired again, disabling another T-62 as *Cossack* swerved closer to Tongak. There was a splash of sparks as the second victim's turret jumped into the air, flipping end over end from the force of the depleted-uranium penetrator. Casey imagined the cries of anguished souls who were obliterated in the microsecond that it took for the hypervelocity SABOT round to strike, melt through the T-62's thin armor, and destroy the weak flesh inside. Three men were tightly packed into the turret of each T-62, surrounded by their unprotected, ready-to-fire 115mm rounds of ammunition. The cruel 120mm SABOT rounds had no mercy. Casey knew that each detonation vaporized the men inside the turret in a violent, fire-charged flash. Each of Graham's rounds struck true, obliterating one enemy tank after another. Casey felt a momentary trace of pity, then thought about his own casualties and quickly got back to the bloody business of war.

Artillery shells fell in front of *Cossack*, spewing smoke in low-hanging bursts of bright, burning white phosphorus. The 2d Platoon was now off to Casey's right, firing rapidly at targets to the northwest.

"Weaver, head back to the northeast. Graham, continue to engage," Casey ordered.

Cossack swerved to the right as Weaver made a hard turn onto the highway and headed east. Enemy tank rounds splashed into the ground and the flimsy metal guardrail on the north side of the road.

"White One, this is Steel Six," said Casey as Graham fired another round at the enemy tanks in Tongak. "Break contact and continue north. I say again, bypass and attack up Viper."

"Wilco, Steel Six. I've got one of Blue's elements with me. The other three have been destroyed. McDaniel didn't make it. I've no idea about their casualties."

"Roger, I'll have Steel ADA check them out," Casey replied, the pain of the loss of McDaniel's men evident in his voice. "Pick up any wounded you can find and get back to me ASAP."

"Wilco," Sellers answered.

The air was suddenly getting colder as the night wore on and the fog disappeared. *Cossack* moved east, then made the turn onto Highway 17 to the north. The 2d Platoon was already moving forward. Charging rapidly up the road, 2d Platoon attacked with two tanks in front and two behind. A Bradley trailed the last two tanks.

A few seconds later the swoosh of two antitank rockets and a flurry of machine-gun fire greeted the lead two tanks. Suddenly a burst of artillery fire detonated to the right of the highway. The enemy round was followed by two, then six, then twelve more.

"Contact, enemy infantry, CS242427," Scott reported over the radio. At the same time, the lead two tanks deployed off the highway to the right of the road, their 7.62mm co-ax machine guns blazing.

"Weaver, move faster!" Casey shouted as he reached for the lever to close the TC's hatch. "Move off the highway to the left."

Roll the dice.

If you roll 2-8, go to Section 58.

If you roll 9-11, go to Section 72.

If you roll 12, go to Section 94.

Section 68

> *Sir, my strategy is one against ten, my tactics ten against one.*
> —Arthur Wellesley, the Duke of Wellington

An American Javelin antitank missile smashed into the top of the turret of the T-72 before the enemy tank could get a round off at *Cossack*. Three other T-72 tanks fired at the American infantry bunker that had fired the missile. The bunker disappeared in the blast of the explosions.

"Damnit!" Casey cursed as Graham targeted and destroyed each of the T-72s in turn. Casey's crew fought like men possessed. The turret floor filled with steel 120mm stubs, ejected by *Cossack's* fast-firing cannon. The battle reached a crescendo. Burning enemy vehicles covered the valley floor. Savage bursts of rifle, rocket, gun, mortar, and artillery exploded in the narrow confines of Objective Dragon.

A dozen more T-72s moved into view and halted. The tank company fired in volleys, hoping to clear the way with their massive firepower. The VTTs followed behind the tanks and rolled toward the center of Objective Dragon. Dismounted infantry ran behind the VTTs. As the Americans demolished one enemy APC after another, more surged forward to replace the ones lost. The enemy seemed to ignore his losses and kept advancing in an all-out assault to crush the Americans.

The smoke began to blow to the south. Soon the northeastern part of the battlefield was clear. Fire from sections of the American line suddenly stopped as many of the defenders ran out of ammunition. Several Americans stood up with their hands in the air in a futile gesture of surrender. A platoon of T-72s closed on the position, only fifty feet away. The enemy tanks gunned them down. Casey's jaw tightened as he saw the slaughter begin. There would be no quarter in this fight, he thought.

"Two tanks, left tank . . ." Casey ordered as he turned the gun onto the tanks that were firing at the American infantrymen.

209

Graham fired before Casey could complete his sentence. The hypervelocity round hit the left T-72, hurling its mangled turret sixteen feet into the air. Graham instinctively moved his sights to the center tank, heard the "Up" for the loader, and fired again. Another T-72 crumpled to a burning, fiery halt. Kriel shouted again as *Cossack*'s breech slammed shut, ready to fire once again.

"On the way!" Graham fired and smashed the third T-72.

"Target, target," Casey yelled. "Weaver, back up!"

Weaver raced the M1 engine and lurched the big tank back thirty feet. Casey looked to his left and saw Andrews's tank smoldering from a direct hit from an enemy tank gun. The enemy hit Andrews's tank in the right front of the turret, directly in front of the tank commander and gunner positions. Andrews's tank cannon dropped to the ground.

"Damnit!" Casey cried out loud, overcome with anger. "Weaver, move forward. Let's get those sons of bitches. Graham, action, right front."

Cossack popped back up to the small ridge.

Roll the dice.

If you roll 2-8, go to Section 33.

If you roll 9-12, go to Section 81.

Section 69

Though we have heard of stupid haste in war, cleverness has never been seen associated with long delays.
                                           —Sun Tzu, *The Art of War*

Casey couldn't move the turret in time. The big, ugly 152mm howitzer fired at a range of less than one hundred meters.

The high-explosive shell hit *Cossack* in the turret. In one horrible moment the turret ripped from the hull and the tank shuddered to a halt. The power of the strike killed Casey and everyone in the turret instantly.

You have been killed in action.
Go back to Section 29, reconsider your options, and try again.

Section 70

> *It is no use to get there first unless, when the enemy arrives, you have also the greater men—the greater force.*
>
> —Adm. Alfred Thayer Mahan

Casey pushed against the right side of the turret as the M1A2 jolted across the rocky ground. He quickly scanned through his vision blocks, trying to direct the tank across the rough terrain.

A bright explosion erupted to the far right as an enemy missile missed *Cossack* and hit a rock. Weaver surged *Cossack* straight toward the bridge.

Casey shot a glance up through his vision blocks. The sky was bright with enemy artillery flares. Graham swung the turret back and forth in short, choppy moves, searching for the enemy.

"Goddamnit!" Casey cursed. "Where's our artillery when we need it?"

Casey shot a glance at his IVIS screen and saw the distribution of his forces and the location of the enemy that had been engaged by

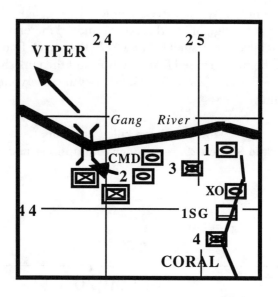

2d Platoon's three tanks. The 3d Platoon, farther behind, was racing to the southwest to get into the fight.

"Identified bunker!" Graham yelled. "Hell, I see three bunkers now. They're firing those missiles from the tops of the friggin' bunkers."

"Up!" Kriel shouted.

"Fire!"

Casey watched through his CITV as an enemy position was engulfed in the explosion of the HEAT round. "Target," Casey yelled. "Fire and adjust!"

Graham began servicing the targets from right to left, destroying the enemy antitank missiles that were closest to the bridge first. After firing several main-gun rounds, he switched to machine gun and plastered the enemy positions with fire.

The three remaining M1A2s of 2d Platoon bulled forward, now only six hundred meters from the enemy defenses guarding the bridge. Casey saw the tank directly to his left explode an antitank mine. The tank pivoted in a vicious turn as its right track split from the force of the mine.

"Minefield!" Scott's voice boomed over the command frequency. "CS244447, attempting to breach with plow."

Another flare burst overhead, illuminating *Cossack* as it ran west along the south bank of the Gang. Suddenly *Cossack* was hit by machine-gun fire from the northwest, from the opposite side of the river.

Roll the dice.

If you roll 2-7, go to Section 62.

If you roll 8-9, go to Section 72.

If you roll 10-12, go to Section 84.

Section 71

There are more ways of overcoming the enemy's army than by storming its positions, just as there are more ways of winning wars than by winning battles.

—B. H. Liddell Hart

Reacting quickly, Casey swung the turret over the back deck and pointed *Cossack*'s cannon in the direction of the enemy tanks to the south.

"Identified, tanks!" Graham shouted.

At the same time, Scott's tank platoon fired a volley to the north, immediately hitting three enemy tanks. The battlefield lit up like daylight from the blast of explosions, burning T-62s, and artillery flares.

"Steel Six, I'm moving west to support you. Hang on!" Stonevitch yelled over the command frequency.

"Fire and adjust," Casey screamed to Graham over the intercom. He pushed his CVC toggle forward to key his radio. "White One, engage enemy tanks to the north. Blue One, engage enemy tanks in the woods to the southwest."

"On the way!" Graham shouted.

Cossack's 120mm cannon roared. The three surviving tanks of Sergeant Scott's platoon blasted away at the attackers to the north. McDaniel's Bradleys fired 25mm and TOW missiles at the tanks in the woods to the southwest.

"Target!" Casey yelled. He saw one of the T-62s burning like a blowtorch. Casey grabbed the TC's override and placed the gun on a T-62 in the wood line to the southwest.

A volley of fire exploded from the wood line. Several 115mm shells landed near *Cossack*. Lieutenant Keeley's thinly armored FIST-V burst into flames as a 115mm tank round smashed into the APC's rear door. The FIST-V exploded in a convulsion of fire and molten aluminum.

McDaniel's Bradleys immediately turned around and fired their 25mm cannons at the T-62 tanks that were firing at them from the wood line at CS245415. A TOW missile fired from one of 3d Platoon's Bradleys, hit a T-62, and smashed it like a bug hit by a sledgehammer. In spite of this gallant effort, however, another Bradley burst into flames as an enemy tank scored another hit.

Suddenly 1st Platoon's four M1A2s entered the battle, firing in rapid sequence from the southeast. Round after round tore into the T-62s in the wood line as 2d Platoon fired with deadly accuracy at the enemy tanks to the north. In a matter of minutes the counterattack had been smashed, but not until another 2d Platoon tank had been hit.

Casey scanned his IVIS screen. He had lost two tanks, three Bradleys, and his FIST-V. In addition, during the confused melee, the enemy had destroyed one of the Wolverine heavy assault bridges and the HEMMT fuel truck.

As the fires burned across the battlefield, Casey made his report to Major Cutter. Faced with the loss of so much of his force and his special equipment, Cutter ordered Casey to return to friendly lines. Reluctantly, Casey gave the order to cancel the attack.

The next morning, as Team Steel limped back to its assembly area and counted its dead and missing, the 1-12th Infantry was overrun.

You have failed to accomplish your mission.
Go to Section 108 and make a different decision.

Section 72

> *The worst obstacle to the tank is the land mine.*
> —B. H. Liddell Hart

Cossack's turbine engine screeched a high-pitched wail as the tank raced across the rough ground. Even with the aid of his DTV, the excellent driver's thermal viewing periscope installed on the M1A2, Pvt. William Weaver never saw the antitank mine that lay directly in *Cossack*'s path.

Wham! There was a sudden sucking in of air, as if the tank had lungs and was taking in a deep breath. Then the inside of the tank ignited with the detonation of the antitank mine in a horrible flash of white-hot flame and molten metal. Casey and his crew died in that same instant.

Go back to the last section that offered you a choice of options
and make a different decision.

Section 73

Captain Casey stood in *Cossack*'s tank commander's hatch, manning his .50-caliber machine gun. He watched as the last volley of 155mm artillery plastered the enemy defensive position just eight hundred meters to the south.

The three American tanks formed a *Y*, the open arms of the *Y* pointing toward the enemy and Casey's tank taking up the southern, bottom stem of the *Y. Cossack*'s turret faced south, over the back deck; the hull was oriented north. Casey intended to continue the attack as soon as the rest of Team Steel reached his position.

The two 1st Platoon tanks that had fought with Casey through Position B faced north, fifty meters from *Cossack*. One tank was positioned on the right shoulder of Highway 21, Direction of Attack Cobra. The other occupied a firing position on the left side of the two-lane asphalt road. The FIST-V, with Lieutenant Keeley, faced north and was parked right next to *Cossack*.

"Steel Six, this is Red Four," the voice of the platoon sergeant of the tank to the northeast of *Cossack* crackled over the company radio frequency. "Request permission to dismount personnel and redistribute ammunition."

"Roger, Red Four. Keep a sharp lookout. We're all alone here in Indian country."

"Wilco," the platoon sergeant of 1st Platoon answered.

Casey pushed his CVC commo switch to intercom. "Kriel, get up here and man the loader's machine gun. I don't want any surprises while we're waiting for the rest of Team Steel to reach us."

"Roger, sir," Kriel replied and opened his hatch.

An abrupt, intense flash erupted to the south, about a kilometer away. Casey trained his binoculars on the area but couldn't make out what was happening in the intermittent light caused by fading flares and brilliant explosions.

"Damn. Power!" Casey cursed as he ordered the command to turn the turret from the tank commander's override. He moved the gun in the direction of the flashes. "Graham, check out what's going on. I think Stonevitch is in trouble."

"Roger, sir, scanning."

"Steel Five, this is Steel Six. SITREP. Over."

"Steel Six, we're under attack from the woods. Stand by."

Casey watched helplessly as the rumble of explosions echoed from the southeast. He raised his binoculars again, but the fog had rolled back in and reduced visibility to only three to four hundred meters. "Graham, what do you see?"

"Lots of hot spots . . . can't make out who's shooting who," Graham replied.

A volley of 120mm tank rounds boomed in the fog.

"Keeley, get me some fire on the woods at CS214415, danger close," Casey yelled.

Keeley, standing in the open rear hatch of his FIST-V, waved acknowledgment and bent down to make radio coordination with the guns.

"Steel Six, we were hit by dismounts and antitank rocket teams. I'm counterattacking. I've lost two or three APCs and one of the heavy assault bridges. I'll give you a complete report when I sort it out."

"Steel Six, this is Steel Seven. That's affirmative. I lost two of the transport M113s and one medic track. One HAB was also completely destroyed and the driver killed. The other one is damaged and can't launch his bridge. I've got two badly wounded with me. We're close to the friendly lines now. I think I should send an APC back with the wounded."

Casey closed his eyes and bit his lip. He'd lost three APCs and one heavy assault bridge. If he sent another armored personnel carrier back, would he have enough to accomplish his mission?

First he had to link up with the 1-12th. That was still not a certainty. The wounded soldiers were a certainty.

"Roger, Steel Seven. Send back one APC with the wounded. Co-ordinate their return through the battalion so they don't get shot up by our own guys when they return to friendly lines. Break. Steel Five, break contact and get here as fast as you can."

The sound of Stonevitch's battle echoed in the valley. The noise of the clash of arms grew, a clear sign to Casey that Team Steel was involved in a major fight. Casey heard the rumble of artillery striking the center of the wood line at CS214415.

"Damnit," Casey cursed out loud, pounding the top of his .50-caliber machine gun with his right fist. "I'm here with two other tanks while the rest of Team Steel is fighting for its life!"

As he brought the binoculars back up to his eyes, he suddenly saw the flash of RPG machine-gun fire only sixty feet away.

Roll the dice.

If you roll 2-3, go to Section 26.

If you roll 4-12, go to Section 103.

Section 74

> But acquiescence society may not have, if it wants an army worth a damn. By the very nature of its mission, the military must maintain a hard and illiberal view of life and the world. Society's purpose is to live; the military's is to stand ready, and if need be, to die.
> —T. R. Fehrenbach, *This Kind of War*

Casey ducked down into the turret to grab more .50-caliber ammunition. *Cossack* cleared the northern berm, then shuddered as if an invisible hammer had slammed into the turret. In spite of the strike, *Cossack* rolled on.

"What was that?" Graham asked. His machine gun continued to fire at the enemy trench line as *Cossack* zigzagged across the rough ground.

"We were hit by an RPG," Casey replied. "Anybody hurt?"

"Up here!" Weaver answered. "No damage to the gun."

"All green here," Kriel echoed.

"I'm okay," Graham reported. "All systems read normal, as if nothing happened."

"Continue mission," Casey ordered, silently thanking God and General Dynamics for the strength of the armor of his powerful war machine.

"Identified bunker," Graham screamed. "On the way!"

As the cannon fired, Casey closed his eyes instinctively to avoid being blinded by the flash of the gun. He opened them a moment later to see a burning bunker to the left as the tank raced by.

"Co-ax on the way!" Graham shouted automatically as he drilled the dazed survivors who stumbled out of the burning bunker.

"Keep moving, Weaver," Casey ordered his driver. He reached up to his CVC helmet switch and keyed the command frequency. "Steel Guns, this is Steel Six. Fire DPICM on Position B after we break through."

"You want me to put the friendly artillery fire behind us?" Lieutenant Keeley questioned.

"Roger. Execute immediately!" Casey reconfirmed. He checked his IVIS screen's POS/NAV indicator and saw that the three American tanks and one FIST-V cleared the 43 grid line. "DPICM in effect."

Cossack's machine guns blazed as the tank moved forward. The FIST-V and the two tanks of 1st Platoon followed close behind, firing on the move, mowing a path through the defenders.

Casey could sense that the enemy's defense was crumbling to the rapid, direct tank assault. In the confusion of the dark and smoke, the enemy infantry could not react rapidly enough to stop the deadly, fast-firing M1A2s. Nothing could stop Casey's tanks.

Machine-gun bullets raced through the night air, making bright arcs of red and green. More artillery flares popped overhead, but the enemy infantry was beaten. *Cossack* clanked forward inexorably, followed closely by the two remaining tanks of 1st Platoon.

"They're running!" Weaver's voice boomed over the tank's intercom. "I can see them in my viewer."

"Not if I get them first" was Graham's bloodthirsty reply.

The 7.62mm machine gun chattered. Unwilling to risk death fighting the unstoppable monsters that had bludgeoned their way through their position, the enemy defense broke.

Casey struggled to reload his .50-caliber machine gun as the three American tanks and the FIST-V exited the north side of the enemy position and moved forward into quieter terrain. Soon all three tanks and the FIST-V climbed onto the concrete, two-lane Highway 21. They raced north, unopposed, along Cobra.

"Weaver. Pull over up ahead and stop," Casey ordered.

"Wilco," Weaver answered.

Cossack slowed to a halt. Lieutenant Keeley's FIST-V, its engine sounding like an overworked washing machine, pulled up next to *Cossack.*

Casey stood in the open hatch and struggled to see the artillery at work. Visibility was steadily improving as the temperature dropped. Casey could now see seven to eight hundred meters in the light of the flares.

Lieutenant Keeley took off his CVC and shouted at his commander. "You know, Sir, you shouldn't draw fire like that. It pisses off everyone around you . . . Sir."

"You know what they say—teamwork is essential. It gives the enemy someone else to shoot at," Casey replied as he raised his helmet, wiped his sweat-stained brow, and smiled. "Glad you made it."

"Me too," the artilleryman replied. "We almost lost you in the middle of the fight. Old Betsy here doesn't run as fast as your big, beautiful M1."

Casey looked up to the south. "When will the DPICM hit?"

"It should be landing right about now," Keeley answered.

Cascading explosions, fire, and noise engulfed the enemy position. Casey watched the brilliant explosions pummel Position B. Hundreds of small bomblets blanketed the enemy position and erupted like a string of huge firecrackers.

"Good job, Keeley," Casey said with a grin. "I think I'll keep you. You got a first name?"

"George," Keeley replied proudly.

Casey nodded, then looked down inside the turret to check the latest digital reports. He watched the artillery fire pummel the few enemy that remained alive on Position B. Then he quickly checked his IVIS screen to determine his combat power:

TM C Unit	M1A2 Tank	M2 IFV	BSFV [ADA]	FISTV	Engr M113	CEV	ACE	HAB Bridge	Medic M113	M88 [Rec]	Fuel HEMMT	M113 APCs
North of PP	3 [1]	3	1	1								
South of PP	5	3			4	1	1	2	2	1	1	15
Total	**8**	**6**	**1**	**1**	**4**	**1**	**1**	**2**	**2**	**1**	**1**	**15**

"We still can make it," Casey yelled down to his young, eager artilleryman. "Is the MLRS ready to fire?"

"Yes, Sir. Once you give me a target, it'll take about two minutes for them to put rockets on it. After that, all we have to do is roll through and pick up the pieces."

"I'll give you the word when I need it." Casey grinned, then put his CVC helmet back on and keyed the radio to transmit. "Steel Five, this is Steel Six. I'll lift the artillery fire as you close on Position B. Find Red One and either tow him out or destroy his tank and evacuate his crew."

"Wilco, Steel Six. I see Red One," Lieutenant Stonevitch answered. "We're taking fire from a few isolated pockets of resistance near the woods at CS213416, but nothing we can't handle. We'll link up with you in about five minutes."

"Bypass everything you can. Take Cobra right up the highway—there's nothing blocking the road. Just get north of Position B as fast as possible."

Casey stood in the tank commander's station, his head and shoulders outside of the tank. The two tanks from 1st Platoon were fifty meters forward in the defile, to the right and left sides. Casey scanned back to the south and saw the last volley of DPICM pulverize Position B.

Roll the dice.

If you roll 2-7, go to Section 73.

If you roll 8-12, go to Section 80.

Section 75

> *For one thing, an impassable area is often confused with an inaccessible one.*
>
> —Carl von Clausewitz, *On War*

As the dust settled, Casey saw from his tank commander's station that the bridge supports were still standing. The enemy had tried to demolish the bridge, but demolitions had not done their job. Casey jumped down and scanned the bridge with his CITV. The bridge remained.

"Weaver, straight ahead. Follow the berm to your right."

Cossack darted toward the bridge, leading the attack. The tank barreled through a triple-strand concertina wire obstacle as if the barrier was made of string. Casey disregarded the mines, then found to his luck that the trail that led along the south riverbank was clear. For some reason, right along the riverbank, the lane was free of mines—probably, Casey thought, because the enemy expected to cover the riverbank with antitank missile fire. They hadn't counted on Team Steel, he mused.

Cossack charged past the minefield. Casey looked to his right. Over the berm that lined the bank he saw a steep drop into the rushing Gang River. The river was fifteen feet below him, an almost vertical drop from the south bank. He knew that he must get to the bridge; there was no other way to cross the Gang.

"Weaver," Casey warned over the intercom, "keep just left of the berm. If you drive up over that berm, we'll fall fifteen feet into the river."

"Roger, sir!"

Sellers's Bradley and McDaniel's 3d Platoon rolled right behind their commander, hugging the riverbank. Sellers turned his turret to the northwest, ready to fire if the enemy shot at them from the north bank of the Gang.

"White One, halt your two remaining tanks and attack by fire!" Casey ordered over the command radio frequency. Casey saw his route register on his IVIS screen. He pushed a button and transmitted the cleared lane to all his units. "Blue One, there's a lane along the south bank. Follow the berm. Move here now!"

"Wilco, Steel Six," McDaniel's voice answered. "I've got the coordinates. We're coming."

Casey scanned the bridge with his CITV. He saw more enemy infantrymen running along the south side of the bridge. He quickly pushed his CVC switch to intercom. "Graham, zap those damn grunts on the bridge!"

"Identified. On the way!" Graham's 7.62mm machine gun drilled the enemy soldiers near the south edge of the bridge, swatting them with red glowing tracer bullets.

Cossack dashed west, throwing up spires of mud in its tracks.

Artillery shells suddenly detonated in the air above the bridge, exploding in orange-red airbursts. Soon a quick, savage volley of fire and steel engulfed the entire length of the bridge, from the south bank to the north bank. Casey watched the figures on the bridge fall to the artillery fire.

The shell fire stopped just as *Cossack* reached the south entrance to the bridge. A dozen dazed and wounded enemy soldiers jumped up to avoid the tank. A few fired small arms at *Cossack*. At this close range, the charging tank had all the advantages.

Cossack bolted over two enemy soldiers while Graham scattered the rest with his machine gun; it churned like a harvester cutting wheat. An RPG team sprang up to challenge the tank. *Cossack* stopped near the entrance to the bridge and Graham chopped them down. At the same time, Sergeant Sellers's BSFV arrived at *Cossack*'s left. The Bradley's 25mm cannon quickly finished off a bunch of enemy soldiers running north along the bridge.

One wild RPG shot hit near *Cossack*, missing the tank and exploding in between *Cossack* and Sellers's Bradley. The round exploded harmlessly, but the BSFV backed up a few meters, not wanting to take chances. Graham gunned down the unlucky grenadier with a short burst of machine-gun fire.

Casey saw a line of trenches to the west and southwest. The enemy intended to defend this bridge but had obviously expected the attack to come from the south, not the east. *Cossack* and Sellers's Bradley suppressed the defenders of these positions while the rest of Team Steel rushed to reinforce the command group.

McDaniel's four Bradleys arrived and raced around *Cossack*'s left flank. Greeted by a weak blast of small-arms fire from the west, the Bradleys bulled farther through the enemy position and machine-gunned the defenders. The M2s quickly pushed aside a hasty roadblock on Highway 17, then annihilated a squad of enemy running to the south. Stunned enemy soldiers struggled in the smoke and chaos of battle to flee. The death-dealing steel monsters didn't give them the chance.

The Bradleys blazed away. McDaniel's infantry dismounted and destroyed several enemy bunkers with antitank rockets. The M-16s and squad automatic rifles rattled away, cutting down the enemy who opposed the American infantry. The enemy finally broke and straggled south, badgered and bloodied by McDaniel's men. In a few more seconds it was over. Team Steel had captured the south portion of the bridge.

Casey thanked his luck. He quickly scanned the southeast portion of the Highway 17 bridge and deployed 1st Platoon, which was still coming along the clear lane through the minefield, to attack by fire the enemy infantry on the north bank of the Gang. Casey then studied the condition of the bridge.

The enemy's explosives had blown a wide hole through the floor of the road in one lane of the two-lane concrete bridge. The left lane was still good, but narrow. Where there any more demolition charges on the bridge, capable of blowing them to hell? Casey wondered. Would the bridge hold a tank?

"Steel Six, this is Blue One!" McDaniel screamed excitedly over the team command frequency. "The bastards are running! The 2d Platoon is catching them in a cross fire as they run south. Do you want me to cross and secure the bridge?"

Casey looked at the long concrete bridge to his front. He had already lost two tanks and his FIST. His combat power was eight tanks, seven Bradleys, and one Bradley Stinger fighting vehicle. He had not lost any of the engineers, APCs, or the recovery or HEMMT fuel truck. He looked at his watch. It was 0318. Time was fleeting. Should he send McDaniel across mounted or dismounted? He had to decide!

If Casey decides to wait, dismount the infantry, and check out the bridge first, go to Section 15.

If Casey decides to order McDaniel to make an immediate, mounted rush across the bridge, go to Section 59.

Section 76

> *Rather few men have the particular combination of intelligence, high manual skills and ruggedness needed by a tank crew. They are not easy to find at all.*
> —Brig. Richard Simpkin, British Royal Amored Corps

A storm of fire burst all around *Cossack*. Brilliant flashes punctuated the night as Casey strained to see through his vision blocks what was going on. He switched his transmitter to radio. "Steel Five, this is Steel Six. Report."

No answer. He checked his IVIS screen. He saw that Steel Five was registering as a mobility kill, possibly having lost one of its tracks to an antitank mine.

"Steel Six, this is Steel Seven," the voice of First Sergeant Washington interjected. "Things are a mess here. Lieutenant Andrews is missing, probably killed in the artillery strike. I've got the allied unit telling me we have to pull out of the passage lane because they think they're under tank attack."

Damn! Casey fumed. Everything that could possibly go wrong has gone wrong. "Steel Seven, this is Steel Six. Move everyone south of me to an assembly area five hundred meters south of Contact Point Bravo, at CS235390. Organize units as they arrive. When you're ready to move north again, call me."

"Wilco, Steel Six," First Sergeant Washington answered. "I'm pulling everyone back, south of the LD now."

A string of artillery flares suddenly burst directly above *Cossack*. The flares burned brightly, illuminating *Cossack* and Sergeant Sellers's BSFV.

"Steel ADA, let's go. We're headed to 2d Platoon's location," Casey shouted over the radio to Sellers.

Artillery churned up the ground two hundred meters to the left of *Cossack*.

"Driver, get us out of here!" Casey yelled over the tank's intercom. There was nothing he could do about the units south of the LD now. "Weaver, move out, northeast. Join 2d Platoon."

Weaver needed no coaxing. Without answering, he shoved *Cossack* into gear. The big, seventy-ton Abrams tank surged forward.

Roll the dice.

If you roll 2, go to Section 25.

If you roll 3-8, go to Section 65.

If you roll 9-12, go to Section 88.

Section 77

> *Every principle of war becomes easy to apply if movement can be accelerated and accelerated at the expense of the other side. . . . The result of such an action is not even within the possibilities of doubt; the latter will certainly be destroyed, for the highest form of machinery must win, because it saves time and time is the controlling factor of war.*[1]

YOU HAVE WON!

Congratulations on your victory! Now let's review the historical examples that this scenario was based on and learn some lessons from history.

The brilliant and unconventional military philosopher, soldier, and strategist John Frederick Charles Fuller wrote the above words in his dissertation on "Plan 1919." Faced with the slaughter and indecision on the battlefields of World War I, men such as Fuller searched for solutions to break the deadlock imposed by the trench and machine gun. The solutions were varied. The Germans developed bold infiltration tactics; the western allies chose technology. In "Plan 1919" Fuller presented a solution that would deliver decisive victory with minimal casualties by penetrating the Kaiser's defenses and paralyzing the German command with a massed tank attack. Fuller's intent was to use the increased mobility and firepower of the tank, allied with new tactical techniques, to gain a decisive advantage over the Germans. He prophesied that the use of tanks and the mechanization of armies was the future of ground combat.[2]

Fuller is now recognized as the father of the modern mechanized military force. His dream is conventional wisdom today; all modern armies are mechanized. The combined-arms team, centered on the tank, rules the open ground. Fast-moving attack helicopters, armed with awesome firepower, race with amazing speed across the face of the earth, regardless of the terrain. Artillery moves on tracks, keeping pace with the tempo of the assault to deliver devastating and accurate firepower.

What relevance can Fuller's words have to professional soldiers who will fight the battles of the twenty-first century? The relevance lies in Fuller's development of tactics and techniques to solve the tactical challenge facing the armies of his time. The riddle of the trenches in World War I required a solution involving mobility, particularly movement under fire. This old debate faces army leaders today in restricted terrain.[3] Instead of trenches, restricted terrain consists of narrow valleys, high mountaintop observation positions, sparse roads, and an excess of natural obstacles to inhibit battlefield mobility. The classic argument is that restricted terrain, like the mountainous areas of Korea, is not "good tank country." Conventional wisdom cries that dismounted infantry must clear and seize the high ground, and then only after massive artillery bombardment.

How do we apply the advantages of firepower, protection, and mobility inherent in today's armored force to the restricted terrain of Northeast Asia? Fuller's words reach out across the decades to answer this question: "Each new or improved weapon or method of movement demands a corresponding change in the art of war." The question is not whether it is "good tank country." The question is how to adapt our tactics, techniques, and procedures to apply the advantages in battlefield mobility of the armored force to restricted terrain. The answer lies in changing our view, or developing it better, on the art of war in restricted terrain. We have the combined-arms instruments; we need only to arrange them in the proper package to reap their maximum potential.[4]

Combined-arms battle in restricted terrain[5] is much more demanding than combat in open terrain. The execution of tactics in restricted terrain must be more precise. There are few opportunities to turn around or move away from the deadly fire of an enemy fire sack when an armored column is fighting in a narrow defile. In this environment, decisive victory with minimum friendly losses will require superbly trained troops and excellent leaders schooled in the tactics of fighting in restricted terrain.

Charged with the task of winning *decisively* with minimal casualties in all types of terrain, professional soldiers should gain insight from Fuller's mental framework and his belief that "at no time in the history of war has a difficulty arisen the solution of which has not at the time in question existed in some man's head, and frequently in those of several."[6] This is particularly important to the evolution of combined-arms tactics, techniques, and procedures in restricted terrain.

Nowhere is the argument for careful study of the nature and method of victory more important today than in Northeast Asia. If the U.S. Army wants to learn the lessons of combined-arms combat and refine the tactics, techniques, and procedures for fighting in restricted terrain, the lessons will be learned in the mountains and valleys of Korea. The U.S. Army fought for three desperate years in Korea against a determined and skillful opponent. When war erupted in Korea in June 1950, the United States was unprepared. Most professional soldiers of that time, trained in the open warfare of World War II, saw the situation in Korea as a purely infantry war. Two of the most illuminating battles of the war, the Battle of Chipyong-ni and the Battle of Heartbreak Ridge, offer a model for the modern application of close operations tactics in restricted terrain. Although the weapons have changed since 1951, the lessons of offensive and defensive operations remain relevant today.

This section addresses methods to use the combined-arms team in the very restricted terrain of Korea to gain decisive victory with minimal casualties. These recommendations for combat are based on tactical lessons learned in 1951, from the defensive battle of Chipyong-ni and the offensive battle Operation Touchdown (which ended the battle of Heartbreak Ridge), and on one commander's METT-T[7] assessment, gained in six years of training in Korea.

The Battle of Chipyong-ni, 13–16 February 1951
The Chinese intervened in the Korean War in late October 1950, altering the nature of the conflict. On 26 November 1950 Chinese armies attacked with approximately 485,000 men. Road-bound, and imbued with a "tactical and psychological dependence on continu-

ous battle lines, such as has been known in Europe,"[8] United Nations' battalions were cut off and chopped up in one battle after another. The linear view of tactics held by the officers of the American army contributed to the debacle. Fearing encirclement, many units lost all sense of cohesion and organization when they discovered the Chinese blocking their line of communication to the south. The Chinese attacks forced General MacArthur's 365,000 United Nations troops back to the thirty-eighth parallel. After the bloody and demoralizing retreat from northern Korea, Gen. Matthew B. Ridgway, the new Eighth Army commander, was eager to restore the fighting confidence of his forces. He launched a general counteroffensive on 5 February.

The Chinese Volunteer Army, veteran and flushed with victory, blunted the blow of the UN offensive. By 11 February the Chinese launched a full-scale counteroffensive of their own. Two Chinese attacks drove south to secure the towns of Hoengsong and Wonju. As the Americans withdrew under the pressure of these attacks, the front lines rolled south almost twenty miles. "Before the Chinese attack, the front lines of X Corps were well ahead of Colonel Freeman's Chipyong-ni perimeter, but as the units went south, sometimes fighting through enemy roadblocks, Chipyong-ni became a conspicuous bulge on the left of the corps' line."[9] Ridgway decided to hold Chipyong-ni and ordered the 23d Regimental Combat Team (RCT) to defend it, even if they were surrounded.

The town of Chipyong-ni, half a mile long and several blocks wide, was situated at a crossroads. A single-track railroad ran through the town. Several brick buildings, including the railway station, occupied the center of the town. Most of the other buildings were mud-and-straw farmers' huts. Half of the buildings had been destroyed in previous fighting. Surrounding the town were eight distinct hills with an average height of 850 feet above the valley. The 12 miles of ridgelines offered an excellent defensive position but would have required a three- to four-mile-diameter defensive perimeter.

The 23d Regimental Combat Team, 2d Infantry Division, arrived at Chipyong-ni on 3 February. The regiment consisted of approximately six thousand troops: four battalions of infantry (one of these was the famed French Battalion—French soldiers using American equipment, a Ranger infantry company, one tank company (dispersed among the infantry battalions), one battalion of towed artillery (105mm), one battery of towed 155mm artillery, one air defense battery (six M16 and four M19 self-propelled antiaircraft machine-gun carriers), and an engineer company. Colonel Paul L. Freeman, the commander of the 23d RCT, positioned his forces in a tight perimeter about a mile in diameter on lower ground.

Freeman directed his battalions to occupy the perimeter in clockwise fashion, with twelve o'clock being north: 1st Battalion from twelve to one o'clock, 3d Battalion from two to five o'clock, 2d Battalion from five to seven o'clock, and the French Battalion from seven to eleven o'clock. The infantrymen set up defenses on the small hills and rice paddies surrounding the town. For ten days the 23d RCT prepared for the Chinese attack. Freemen's men used the time to their advantage:

> The infantry companies dug in their machine guns, registered their mortars, sowed antipersonnel mines, and operated daily patrols to the encompassing high ground. The regimental Heavy-Mortar Company divided the fires of its platoons and sections among the sectors of the perimeter, the artillery registered on all probable avenues of approach, and all units established good communications lines. There was time to coordinate the infantry, artillery, and air support into an effective combat team.[10]

The Americans in Chipyong-ni were mostly veterans. They knew that the Chinese were worthy foes and had proved themselves the masters of the night infiltration attack. "In attack, the Chinese usually made one or more frontal assaults and sent a sizable force around a flank to cut the main exit road behind those they were attacking. They were adept at picking ridgelines or hills close to the road, overlooking the point where they put their fire and roadblocks."[11]

Forced to travel and resupply their forces on Korea's narrow roads, the Americans could be held up at a single position for hours. Because close air support was effective only during daylight,

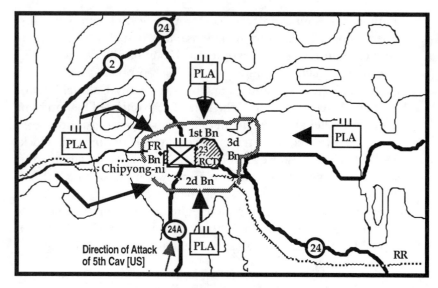

Battle of Chipyong-ni

the Chinese almost always attacked during periods of limited visibility. At night the Chinese would infiltrate squads, platoons, or whole companies into American positions. These tactics usually unnerved their enemies and led to the quick collapse of the defender.

Chinese patrol activity increased in the Chipyong-ni area on 13 February. The 23d RCT's Tactical Air Control Party (TACP) called in forty flights of aircraft against the Chinese. Artillery from within the perimeter fired on the advancing Communist columns, causing heavy casualties.

On the evening of 13 February Colonel Freeman called an orders group meeting of his subordinate commanders and informed them that their position was surrounded by Chinese. "We'll stay and fight it out," he said,[12] confident in the ability of his troops and the strength of his position. Between 2200 and 2300 enemy mortar shells landed inside the Chipyong-ni perimeter, announcing that the defenders of Chipyong-ni were now the main target of the Chinese offensive.

Heavy mortar and artillery fire preceded the Chinese attack, striking the northwest (French Battalion), north (1st Battalion), and southeast (2d Battalion and French Battalion seam) of the perimeter. By 0100 the Chinese had launched strong attacks on the 1st and French Battalions. At 0215 the attacks switched to the southwest and southeast to focus on the 2d Battalion. The Chinese attacked in platoon and company-sized strength searching for a gap in the 23d RCT's defenses. None was found. The American perimeter held, but the stubborn Chinese kept up the pressure until about 0730, when the battle tapered off.

The Chinese withdrew quietly, leaving dozens of dead in front of the American positions. Intermittent mortar shelling covered their withdrawal. Although the Chinese considered the action on the night of the thirteenth merely a probing attack, they were surprised at the stubbornness of the American defense. Mortars and pack howitzers were positioned for firing. Ammunition was brought up and cached near the guns. Unable to penetrate the perimeter in stride, the Chinese planned to launch a major attack on the night of the fourteenth to wipe out the Americans and their French allies.

During the day the infantrymen, tankers, and gunners of the 23d RCT rebuilt their defenses. The defenders redistributed ammunition and prepared for another onslaught. The artillery inside the perimeter fired at observed enemy positions in the surrounding hills throughout the day. On the afternoon of 14 February, the TACP brought in three air strikes to the south, and the 23d RCT received twenty-four airdrops of ammunition.[13] Other than this activity, the fourteenth was a quiet day for the six thousand men of the besieged 23d Regimental Combat Team.

As the sun went down on 14 February, Saint Valentine's Day, the Chinese moved to their line of departure to conduct the decisive attack. At 2000 flares suddenly appeared in the sky. The sound of bugles, whistles, and yells filled the cold night air. The Chinese attacked in the north, hitting C Company of the 1st Battalion in force. Colonel Freemen described the Chinese attack of his prepared defenses with satisfaction:

> The Chinese assault wave bungled into the trip flares, antipersonnel mines and booby traps in front of C Company. With the resultant confusion in enemy ranks, down came the artillery

and mortar barrages and the terrified enemy recoiled. . . . Despite his initial clobbering the fanatical enemy came back for more. Not a small arm was fired until he hit the barbed wire in front of the main positions. Then, in the light of 155mm illuminating shells, the machine guns cut loose. At the same time "meat choppers" [M-16s—quad .50-caliber machine guns mounted on armored tracks] and tanks near the road between the French and 1st Battalion contributed their heavy volume of fire.[14]

Repulsed in the north, the Chinese effort shifted to the south. The main attack started at midnight with an intense mortar barrage directed against George Company, 2d Battalion. The Chinese attacked ferociously all night, pressing their attacks in squad and platoon groups. Flares lit up the night sky as "Chinese infiltrators began to infiltrate over the low hills, carrying pole and satchel charges. They poured into George Company, killing many men by dropping explosives into the foxholes. George was piling up the dead by the hundreds, but too many of the enemy were getting close . . . fighting a determined battle for each foxhole."[15]

George Company's valiant defense was eventually overwhelmed, and the survivors moved down the hill to the center of the defensive perimeter. The Chinese had broken through the perimeter. Official Chinese reports stated: "Nearly a hundred enemy were killed and five captured . . . information was received from the interrogation of the prisoners that the enemy forces were highly concentrated and had constructed strong field works."[16]

Several hasty and poorly coordinated counterattacks with the Ranger Company and tanks stunned the Chinese but were repulsed with heavy casualties. Poor tank-infantry-artillery communications and the lack of counterattack planning and rehearsals caused the attacks to fail. Piecemeal counterattacks were not enough to dislodge the determined Chinese, who now dug into George Company's positions. "The enemy attack continued without let-up. It was not one calculated to overrun the entire hill but a persistent, gnawing assault that progressed from one hole to the next."[17] The 23d RCT was in danger of defeat.

But the Chinese were spent and demonstrated what would be proved again and again in Korea: "They could crack a line, but a force lacking mechanization, air power, and rapid communications could not exploit against a force possessing all three."[18] Unfamiliar with the ground and the enemy defenses, Chinese reinforcements got lost in the dark. Chinese fire support, consisting of 76mm howitzers and 120mm mortars, was poorly coordinated. In addition, their command and control was disorganized and ineffective. Bugles and horns did not transmit orders in time to move forces forward to take advantage of the rupture in the 23d RCT's perimeter.

The Chinese admitted that their failure on the night of the fourteenth was a failure of coordination. "Our firepower was not adequately organized because of the enemy's superior firepower and the open terrain. For this reason we failed each of the three times we attacked, with our troops suffering heavy casualties."[19]

Daylight came, and with it American close air support. As the sun rose, devastating air attacks rocked the Communist lines with high explosives and napalm. Napalm fell all around the outside of the American perimeter. The Chinese "went to ground," or withdrew, to avoid the terrifying air attacks. Colonel Freeman followed up the air attacks with a coordinated combined-armor, infantry, and artillery counterattack that recovered most of George Company's position, plugging the gap. In this effort, Baker Company led the way. "B Company was unsuccessful in their counterattacks until 1400 hours when air strikes and napalm drops routed the enemy from his position."[20]

The crisis of an imminent Chinese breakthrough of the perimeter was over, and the Chinese assault on Chipyong-ni had been stalled. Although the 23d RCT's coordination of combined-arms counterattacks had been poor, the massive firepower of machine guns, tanks, air defense guns, artillery, and close air support drove the enemy back into the hills with tremendous casualties. "The Chinese had been held off, but they still surrounded Chipyong-ni. What was needed now was a rescue by a strong force. It was on its way."[21]

Task Force Crombez of the 5th Cavalry Regiment was fighting its way north along a narrow, heavily defended road to rescue the besieged defenders of Chipyong-ni. The stripped-down armored task force consisted of twenty-three tanks. It was specifically organized to penetrate the enemy lines along a narrow secondary road. Infantrymen rode on top of the tanks. Artillery fire was not planned, but planes bombed and strafed ahead of the column. Chinese small arms raked the sides of the tanks, wounding many of the infantrymen on top of the tanks. When the tanks stopped in the gauntlet of Chinese fire, the infantrymen jumped off to find cover.

The tanks continued moving, but because of poor tank-infantry cooperation—largely due to the lack of training of both the infantry and armor in combined-arms operations—many infantrymen were left behind. This sad event was repeated at several Chinese ambushes along the direction of attack. Some infantrymen were able to fight their way south, back to friendly lines; others were surrounded, killed, or captured. Of the original 160 infantrymen who rode on the tanks, only 23 made it to Chipyong-ni.[22]

Chinese lined the gauntlet, firing small arms, throwing satchel charges, and launching antitank rockets. A critical point occurred just south of Chipyong-ni when the lead tank was hit by a Chinese bazooka. The tank burst into flames, its crew inside the turret killed. The driver continued to drive the tank through a narrow choke point even though his tank was on fire; he thus kept the direction of attack clear for following vehicles. Pushing forward relentlessly, the armored task force broke through and linked up with the 23d RCT at 1700 on 15 February.

It took only an hour and fifteen minutes for the tanks to penetrate six miles of enemy territory. Three tanks were damaged; only one tank, the lead tank of the company commander, was destroyed. The official Chinese Communist after-action reports expressed the value of the armored task force attack very succinctly:

> The tanks surprised us and arrived "almost at the door of the Regimental CP before they were discovered, seriously threatening the flanks and rear of the 2d battalion [Chinese]. The Regiment immediately ordered the displacement of the 2d battalion . . . we have underestimated the enemy. In view of their past characteristics in battle, we expected them to flee at Chipyong-ni . . . we have been taught a lesson at the expense of bloodshed." [23]

The Chinese lost an estimated 4,946 men to the 23d Regimental Combat Team and an additional 500 to Task Force Crombez. The 23d losses were 52 killed, 259 wounded, and 42 missing. Task Force Crombez lost 12 killed, 40 wounded, and 19 missing from L Company—the infantry who rode on top of the tanks.

Until the battle of Chipyong-ni, the bold infiltration tactics of the Chinese had swept all before them. The battle showed that combined-arms operations in restricted terrain, in spite of the tank-infantry coordination problem, were effective. Infantry provided the shield, defending the perimeter; machine guns, tanks, artillery, and close air support did most of the killing. Careful preparation of a well-designed perimeter defense, and the psychological willingness to fight when surrounded, confounded the enemy. Aerial resupply enabled the defense to continue. The rapid armored penetration of the Chinese defenses by the 5th Cavalry broke the back of the Chinese and forced them to redeploy, defeating their plan to annihilate the defenders at Chipyong-ni. Task Force Crombez penetrated the Chinese lines so rapidly that the Chinese could not respond in time. Movement *was* accelerated—at the expense of the other side. In restricted terrain, an armored combined-arms force can be the weapon of choice for counterattacks.

In spite of the casualties, Gen. Matthew Ridgway believed that "Task Force Crombez, in its relief role, epitomized the offensive spirit." Although placing infantry aboard the tanks had proved costly, Ridgway judged Colonel Crombez's decision to advance with armor when his infantry moved too slowly to be one of the best local decisions of the war.[24]

The battle of Chipyong-ni and the relief of the siege by Task Force Crombez became one of the decisive battles of the Korean War. Like the battle of Gettysburg, the three-day battle for Chipyong-ni turned the tide of battle in Korea for the United Nations forces. After Chipyong-ni, "a new pattern was set. Eighth Army had risen from its own bitter ashes. It would not fall again."[25] As a defensive model in restricted terrain, the battle of Chipyong-ni has valuable lessons for modern combined-arms combat.

Operation Touchdown, 17–23 October 1951
The 2d Infantry Division began the attack on Heartbreak Ridge on

13 September 1951, expecting light resistance. Resistance, however, was anything but light. The reconstituted North Korean army, the Inmun Gun, was more fanatical, stubborn, and resolute than in 1950. They fought fiercely for each position. The artillery would not move them. The North Koreans—who named Hill 851Kim Il Sung Ridge after their cruel leader—would not give up easily.

The 2d Infantry Division attacked the North Koreans with infantry and artillery, climbing the steep slopes under murderous fire. In spite of overwhelming artillery support and undisputed control of the air, the infantry battalions of the 2d Infantry Division were repulsed in one fruitless attack after another. "Again it was the work of riflemen, grenadiers, and flame-thrower operators. Tanks could support by fire only from the base of the hills, and artillery alone could not demolish

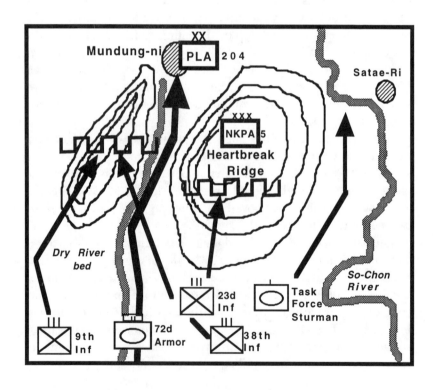

Heartbreak Ridge, Operation Touchdown

the deep NKPA fortifications, though the 2d Infantry Division Artillery fired 229,724 rounds."[26]

After weeks of piecemeal assaults and massive casualties, General Young, the new commanding general of the 2d Infantry Division, decided on a coordinated, combined-arms attack. The plan involved penetrating the Mundung-ni and Satae-ri Valleys and cutting off Heartbreak Ridge at Mundung-ni from enemy reinforcement. To conduct this decisive end run, Young picked the 72d Tank Battalion. The plan to win Heartbreak Ridge was named Operation Touchdown.

Operation Touchdown was designed to use mobility *and* firepower to push the Reds off balance. The infantry and artillery would fix the defenders. The 72d Armor would deliver the main attack down the Mundung-ni Valley. Another tank force, a reinforced company named Task Force Sturman, would attack up the Satae-ri Valley to the east of Heartbreak Ridge. Task Force Sturman's mission was a supporting attack to fix the enemy's attention in the east while the 72d Armor delivered the knockout punch in the west.

After a full day of furious artillery and air bombardment, Operation Touchdown kicked off on 5 October with a night attack conducted by all three of the 2d Infantry Division's infantry regiments. The American infantry pushed forward, making steady but costly progress as they pressed up the steep slopes. In the meantime the 2d Engineer Battalion blasted the mines and boulders from the Mundung-ni Valley trail to prepare the direction of attack for the tanks. By 9 October the Indianhead Division, despite fanatical opposition from the Communists, had taken the southern approaches of Heartbreak Ridge. The North Koreans still dominated the ridge, but the entrance battle had been won.

Early on the mist-covered morning of 10 October, the tanks of the 72d Armor rumbled forward.[27] A coordinated artillery and air attack blasted the high ground on each side of the valley that snaked north to Mundung-ni. Marine Corsairs preceded the advance of the tanks.[28] A field artillery observer attached to the 72d Armor occupied an observation post in the southern end of the Mundung-ni Valley. His critical observation site allowed him to see the entire approach just short of the village of Mundung-ni. From this perch he directed accurate artillery fires on the enemy antitank and machine-gun positions along the walls of the valley.

The pace of the 72d column was slow at first, only five miles an hour, as the artillery and air did its work. Then, after the tankers became confident that the engineers had cleared the minefields, the rate of march increased to fifteen miles per hour. The tanks pushed on as machine-gun fire ripped at their sides. Tanks stopped and the gunners quickly searched out their targets and fired, silencing one enemy bunker after another. North Korean artillery and 120mm mortar shells peppered the advancing tank column, producing huge spires of dust. Most of the enemy fire was ineffective, however, with only one tank taking a direct hit in the tank commander's hatch.

The detailed planning was paying off. Except for this one tank's unlucky break, the rest of the column was charging ahead. The lead unit, Baker Company, now with eleven M4A3E8 tanks, roared through the Mundung-ni Valley. The tanks bypassed obstacles, avoided the craters in the road, took to the streambed to move around a minefield, and kept moving north. Baker's tanks swept the sides of the ridgeline with machine-gun and 76mm cannon fire. Every few feet a tank would deploy off the line of march and swivel its cannon to the flanks of the steep defile to knock off a row of North Koreans who bravely tried to block the armor onslaught. Every time a North Korean rose to fire an antitank gun or lob a grenade, the searching bullets of the tanks cut him down. The mobility and accurate machine-gun fire saved the Americans as the North Korean antitank gunners missed their targets in the swirling smoke and dust.

The infantry regiments of the 2d Infantry Division continued to attack across the front, assaulting the hills of Heartbreak Ridge in coordination with mortars, artillery, and close air support.

The tanks raced north, picking up speed, all guns blazing. A few more tanks were hit, but the column continued relentlessly. Repeated Chinese and North Korean attempts to stop the tanks with grenades, satchel charges, and antitank guns failed. As the tanks exited the defile, they entered into more open ground where they pulled abreast, firing all the way. The village of Mundung-ni stirred like a rattled hornets' nest. An entire Chinese infantry division, preparing to counterattack to reinforce Kim Il Sung Ridge, occupied an assembly area in Mundung-ni, using the village to hide from the ever-searching eyes of the American Corsair fighter-bombers. Baker Company charged into the town of Mundung-ni. With only eleven tanks, Baker Company took on thousands of Chinese.

Unprepared for the swift tank attack, the startled Chinese panicked and were slaughtered by the tanks' cannon and machine-gun fire. Most of the frightened enemy took to the hills to the north and the safety of friendly lines. Those who didn't run fast enough were quickly shot down or run over. The rest of the 72d Armor moved into and around Mundung-ni, gunning down the fleeing Chinese.

The Chinese and North Koreans defending Heartbreak Ridge heard the roar of the tank cannons to their rear. Soon the word spread that Mundung-ni had been captured by the Americans. This put the Communist defenders in a precarious position. Heartbreak Ridge could no longer be supplied or reinforced. The North Korean and Chinese defenders, battered by artillery fire, withdrew to the north. By nightfall the battle was won and Heartbreak Ridge was occupied by the 2d Infantry Division.

The next day the men of the 72d Tank Battalion counted more than 600 dead enemy soldiers, one self-propelled gun, 11 machine guns, three mortars, several ammunition dumps, and 350 captured bunkers. No one knows how many Communists were killed in the bunkers; the tankers were too busy to go in and count. In return, the 72d Tank Battalion lost three killed, five wounded, and eight tanks lost to enemy action.

During Operation Touchdown the accelerated movement of the 72d Armor through the "impassable" Mundung-ni Valley sealed the victory for the 2d Infantry Division by disrupting an entire Chinese infantry division. This attack was the result of careful preparation and the rapid advance of a well-equipped combined-arms force. Operation Touchdown proved that a combined-arms task force could be decisive, even in restricted terrain.

The fighting prior to Operation Touchdown had demanded a change in tactics. Sadly, the lesson was learned too late for many. The 2d Infantry Division lost more than 3,700 casualties from 13 September until 12 October 1951. Communist casualties were estimated at more than 25,000. The last two days, from 10 to 12 October, when the division attacked with three regiments abreast and hurled the 72d Armor down the Mundung-ni Valley, won the battle. The truce talks at Panmunjom, which were broken off on 22 August, resumed on 25 October, partly because of the fighting at Heartbreak Ridge.

Combat in Restricted Terrain Today

The lessons of Chipyong-ni and Operation Touchdown dramatically depict the value of combined-arms combat in restricted terrain. When combined-arms tactics were employed, casualties were reduced and the opportunity for decisive victory was enhanced. The lessons learned offer a metaphor for combat in restricted terrain based on J. F. C. Fuller's combat tactics of protecting and hitting: a shield and sword. At Chipyong-ni the infantry acted as a shield, pinning the enemy; Task Force Crombez was the sword that hastened the defeat of the enemy. A variation of the same method was employed in Operation Touchdown to win Heartbreak Ridge. The infantry battalions fixed the defenders, and the armored task force enveloped the position in the west. Fixing and enveloping is the basis for all tactics.

This situation is applicable to U.S. forces assigned to Korea today. The U.S. battalions in Korea are vastly superior to similar North Korean units by almost every means of measure—technological, organizational, and operational (which includes training). This fact, although comforting to many, is not the most decisive element of victory. The U.S. forces outmatched the North Koreans and Chinese in almost every measure of technology during the Korean War. The common phenomenon of armed forces to "act according to mistaken expectations of their own vast superiority, and therefore rely overmuch on linear logic to optimize the administration of their own means,"[29] should not cloud our need to develop tactics and training that will maximize our technological, organizational, and operational advantages.

Single solutions are simple but dangerous. The commander who believes that army aviation or attack aircraft will provide him the maneuver of direct combat power to destroy an enemy attacker in restricted terrain assumes that the enemy is a "C" student. What if the enemy learned the lessons of Desert Storm and has improved air defense? What if the cloud cover, so often too low to fly in mountainous regions, precludes the free use of airpower? Can a commander afford to choose a single-arms solution to win the battle in restricted terrain? The historical vignettes of Chipyong-ni and Operation Touchdown answer this question with a resounding "no." The operational and tactical level commander can increase his options for decisive victory by possessing an all-weather combined-arms force of great mobility and armored protection. A properly trained combined-arms force, employing intelligent tactics that have been practiced and tested for combat in restricted terrain, is an important part of the solution.

In restricted terrain, U.S. commanders will require both firepower and maneuver solutions to win decisively with minimal casualties. The tactical commander is concerned with finding, fixing, fighting, and finishing the enemy. To do this he uses his firepower to gain an advantage over the enemy and destroys him with a combination of fire and movement.

In restricted terrain, innovative tactics and increased emphasis on combined arms is the answer. This combined-arms task force—using the increased mobility of Bradleys, M1A1 tanks, Kiowa Warriors, and Apache helicopters—provides the weapon of choice for decisive battle with minimal loss. Taking advantage of every possible mobility corridor, the task force employs a combined-arms team to crack open a critical weak spot in the enemy's dispositions. This force would then penetrate the enemy's defenses with mobile direct-fire weapons, fighting asymmetrically, destroying the opponent's artillery or command and control. Once the critical enemy center of gravity—the brigade and division and corps artillery groups[30]—is destroyed, then the combined-arms force would either defend and wait for linkup with follow-on forces or continue to attack back toward friendly lines.

In restricted terrain, an infantry-heavy combined-arms force can fix the enemy and channelize his movement. Infantry that occupies prepared defensive positions in rough ground represents the shield. A determined combined-arms defense, prepared to fight even if surrounded, can usually stop an enemy from attacking down most valley avenues of approach. Infantry can enhance their defensive power by occupying built-up areas or using terrain that blocks the enemy's critical avenues of approach. Firepower is the key to this kind of defense. The intent must be to block, fix, and trap the enemy.

The mobile, armored combined-arms force is the sword that will snap the trap. The penetration attack should be launched against an enemy flank and aimed at an objective that will cause the decisive defeat of the enemy force.

The armored combined-arms force is still the weapon of decisive attack on the conventional battlefield. The greater the training and coordination of the combined-arms force, the faster the penetration. The faster the combined-arms force moves to its objective, the greater the success and the smaller the friendly losses. Concentration at the tip of the sword is critical for success in restricted terrain.

Regardless of the objective, mobile combined-arms task forces, providing the decisive knockout punch, can be task organized into a combined-arms penetration package of mechanized infantry, tanks, artillery, aerial observation, and attack aircraft (helicopter and close air support) to rapidly attack and penetrate the enemy's flank. Under the command of an armored or a mechanized task force commander, they would be a tactical maneuver force for the division commander.

Attacking with amazing power and directed with information-age intelligence, the armored combined-arms force must be trained to expect to operate "deep in enemy territory; the presence of the enemy to the front, flanks, and rear is a condition to be expected. All personnel must be conditioned to consider such conditions more normal than otherwise. . . ."[31]

In restricted terrain the enemy's flank will, more than likely, be guarded by terrain cross compartments consisting of high mountain ridges. Today this task could be accomplished by a well-organized package of combined arms—a "penetration package"—of tanks, mechanized infantry, engineers, armored air defense systems, artillery supported by observation helicopters, attack helicopters, and close air support.

The commander must organize a penetration package based on several important assumptions: (1) the quality and training of his forces versus the enemy and (2) the requirement for combat multipliers to set the conditions for success of a penetration of an enemy defense with one hour, four hours, twelve hours, and twenty-four hours of preparation. The higher the quality of his forces and the less time the enemy has for preparing defenses, the smaller the penetration package can be and still achieve success.

The training required to turn theory into practice is the next critical step. Winning in restricted terrain will require a lot of training in combined arms. In restricted terrain this is a very challenging task. Once movement down a narrow mountain road begins, there may be only a few opportunities to turn around. Turning around a battalion task force of 235 armored and wheeled vehicles is often impossible in these circumstances. In short, combat in restricted terrain is unforgiving. Providing combined-arms training, and focusing on the penetration packages required to fight in restricted terrain, are major training and resourcing challenges. Commanders should strive to put this training together and practice with a frequency that will produce mastery of the techniques that win in restricted terrain.

If we expect to win our wars rapidly, with minimal casualties, we must train to win every skirmish, engagement, and battle decisively. Pushing back the enemy will not produce a decisive victory. Our tactics must be to trap the enemy; to trap him with maneuver, to trap him with fires, to maintain the initiative and never give him a chance to recover.

Conclusion

U.S. Army doctrine on fighting a tank or mechanized force in restricted terrain is sparse.[32] Many potential battlefields, however, are located in areas with mountainous terrain. Many of our potential enemies, primarily Second Wave[33] military forces, will try to leverage the terrain to make up for their training and technological disadvantages. In Northeast Asia today, the U.S. Army is deployed in a near wartime footing,[34] facing a dangerous, unpredictable, and implacable foe whose economy and political stability is crumbling, a foe that also has a large conventional military force, an offensive arsenal of chemical weapons, and, very probably, rudimentary nuclear

245

weapons. The North Korean situation, therefore, is volatile, one that will end in the next few years in either "explosion or implosion."[35] In 1951 Gen. Matthew B. Ridgway, the commander of the Eighth Army during the battles of Chipyong-ni and Heartbreak Ridge, understood the problems of maneuver in restricted terrain. He admitted that had it not been for "our massive firepower, our constant close air support and our tight control of the seas, China might have overwhelmed us. It was our guns—our ability to concentrate untold amounts of hot steel at any point along the battle line—that gave us superiority."[36] But he also admitted that, with experience and training, his units had learned to use the terrain to their advantage—obviously with Task Force Crombez and Operation Touchdown in mind. These battles vividly illustrate how maneuver in restricted terrain was decisive during the Korean War (1950–53). Superb combined-arms leaders demonstrated that "on numerous occasions they could operate effectively in terrain that doctrinally was considered completely unsuitable for tanks."[37]

The battle that you have just experienced in this tactical decision game was similar to the situations at Chipyong-ni in February 1951 and Heartbreak Ridge in October 1951.

Notes

1. Col. John Frederick Charles Fuller, *Memoirs of an Unconventional Soldier* (London: Ivor Nicholson and Watson, Ltd., 1936), pp. 323–24.

2. The French General staff strongly believed that massed firepower was the answer. They, and their British counterparts, opposed Fuller's plans to mechanize. Their argument was vividly expressed in the aphorism "Artillery conquers, infantry occupies."

3. Department of the Army, "FM 34-130 Intelligence Preparation of the Battlefield" (Washington, D.C.: U.S. Army, November 1993), pp. 2–15. Restricted terrain is defined as "terrain that hinders movement to some degree. Little effort is needed to enhance mobility but units may have difficulty maintaining preferred speeds, moving in combat formations, or transitioning from one formation to another. Restricted terrain slows movement by requiring zigzagging or frequent detours. Restricted terrain for armored and mechanized forces typically consists of moderate to steep slopes or moderate to

densely spaced obstacles such as trees, rocks, or buildings. . . . Severely restricted terrain hinders or slows movement in combat formations unless some effort is made to enhance mobility. This could take the form of committing engineer assets to improving mobility or of deviating from doctrinal tactics, such as moving in columns instead of line formations or at speeds much lower than those preferred."

4. Mary Lee Stubbs and Stanley Russell Connor, *Armor-Cavalry Part II: Army National Guard* (Washington, D.C.: Office of the Chief of Military History, U.S. Army, 1972), p. 77. "Although the rugged terrain in Korea had been considered generally unsuitable for tank employment, Russian-made T-34s were used with success by the North Koreans during the early days of the war. American tanks were rushed to the scene in support of the United Nations and engaged in their first combat on 10 July. For several weeks they were outnumbered, and it was not until late August that the tank balance in Korea was tipped in favor of the United Nations. By then more than 500 U.S. tanks were in the Pusan Perimeter, outnumbering the enemy's there by over five to one. For the remainder of the war, tank units of battalion size and smaller were in most combat actions."

5. The U.S. Army is the undisputed master of combat in open terrain and trains, almost exclusively, for combat in open terrain.

6. Fuller, *Memoirs of an Unconventional Soldier,* p. 325. It is interesting to note that few armies in history have been tasked to deliver victory *and* minimal casualties as a method of war. Although minimal casualties have been the goal of every enlightened commander, casualties have now become a defining factor in the American way of war. The requirements of this demand are exacting when opposed by an enemy that will not surrender. It is, therefore, required that the tactics of fighting in the restricted terrain of Korea be studied and perfected.

7. METT-T is a common U.S. Army acronym that stands for mission, enemy, terrain, troops, time available. It is a method to help commanders analyze tactical situations.

8. T. R. Fehrenbach, *This Kind of War: A Study in Unpreparedness* (New York: Macmillan Company, 1963), p. 158.

9. Russell A. Gugeler, *Combat Actions in Korea* (Washington D.C.: Office of the Chief of Military History, U.S. Army, 1970), p. 104.

10. Gugeler, p. 101.

11. Lt. Col. Roy E. Appleman (USA ret.), *East of Chosin: Entrapment and Breakout in Korea, 1950* (College Station: Texas A & M University Press, 1987), p. 67.

12. Gugeler, p. 104.

13. Headquarters, 23d Infantry Regiment, 2d infantry Division, "Command Report from 1 February 1951 to 28 February 1951, signed by LTC John H. Chiles" (Department of the Army, Adjutant General's Office, 21 February 1952, declassified 28 September 1970), p. 10.

14. Col. Paul Freeman, *Wonju through Chipyong: An Epic of Regimental Combat Team Action in Korea* (found in the U.S. Forces Korea/Eighth U.S. Army Staff Ride Read-ahead Packet: "Battle of Chipyong-ni 13–15 February 1951," edited by Thomas M. Ryan, 30 August 1992), p. 477.

15. Fehrenbach, p. 392.

16. Chinese Communist forces, Headquarters XIX Army Group, "A Collection of Combat Experiences" (29 March 1951 Critique of Tactics Employed in the First Encounter with the Enemy at Chipyong-ni, Annex Number 1 to Periodic Intelligence Report Number 271, 2d Infantry Division, translated by ATIS, 29 June 1951), p. 1.

17. Gugeler, p. 115.

18. Fehrenbach, p. 394.

19. Chinese Communist forces, Headquarters XIX Army Group, "A Collection of Combat Experiences" (29 March 1951Critique of Tactics Employed in the First Encounter with the Enemy at Chipyong-ni, Annex Number 1 to Periodic Intelligence Report Number 271, 2d Infantry Division, translated by ATIS, 29 June 1951), p. 2.

20. Capt. Donald T. Murphy, "Allied Cooperation in a Combined Arms Battle: The French Battalion at Chipyong-ni, Korea, February 1951" (Fort Leavenworth: Command and General Staff College, MMAS thesis, 1976), p. 7.

21. Edwin P. Hoyt, *The Bloody Road to Panmunjom* (New York: Stein and Day, 1984), p. 181.

22. Gugeler, p. 134. "Hindsight clearly indicates in this instance

[that] not one soldier should have ridden on top of the tanks. Friendly artillery and the tanks with their own machine guns could have provided adequate close-in protection for the armored column. No engineers were necessary to remove mines."

23. Chinese Communist forces, Headquarters XIX Army Group, "A Collection of Combat Experiences" (29 March 1951Critique of Tactics Employed in the First Encounter with the Enemy at Chipyong-ni, Annex Number 1 to Periodic Intelligence Report Number 271, 2d Infantry Division, translated by ATIS, 29 June 1951), pp. 2–4.

24. Billy C. Mossman, *Ebb and Flow, November 1950–July 1951* (Washington D.C.: Center of Military History, 1992), p. 300.

25. Fehrenbach, p. 396.

26. Fehrenbach, p. 521.

27. The tank battalions in Korea consisted of the 6th, 70th, 72d, and 89th. Each battalion averaged sixty-nine tanks. The 6th was equipped with M46 Pattons; the other battalions were about equally divided between M26 Pershings and M4A3 Shermans. The 72d was equipped with the M4 Sherman, many of which were retrieved from Pacific War battlefields. In spite of this, it was no secret that the tankers preferred the reliable M4A3 Sherman to the M26 Pershing.The tankers called the M4A3E8 "easy eights." The name was derived from the nomenclature of the E8 designation. The "easy eights" were sturdy, good on fuel consumption, mechanically dependable, and highly maneuverable. The wide tracks allowed the tank to move through most rice paddies without problems. These Sherman tanks were armed with a 76mm cannon, a .50-caliber M2HB Browning machine gun forward of the turret for the tank commander, a .30-caliber Browning bow machine gun in the front of the tank, and a .30-caliber machine gun mounted coaxially with the 76mm cannon. A Sherman had a crew of five men.

28. Hoyt, pp. 188, 298–99: "The trouble, the ground marines complained, was that the marine air wings were just too good. The U.S. Army and the British Commonwealth commanders had all requested marine air when it came to close air support, because they saw how effective it was" (p. 188). "The coordination of air force and army units in the field never achieved anything like the effectiveness of the marine air and ground units. Later in the campaign, when air

support was vital, the army units showed a marked preference for marine air" (pp. 298–99).

29. Edward N. Luttwak, *Strategy: The Logic of War and Peace* (Harvard: Belknap Press, 1987), p. 16.

30. Carl von Clausewitz, *On War,* ed. and trans. by Michael Howard and Peter Paret. (Princeton: Princeton University Press, 1976), p. 619. Clausewitz determined that the first task in planning for a war is to "identify the enemy's centers of gravity, and if possible trace them back to a single one. The second task is to ensure that the forces to be used against that point are concentrated for a main offensive."

31. Department of the Army, "FM 17-32 Tank Platoon and Tank Company" (Washington D.C.: U.S. Government Printing Office, 8 October 1952), pp. 2–3.

32. The only U.S. Army field manual that explains how to fight in mountains is FM 90-6, published in June 1980.

33. The concepts of Alvin and Heide Toffler, as found in their book *War and Anti-War.* The First Wave, which occurred during the agricultural revolution, was characterized by hand-to-hand combat; the Second Wave, which occurred during the industrial revolution, was represented by wars of mass destruction, such as World Wars I and II; the Third Wave, the ongoing information revolution, is knowledge-based warfare as evidenced in Operation Desert Storm.

34. The 2d Infantry Division in Korea remains the only U.S. Army division with an alert status measured in a few hours and has all of its tanks, Bradleys, and howitzers uploaded with live, "go to war" ammunition at all times.

35. Comments made by Gen. Gary Luck, commander in chief, U.S. Forces Korea, at Camp Red Cloud on 3 July 1996.

36. Gen. Matthew B. Ridgway, *The Korean War* (Garden City, N.Y.: Doubleday & Company, 1967), p. 195.

37. David A. Niedringhaus, "U.S. Army Armor in Limited War: Armor Employment Techniques in Korea and Vietnam," Master's Degree thesis: Ohio State University, 1987, p. 27.

Section 78

Sergeant Scott's tank inched forward across the southern concrete section of the bridge. The concrete shuddered as the tank slowly shifted onto the metal heavy assault bridge, which groaned like a wounded animal under the weight. The tank surged forward, clearing the bridge and making the north side of the Gang River. Then, in a shower of dust and broken concrete, the southern edge of the bridge collapsed, sliding down the steep slope to the river, thirty feet below. The metal bridge followed the concrete into the flowing water.

Casey stood on the north bank as he watched the calamity. The heavy assault bridge was a total loss. They would never recover it. Now, there was no way to cross the Gang. He had two tanks, three Bradleys, the BSFV, and Keeley's FIST-V on the north bank, with no way to get anything else across. With the southern section of the bridge washed out, the gap was almost seventy feet long. The remaining heavy assault bridge could not span that long a gap. His force on the north bank was stranded.

Lieutenant Stonevitch stood on the south bank. He looked across the gap at Casey and shouted, "What now, sir?"

"We're already committed," Casey yelled back with fire in his voice. "I'll fight my way through with what I have here. You defend there for the time being. Contact Major Cutter and tell him what I plan to do."

"Wilco," Stonevitch answered. "Good luck!"

Casey turned, ran back to *Cossack*, and climbed into the turret. He issued quick instructions to his small group. Casey and Scott would move forward on-line with Scott to Casey's right. McDaniel's 3d Platoon would follow on Casey's left rear. Keeley and Sellers would follow Scott. This echelon arrangement would be the battering ram that would force its way into Objective Dragon.

Casey looked at his watch. It was already 0800. He still had a full day of fighting ahead of him. He contacted the commander of the 1-12th on their battalion radio frequency. He was told that Captain Gabriel was wounded. A captain named Broughton, now in command, explained that the battalion was down to less than a hundred men. Although they still had small-arms and machine-gun ammunition, the defenders were down to their last three Javelin antitank missiles.

"I've got sergeants commanding companies and wounded all over the place," explained Broughton. "When will you get here?"

"In about fifteen minutes," Casey replied.

"We see some T-62s to our south, on Highway Seventeen," Broughton said, "so watch out for them. We'll hold our fire as you turn the bend onto the highway."

"Roger, hang tough. We're on our way," Casey promised.

Casey's small force moved forward. Keeley shifted the artillery to fire high explosive and variable time shells ahead of the column's advance, as he had along the defile in Cobra. Communications with battalion and the artillery FDC grew intermittent. The high mountains surrounding Objective Dragon interrupted the direct line of sight of the FM signal.

Scott's M1A2 led, followed by *Cossack*, Sellers's Bradleys, and Keeley's FIST-V. The column picked up speed and charged to the northeast as fast as they could drive. Casey cleared a small ridge and couldn't believe his eyes. More enemy infantry than he had ever seen were massed at CS223460. Casey quickly realized that he had run into an entire enemy infantry regiment. The enemy appeared to be massing for a final assault on Objective Dragon. Casey was going too fast to stop. The only way was forward. His strength lay in surprise, mobility, and firepower. With machine guns and the force of their tracks, Team Steel attacked with a vengeance.

Caught with their pants down, the enemy in the assembly area stirred like a rattled hornets' nest.

Casey immediately spotted five T-62s near Highway 17, surrounded by a mass of infantry. The enemy tanks faced north and were lined up to fire shells at Dragon. Casey and Scott charged right toward the tanks, cutting a swath through the helpless infantry. Enemy troops scattered as *Cossack* and Scott's tank fired on the move.

The T-62s reacted, but they never stood a chance. In rapid succession Casey and Scott destroyed the enemy tanks with five well-placed SABOT rounds. In seconds the tanks were flaming wrecks.

The huge tactical advantage of surprise worked to Casey's advantage. The dazed enemy infantrymen staggered into the swath of the advancing American fire. Stunned by the sudden appearance of the Americans, the enemy could neither run nor hide.

Cossack rolled on at high speed. The two M1A2s surged forward, protecting the boxy FIST-V and the M2 Bradleys that followed close behind their bigger brothers. The Bradleys fired their 25mm cannons, knocking down any sign of resistance. The enemy, unable to react to the attackers until they were face to face with the snarling death machines, melted away.

Cossack and Scott's tank blasted both sides of the roads, knocking down anyone who rose above ground level. Two more T-62 tanks, which were refueling next to a large fuel truck, burst into flames as Graham rapidly picked them off. The exploding fuel truck burst in a huge mushroom cloud and created an inferno of liquid fire that squirted in a wide circle around the site, catching hapless foot soldiers on fire.

Black smoke covered the battle area. A VTT-323 APC and a BTR—a Russian-made six-wheeled armored personnel carrier—suddenly plunged through the smoke and were just as quickly destroyed by Scott's tank. By the time *Cossack* reached the point of the short skirmish, the burning hulls of the shattered APC and BTR lined the road. Casey glanced at the burning BTR through the slit in his tank commander's hatch. The remains of the crew of the burning vehicle were clearly visible, each slumped in his position like the charred wick of a candle.

The VTT partially blocked the road. *Cossack* unceremoniously smashed into the wreck's side, pushed it out of the way, and continued northeast. The smoldering VTT burst into flames and shot burning fuel in all directions.

"Steel Six, White One. I see hot spots all over the place!"

Casey saw the hot spots that Scott reported; they were the burning T-62 tanks, a few scattered APCs, trucks, and hundreds of enemy soldiers. Casey realized that he was in what his officers' course at Fort Knox would consider a "target-rich environment."

"White One, cut your way through. Keep moving! Get to Dragon!"

The American armored vehicles fired on the move, launching a blast of fire to both sides of their column. The firing increased as the enemy turned to stop the Americans. Enemy machine guns and RPG rounds flew wildly at Team Steel, but a moving tank or Bradley is hard to hit when you are ducking machine-gun fire. The enemy rounds missed, detonating harmlessly to both sides of the fast-moving column.

Suddenly Casey saw three enemy soldiers dart into the road. The men fired an RPG at the rear of Scott's tank. The grenade exploded in a burst of sparks but missed its mark.

"Identified! On the way!" Graham screamed over the intercom as he quickly laid the gun to the right front. The enemy antitank team bravely tried to reload. Graham was faster. The gunner's 7.62mm machine gun rapidly cut them down. The RPG team crumpled to the side of the road as if crushed by an invisible hand.

"Graham, there's a tank to our right!" Weaver shouted over the intercom. "It just drove up to the road. Right front!"

Casey shot a glance to the right and saw a T-62 lumbering through the black smoke of a burning VTT. The T-62 jerked to a halt to fire. Casey heard Kriel cry, "Up!"

Casey swiftly grabbed the TC's override controls and turned the turret to the right, like a gunfighter in a western movie getting a bead on the bad guy. In less than three seconds, Casey lay the cannon on the target and fired.

"Target!" Graham screamed. "You blew the fucker's turret right off."

Cossack raced past the flaming T-62.

Bullets flew everywhere as the enemy infantry reacted to the tanks. McDaniel's 25mm cannons plastered the enemy infantry. Hundreds of soldiers ran for cover to escape the Bradley's rapidly firing guns. McDaniel's Bradleys dashed right behind the command group, blasting the enemy infantry with fire as the column raced by.

"Graham, get the infantry," Casey ordered, swinging the turret to the left. Graham caught a mass of enemy stragglers running north on the far paddy dike. Graham and the Bradleys dropped dozens of terrified enemy soldiers as they frantically tried to flee.

The enemy couldn't get away from Casey's guns. Unable to flee, the enemy turned on their attackers in a last-ditch, futile counterattack. *Cossack*'s 120mm gun roared. Machine guns chattered and chewed up the rice paddies in spires of muddy water. The accurate fire staggered and stopped the enemy's forlorn attack. Enemy soldiers, desperate to survive, fled like quail in all directions. Casey's vehicles were now perpendicular to the enemy's route of escape; the tanks cut down the enemy like a scythe. The enemy dropped into the muck of the rice paddies, never to get back up.

In the wake of this destruction, Casey's force reached Highway 17. *Cossack* then rolled into Objective Dragon and slowly moved to a berm that offered protection and an excellent firing platform from which to shoot to the east. Casey deployed Scott's tank in the north and the Bradleys in the south. Keeley's FIST-V and Sellers's BSFV moved next to *Cossack*.

The survivors of the 1-12th Infantry cheered when they saw the column move into Dragon, thinking that they had been saved.

Within the relative safety of the 1-12th's defensive position, Casey opened his hatch and surveyed the scene. The infantry occupied an old bunker complex designed as a firing position for an allied artillery battalion. These bunkers had saved the 1-12th and permitted their staunch defense. The defense, however, had been costly. The dug-in positions that marked the American defensive perimeter bore grim testimony to the fierceness of the struggle. Charred holes outlined the scene of the most vicious fighting.

Casey immediately tried to report his linkup with the infantry to Major Cutter. In spite of his long whip antennas, however, neither Casey nor Keeley could reach the artillery FDC, Lieutenant Stonevitch, or Major Cutter. Something must have happened to the battalion and brigade radio retrans sites, Casey concluded. With the bridge down and radio communications inoperable, Casey was truly on his own.

Section 78

Someday, he thought, our radios will point up to satellites rather than the present method of sending FM radio signals across the rugged terrain, trying to bend the waves around tall mountains to gain line of sight. He shook off the idea; his problem was here and now.

"Steel Six, this is Bayonet Four. Man, are we glad to see you!"

"Roger, Bayonet Four," Casey radioed. "It took quite a lot to get here. What's your situation?"

"We've been sniped at all night. Took heavy casualties yesterday. Repulsed two attacks this morning. The enemy's stopped hitting us with just infantry. Now he's moving up tanks and more artillery. I've got about eighty effectives and more than a hundred wounded. When does the rest of your force arrive?"

"This is it, Bayonet Four. The bridge on Highway Seventeen collapsed. We're all there is until tomorrow morning."

There was a long silence on the radio. Suddenly an explosion blasted about eighty meters to *Cossack*'s left flank. Enemy mortar rounds began falling nearby, billowing in geysers of dust and smoke. Soon heavy artillery shells smashed into the American perimeter, adding to the fury of the mortar bombs, as if in angry response to the surprise American attack on the southern edge of Objective Dragon. Hundreds of shells blanketed the defenders. High-explosive 152mm shells pulverized the hill into a cloud of dust and debris. The pounding was horrific. The barren ridge took each hammer blow in silence. As the storm of steel burst overhead, the American infantrymen hugged the bottom of their bunkers.

The pounding continued for ten minutes, then suddenly stopped. The quiet echoed in Casey's soul as intensely as the explosions that had resonated in the valley only moments before. Suddenly Casey realized how tired he was. The need for sleep—just fifteen minutes of rest would do—beckoned him like a siren's call. His eyes blinked, his mind wandered off to unconsciousness; then fear jolted him back to reality. The enemy was out there, hoping to kill him and his men. Casey waited in *Cossack*'s turret, searching through the narrow vision blocks of the commander's weapon station, and prayed for a miracle.

Graham quickly scanned the northeastern ridge with his thermal sight and reported no movement. It appeared that the latest enemy infantry attack had been crushed, but he knew it wouldn't be the last attempt to annihilate the Americans.

Things were happening too fast, Casey thought. We're slaughtering the enemy, but we can't keep this up for much longer. We're reacting to their moves. They retain the initiative.

Casey checked his IVIS screen and read the latest ammunition report. Sergeant Sellers's Bradley was out of 25mm. The three remaining tanks were almost out of machine-gun ammunition. Casey knew how critical his machine guns were to fighting enemy infantry in restricted, mountainous terrain.

Casey popped his hatch to survey the battlefield. The few remaining survivors of the 1-12th, about seventy men, quickly crawled out of their bunkers and reoccupied their fighting positions. Soldiers moved wounded men quickly inside the bunkers, which were now crammed with casualties.

Casey's stomach tightened as he watched a soldier drag a dead comrade into a bunker. The infantry had fought hard. They deserved better than to be left here. How much longer can we hold out, Casey wondered. I've got to do something!

Casey looked to the east and, just by chance, saw a green signal flare shoot high over the slope of the hill behind him. The enemy must be organizing another attack, Casey thought; it was just a matter of the enemy coming in for the final kill.

Anxiety seemed to hover over the battlefield as Casey thought of survival and played out each possible scenario of life, death, capture, or injury in his mind. He knew that he was fighting now out of simple, naked fear.

Casey kept watch to the northeast. After a few seconds the ground rumbled with the approach of enemy tanks. Casey listened to the growing tumult of their approach. This is it, he thought, our last stand. A thought flashed through his mind; he didn't want to die so far from home. He smiled suddenly, embarrassed by the thought. It seemed silly to worry about where you died. More important, however, was the strong desire not to let his soldiers down. He steeled his soul, realizing that he must remain strong and focused to lead. He resigned himself that if he must die, he would die fighting.

"Identified T-72s!" Graham shouted, riveting the commander's attention back to the threat at hand.

"Here they come again," Casey announced over the radio. He quickly turned to the northwest. He saw the squat, ugly T-72s as they maneuvered into view, in paradelike fashion, moving from column to platoon line formation. There were about ten T-72s moving toward them—at least a company, with more probably on the way.

"Steel elements. Depth. I'll take the near targets," Casey ordered over the radio. "Wait until they turn onto the highway."

"Roger," Scott's voice answered.

"Wilco," replied Scott's wingman.

Machine guns opened up from the surrounding hills. Enemy mortar fire slammed into the defenders' positions. A volley of antitank missiles arced toward the American lines as the enemy supported the tanks in an all-arms assault.

"Tanks, nine hundred meters and closing," Graham announced. "The lead platoon has turned the bend and is in the open."

"I see 'em," Casey replied with a voice so calm that it surprised him. "Steady. Wait for my command."

The lead enemy tank platoon opened fire while they moved. Their volley of 125mm shells smashed into the American defenses, sending up big spires of dirt and rocks.

Casey could sense his heart beating fast in his chest. He strained to see the enemy through his sights.

A second enemy tank platoon entered within range, then a third. An entire enemy tank company was packed into Casey's field of vision.

"Fire!" Casey commanded over the radio.

"On the way!" Graham yelled on the intercom.

The tank jerked from the gun's recoil. The round screamed forward, hitting the leftmost enemy tank in the front at the driver's compartment, stopping it in its tracks. The force from the strike tore apart the lead T-72. Undaunted, the nine remaining T-72s now raced toward Casey's position, moving fast.

"Target. Right tank," Casey yelled.

Casey heard the sound of tank fire to his left. Looking through his vision blocks he saw Sergeant Scott's tank, blasting away at the enemy tank formation.

Graham's round hit another T-72, sending another turret sky-ward. Casey saw the T-72's turret fly into the air. The Russian-designed T-72 tank has a three-man crew. Loading is accomplished by the tank's automatic loading system. The automatic loader, how-ever, was not much of an advantage. The T-72 tank carries its 125mm ammunition in an open carousel around the turret ring to facilitate this loading system. If the tank's turret armor is penetrated, the combustible-cased ammunition usually explodes, blowing the turret into the heavens and disintegrating the gunner and tank com-mander in an agonizing, instantaneous flash of molten steel. Not a very pleasant way to go.

With his heart pounding, Casey watched the SABOT rounds tear through the enemy tanks, clanging against their special reactive ar-mor in a dazzling shower of bright sparks. Mushroom-shaped black clouds lifted skyward from the burning turretless hulls as the M1A2s did their deadly work.

Casey surveyed the attack. The enemy seemed to be ignoring his losses. The T-72s fired as they moved and maintained a steady ad-vance to overrun the defenders. VTTs followed behind the tanks. Dis-mounted infantry ran behind the VTTs. Apparently, Casey guessed, the enemy is making an all-out assault to crush us.

The tension inside *Cossack*'s turret mounted as the endless array of targets got closer and closer. Casey's crew fought like men pos-sessed. Graham locked onto each target and fired the main gun as soon as he heard an "Up!" from Kriel. Kriel loaded the heavy 120mm tank rounds with lightning speed. The turret floor filled with the steel 120mm stubs ejected by *Cossack*'s cannon.

The battle reached a crescendo as the savage explosions of rifle, rocket, gun, mortar, and artillery devastated the cramped battlefield. An American Javelin antitank missile fired and smashed into the top of the turret of a T-72. Three enemy tanks moved around the de-stroyed hulk of their comrade and angrily blasted away at the Amer-ican infantry bunker that had fired the missile. The three enemy tanks volley-fired at almost the same time. The bunker disappeared in the force of the explosions.

The fire from portions of the American line ceased as the de-fenders ran out of ammunition. Several Americans stood up and put their hands in the air. It was a futile gesture. A platoon of T-72s closed on the position and gunned them down. Casey's jaw tightened as he saw the slaughter. There would be no quarter in this fight, he thought.

"Three tanks, left tank!" Casey ordered as he aimed the gun toward the enemy tanks to the northeast.

The hypervelocity round smashed the left T-72, hurling its mangled turret six feet into the air. Graham fired again. Another T-72 crumpled to a burning, fiery halt.

"On the way!" Graham fired and smashed the third T-72.

"Target, target, target," Casey yelled. "Weaver, back up!"

Weaver raced the M1 engine and lurched the big tank back thirty feet. Casey looked to his left and saw Scott's tank smoldering from a direct hit from an enemy tank gun. The enemy had hit Scott's tank in the right front of the turret, directly behind the tank commander's and gunner's station. Scott's tank cannon dropped to the ground. *Cossack* was the last remaining American tank.

"Damnit!" Casey cried out loud, overcome with anger. "Weaver, move forward. Let's get those sons of bitches. Graham, action, right front."

Cossack popped back up to the small ridge.

Graham immediately fired as the cannon cleared the ridge. There were plenty of targets to shoot at. Graham hit a tank, then turned the turret quickly to fire at a VTT.

Casey, looking to his left, saw a more dangerous target. An enemy tank platoon had maneuvered to his far left. They had obviously been the tanks that had hit Scott. Flashes of red and yellow light burst against the hard armor of the lead enemy tank as an American machine gun tried in vain to stop the tank's advance. The T-72's turret turned toward *Cossack*. Taking control of the gun, Casey swung the turret hard to the left.

Roll the dice.

If you roll 2-8, go to Section 34.

If roll 9-12, go to Section 53.

Section 79

Casey suddenly knew that it was his curse to see things clearly that had not yet happened. Somehow, in an instant, he knew. Like Cassandra who foretold the destruction of Troy, Casey looked up at the flares and saw his end before it happened.

As Casey struggled with the heavy hatch of his commander's weapon station, a 152mm artillery shell detonated directly above *Cossack*. The shell exploded twenty feet off the ground in a fierce airburst of orange and red flames. Dozens of hot, burning metal fragments pelted the top of the M1A2 tank, striking the tank commander with terrible force.

Casey was smashed by shell fragments before he could close the hatch. The screaming metal tore into his Kevlar CVC helmet and ripped into the back of his neck, severing his head from his shoulders. He died before his senses could really register the pain.

Go back to Section 8 and make a different decision.

Section 80

Rifle fire banged against the FIST-V's side. Keeley's lightly armored APC sat only a few meters away from *Cossack*. Moving like a boxer in a ring, Lieutenant Keeley quickly delivered a knockout blow to the RPG team with a long burst of 5.56mm bullets from his M-16. The enemy soldier with the RPG on his shoulder crumpled to the ground before he could launch his rocket.

"Action rear!" Casey screamed as he grabbed the tank commander's override control. In one quick jerk he slewed the turret to the right rear.

Weaver revved *Cossack*'s engine. Casey laid the turret in the direction of the enemy as Weaver accelerated the right track and neutral-steered the tank around.

"Fire and adjust," Casey shouted into the intercom as he forced the machine-gun bolt of his .50 caliber to the rear.

Flares popped overhead as the enemy used hand-fired flares and mortar illumination to light up the battle area. Bullets ricocheted off the right side of the tank. The small-arms fire made a dull, whacking sound as the lead splashed against *Cossack*'s turret in a shower of sparks.

It'll take more than rifles and machine guns to stop us, Casey thought. Weaver threw the seventy-ton beast into gear. *Cossack* darted forward. Within seconds Casey's .50-caliber machine gun was rattling loud, long bursts of fire to the south. Casey stood with his head outside the turret to see his attackers on the ridge to his right and rear. Hot .50-caliber brass casings fell inside the turret as Casey swung back and forth wildly in his tank commander's weapon station. Perspiration streamed down his face.

"RPG team, direct front!" Private Weaver yelled over the tank intercom.

Graham swung the turret forward and quickly fired a searing burst of 7.62mm machine-gun ammunition into the RPG team. The RPG gunner and his ammo bearer ducked to the ground. *Cossack* jerked forward, racing out of the ambush area, crushing the RPG team in its heavy metal tracks. The FIST-V, with Lieutenant Keeley in the back emptying his M-16 at the enemy, followed close behind.

"Steel Guns, Red elements, move now, three hundred meters north!"

A dozen more attackers rushed out of the darkness toward the moving tank. Casey could barely believe what was happening. The enemy was willing to sacrifice several companies of riflemen to stop his tanks. Without mercy Casey swung to the right and blasted them. At the same time, Graham swung the turret to the left and fired the co-ax. The movement of the turret made Casey's shots wild, but enough lead sprayed the area to worry the enemy. Tracers lit up the night, bouncing off the moving tank's sides and ricocheting in all directions. Graham's machine gun ripped into the attackers, forcing them to the ground and leaving a trail of dead in *Cossack*'s wake.

Suddenly the steady hammer of the .50 caliber stopped. Casey quickly realized that he was out of ammunition. Graham kept firing the cannon, swinging the turret right and left to the rear. The captain ducked down into the turret and reached for another box of .50-caliber machine-gun ammunition in the vertical tray near his feet.

Roll the dice.

If you roll 2-7, go to Section 83.

If you roll 8-12, go to Section 84.

Section 81

> *The more mechanized become the weapons, the less mechanized must be the spirit which controls them. It is the soldier's spirit which determines success on the battlefield.*
>
> —J. F. C. Fuller

Cossack charged to the berm. Two T-72s anticipated Casey's move and fired their special 125mm rounds into *Cossack*, hitting the M1A2 in a fiery clang of metal against metal.

One 125mm round hit the turret but glanced off the M1A2's superb turret armor. The second supervelocity round was a lucky shot. It tore through the top of the tank commander's station and spilled hot lead and flame into the TC's hatch. Casey had nowhere to turn and no time to act. The superheated metal disintegrated his head and shoulders. He died instantly in the tank commander's seat.

You have died in action.
Go back to Section 59 and try again.

Section 82

> *An important difference between the military operation and a surgical operation is that the patient is not tied down. But it is the common fault of generalship to assume that he is.*
>
> —B. H. Liddell Hart

In a fast move, Casey pulled his 9mm pistol from his shoulder holster and fired two shots. The 9mm slugs hit the RPG gunner in the shoulder. The man crumpled to the ground as if an unseen hand had hammered him with a baseball bat.

Kriel heard the pistol shots and opened his hatch. "Sir?"

Casey pointed to the dead man lying in the road just south of the bridge. The black figure twitched on the ground, then lay still. The grenade launcher, loaded and cocked, lay at the enemy soldier's side.

"Man the loader's machine gun," Casey ordered calmly. "We don't want any more surprises."

Kriel nodded and swung the 7.62mm machine gun to the side of the tank.

In the meantime the Wolverine heavy assault bridge was hard at work. Jacobs quickly laid the bridge and moved the Wolverine launch vehicle to the side. Casey rolled *Cossack* across first. Sergeant Sellers's Bradley and Lieutenant Andrews's 1st Platoon followed. Casey patiently waited on the north side of the Gang River as the tanks of 1st Platoon and the Bradleys of 3d Platoon assembled to continue the attack to the northwest to link up with the 1-12th Infantry.

"Steel Six, this is Steel Five," Stonevitch announced over the radio. "I've got the fuel HEMMT and the APCs with the fuel bladders. Do you want to refuel here?"

Casey realized that he was in a vulnerable spot, but he also realized that he might not get a chance to refuel on Objective Dragon. Time, however, was equally critical. "Negative. Give the tanks on the south side a quick shot of fuel, then send the HEMMT to me. Tanks get priority. We'll wait until the rest of the force gets over here, but make it as fast as you can."

"Wilco," Stonevitch answered.

Casey waited in the open hatch of his tank as the time ticked away. He grew more apprehensive as each minute passed. After fifteen minutes 2d Platoon completed refueling. Stonevitch sent 4th Platoon's Bradleys across the bridge.

Roll the dice.

If you roll 2-7, go to Section 35.

If you roll 8-12, go to Section 60.

Section 83

The first law of war is to preserve ourselves and destroy the enemy.
—Mao Tse-tung

Casey's soul was in a rage but his mind was in focus. He knew that his survival in battle in restricted terrain depended upon uninterrupted movement and firepower. He shouldn't have waited in one place so long.

Wars are often lost by waiting, he thought. It's better to force the fight before the cycle swings against you.

Still, he had been lucky.

In a few seconds they were out of range of the enemy infantry. Casey looked behind him and saw the FIST-V and only one of the M1A2s following him. The other tank was still in its original halt position, its tracks destroyed by RPG rounds and enemy infantry swarming all over. An explosion erupted from the stationary M1 as an enemy rocket found its mark.

Graham swung the turret to the south and aimed raking fire on the dying tank. Shadows all around the burning vehicle slumped to the ground.

Casey keyed his radio. "Steel Guns, get artillery fire on our old position ASAP. Take out that infantry! Red elements, keep moving south."

Casey looked back through the thinning smoke and strained to see his surrounded tank through his binoculars. He saw flames shooting up from the open turret hatches of the stricken M1. He closed his eyes in anguish. He had lost another tank and crew.

Graham continued to fire until he ran out of machine-gun ammunition. "Sir, we can't leave them there."

"We don't leave anyone," Casey replied in anger. "As soon as I get some fire on the enemy, we'll move back. Reload the machine gun. We're going to need it."

As if to answer his rage, artillery screeched overhead. A second later a volley of deadly 155mm shells fell on his old position. The variable time fuse shells burst all around the burning tank, showering the area with shell fragments. The artillery fire lasted for three minutes. The shells struck the area along the highway and on both flanks of the road. Finally, the bombardment stopped.

Cossack moved back to the burning tank with the two tanks from 1st Platoon. Several tankers from the platoon dismounted to check the crew of the damaged M1A2. Miraculously the driver was still alive.

The tankers counted at least sixty dead enemy soldiers scattered about the battle area.

Casey took little joy in the lopsided casualty figures. The enemy had plenty of replacements. Casey had only six operational tanks. The radio suddenly crackled to life. Casey slowly reached for his CVC helmet to receive the transmission.

"Steel Six, this is Steel Five. I've lost one Bradley, two APCs, and an ACE, but we broke contact and bypassed the enemy. We'll be at your location in a few minutes. One of the Wolverine assault bridges got shot but somehow got through without a scratch. I sent one APC back with the wounded. I see firing at your position. What's your situation?"

Casey took a deep breath. He couldn't think about casualties now. He had to focus on the mission. "We're on Cobra at CS217430. Just got attacked by dismounts. Shoot at anything that moves as you come forward. Look for our thermal panels so you don't shoot us up when you get here."

"Wilco. Steel Five. Out."

"Steel Six, this is Red One," Lieutenant Andrews's voice boomed over the radio. "I've short-tracked my tank and can move. I copied your location. My tank and the BSFV are headed there now."

"Good job. Get here as fast as you can," Casey replied, happy to hear some good news for a change. He glanced down at his IVIS screen and checked his combat power:

TM C Unit	M1A2 Tank	M2 IFV	BSFV [ADA]	FISTV	Engr M113	CEV	ACE	HAB Bridge	Medic M113	M88 [Rec]	FUEL HEMMT	M113 APCs
1 Plt	2											
2 Plt	4											
3 Plt		3										
4 Plt		2										
Engr Plt					4	1	0	2				
HQTnk	2		1	1								
Mech												1
1SG									2	1	1	1
M113s												10
Total	8	6	1	1	4	1	0	2	2	1	1	12

"All Steel units. Rally on my position. We'll continue the attack to the north, up Cobra," Casey ordered over the radio, trying to sound confident. He waited in apprehension until Lieutenant Andrews's tank and Sergeant Sellers's Bradley arrived. Finally the lead tank of Stonevitch's force, commanded by Sergeant First Class Scott, barreled down the road. Casey flagged it forward to take the lead.

Casey thought over his options. Time was running out; it was already 0430. He knew that his enemy was determined and smart. He knew that they would try to defend the defiles against an armored penetration by reinforcing their defense with the terrain. Keyhole positions—defensive positions that allow for single or multiple flank or rear shots at the enemy during limited windows of opportunity, without directly giving away the firing position—along the fingers of the defiles and valleys will anchor the defense. Casey knew that if the enemy was waiting in ambush along Cobra, it would be like firing at his lead tanks through a keyhole as his force passed down a narrow hallway. He needed to concentrate decisive combat power at the point of penetration to win the close-range direct firefight at the tip of the attack—the tip of the spear. To increase the density of force at the tip of the spear, he put Sergeant Scott's 2d Platoon, which was relatively fresh, in the lead.

Scott's first requirement was to use the mobility, protection, and overwhelming firepower of the M1A2 to burst through the enemy's defense. Scott's tanks would have the lead all the way to the objective. Casey knew that only tanks could provide the necessary devastating direct fire and employ mechanical breaching equipment, with his two mine plows, to punch through hasty obstacle belts.

"White One, you will lead the assault up Cobra once we get started."

"Wilco," Sergeant Scott's steady voice responded.

"Steel Guns, be prepared to fire the MLRS on the exit of Cobra at CS220443 on my command. Plan a series of 155mm targets to fire as we move up Cobra. I want the shells falling five hundred meters in front of the lead tank platoon and moving ahead of them along the route. If the enemy is waiting in ambush for us there, I want to smash them with artillery before we arrive."

"Roger, Steel Six," Lieutenant Keeley replied over the radio. "That'll be hard to do."

"Just follow them on the IVIS screen and send in the targets digitally," Casey answered like a teacher patiently assisting one of his star pupils in school. "You can handle it, White One. Move as soon as the rockets fire."

"Wilco, Steel Six. We're ready to move."

The minutes ticked by as Casey reorganized his company team for the attack. He chafed at the loss of precious time. Nothing happened fast on a dark night in the middle of a battle. He also knew that he couldn't afford any more mistakes. The attack up a defile cannot be a piecemeal assault. He ordered the infantry of both platoons to consolidate under Lieutenant McDaniel's command. Casey then quickly laid out a new plan of attack and sent a digital transmission to all his vehicles with his IVIS:

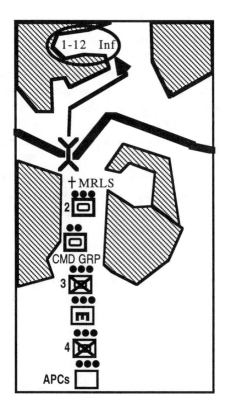

In twenty minutes everyone was ready to go. Casey ordered Lieutenant Keeley to fire the MLRS. Within a few more minutes the shrill scream of rockets raced overhead in the dark, cloudy sky.

A terrible rumble, followed by the brilliant flash of multiple explosions, lit up the northern horizon. Casey saw the flashes as the MLRS strike landed just south of the bridge on Cobra. The ground rumbled with the strike of the huge rockets. Each warhead carried hundreds of grenade-sized bomblets, enough to plaster an area the size of a football field with each strike. The MLRS was capable of providing a large volume of firepower in a short time and was devastating to lightly armored targets such as APCs and troops.

If Casey wanted to take advantage of the disruption caused by this fire strike, he needed to move fast. The radio crackled suddenly with a call from battalion. Casey reached for his CVC helmet to receive the transmission.

"Steel Six, this is Dragon Six," Major Cutter's voice sounded over Team Steel's command frequency. "Brigade and division are jamming every enemy radio frequency they can find. Our latest radio intercept picked up an enemy report to destroy the Highway Twenty-one bridge along the Gang. Your attack must have shaken them up. We don't know if the bridge is down yet or if the order was received. We only intercepted and tried to jam the order to destroy it. I've already received your latest combat power report. Do you still think you can make it?"

Casey's hopes sank lower. The Gang River was too deep and too wide to ford. What if the bridge was destroyed? A heavy assault bridge was capable of crossing a twenty-four-meter gap. The Gang River was almost fifty meters wide, according to the latest intelligence information. What if he couldn't get across the Gang?

Don't take counsel of your fears, Casey reminded himself. His jaw was tight. "Roger, Dragon Six. I'll find a way or make one. We've broken through the security zone positions along Cobra. I'm continuing the attack. Over."

"Roger. Nothing further. I'll see you tonight on Objective Dragon. Good luck! Dragon Six. Out."

Standing in the commander's weapon station, Casey watched the flashes on the northern horizon. Checking his watch he saw that it was already 0450. He noticed that the rain had stopped, and he felt the cold early-morning air slowly clear away the fog. The night was still as dark as tar to the naked eye, but Casey had clear vision through his thermal sights.

It would be daylight in less than an hour. Casey knew that he held the advantage in the dark. If he didn't secure the bridge before sunrise, he'd lose what little advantage and surprise he may have left.

"White One, move out. You must seize the bridge along Cobra at CS213447. Don't stop for anything."

"Wilco, Steel Six. Moving now."

The attack up the defile was on. Casey knew now that everything depended on the lead platoon. They had to find a way to cross that bridge!

"Weaver, move out. Follow 2d Platoon," Casey ordered, then pushed forward the radio switch on his CVC helmet. "Steel Guns, is the artillery ready?"

"Affirmative!" Lieutenant Keeley said exuberantly. "I'm following 2d Platoon on my IVIS. The rounds will land danger close in front of him and move up the highway. Tell him to keep buttoned up."

The 2d Platoon, with Scott's mine-plow tank in the lead, raced ahead. *Cossack* rattled forward, following the trail tank in Sergeant Scott's column. Lieutenant Keeley's FIST-V and Sergeant Sellers's Bradley followed close behind *Cossack*. The rest of Team Steel deployed in the prescribed order of march.

The artillery blasted Cobra to the north. Scott's tanks raced at twenty miles an hour along shell-marked Highway 21. Scott led in his plow tank in the right lane while the second tank, staggered thirty meters to his left, trailed in the left lane. Two more tanks followed the lead section in the same formation. Casey's command group followed in column—*Cossack*, the Bradley Stinger fighting vehicle, and the FIST-V—down the center of the road.

A bright flash suddenly brought the left lead tank to a halt. The M1A2 swung fiercely to the left, turning sideways in the highway as its left track rolled off its seven huge steel road wheels.

The right trail tank slammed on the brakes. The column stopped abruptly. Casey smashed against the .50-caliber machine gun.

"What the hell!" Casey cursed angrily as he scanned the road ahead. "Don't stop! White One, continue the attack! Weaver, pull around to the right."

Cossack quickly surged off to the right of the stopped 2d Platoon tank.

"Minefield!" came the agonized shout over the radio.

Roll the dice.

If you roll 2-7, go to Section 72.

If you roll 8-12, go to Section 109.

Section 84

> *In all battles, the percentage of human failure is far higher than history ever records.*
>
> —B. H. Liddell Hart

Before Casey could duck down for more ammunition, three enemy soldiers sprayed *Cossack*'s turret with small-arms fire. The bullets flew wild, but one struck the captain in the head and two more penetrated his shoulder. He fell inside the turret.

"Captain's down!" Kriel yelled.

Weaver jerked the tank forward. The last thing Casey heard before he died was the churning of the tank's tracks as Weaver ran over Casey's attackers.

You have been killed in action.
Go back to the last section where you could
make a decision and consider your options again.

> *War is mainly a catalogue of blunders.*
>
> —Winston Churchill

Section 85

There was a tremendous roar as an AT-4 missile hit Casey's tank. *Cossack* shuddered brutally from the blow but kept moving.

"Identified, AEE TEE," Graham screamed as he jerked the turret and laid the gun on a target at the western edge of the town.

"Up," Kriel yelled as he pushed the cannon's mechanical safety lever to the fire position.

Cossack surged forward at fifteen miles an hour across the bumpy gravel trail. Graham aimed the cannon. The M1A2's gun stabilization system steadied Graham's aim on the area of the enemy antitank missile launch as *Cossack* bolted ahead.

"Fire!" Casey screamed.

The high-explosive antitank round shot from the muzzle of *Cossack*'s cannon. The breech recoiled, opened, and shot the small metal base stub to the turret floor. Kriel immediately rammed another round into the opening. "Up!"

"Target!" Casey shouted over the intercom, his right eye glued to his CITV thermal sight. Casey pushed a button and sent a digital contact report over his IVIS system to the rest of the company. This report traveled automatically to every M1A2 in Team Steel and allowed other vehicle commanders to see the exact location of the enemy. "Scan! Do you see any more?"

The surreal, artificial light of flares and explosions lit the sky. *Cossack*'s hull faced northeast as it followed Coral; the turret was twisted due east toward Masan. The turret moved back and forth as Graham scanned for additional threat targets. *Cossack* pitched violently as it raced across the trail.

Kriel pushed the safety handle to fire and yelled, "Up!"

"Identified!" Graham shouted.

"Fire and adjust," Casey ordered, releasing the gunner to control the firing at his own pace.

Graham identified another target in Masan. *Cossack*'s cannon fired again. The gun leapt back in its carriage, depositing another aft cap onto the turret floor. Kriel executed his drill again, loading another HEAT round into the cannon.

Masan was receiving a healthy volume of fire. Casey shot a glance to his left front at the four tanks leading the way up the gravel road. All four tanks were firing on the move at the western edge of Masan. Behind him, Casey saw the pinpoint light of 25mm tracers as McDaniel's Bradleys sprayed the town with fire. There were brilliant explosions and the sparkle of armor-piercing machine-gun rounds as they smashed against metal and masonry.

The western edge of Masan burned fiercely, but the enemy wasn't through yet. An eruption of mortar flares in the sky over the area north of Masan told Casey that the enemy still wanted to stop Team Steel.

"Action right front! Missile launch!" Sergeant Scott screamed over the command frequency.

Weaver jerked the tank to the left.

Roll the dice.

If you roll 2-9, go to Section 29.

If you roll 10-12, go to Section 11.

Section 86

Find out where your enemy is. Get at him as soon as you can. Strike at him as hard as you can and as soon as you can, and keep moving on.

—Gen. U. S. Grant

Two blackened and busted hulls that were once VTT-323 armored personnel carriers smoldered near the entrance to the bridge. An MT-12 antitank cannon lay near one of the VTTs, smashed in half on its carriage. Six enemy soldiers lay in gruesome, contorted poses on the south side of the bridge, paying testimony to the skill of Sergeant Scott's machine guns. Unfortunately, Casey thought, Scott's tanks did not kill them all before the enemy detonated the center section of the bridge into shattered chunks of concrete.

Team Steel's long column of armored vehicles assembled in the open area south of the bridge. Each unit peeled off to designated sectors to form a portion of a perimeter to secure the south side. A few scattered rifle and machine-gun shots signified that some of the enemy had still not given up.

Casey stood in his turret, scanning the far side of the river with his binoculars. Private Kriel opened the loader's hatch and manned his 7.62mm machine gun.

Dawn was breaking. In the dim, early-morning light, Casey saw that the sides of the river were too steep to lay a bridge or ford. A winding footpath to the west of the bridge offered a means to get down to the south bank of the Gang.

"Graham, man the fifty," Casey ordered. "I'm going to look at the bridge."

Casey unhooked his CVC helmet, grabbed his chemical protective mask, and jumped out of the commander's weapon station. After quickly climbing down *Cossack*'s right front slope, he ran over to the demolished bridge.

The center bridge span lay in a pile of rubble in the fast-flowing Gang River. Rusty steel rods and cracked concrete protruded from the jagged edge of the northern section. The southern portion looked sturdy. The blast had destroyed only the center section.

Casey quickly scanned the north bank to the left and right of the bridge. As far as he could see, the north bank was a sheer six-foot wall of rock. Without an exit on the north bank, the option of swimming his Bradleys and APCs was out of the question. The bridge was the only way to cross the river.

Crom, Lieutenant Stonevitch's tank, rolled up next to *Cossack*. The thin executive officer crawled out of the turret and climbed down the tank.

"Any way we can ford?" Stonevitch yelled to his commander as he walked up to the edge of the bridge.

"No. There's no way to climb out of the river on the north side," Casey answered, the anger rising in his voice. "So damn close. The 1-12th is just over there."

Casey pointed to the hills to the northeast. The sound of exploding artillery shells echoed from the north. Casey knew that the 1-12th was catching hell. They wouldn't be able to hold out much longer.

"Sir, I've got a Captain Gabriel on our command frequency. He says that he's the commander of the 1-12th," Sergeant Graham shouted from *Cossack*'s turret. "He says come on, for God's sake. They can't hold out much longer."

Casey waved to Graham, noting to himself that a captain was now the commander of the 1-12th. Casey considered the options. If he could place one of the heavy assault bridges across the concrete bridge's missing span, he might be able to get across the Gang River and complete the mission. He didn't have time to try to backtrack and attempt to attack along Direction of Attack Viper or Coral. The only other thing to do was to tell the 1-12th to try to fight their way to him. He looked at the jagged gap in the bridge, then down at Stonevitch.

"This gap in the bridge is only eighteen to nineteen meters wide," Casey announced. "We can span it with the heavy assault bridge."

"The concrete bridge sections will never hold," Stonevitch replied, shaking his head as he stared up at the underside of the damaged concrete bridge. "This was a forty-ton bridge before they punched holes in it. The M1A2 requires a seventy-ton bridge to be perfectly safe. We've crossed forty-ton bridges with no problem in training, but those were caution crossings across bridges in good shape. Do you really think that this damaged forty-ton bridge can support the weight of a twelve-ton assault bridge and a seventy-ton M1A2 tank?"

Casey looked at the gap and at the deep, rushing water below.

The sharp sound of explosions echoed again in the north as if to emphasize that time was pressing.

"What do you want to do, sir?" Stonevitch asked.

**If Casey decides to hold where he is and tells
the 1-12th to fight its way to him, go to Section 96.**

**If Casey decides to risk spanning the damaged bridge
with a heavy assault bridge, go to Section 101.**

Section 87

> *The greatest general is he who makes the fewest mistakes.*
>
> —Napoleon

Dozens of large-caliber artillery shells pounded the muddy ground all around *Cossack,* shooting up spires of water, rock, and whizzing steel. Casey scanned through his vision blocks, trying to see if the enemy was following up the barrage with another assault.

The shelling was overpowering. Inside the confined walls of the tank, Casey felt as if even the air was crushing in around him.

He shot a glance toward the loader. Graham was sitting in front of him, gripping the turret controls with both hands. Kriel had taken off his helmet and was braced against the side of the turret, sitting on the turret floor, shaking.

"Kriel, are you okay?" Casey yelled.

The noise of a nearby explosion drowned out Casey's voice. The tank rocked from the near miss like a ship at sea in a gale. Casey bent down to get closer to Kriel.

"Kriel!" Casey shouted. "Are you hit?"

Kriel looked up at his captain with wild, desperate eyes.

Suddenly a large shell fragment hit the turret of the tank. The sound echoed inside the turret like a hammer hitting a bell. Casey shot back up to his seat and checked his instruments. He pushed the switch on his CVC helmet to the rear, to speak on intercom. "Graham, status report."

Before Casey knew what was happening, Kriel had opened the hatch and leapt onto the top of the turret.

"Captain, Kriel's gone!" Graham shouted over the intercom.

Casey unsnapped his CVC helmet from its radio cord and leapt up to the open loader's hatch. Kriel jumped off the tank and fell into a ditch to the left.

The ground rocked as another enemy shell exploded and showered the top of the tank with dirt. "Kriel, get back inside!" Casey screamed as he climbed out of the turret and onto *Cossack*'s back deck.

Kriel lay in the ditch, hugging the dirt. Casey got ready to jump down to join him.

That was Casey's last act. As he started to jump, a 152mm shell burst nearby. The blast threw him through the air as the shrapnel from the shell hit his body at two hundred miles an hour and blew him to pieces.

You have fought gallantly but failed.
Return to Section 10 and try again.

Section 88

> *Weigh the situation, then move.*
>
> —Sun Tzu

Casey moved to close his hatch, but the enemy's artillery beat him to the punch. He had waited too long in the enemy's fire sack. A 152mm shell landed right on top of *Cossack*, guided to its target by an enemy observer using a laser designator. The powerful explosion ripped into the top of the tank, killing the captain and his crew.

• • •

Intelligent adversaries will recognize U.S. shortcomings and devise asymmetrical responses that negate U.S. technological superiority. Most of our potential adversaries will try to counter America's excellence in mounted warfare with artillery firepower. This will become easier and cheaper as precision weapons technology floods the world's arms markets, allowing any nation with money to purchase a dramatic increase in artillery weapon effectiveness. Even with conventional "dumb shells," Third World "artillery armies" will employ large concentrations of artillery to destroy and disorganize attacking armored forces. Destroying a mobile force, even with precision munitions, is much more difficult than destroying a stationary force. An armored force, standing stationary in front of the enemy's defenses, is a disaster waiting to happen.

An armored force, therefore, finds protection in movement. If the armored force continues to move, maintaining a tempo of battle that denies the enemy the ability to concentrate his artillery in time and space, it gains a tremendous advantage. Mobility is almost always superior to immobility, and action is always superior to reaction.

You have failed in your mission.
Go back to Section 110 and try again.

Section 89

At a specified time and in a specified place, concentration against fragmentation is exerting the greatest power at a point of certain victory, thus striking a blow against the enemy and giving you certain superiority.

—Sun Tzu

Three T-62s fired almost simultaneously. The first shell splattered in a huge fireball against a rock. The other two struck home, hitting *Cossack*'s turret.

Although the power of a T-62's SABOT round is not enough to penetrate the armor of the M1A2 Abrams main battle tank, it is more than adequate to sever the head and shoulders of anyone above the commander's weapon station.

The explosion splattered Casey with molten splinters. The searing metal from the explosion smashed into his head and shoulders, killing him instantly.

Return to Section 111 and choose a different option.

Section 90

> *That's the way it is in war. You win or lose, live or die—and the difference is just an eyelash.*
>
> —Gen. Douglas MacArthur

Cossack's turret pointed northeast as Graham blasted another advancing T-72. Casey saw a more dangerous target to his right and realized that the most vulnerable part of the turret lay in the direct aim of the enemy's gun.

Before Casey could move the turret, the enemy tank fired. The special hypervelocity round tore into the tank with a shudder. At the same second, Kriel had opened the ammunition doors to load another round. The force from the strike penetrated *Cossack*'s turret ammo storage area and sent a huge fireball into the turret.

Unable to breathe or escape through the hatches, *Cossack*'s crew burned to death in several horrible seconds.

You have been killed in action.
Return to Section 29, reconsider your options, and try again.

Section 91

Casey peered through his tank's vision blocks and watched in disbelief as a number of the exploding shells discharged spires of wispy yellow smoke.

"Gas!" an anonymous voice shouted over Team Steel's radio speakers.

The verbal warning registered on Casey's tired mind and shot through his nervous system like liquid fire. He and his crew reacted automatically—frantically—and quickly struggled with their protective masks, executing a drill that they had practiced more than a hundred times in training and hoped they would never have to test in war.

Casey jerked off his CVC helmet, pulled the straps of the mask over his head, and forced out a hard breath to clear his mask. As he began breathing filtered air, he pulled the plastic hood over his short-cropped hair and tightened the side straps. He grabbed the CVC helmet in his lap and put it back on. Next, he disconnected the voice mike from the CVC helmet and stuck an identical connection from the mask into his CVC boom microphone.

"Crew report!" Casey ordered, the words flying from his mouth as he found himself almost out of breath. He knew that the overpressure system of the M1A2 tank would keep out the enemy's chemical agents, but a tank is hardly an airtight vehicle, even with an overpressure system. The drill is to put on your protective masks whenever you anticipate chemical agents.

"Gunner up, scanning for targets. Bastards! I can't believe they gassed us!"

"Loader up," Kriel replied, his voice muffled in the gas mask microphone.

"Driver up!" Weaver shouted. "Sir, don't you think we ought to get out of here?"

Casey didn't answer. Where could they go? Leaving the infantry was out of the question. God . . . , Casey mused. The infantry. The wounded wouldn't stand a chance of survival in a chemical environment. Armageddon, he thought.

More explosions blanketed the position. Smoke shrouded the battlefield again. High-explosive shells detonated nearby, missing *Cossack* by meters and hammering the sides of the tank with shrapnel, rocks, and debris. Casey struggled uncomfortably in his protective mask to see the battlefield through his vision blocks. Graham moved the turret back and forth, scanning for targets. Anyone caught out in the open was dead meat, Casey thought—killed by the shrapnel or gas.

"Damn them," he cursed. "Damn the bastards to hell."

Dragon exploded in a riot of artillery shells. A brilliant flash erupted to *Cossack*'s left as a 152mm artillery shell slammed directly on top of Sergeant Sellers's Bradley. Sellers and his crew didn't have a chance. The explosion tore apart the thinly armored Bradley as if it was cardboard. Debris, twisted metal, and flesh shot out in a geyser, spreading an inferno over a fifty-meter area.

Cossack shuddered with the impact of each artillery shell. The high-pitched whine of the tank's chemical pressure system kicked in. Casey looked outside the tank and saw an American soldier climb out of a trench. The man wasn't wearing a protective mask. Gagging for air, the man fell to the ground and started kicking madly, tearing at his throat and eyes. Casey watched, powerless to help, as the man died in agony.

Just when Casey thought he could stand no more, the artillery fire slackened. Finally it stopped.

"Kriel, get a Two-Five-Six kit started," Casey said, his ears ringing from the constant bombardment. He glanced over at the loader. Kriel's eyes looked as big as silver dollars inside the eyepieces of the black protective mask. Casey recognized a state of panic and shock in those eyes. "Kriel, do you understand?"

Kriel nodded slowly, then reached for a chemical detection card to determine the type of chemical agent. Casey peered through his vision blocks. He heard the distinct crack of small-arms fire.

"Okay, let's keep our cool," Casey announced loudly, as much for himself as his crew. "We'll make it as long as we work together."

The sound of small-arms fire and tank machine guns erupted all across the perimeter. The intensity of the fire of the defenders was much less than before. Casey knew that the chemical strike had done its deadly work.

"Here they come. Identified, troops, northeastern ridge," Graham's muffled voice announced as he quickly turned the turret toward the enemy. "I see 'em. The bastards are wearing gas masks. I have two hundred and fifty rounds of machine-gun ammunition left."

"Roger. Save the machine gun for when we get closer. Fire HEAT," Casey ordered, forcing himself to pronounce the words clearly while wearing his hot rubber mask.

"On the way," Graham shouted. The gun screamed. Casey saw the target—a dozen enemy riflemen who were firing at the American infantry—disappear as the shell exploded. The blast scattered dirt, rocks, and pieces of enemy soldiers all over. The enemy pressed on, determined to overrun the defenders. Advancing in groups of three or four, the enemy infantry fired RPGs and hurled grenades in a fanatic, supreme effort to destroy the Americans.

Cossack and the survivors of Team Steel tanks fired desperately to stem the tide of enemy infantry. For every enemy killed, three seemed to rush out from behind the ridge. The enemy dead were stacking up in small mounds, but more enemy infantrymen kept coming. They popped up near Casey's position. Two Bradleys were hit in the south. Casey looked to his left. Suddenly there was a blinding flash that registered through the vision blocks.

"Troops, right front!" Weaver shouted. "They've got RPGs."

Graham swung the turret into action and immediately ripped off a short burst of 7.62mm. The machine gun stopped.

"Out of ammo!"Graham shouted. "Load HEAT."

Casey saw men running everywhere. Groups of enemy soldiers rushed the tank as other enemy elements fired RPGs and grenades. Instantly Casey realized that the enemy had climbed the high ground to the west and hit him from the rear of Dragon.

Kaboom! An RPG exploded against the turret.

"What in the hell?" Graham screamed.

"Weaver! Back up!" Casey cried over the intercom, trying to place his heavy armor toward the threat. "Hold your right track!"

Cossack lurched backward, pivoting in a violent, quick jerk.

"Weaver, move forward!" Casey yelled. "Charge them . . . move. . . . Move!" *Cossack* raced up the rough, high ground toward the enemy.

An earsplitting crash resonated against the turret. *Cossack* lurched to the left in a wild, uncontrolled spin, then pitched to the side, throwing the crew against the turret. The tank canted to the right, leaning like a ship sinking at sea.

Stunned momentarily, Casey recognized the agonizing sound of twisting metal. He struggled to see out his narrow vision blocks. "Back up!" he cried.

"She won't respond, sir!" Weaver yelled as *Cossack*'s engine raced and the tank jerked from the power of one track tearing at the dirt. "We've lost a track."

Wham! A violent blast shoved the turret to the right. Casey was hurled against the side of the tank commander's station. Kriel slammed against the breech block, then fell to the floor in an unconscious heap. Graham struggled to move the turret.

"Can't see anything. The damn turret won't move!" Graham cursed in frustration.

"I see 'em, must be a dozen or more," Weaver mumbled, his voice barely audible over the intercom. The engine was screaming, as if it was ready to burst. The tank shuddered back and forth as the left track tried in a fruitless effort to move the seventy-ton beast out of the ditch that was holding it in a death grip. "They're all around us."

Casey grabbed his 9mm pistol from his shoulder holster. "I'm going for the loader's machine gun. Use your pistol!"

Graham nodded, his heavy breathing in his protective mask coming over the intercom. He forced out the word "okay."

Casey strained to hear signs of the enemy. He listened as an animal at bay listens to a pack of wolves closing in for the kill. For several seconds he waited. He knew he would have to act quickly. He grabbed the handle of his TC hatch, then hesitated. The sweat formed on his face. He could barely see through the face piece of his protective mask.

Hell, he thought, it's now or never. He grabbed the handle again and with a mighty heave forced the hatch open.

Two enemy soldiers stood only a few feet away. Casey fired his pistol, hitting one man with several shots before the second blasted him with a full magazine of Kalashnikov fire. Casey sank against the side of the tank commander's weapon station and died as the enemy rifleman shoved a grenade past his limp body and into the turret.

You have fought a hard and gallant fight but failed.
Return to Section 29, make a different decision, and fight again!

Section 92

> *Most victories in history have been won by seizing opportunities from the loser.*
> —B. H. Liddell Hart

Casey looked to the north. A burst of bright light designated the launch of the enemy antitank missiles that had survived the MLRS strike.

Casey reached for the grenade button and screamed, "Grenades."

Both banks of red phosphorus grenades spewed out in a semicircle in front of the tank. The grenades exploded in midair, showering the tank in a blanket of white smoke.

"Weaver, back up. Let's get out of here!"

"Identified PC!" Graham yelled over the intercom.

"Fire and adjust!" Casey replied.

Cossack's cannon boomed as Graham fired at one of the enemy armored personnel carriers that had fired an AT-4 missile at the Americans. *Cossack* jerked violently backward as Weaver raced the engine in reverse, the frontal armor still facing the enemy.

Section 92

"Weaver, slow down and turn around so you can see where you're going," Casey shouted.

Casey slammed against the side of the turret as Weaver brought the tank to an abrupt stop.

"Break. White elements, send one tank to the tank that hit the mine and take on their crew. Abandon that tank and destroy it. We're heading back."

"Steel Six, Wilco," a voice from 2d Platoon answered over the radio, sounding lost and defeated.

"Steel Six, this is Steel Five," Lieutenant Stonevitch asked. "What's going on?"

"Steel Five, this is Steel Six. I just lost the FIST. We won't make it without artillery support. I won't send in good money after bad. We're turning back."

"Retreating?" Stonevitch questioned. "We can't! We have to try!"

Casey faltered. He looked at the spot where the ruins of the FIST-V were burning white hot.

"Negative. We've already lost too much combat power. This mission is suicide. Withdraw. Return to Contact Point Alpha. Get Steel Seven to assemble the elements as they arrive."

"There's always a way!" Stonevitch insisted. "Let's regroup and try another way. What about Coral?"

"Negative, damnit!" Casey screamed on the radio. "I'm not going to lose any more men. I'm in command. Execute my orders or I'll relieve you right now!"

"Wilco. Out," Stonevitch answered, not trying to mask the contempt he had for Casey's decision.

Go to Section 37.

Section 93

> *I always located where I could see and hear what was going on in front; that is near the enemy and around myself—namely at the focal point.*
>
> —General Manteuffel

"Weaver, move straight ahead. Fast!" Casey ordered as he reached for the grenade button and screamed, "Grenades!"

Red phosphorus grenades shot out in a semicircle in front of *Cossack* as the tank lurched forward for the kill.

"Identified PC!" Graham yelled over the intercom.

"Fire and adjust!" Casey replied.

Cossack's cannon boomed as Graham fired at one of the enemy armored personnel carriers that had fired an AT-4 missile at the Americans. *Cossack* jolted across the rough, open ground at twenty miles an hour, undeterred, inexorable.

"On the way!" Graham shouted as *Cossack* fired another round at the enemy.

Casey braced himself against the turret as the tank fired. Machine-gun fire rattled harmlessly against *Cossack*'s tough armor. Casey glanced through the opening in his hatch and saw that artillery shells were still bursting over the enemy trench line, peppering the defenders with deadly slivers of steel.

"Steel Six, this is Steel Five," Lieutenant Stonevitch radioed. "We're headed your way. What's the situation?"

"Steel Five, this is Steel Six. I just lost the FIST. I'm taking heavy fire from Position B. Get in touch with the artillery and keep up the artillery fire. Vee Tee in effect. Over. Continue the attack!"

"Wilco, Steel Six," Stonevitch answered. "Do you want us to clear Position B or bypass?"

Machine guns chattered in a futile wave of desperate fire to stop Casey's three advancing M1A2 tanks. An angry stream of machine-gun tracers shot at *Cossack* from the trench. At the same moment, a loud crash to *Cossack*'s left signified the strike of another enemy anti-tank missile. It was clear that artillery alone would not silence the enemy in Position B.

For one long, angry moment Casey scanned the area to his left and right and considered his options.

"Steel Six, this is Steel Five. I say again, do you want us to clear Position B? I can attack in the northwest and clear from west to east. Over."

Casey had to decide whether to clear Position B or penetrate the enemy position and bypass the defenders.

If Casey decides to order the team to penetrate Position B and bypass enemy resistance, go to Section 74.

If Casey decides to clear Position B, go to Section 98.

Section 94

> *In war all turns on the time factor.*
> —B. H. Liddell Hart

Casey watched in horror as the enemy's 152mm artillery shells burst all around. They sliced through the air in a steady rain of searing metal. The pounding rocked *Cossack* like a ship in a squall.

Casey struggled with the hatch, but it was too late. An enemy shell exploded in the air directly above *Cossack*. The force of the explosion hit Casey like a ten-pound hammer smashing a bug. He died a millisecond after the flash.

You have failed in your mission.
Go back to Section 110 and make a different decision.

Section 95

*Here in a nutshell is the key formula of all tactics, great or small—
that of fixing combined with decisive maneuver, i.e., while one limb
or part of your force, whether an army or a platoon, "fixes" the enemy,
the other part strikes at a vulnerable and exposed point—usually a
flank or communications in war just as it is the chin or solar plexus
in boxing.*

—B. H. Liddell Hart

"Identified two tanks," Graham shouted as he moved the crosshairs
onto the lead enemy tank.

"It's time to help Red," Casey ordered. "Fire and adjust."

Graham fired and hit one of the T-72s on the front slope, just below the turret at the point where its armor is thickest. The depleted-
uranium SABOT round punched right through the metal. A flash
of flame and spall—molten metal from the inside wall of the tank—
shot out of the T-72's engine compartment. The tank stopped immediately, shuddered, smoldered, then exploded as the on-board
ammunition cooked off. The turret flew into the air like a giant
Frisbee.

The second T-72 fired and hit Lieutenant Andrews's tank. Graham
destroyed this T-72 before the enemy tank could get off another
round. The last T-72 incinerated in almost the same instant, proof
of the accuracy of 1st Platoon's gunnery. Flames shot out of every
opening in the shattered enemy tank. In quick succession the enemy's deadly T-72s became burning tombs. The three remaining
tanks of 1st Platoon fired relentlessly until every enemy vehicle was
hit and burning.

Then, just as suddenly, it was over. A battalion's worth of VTT-323s
and tanks were smashed into junk in a few minutes. The valley was
littered with thirty or more burning enemy vehicles.

Casey looked through his vision blocks at Lieutenant Andrews's
smoldering tank. The new, improved 125mm shell had hit the tank

right between the turret and the hull. Casey breathed in relief as he saw the hatches open and all four crew members bail out. The dazed tankers ran over to other tanks in the platoon and squeezed inside their turrets.

"Steel Five, this is Steel Six. SITREP. Over."

"Six, this is Five. We've established the crossing site. I've sent the Bradleys and APCs across. We'll wait for you, then cross the rest of the tanks."

"Negative. Get everyone across. I'm on my way to your location now."

Cossack was the last vehicle to roll into the 2-72d Armor assembly area; it was just before dark. Casey's mission had been a success. He'd taken casualties—one tank, two Bradleys, two APCs, and a HEMMT. Team Steel lost fourteen men killed and twenty-three wounded. Most importantly, the 1st Battalion, 12th Infantry, had been rescued.

Lieutenant Stonevitch walked up to *Cossack* and yelled. "Sir, the battalion commander wants to see you in the TOC."

Casey climbed down *Cossack*'s side and met Stonevitch. "Tell me, Stoney, why is this tank named *Cossack*?"

"Shit, Sir, I thought you'd never ask," Stonevitch said, beaming a smile from ear to ear. "It's an old superstition in Team Steel. Back in the 1980s one of the company commanders named his tank *Cossack*. The tank company always led the way in tactics and tank gunnery. Since then, every C Company commanders tank has been named *Cossack*. The legend says that as long as Team Steel is led by a *Cossack*, the unit will be okay."

"You believe in that kind of stuff?" Casey asked.

"I guess it worked for you," Stonevitch replied.

"I guess it did," Casey said with a laugh.

"Sir, I just want to say—" Stonevitch offered, but he was cut off by the wave of Casey's hand.

"Stoney, you're the best XO in the business. Now we have a team to see to. Take care of the troops and get a schedule with a support platoon to refuel and rearm Team Steel. In the meantime, I'd better go see the old man. If I don't come back, you'll get your chance to command."

"Yes, sir!" Stonevitch smiled, then offered a salute. "You'll be back; I wouldn't want it any other way."

Casey returned the salute, then walked into the battalion tactical operations center. As he entered, every voice hushed.

Casey walked up to Major Cutter and saluted. "Sir, I'm back. You can arrest me if you like."

"Arrest you?" Cutter looked at him seriously. "I just want to know one thing."

"Yes, sir?" Casey replied.

"Did you smoke the cigar I gave you?"

Casey looked dumbfounded. "The cigar? I forgot all about it. It's here in my pocket."

"Well, then, pull it out and light it up." Cutter beamed a wide smile and reached out his hand. "You've certainly earned it. Hell, Tom, you did a great job! No one could have done it better!"

Go to Section 77.

Section 96

> There are two things never to be lost sight of by a military commander: always mystify, mislead and surprise the enemy if possible. . . . The other rule is never fight against heavy odds, if by any other possible maneuvering you can hurl your own force on only part, and the weakest part, of your enemy and crush it. . . .
> —Gen. "Stonewall" Thomas Jonathan Jackson

Casey ran back to his tank, climbed into the commander's weapon station, and connected his CVC helmet. "Dragon Six, this is Steel Six. The bridge on Cobra is destroyed. The center section is gone and it's too risky to try to cross with heavy assault bridges."

"Any way you can ford the river?" Major Cutter asked.

"There's no way to ford the Gang on Cobra," Casey replied. "I recommend you coordinate for the 1-12th to fight their way to me. Over."

"Steel Six, this is Dragon Six," the voice of Major Cutter answered. "Negative. They can't break through to you. Is there any way you can cross the Gang? Any way at all?"

"I say again, negative. I can't risk a tank crossing the bridge," Casey replied. "It just wouldn't hold a tank and a heavy assault bridge. Over."

The ground rumbled as artillery churned a hundred meters to *Cossack's* left. Soldiers scurried to get under the protection of their armored vehicles.

"Steel elements, this is Steel Six. Withdraw down Cobra five hundred meters," Casey yelled in vain as he reached to pull the hatch closed.

Go to Section 79.

Section 97

> *There is no teacher but the enemy. No one but the enemy will ever tell you what the enemy is going to do. No one but the enemy will ever teach you to destroy and conquer. Only the enemy shows you where you are weak. Only the enemy tells you where he is strong. And the only rules of the game are what you can do to him and what you can stop him from doing.*
>
> —Orson Scott Card, *Ender's Game*

As Scott's tanks raced to the bridge, machine guns blazing, artillery burst above the enemy in sharp, bright explosions. With the protection of this fire, Scott's M1A2s reached the southern end of the bridge and gunned down the defenders, but not before the enemy force completed its task to deny the bridge to the Americans.

With a tremendous roar and a brilliant flash of fire and smashed concrete, the bridge collapsed into the river. Casey watched helplessly. The only means of crossing the Gang River disintegrated in front of him. What the enemy couldn't do with antitank weapons and mines he had accomplished with dynamite. He had stopped Team Steel.

Cossack pulled up to the bridge. Scott's two remaining tanks deployed on-line on the south bank of the Gang and faced north. Mc-Daniel's Bradleys arrived, the back ramps lowered, and infantry jumped out to disarm the last remaining group of enemy soldiers. Five dazed defenders stood up from a trench to the east of the bridge, their hands high in the air.

The blackened and busted hulls of two VTT-323 armored personnel carriers smoldered near the entrance to the bridge. An MT-12 antitank cannon also lay smashed in half near one of the VTTs. Six enemy soldiers lay in gruesome, contorted poses on the south side of the bridge, in testimony to Scott's accurate machine-gun fire.

Unfortunately, Casey thought, Scott's tanks did not kill them all before the enemy blew the center and southern sections of the bridge into shattered chunks of concrete.

The American armored column closed on the open area south of the bridge. Casey ordered the platoons to defend a portion of the defensive perimeter.

A sudden quiet descended on the battle area. The sky lightened as dawn broke. Casey stood in his turret, scanning the far side of the river with his binoculars. Private Kriel opened the loader's hatch and manned his 7.62mm machine gun.

Casey pulled out his binoculars and searched the north bank of the river. In the dim, early-morning light he studied the steep sides of the Gang. A winding dirt trail to the west of the bridge offered a means to get down to the south bank of the Gang, but there was no means of getting vehicles down the south bank or up the north bank on the other side.

"Graham, man the fifty," Casey ordered. "I'm going to look at the bridge."

Casey unhooked his CVC helmet, grabbed his chemical protective mask, and struggled out of the commander's weapon station. After quickly climbing down *Cossack*'s right front slope, he ran over to the demolished bridge.

Casey surveyed the bridge. Its southern and center span lay at the bottom of the fast-flowing Gang River. Rusty steel rods and cracked concrete protruded from the jagged edge of the northern section of the bridge. As far as he could see, the north bank was impassable; it was a sheer six-foot wall of rock. Without an exit on the north bank, the option of swimming his Bradleys and APCs was out. The bridge was the only way to cross the river.

Crom, Lieutenant Stonevitch's tank, rolled up next to *Cossack.* The thin executive officer crawled out of the turret and climbed down the tank.

"Any way we can ford it?" Stonevitch yelled to his commander as he walked up to the edge of the bridge.

"There's no way to climb out of the river on the north side," Casey answered, the anger rising in his voice. "So damn close. The 1-12th Infantry is just over there."

Casey pointed at the hills to the northeast. The sound of artillery explosions echoed in the north. Casey knew that the 1-12th was catching hell. He knew that they wouldn't hold out much longer.

"Sir, I've got Dragon Six on our command frequency," Sergeant Graham shouted from *Cossack*'s turret. "I told him that the bridge is down. He says he needs to talk to you."

Casey waved to Graham, then looked at the destroyed bridge and the deep, rushing water below. The sharp sound of explosions echoed again.

"Maybe the 1-12th can fight their way out to us," Stonevitch offered.

Casey shook his head. "Doesn't sound like it. I'd better get on the radio and talk with Dragon Six."

He ran back to his tank and climbed *Cossack*'s battle-scarred sides. Graham handed him the spaghetti-cord connection for his CVC helmet. Casey twisted the connection together and pushed forward his helmet transmission switch.

"Dragon Six, this is Steel Six. The bridge on Cobra is destroyed. I can't cross here, even with two heavy assault bridges. Recommend you coordinate for the 1-12th to fight their way to me. Over."

"Steel Six, this is Dragon Six," Major Cutter answered. "Negative. They can't break through to you. Is there any way you can cross the Gang?"

Casey considered the options. What could he do? "Negative, Dragon Six. The bridge is the only way to cross."

There was a cold, lonely silence on the radio for almost thirty seconds.

"In that case, we've failed," Cutter's reluctant voice announced. "The 1-12th can't break out and you can't reach them. Stand by, Steel Six."

Casey stood silently in the turret. The wait was difficult. He thought about his casualties and how hard his men had fought to get this far. He thought about the poor, bloody infantry, surrounded by enemies. He looked to the northeast and heard the rumble of explosions that punctuated their death fight.

"Collect your force, Steel Six. We can't afford to take any more casualties for nothing. Your mission is canceled. Stand by for instructions on your passage of lines and how you will return to the assembly area."

Casey's heart sank, but he knew that there was nothing else he could do. Was there an approach he hadn't considered?

You have fought hard but failed in your mission.
Go to Section 104 and make a different decision.

Section 98

If you start to take Vienna—take Vienna.

—Napoleon

295

Casey gritted his teeth. He couldn't afford to leave an enemy behind him that could shoot up his column as he moved north. If the enemy was left behind, they might establish blocking positions on Cobra and break his column in two. No. He would clear them all out.

Pushing forward the transmitter switch on the right side of his CVC helmet, he rapped out a series of orders. The two tanks with him would lay down rapid fire on the enemy positions to the northeast and support the attack by fire. Lieutenant McDaniel's three Bradleys, reinforced with the three Bradleys of 4th Platoon, would move to the northwest point of the enemy position and assault the trenches from west to east. Fires would shift west to east as the squads progressed. Sergeant Scott's 2d Platoon, four M1A2 tanks, would move to Casey's right and join in on the support fire. The artillery, now managed by Lieutenant Stonevitch, would shift to the east as soon as the infantry dismounted.

Casey sketched a quick outline of the attack and sent it to the platoon leaders:

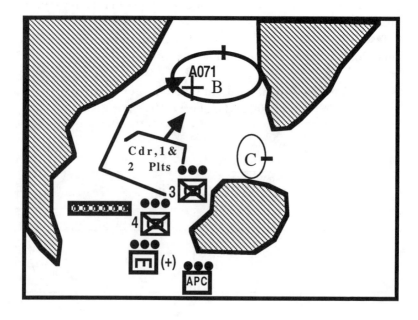

The enemy increased their fire. The two M1A2s with *Cossack* blasted the trenches from close range with a devastating, rapid fire. At the same time, the American artillery hammered the enemy positions with intense, overhead explosions. In spite of this awesome firepower, return fire shot out from the enemy's trench line and bunkers.

Casey scanned the enemy battle position in the light of the flares. He was impressed by the stoicism and fierce resistance of the enemy forces, but he knew that courage was not enough. They may be dug in like Alabama ticks, he thought, but they are going down.

McDaniel's assault element rumbled behind Casey, then moved northeast, hugging the eastern edge of the mountain. The maneuver took time as the Bradleys moved carefully across the broken ground. Casey checked their movement through his CITV, then watched the artillery smash into Position B. The heavy 155mm shells exploded too far to the north, missing their intended target.

Casey lazed to the target and sent a digital call for fire to the FDC. After several minutes the rounds adjusted and fell right on target, lighting the trace of the enemy trench line with dazzling bursts of fire. The tanks to either side of *Cossack* fired a volley of HEAT rounds at the bunker line, adding to the enemy's destruction.

Twenty minutes had passed and the infantry was still moving into position to assault the bunkers.

"Steel Six, this is Steel Five," Stonevitch called on the command frequency. "Rounds complete for the artillery. They have to move the guns."

Casey looked at his watch. The tanks supporting the Bradleys had been in the same spot for more than twenty-five minutes. Now, there was no artillery fire.

"Get me mortars," Casey ordered, wishing that Lieutenant Keeley was still with him. "Break. Blue One, this is Steel Six. Status. Over."

"We're dismounting now. Shift fires to Position B center and east. Over."

Casey saw the Bradleys start support fire with their 25mm cannons. Then, like an avalanche from heaven, the sky erupted in fire. Hundreds of artillery shells fell all around *Cossack*. In an instant Casey recognized his mistake: he had placed his tanks in the center of the enemy engagement area, a place registered as a fire box for their multiple rocket launchers.

As Casey struggled with the hatch, a volley of 120mm rockets detonated directly above *Cossack*. The force of the explosion killed Casey before he had a chance to close the hatch.

**Go back to Section 104,
make a different decision, and try again.**

Section 99

> *You don't hurt 'em if you don't hit 'em.*
> —Lt. Gen. "Chesty" Puller

"Well, Weaver, it's up to you and me. The 1-12th Infantry won't last long if we don't cross this bridge. Are you ready?"

"Roger, Sir, let's give it a whirl," Weaver replied.

"Move out, nice and steady."

Cossack inched forward. The southern concrete section of the bridge shook as the tank's weight shifted onto it. Dust fell from the concrete as *Cossack* moved onto the metal assault bridge, which groaned and creaked as *Cossack* centered on it.

Then, in a shower of dust and broken concrete, the southern edge of the bridge collapsed, sliding down the steep slope to the Gang, thirty feet below. *Cossack* slid backward as the metal bridge fell with the concrete section. In seconds, *Cossack* lay on its side under eight feet of water.

Knocked out from the concussion of the fall, and pinned underwater in his tank commander's station, Casey drowned in the cold waters of the Gang.

**You have risked everything but failed in your mission.
Go back to Section 80 and try again.**

Section 100

"Bayonet Four, this is Steel Six. We're not going to have any ammunition left by the time the task force links up with us tonight. I want you to mount up all your troops in my vehicles. Our only way out is to fight our way south to my platoon holding the bridge on Cobra."

There was a pause on the radio while Bayonet Four considered this decision. "You're right. Do you have enough room for all of us?"

"We won't leave anyone behind. I have room for about one hundred and four men in the APCs, if we cram them in tight. My engineers and Bradleys can probably carry another thirty. If we have to, some can ride on top of the APCs and Bradleys while the tanks cover their withdrawal."

"Okay, how do you want to do this?" Bayonet Four asked.

"I'll keep them pinned down with the tanks and Bradleys. You pull in your men from the north and center of the perimeter. Collapse on the southern perimeter where most of the M113s are. Load them as fast as you can. Call me when you're ready. Once you call, I'll send my XO with a few tanks and all the Bradleys to fight their way back to the bridge. I'll keep them busy here until you get out."

"Wilco," Bayonet Four replied. "It'll take us about twenty minutes."

"Hurry, we may not have much time left," Casey replied.

The burning wrecks of the enemy's shattered attack burned black, covering the battlefield with a smoky haze. Casey watched as the infantry loaded the wounded into the APCs. The tanks fired HEAT rounds at any attempt by the enemy to infiltrate infantry over the top of the northern ridge. For a short while Casey knew that he held the initiative. It would be a race against the clock to see if he could maintain it.

The enemy lobbed mortar shells into the perimeter but refrained, for the time being, from any more major assaults. While the harassment shelling occurred, the infantry frantically loaded every available vehicle. The M113s, including the engineer, medics, and all the Bradleys, were filled. Most of the M113s carried more than eight men. Some had men riding on the tops of the vehicles. The vehicle crews dumped every piece of excess equipment to make room for the infantry. Finally, every living soul was loaded.

Casey gave the word to Stonevitch to take his tank, Lieutenant Andrews's two tanks, and the Bradleys and dash south.

"Don't stop for anything," Casey ordered. "Get across the bridge and wait for us there. We'll be close behind you."

"Wilco," Stonevitch answered.

Crom led the way south, followed by the two 1st Platoon tanks, four Bradleys, the BSFV, Keeley's FIST-V, the engineers, and the M113s.

Casey watched as small-arms fire erupted to the south. The boom of Stonevitch's cannon smashed through the hasty opposition that the enemy placed to block the column's advance. Nothing was going to stop Stonevitch from breaking through.

The enemy's artillery fire smashed into Objective Dragon to support a combined-arms assault of T-72s and VTTs. The attack rolled down Highway 17 while dismounted infantry ran over the northern ridgeline. The enemy seemed determined to stop the Americans from escaping their trap.

Casey had four tanks—his tank and three tanks from Scott's platoon. *Cossack* and Scott's tanks immediately started to fire on the T-72s and the VTTs as they popped in and out to fire at the defenders of Objective Dragon. There was no wild charge down Highway 17 this time. The T-72s and VTTs fired from carefully selected positions. The infantry rushed to the flanks, trying to overrun Casey's tanks from north to south. Scott's northern tank fired at the northern ridge, sending lethal rounds into the ranks of dozens of enemy infantrymen as they advanced in squad groups over the ridge.

In a tremendous strike of hypervelocity penetrator against Chobham armor, a volley of 125mm rounds struck the northernmost tank. The tank smoldered and the hatches opened. The crew bailed out, only to be cut down by machine-gun fire from the north.

The enemy infantry continued to move in bounds down the northern ridge. Scott's tank, now the one farthest north, turned its turret to the left and engaged the infantry with machine-gun fire. The fire slowed, but did not stop, the enemy's advance.

Casey glanced at his IVIS screen as Graham fired and destroyed a T-72. Casey was waiting for Stonevitch's tank to reach the bridge. After a few minutes, Casey saw the icon on his screen reach the decision point.

"White. Move south, now!"

"Wilco," Sergeant Scott answered. "We should move in bounds. I'll cover your move."

"Negative," Casey answered. "I'm in a better position. You move while I support by fire. Execute now!"

Sergeant Scott's tank fired his smoke grenades, then backed out of his firing position. The tank to Scott's right did the same. Both tanks dashed south. *Cossack* was the last remaining defender of Dragon.

"Graham, you take the tanks, I'll take the infantry," Casey ordered as he popped open his hatch and pulled back the charging handle of his .50-caliber machine gun. "Caliber fifty!"

The enemy infantry rushed forward; they were now only a few hundred meters from *Cossack*. Casey blasted away with his .50 caliber as an enemy squad advanced over the top of a nearby bunker. Casey ducked as bullets sparked off the M1A2's thick metal turret.

"Weaver, back up. Let's get out of here!" Casey ordered, too late. In a flash he saw an RPG gunner standing behind his tank and saw the missile launch.

Major Cutter nodded as Stonevitch finished his report. The column had fought its way back to friendly lines, taking heavy casualties along the way. In the end, Stonevitch made it back with only three tanks, two Bradleys, a CEV, the FIST-V, and seven M113s. Of the total force, Team Steel was reduced to a third of its original strength. Still, they had broken through and rescued about seventy soldiers of the 1-12th.

Lieutenant Stonevitch sat in a metal chair, looking down at the muddy ground. The rain had picked up again, adding to the gloom.

"Maybe if we hadn't come back on the same route we attacked up," Stonevitch offered. "Maybe I should have done more to make it work. I didn't—"

Cutter put up his hand, cutting off the conversation. "It's over. You've got to put it behind you and get ready for tomorrow. Learn from this, and figure out how to put the odds in your favor next time. Next time, you may be faced with even tougher odds."

Stonevitch looked at Cutter with tired resignation.

"You did all you could," Cutter added. "The enemy knew that you had to cross one of the bridges. The latest intel shows that they were both heavily defended. Just put it behind you."

"Any final word on Casey?" Stonevitch asked.

"Graves registration found his body this morning, along with the rest of his crew," Cutter said, terminating the briefing. "Now I want you and your men to get some rest. We move out to continue the attack tomorrow."

You have fought well, but you have won a Pyrrhic victory.
Return to Section 104 and try again!

Section 101

> *Time is the controlling factor of war.*
>
> — J. F. C. Fuller

Scott's three M1A2s fired in quick succession at the enemy's S-300 mobile SAM systems that were north of the bridge. Although the S-300s were aware of the Americans, they suddenly halted, hesitating within easy range of the American tanks.

"They're here to protect the bridge," Casey said with grim satisfaction as he looked through his binoculars. "The bastards are probably waiting for orders to withdraw."

A tank fired as Casey finished his sentence. Scott's tank scored a direct hit on the left S-300. A second later, the other two tanks hit their marks. All three of the enemy's prized air defense systems were now nothing more than burning hulks.

"That's what happens when your command and control is too centrally controlled," Casey remarked.

"We don't have much time," Stonevitch said, pointing to the bridge. "The enemy must know we're here. Every minute we waste takes away what surprise we may have left. But can we risk a crossing on this piece of shit?"

"Stoney, I took an oath a few years back. Gave my word to protect and defend the Constitution and keep faith with my comrades. Part of that faith also involves not leaving anyone behind."

Stonevitch nodded in agreement.

"We'll cross with the assault bridges," Casey said, the determination in his voice ending all further discussion. "It's our only chance to break through to the 1-12th. Get the bridges up here."

"Right away," Stonevitch answered. "But I want to be the first to cross."

Casey smiled. His XO was definitely a fighter. "No, Stoney. That's my job. Bring up the HEMMT and fuel the tanks, then the Bradleys."

"Wilco," Stonevitch answered. The lieutenant stroked his chin and looked at the map he carried in his left hand, then pointed to the southeast, near the town of Sori. "Top has collected our wounded with the trains and the M113s at Sori. If we can secure a landing zone there, where their S-300s will be masked by these high hills and unable to get a clear shot at the helicopters, battalion might be able to send us some Blackhawks and move the infantry by helicopter."

"That might work," Casey replied. He suddenly realized, now more than ever before in his life, that leadership was more about empowering teams than about great men. "Get on the radio with Major Cutter and see what you can work out. I'll take care of the crossing."

Stonevitch nodded and headed back toward his tank.

Lieutenant Keeley ran up to the captain. "Anything I can do, sir?"

Casey looked at his eager artilleryman. "You've done a great job, George. Now I need you to buy me some time. Get a smoke screen going north of this bridge to cover our crossing."

"I'll have it falling in a few minutes," Keeley replied, then saluted and ran back to his FIST-V.

In a few minutes the heavy assault bridge clanked up to the concrete bridge. About eight hundred meters north and northeast of the bridge, 155mm smoke rounds burst in a linear sheaf. The HEMMT fuel truck moved up to *Cossack* first and gave the commander a quarter tank of JP8, approximately 120 gallons.

We may just make it yet, Casey thought.

Casey stood at the bridge, looking at the gap during the refueling. The sun was breaking over the horizon. Although the sky was still ominously dark and cloudy, several streaks of sunlight broke through. Casey looked to the northeast and saw smoke coming from the area where the 1-12th was defending against uneven odds.

Sergeant Jacobs, the grimy and fatigued heavy assault bridge section leader, dismounted his huge vehicle and ran up to his commander. He saluted, took a quick look at the bridge, and said, "Piece of cake, sir. I'll have it set in fifteen minutes."

Casey returned the salute. "Think I can get my tanks across?"

"There's only one way to find out," Jacobs replied. "You willing to risk it?"

The sound of explosions in the hills to the northeast echoed in the valley. "Do you need to ask that question?" Casey replied.

"Nope, I guess not," Jacobs answered with a grin, then saluted and ran back to his bridge layer. He quickly maneuvered the heavy assault bridge up to the concrete bridge and drove onto the southern section. The concrete structure creaked and moaned; dust fell to the water below, but the southern side held.

Jacobs deployed the bridge layer's spade at the front. With a loud screech the spade nestled onto the concrete. The bridge sections enlarged, extended horizontally, then slowly lowered into place. In less than five minutes Jacobs laid the bridge over the gap, resting the metal bridge on the southern and northern sections of the concrete bridge. Jacobs pulled the launcher chassis out of the way, parked his vehicle, and dismounted to check his handiwork. After a few minutes of inspection, he crossed the bridge, then waved to Casey from the north side of the Gang River.

Casey had already arrived at the bridge and was walking across the metal section that spanned the eighteen-meter gap in the concrete. He waved for Graham, who was standing in *Cossack*'s tank commander's hatch, to move forward.

"Just take it slow, Captain. Nice and steady as you cross," Jacobs said.

"You can count on it, Jacobs. Good job." Casey ran back to his tank and climbed up the right front slope to the turret. He quickly occupied the TC's station and ordered Graham and Kriel to wait on the south bank until he tested the bridge's capability. Following Jacobs's hand signals, Casey guided Weaver to drive the heavy M1A2 up to the southern edge of the metal bridge.

Roll the dice.

If you roll 2-7, go to Section 99.

If you roll 8-12, go to Section 107.

Section 102

> *"Why me?" That is the soldier's first question, asked each morning as the patrols go out and each evening as the night settles around the foxholes.*
>
> —William Broyles, Jr.

A tremendous violet and yellow explosion erupted in front of *Cossack,* missing the tank by a few feet.

Lieutenant Keeley's thinly armored APC wasn't as lucky. The second antitank missile slammed into Keeley's vehicle, engulfing the FIST-V in a brilliant, white-hot explosion. Keeley's APC blew apart in an instant, then burned down to its tracks, like a paper box that had been doused with gasoline and set on fire. White and red sparks gushed skyward where the FIST-V had once been.

No one survived the explosion. Casey ducked inside *Cossack's* turret and watched the FIST-V burn for one long, terrible minute. Losing his FIST meant that he had little artillery support unless he could call in howitzer support by some other means. Could he call for artillery fires in the thick of the fight without his FIST?

Graham turned the turret in the direction of Position B. The night sky reflected the light from the flames, illuminating the three M1A2 tanks located next to the remains of Steel Guns. The two M1A2 tanks to Casey's left, the survivors of 1st Platoon, fired their cannons angrily in the direction of the enemy's missile launch. Their HEAT rounds added to the explosions of the DPICM falling on Position B.

Casey checked his combat power:

TM C Unit	M1A2 Tank	M2 IFV	BSFV [ADA]	FISTV	Engr M113	CEV	ACE	HAB Bridge	Medic M113	M88 [Rec]	Fuel HEMMT	M113 APCs
Total	8	6	1	1	4	1	1	2	2	1	1	15

Casey had lost too many good men just breaking through the enemy's first line of resistance. He thought about Lieutenant Andrews, stranded to the south of Position B in a disabled tank guarded by the Bradley Stinger vehicle. Could Casey leave them there? Should he continue the mission and pursue the attack north along Cobra? Could he still succeed?

Casey had to make a decision: continue to attack with whatever can still fight and move, or pull back?

**If Casey decides to reduce casualties and pull back,
go to Section 92.**

**If Casey decides to continue the attack,
go to Section 93.**

Section 103

"The enemy's all over the place!" Casey screamed as he grabbed the tank commander's override control and slewed the turret to the right rear.

Rifle fire drilled against the FIST-V next to *Cossack*. Keeley, trapped in his APC like an animal ready for a snake to strike, closed the hatch.

A sudden bright flash and a wave of hot air forced Casey back inside the turret. He couldn't move. He felt dazed. His arms and legs didn't want to work. His mouth was very dry and his heart was racing. He couldn't find the strength to push his body up to stand on the loader's seat and man his machine gun.

Kriel stood up in the turret just as the high-explosive warhead hit the top of the tank commander's hatch. The force of the blast cut Kriel in two, leaving the top part of his bisected torso hanging from the loader's hatch. Casey's eyes burned from the exhaust of the blast. He rubbed his eyes and discovered that he was inside the turret facing the bloody body of his loader.

"Kriel!" Casey yelled. He recoiled in horror as the lifeless torso gushed blood into the turret. The turret started to smoke as pieces of burning cloth and debris fell in through the tank commander's position. The lower part of Kriel's smoldering body lay crumpled at the bottom of the turret, the open cut facing Casey.

"Damnit!" Casey cursed, white hot with anger. He pushed against the side of the turret and stood up to fire the .50-caliber machine gun. Within seconds the machine gun was rattling loud, long bursts of fire.

Enemy tracers replied in turn, bouncing off the tank's sides and ricocheting in crazy directions. Graham's machine gun ripped into the attackers, who seemed to pop up from both the east and west sides of the road.

Casey blasted to the right as Graham swung the turret to the left. Casey fired wild as the turret turned. Suddenly the steady hammer of the .50 caliber stopped. Graham kept firing, swinging the turret right and left.

Three enemy soldiers were right on top of them.

Bullets ricocheted off the top of the tank. Casey quickly realized that he was out of ammunition. He ducked down into the turret and reached for another box of .50 caliber. In shear panic he realized that someone had jumped onto the back deck of his tank. Casey's senses abruptly sharpened, like those of an animal making his last stand against a predator. Casey feverishly reached for the tank commander's hatch release, pulled hard, and closed the hatch. He keyed his radio. "Steel Guns, get Vee Tee fire on our position ASAP."

"RPG team, direct front!" Private Weaver yelled over the tank intercom.

"Move! Run him down!" Casey screamed.

"Engine won't start. . . . I've got an abort light!" Weaver screamed. An explosion erupted from the FIST-V as an enemy rocket found its mark.

"They've hit the FIST-V!" Weaver shouted. "I still have an abort light!"

Graham swung the turret forward and fired a full burst of 7.62mm machine-gun ammunition at the RPG team. The enemy crumpled to the ground.

"I'm almost out of machine-gun ammo!" Graham reported.

Suddenly a terrible sound screeched overhead, followed by the rumble of explosions. Keeley must have gotten through before he was hit, Casey thought. *Cossack* shook from the thunder of hundreds of small explosions. The fire scraped against the tank, striking the outside with shards of flying steel. Casey could hear the dull whack of lead plastering the tank's hard sides. His chest tightened; it was difficult to think, hard to breathe. He felt that this was the end. He closed his eyes, waiting to be eaten by the red, horrible monster of war.

The artillery fire lasted for several minutes. Graham continued to fire until he ran out of machine-gun ammunition. Finally, the artillery stopped.

Casey waited for several minutes. He realized that there wasn't anyone on top of *Cossack* anymore. He moved back to the commander's weapon station and surveyed the scene from inside the buttoned-up tank. He turned the turret in all directions, scanning for the enemy.

One of the M1A2s to the north was on fire. The other one was racing up the road, firing its co-ax 7.62mm machine gun to the left and right. Suddenly, it stopped, and smoke and flame billowed from its engine compartment.

Casey waited; then when he thought it was safe, he pushed open the hatch. The fresh air swept into the turret. Casey climbed onto the top of the tank. Graham followed right after him, carefully avoiding the bloody body lying in a heap on the turret floor.

Casey drew his 9mm pistol and searched for the enemy as he walked on top of the tank. Pieces of dead enemy infantrymen lay everywhere. Clumps of mangled bodies were strewn on the ground, as if the bodies were seeking company in the mournful sorrow of death. No one in the open had survived the bombing. No one could have survived.

The FIST-V and both of the M1A2s from 1st Platoon lay smoldering in a graveyard of dead and dying men. Smoke and the smell of cordite filled the thick night air. The smoke, the smell of burning diesel fuel, and the scenes of the dead dominated Casey's senses. Choking from the smoke, he took off his CVC helmet, threw it on the turret roof, and vomited over the side.

He didn't try to look for Keeley and his crew. He knew they were dead. No one could have survived the explosion of the APC.

Casey realized that he should have kept his tanks moving, that a tank force that is stationary in restricted terrain is a prime target for close-in infantry attack. In restricted terrain, movement and firepower are the keys to success for an armored force, particularly against a determined enemy who is willing to sacrifice his infantry by the hundreds to stop a tank penetration of his defenses.

Casey wondered how much of the rest of Team Steel had survived. The radio suddenly crackled to life. Casey slowly reached for his CVC helmet and reconnected the spaghetti cord to receive the transmission.

"Steel Six, this is Dragon Six," Major Cutter's voice sounded over Casey's radio. "Intel reports that the bridge along Cobra at CS213447 has been destroyed. You may be able to span the damaged bridge with your heavy assault bridges. What is your situation?"

Casey sadly reported his losses to Major Cutter. The loss of one heavy assault bridge and the damage to the other bridge made Cobra an untenable option. There was a long pause on the radio, then Cutter ordered Casey to collect his force and report back to him when he was ready to move.

Go to Section 37.

Section 104

> *They've got us surrounded again, the poor bastards.*
> —Gen. Creighton W. Abrams

Stonevitch and Casey looked at the map.

"They've got the 1-12th in a vice grip," Stonevitch offered. "It looks as if the enemy wants our guys bad."

Casey nodded, noting the location of the enemy units on the map. Stonevitch pointed to the town of Tongak.

"As far as the direction of attack, this shows at least a tank platoon at Tongak. Where there's one platoon, two more will be close by. That means they have a tank company, probably with infantry support, guarding Viper."

"You're probably right," Casey answered, nodding his approval of Stonevitch's assessment. "This also shows two infantry companies along Highway Twenty-one and another one north of the bridge at CS212447. What worries me more than the infantry is that the bridge over the Gang along Cobra is only a forty-ton bridge."

"We cross forty-ton bridges all the time with M1A2s. It's no problem—we'll treat it as a caution crossing," Stonevitch replied in a tone that ranged between arrogance and pride. "Besides, what choice do we have? The Gang River is swollen. We can cross the Gang only at the bridges."

"Yeah, I heard that from Cutter," Casey answered. "The enemy knows that too. Viper is the best bridge and has the widest fields of fire. Cobra has a smaller bridge but a very restricted direction of attack. Cobra is so narrow that we'd be lucky to move forward with two or three tanks abreast."

"Welcome to combat in restricted terrain," Stonevitch said with a smirk. "This ain't the National Training Center, or Kuwait. Fighting in the mountains is much tougher than in the desert. We'll have to clear the high ground with infantry before we move forward."

"No one has that much infantry," Casey observed. "With only thirty-one riflemen, we'll never make it that way."

"It beats getting smacked with an AT-4 and slammed with RPGs."

"How much infantry does it take to beat a dug-in enemy platoon?" Casey quizzed.

"The book says I need three to one," Stonevitch answered. "A company."

"Taking the high ground is a bloody solution for not thinking. Those hills can be as strong as a fortress. It might take six times that amount of infantry to climb up under enemy fire and to take out an enemy platoon that's in prepared positions. We don't have that much infantry, can't afford those kinds of casualties. And we don't have that much time. Furthermore, if we don't break through to the 1-12th Infantry by early tomorrow morning, they won't last."

Stonevitch eyed his new commander carefully. "Okay. I see what you're getting at. What do you suggest?"

"We'll have to use the strength of our tanks and Bradleys to get around the enemy's defenses," Casey offered, pointing to the map. "He can't be strong everywhere. We might move around Tongak, for instance, to the east and bypass the enemy tank company. We could then attack up Highway Seventeen, along Direction of Attack Viper, and take the stronger, seventy-ton bridge."

"I don't agree," Stonevitch answered firmly. "That's exactly what

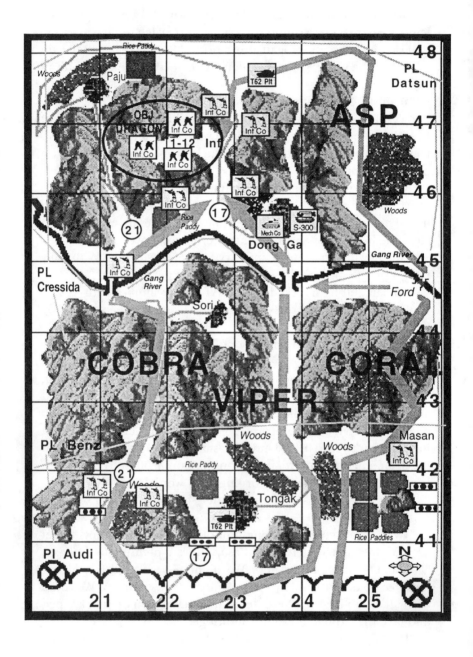

the bastards want us to do—attack right into their prepared engagement area. That's not what I would do."

"Okay, what about Coral? What if we took the Highway Seventeen bridge from the east?"

"I know that Viper won't work, but I haven't thought much about Coral," Stonevitch replied, tugging at his ear. "Coral looks like a goat trail compared to Viper. If you're worried about narrow approaches, Coral is the worst. Maybe we could get the UAV to check it out."

"No time," Casey countered, shaking his head. "Major Cutter had to beg just to get the UAV to see if the bridges were still up. With our satellites down, the UAVs are now strategic assets. We don't have time."

Casey hesitated. He saw three possibilities. Cobra would be a tough fight through two enemy infantry companies, maybe more, and then a race to the bridge. If the bridge was still standing when they got there, Cobra offered a direct route to the beleaguered infantry.

Viper, on the other hand, had the best field of fires to conduct a combined-arms battle. Viper was also, as Stonevitch pointed out, probably the most heavily defended, because it was the only route to the only seventy-ton bridge in the area of operations. Casey needed a way to cross the Gang with tanks. A seventy-ton bridge would do nicely.

Coral, the end around, gambled everything on the chance that they could get through the narrow mountain trail and then take the Highway 17 bridge on Viper from the east. A couple of well-placed minefields along Coral could bottle up the entire team and leave Casey without options. Without better intelligence, could he risk his entire force down Coral?

"I wish I had more information," Casey complained.

"As you've said, we don't have much time," Stonevitch insisted. His cold blue eyes stared into Casey's eyes. "The platoons need to plan, and we have to rehearse this on a terrain model at least once before dark. We should decide right now and get things rolling ASAP."

Casey hesitated. He looked at the map. Suddenly he realized that the moment of truth had arrived. All his previous experience came down to this decision. If he waited for more information, he'd waste valuable preparation time. Should he plan the attack up Cobra, or could he delay the decision and try to gather more information?

"Well?" Stonevitch pressed. "Every second we delay works against us."

If Casey decides on Cobra, go to Section 5.

If Casey chooses to take more time to decide, go to Section 7.

Section 105

> *On 17 January, I started with 39 tanks. After 38 days of aerial attack, I had 32, but in less than 20 minutes with the M1A1, I had zero.*
>
> —Comment by an Iraqi battalion commander captured in the 1991 Gulf War

Team Steel rolled northeast, firing in all directions along the same path that had led them into Objective Dragon. The column cut back into the shattered remains of the enemy artillery group. The order of march was 2d Platoon, 3d Platoon, the command group, the trains with all the APCs carrying the infantry, the engineers, 4th Platoon, and 1st Platoon.

Even with his tanker's helmet on and the whine of *Cossack*'s engine, Casey could hear the distinct loud bang of tank cannons and the rattling of tank machine guns. The road was strewn with wreckage. A blazing 152mm self-propelled gun lay on its left side among scattered items of individual equipment, bodies, and bits of bodies.

The M1A2s, Bradleys, APCs, and Wolverines raced on, making the turn on Asp to the south. The noise of the battle was tremendous. Rifle tracers filled the incandescent sky as the enemy attempted to defend his positions. The M1A2s returned fire with a volley that overwhelmed the confused defenders. Enemy artillerymen crumpled to the ground, cut down by the merciless tanks. Lethal flying metal zinged over the battle area. Green and red tracers filled the air.

"Steel Six, this is White One," Sergeant Scott reported, his voice charged with excitement. "We're cutting through them without a problem. Nothing is getting out on our end. We've destroyed at least thirty self-propelled howitzers. The enemy is running."

"Roger, White. Be careful if they try to surrender," Casey replied. "Just send them away."

"No problem, Steel Six. Anyone without his hands in the air dies."

Something told Casey that he should say something to make sure that prisoners were not shot out of hand. He knew how difficult it was for tankers to take prisoners. If the enemy surrendered, how would his men guard them? He couldn't stop to take prisoners, but he wasn't going to allow anyone to shoot soldiers who were surrendering.

"White One, keep moving. Fire at anyone who resists. Anyone with his hands in the air, trying to surrender, just let him pass."

"Roger, Steel Six. They haven't all quit yet," Scott responded. A volley of tank fire indicated that Scott's response was accurate. "There are still plenty of them fighting right now!"

Casey strained to look ahead as he held tightly to the sides of his tank commander's station. The tank moved rapidly, running over pieces of debris in the road. Burning vehicles lined the highway. The M1A2s pushed them off the road. The wrecked vehicles lay at various angles, some on their side, others completely upside down. The fires were intense.

An RPG exploded to *Cossack*'s left front, another indication that Scott was correct. A clump of dismounted enemy soldiers appeared to the left front, hiding behind an overturned command car. Casey slung the turret to the left and fired a HEAT round. The shell detonated against the belly of the overturned armored car, which disintegrated into a dozen flaming pieces.

Thick lines of smoke rose into the sky, reached a certain level high above the valley, then floated north like a black blanket. Hundreds of burning armored vehicles—BTRs, self-propelled howitzers, and trucks—lay wrecked in the smoke-filled valley. It was as if some unstoppable force had swept in, killed and crushed everything in sight, and suddenly left. The enemy, gripped by panic, ran away to the east and north.

The tanks raced along the two-lane concrete road, spreading overpowering destruction in their wake. Fifty feet to Casey's right, a wrecked BRDM command car smoldered. The side of the vehicle was torn open, revealing a knot of mangled bodies. One of the disfigured shapes on top of the armored carrier flapped its arm in a frantic, useless gesture for help. Casey turned away. He recognized that the reality of modern warfare was brutality and death. The faster he killed the enemy, the sooner this madness would end.

Cossack arrived at the edge of the woods on Asp at CS249468. Casey ordered Weaver to pull to the side of the road, then waved the rest of the column on. Casey turned his CITV to the north.

He saw a formation of T-72s headed his way. From the scene through Casey's CITV, the enemy was in battalion strength—Casey guessed a reinforced tank battalion of thirty tanks and a dozen VTT-323s with infantry.

Lieutenant Stonevitch's tank, *Crom*, thundered past, its gun tube over the left rear side pointing toward the enemy. "Steel Six, this is Steel Five. Why are you waiting?"

"We've got company coming," Casey reported. "An enemy tank battalion is five minutes out. I'll peel off 1st Platoon and slow them down. You take charge of the crossing site and get everyone across."

"Wilco," Stonevitch replied. "We'll wait for you."

"Roger. Break. Red One, did you copy what we're going to do?"

"Affirmative, Steel Six," Lieutenant Andrews reported. "I'll be at your location in two minutes."

Casey watched as the Wolverines and the Bradleys of 4th Platoon passed *Cossack*. A minute later 1st Platoon arrived and deployed in a jagged W oriented to the north and northeast.

Right on schedule the artillery began to fall. The area was consumed with patches of dense white smoke.

The enemy tank battalion attacked in a long column of vehicles, moving at twelve kilometers per hour through the smoke, with their hatches buttoned down tight. Casey peered through his CITV. The M1A2's thermal sight registered the targets as white hot spots moving across a dark background.

Casey knew that the enemy couldn't see his tanks in the smoke. Hell, he thought, with their hatches locked down tight they could barely see the road.

"They're twenty-one hundred meters and closing," Graham reported over the intercom. "Time to start shooting, Sir. In the words of my old drill sergeant, 'If the enemy is in range, so are you.'"

Casey didn't reply. He stayed glued to the CITV, searching the enemy formation to see if any more vehicles were following.

"Steel Six, this is Red One. They're getting awful close," Lieutenant Andrews called over the radio. "When are we going to open fire?"

"Steady, wait for the word," Casey clicked back a reply.

The third enemy tank platoon came into view. The lead elements were now fifteen hundred meters away, deploying straight across the rough ginseng fields in platoon columns. Through the thermal image in his CITV, Casey saw the distinct outline of a VTT-323 APC; it was nineteen hundred meters away. Casey glanced down to his left. Kriel stood in the loader's station, prepared to load on command. He looked anxious but ready.

"Identified PC!" Graham screamed, his palms sweaty and his trigger finger eager to send a HEAT round into an enemy vehicle. The enemy was moving south in perfect column formation. The T-72s and VTT-323s were about twenty-five meters apart, maintaining their formation as if they were on parade.

"Red, this is Steel Six. Direct-fire hot. You get the tanks, I'll take the Vetts."

"Roger, Steel Six," Andrews answered coolly.

"Fire!" Casey shouted over the company command net.

The four well-trained M1A2 tank crews of 1st Platoon fired almost simultaneously. Four enemy tanks went up in flames, their wreckage thrown about in fantastic contortions of busted metal and burning rubber. Other enemy vehicles quickly bypassed these burning wrecks.

The enemy column picked up speed. Several sections broke off the main road and formed platoon columns.

Graham fired. A VTT-323, the target of Casey's cannon, disintegrated from the impact of the 120mm high-explosive round. Graham quickly switched to another APC and shattered it in turn.

The enemy was looking to the south, straight ahead, Casey thought. He hit the slave button on his override and placed Sergeant Graham on the center of mass of another enemy APC. Casey grinned. The black smoke from burning artillery pieces concealed the M1A2s nicely. The enemy still didn't know where he was. Through the wreckage and smoke, the enemy was dying to a force they could not see.

The lead enemy tank company melted in front of 1st Platoon's guns. The engagement spawned two dozen bonfires in the first few seconds. The two lead T-72s of the next company halted to return fire at their unseen foe. Confused as to where the firing was coming from, the enemy tanks formed a firing line facing south. Stalled by the tanks in front of them, more T-72s and an APC were destroyed in rapid succession.

"Gunner, two tanks," Casey shouted, swinging the gun in the direction of the enemy tanks. "Left tank."

"Identified!" Graham replied.

"Fire!" The shot from Casey's gun tube hit the first enemy tank squarely on its turret. The T-72 tank shuddered from the strike and jerked quickly to a stop from the force of the explosion. Through his thermal sight, Casey saw flames shooting skyward from the turret hatches of the dead tank. "Left tank, fire SABOT."

Kriel loaded another depleted-uranium SABOT round. "Up."

"On the way!" Graham screamed.

This round punched right into the second enemy tank. The T-72 smoldered for a brief second, then exploded in a shower of sparks and orange flame. The turret was tossed into the air as if the tank had been a toy.

Undeterred, the enemy kept coming. Spires of dirt erupted near *Cossack* as the enemy guns found the range. The enemy had finally seen their foe. Two T-72 tanks appeared in Casey's tank sights, pointing their long 125mm cannons at *Cossack*.

Roll the dice.

If you roll 2-3, go to Section 90.

If you roll 4-12, go to Section 95.

Section 106

> *In war, as in life generally, the longest way round is often the shortest way there. More precisely the shortest way in space rarely proves the shortest way in time. Shortness is relative to the obstacles in the way.*
>
> —B. H. Liddell Hart

"Dragon TOC, this is Steel Six. Over."

"Steel Six, this is Dragon TOC. You're coming in weak but readable."

Casey could barely hear Dragon TOC. He pushed the square button on the side of the hand mike. "I've linked up with the 1-12th. I'm moving them with me. We will attack reverse Asp to Coral. Over."

"Negative, Steel Six. Dragon Six and Three . . . here. We don't have authority . . . change the plan. . . ."

Casey couldn't hear the rest of the transmission.

"Dragon TOC, you're breaking up. Let me talk to Dragon Six."

"I say again, Dragon Six and Dragon Three . . . brigade . . . brigade rehearsal," the voice on the other end screamed. "Your orders are . . . with the 1-12th and defend Objective Dragon. My orders are to tell you to . . . ."

Casey tried again several times but heard only static. He knew that they didn't have any time to lose. He either had to prepare to defend or get out of Objective Dragon.

If Casey decides to obey his original orders, go to Section 43.

**If Casey decides to disobey his original orders
and fight his way back to friendly lines, go to Section 61.**

Section 107

> *Courage is fear holding on a minute longer.*
> —Gen. George S. Patton Jr.

Standing in the commander's weapon station, head and shoulders above the turret, Casey listened to the heavy 155mm shells hurtle through the early-morning sky. Seconds later, as proof of Keeley's promise, a mass of white smoke burst in angry puffs about eight hundred meters north of the bridge.

Casey studied the heavy assault bridge that spanned the gap, a forty-ton concrete bridge crossing the Gang River. "Well, Weaver, it's up to you and me. If we can't get these tanks across, we'll never break through to the infantry. Are you ready?"

"As ready as I'll ever be, Sir," Weaver replied.

"Move out, nice and steady. Hatches open."

Cossack's engine whined. Graham opened his driver's hatch and shifted the tank into gear. The heavy M1A2 inched forward and rolled onto the bridge. The southern concrete section settled a few inches as the tank's weight shifted onto it. Concrete dust fell into the swiftly flowing river.

Cossack kept moving and climbed onto the metal assault bridge, which creaked under the weight. Cossack rolled slowly over the bridge, guided by hand and arm signals from Sergeant Jacobs.

A collective cheer rose from Team Steel as Cossack cleared the northern section and safely touched the far bank of the Gang.

Okay, Casey thought. The bridge can take a tank. Let's get the rest of the most critical elements across. "Steel Five, send the command group across. After that, send 3d Platoon's Bradleys, then in sequence 2d Platoon, the engineers, and the M113s. We'll leave 4th Platoon here to guard the bridge. Attach the heavy assault bridges and the M88 to 4th Platoon."

"Roger, Steel Six," Stonevitch answered, the newfound respect for his commander evident in his voice. "We might just make it."

"Of course we're going to make it," Casey replied in mock astonishment. "Did you ever doubt it?"

Team Steel kicked into high gear, refueling, reorganizing, and slowly crossing the bridge. The BSFV and Keeley's FIST-V crossed without mishap.

The 3d Platoon was the next across. The Bradleys, lighter and narrower, lined up on the south side. The infantrymen dismounted and crossed on foot. After they were safely across, the Bradleys moved over the bridge, one at a time. The bridge continued to creak and groan as each vehicle crossed. The southern concrete span settled a few more inches with each crossing. Worried Bradley drivers followed Sergeant Jacobs's directions, crossed, then beamed grins of relief. Once across, McDaniel's 3d Platoon rapidly deployed into a firing line on the north side. Casey finally had his tank, the BSFV, the FIST-V, and 3d Platoon on the north side of the Gang.

Now it was time for more tanks. Nervously, Casey watched as Sergeant Scott's tank slowly crossed.

Roll the dice.

If you roll 2-4, go to Section 51.

If you roll 5-12, go to Section 78.

Section 108

The rain drizzled down.

"Did I ever tell you what my old drill sergeant used to say," Sergeant Graham announced as *Cossack* moved into Team Steel's assembly area.

"Okay, I'll take the bait," Casey answered, wondering just what kind of fellow his gunner was. "What did he say?"

"'All battles are fought in the rain.'"

Cossack's engine rumbled quietly as Casey directed his driver carefully through Team Steel's assembly area. The reconnaissance had been well worth the effort, in spite of the dense fog. Each leader traveled the route from the assembly area to the passage lanes—a valuable rehearsal even for vehicles equipped with state-of-the-art global positioning navigation systems. The M1A2's thermal sights aided the recon by enabling the leaders to see through the fog. Each platoon leader saw the passage lanes and the key terrain on the enemy side of Phase Line Audi, and even identified a group of enemy soldiers placing mines at CS210414 and at CS225410.

Casey talked over Team Steel's movement from the assembly area to the passage lanes. He described the actions to take if his men ran into enemy obstacles. He outlined each of the possible directions of attack. As an added bonus, Casey and Stonevitch were coming to terms. The XO's sharp edge, largely the result of the tension and anxiety of combat, dulled against Casey's determined but respectful manner.

In spite of this, Stonevitch was still dead set against Viper, a point that Casey now agreed with after seeing the enemy placing mine-fields. Unfortunately, Casey still didn't have a clear picture of what was on the other side of the hill.

Casey looked at his watch. It was 1430. He scanned his IVIS terminal again for any additional information on the enemy from brigade. The only new reports cited vehicle noises in the vicinity of CS225415, near Direction of Attack Viper. Casey knew that he would have to decide soon, and with very little information on the location and composition of the enemy.

Casey's thoughts wandered as the tank moved into position in the center of the assembly area—an ever-widening arc of vehicles that belonged to Team Steel. Casey thought about the name of his tank, christened *Cossack* by the late Captain Buford. All the tanks in C Company were named with names starting with the letter *C*. Casey liked the name, thinking that it fit the mission—a raid behind enemy lines like the Russian Cossack cavalry might have conducted against one of Napoleon's corps in the nineteenth century. Casey could understand why Stonevitch might have called his tank *Cossack;* instead, Stonevitch's tank had the name *Crom* emblazoned on the bore evacuator of the 120mm gun tube. Why did Buford name his tank *Cossack?*

Casey saw that the thirteen M113s and two huge Wolverine heavy assault bridges (HABs) had joined his group, bringing his force up to the full numbers promised by Major Cutter. More importantly, every vehicle that Casey passed in the assembly area was a beehive of activity. All weapons were mounted and most of the tanks and Bradleys had boxes of extra ammunition and smoke pots in the bustle racks and on the top of their turrets. To Casey's trained eye, the company team certainly *looked* combat ready.

"Stop here and I'll have Sergeant Graham ground-guide you into position," Casey ordered his driver, Pfc. William Weaver, over the tank's intercom system.

The tank halted. Casey, Stonevitch, and Scott dismounted. Casey and Stonevitch walked over to the first sergeant's APC as Graham positioned the commander's tank. First Sergeant Washington sat in the back of his M113 with the ramp down, watching the two officers approach.

"Greetings, Captain," First Sergeant Washington said, throwing his commander a salute. "Team Steel is assembled, fueled, fed, and loaded for combat. I just finished my precombat inspection of all vehicles with the platoon sergeants. Every platoon knows the possible directions of attack. We've got a few things left to do—we're short combat lifesaver kits and some grenades and 9mm ammo—but we'll be ready when you give the word."

"Good job, Top," Casey replied, stepping inside the armored personnel carrier. The captain took a seat on the narrow troop bench and faced First Sergeant Washington. Stonevitch followed and sat to the commander's left.

Casey studied his first sergeant for a minute in the dimly lit M113. They hadn't had much time to get acquainted, only a short talk before Casey left for the reconnaissance. During that talk, Casey saw that Washington was a professional whom he could trust. The first sergeant had prepared Team Steel for battle. Casey was delighted.

"Top, Stonevitch and I are about to decide on the direction of our attack," said Casey. "I say 'about to decide' because I want your ten cents' worth first."

"Captain, I've read the brigade's OPORD. Whichever way we go— Cobra, Viper, or Coral—we have to blast through and keep moving. I've been down all three of these routes before the war," the veteran first sergeant replied, reaching for Casey's map. Washington opened the map and quickly taped it to the inside wall of the APC.

"What do you recommend?" Casey queried.

Washington pointed to the map. "I'm worried about Viper. I agree with Lieutenant Stonevitch that the enemy will be ready for us along Viper. It's too obvious and direct a route for an attacking force to reach the 1-12th Infantry. I think they want to trap us there."

Casey followed Washington's finger as it traced Viper on the map.

"The U.S. Army has a habit of taking the best course of action and using the least effective as the deception. We fight through with our firepower, regardless of the enemy. But all warfare is based on deception."

"Keep going, I'm following you so far," Casey said, feeling curiously like a pupil in school as he was mentored by this veteran soldier. His respect for First Sergeant Washington was growing.

"We're a small force—powerful, but small. Our mission is to get to the 1-12th Infantry. We should do everything we can to avoid a fight. We should take the least obvious approach. The greatest means to increase speed is to avoid contact. The way I see it, we should attack along Coral and take the ford."

"Top, we've already thrown out that idea," Stonevitch snapped, shaking his head. "We don't know what the enemy has along Coral. One well-placed platoon could stop us cold if we try to take the entire team down that narrow defile. Besides, we can't cross the river. The Gang is too deep to ford and it's too wide to bridge, even with the new assault bridges."

"What if I told you that I know a way that we can ford the Gang?" First Sergeant Washington offered. The first sergeant waved his arm, signaling to someone at the front of the APC. "Let me introduce you to Sergeant Jacobs, our resident expert on the heavy assault bridge."

"Sergeant Jacobs reporting as ordered," Jacobs announced with a broad grin and a jaunty salute. "I understand you have a puddle to cross."

Casey smiled. "Glad to see you're with us, Jacobs. I guess you found a Wolverine."

"That's right, sir, and they're brand-new ones too," Jacobs said with a wide smile. "Top and I think we have a solution to your problem."

"I'm listening."

"Sir, if you'll come with me, I'll show you," Jacobs said.

"You go on, Sir," First Sergeant Washington told Casey. "I have to stay here and wait for two more reports." Washington handed Casey back his map. "I think you'll like what Jacobs has to show you."

Lieutenant Keeley arrived as the APC opened.

"Keeley, you're just in time," Casey announced. "Come with us."

Casey and Stonevitch stepped outside and walked with Keeley and Jacobs to the engineer sergeant's newly assigned heavy assault bridge section. A terrain model, outlined with fist-sized rocks, depicted the rough outline of the Gang River along Direction of Attack Coral. A line of twigs stuck into the sand indicated the crossing point.

"Who made this?" Stonevitch asked.

"I did, sir," Jacobs answered, beaming with pride. "Sir, I can lay the heavy assault bridges at the ford site and you can cross the Gang."

"This is a waste of time," Stonevitch interrupted, shaking his head. "The heavy assault bridge can only cross a twenty-four-meter gap. The latest reports put the river's width at the crossing on Coral at thirty to thirty-five meters and six feet deep. The Gang is too wide for the assault bridges and too deep to ford. We'd never get the tanks across."

"He's right, Jacobs," Casey said. "If we attack up Coral and can't cross the river, we're screwed."

"But what if we lay the bridge underwater?" Jacobs suggested, pointing to the terrain model. "I can overlap the assault bridges. That would allow us to cross a forty-eight-meter gap. A tank crossing the underwater bridge could cross six feet of water. I can mark the sides of the bridge with poles, and the tanks can drive between them."

Casey stroked his chin and stared down at the terrain model.

"If I overlap the bridges at the ford on Coral, I know you can make it," Jacobs persisted, his face turning serious.

Casey looked at his map and then at Stonevitch, scratched his head, and suddenly beamed a wide grin. "Hell, that's a great idea! We can cross where they don't expect us."

Stonevitch looked at the terrain model in disbelief, "I don't know. I've never crossed stacked bridges before. It's a hell of a risk. What if it doesn't work?"

"I don't think we can afford to pass it up," Casey replied. "If we can attack along Coral and cross the ford on underwater bridges, we might catch the enemy by surprise."

"It will work," Jacobs added. "I guarantee it!"

Casey placed his map on the wet, flat spade of the Wolverine heavy assault bridge. He took out an alcohol pen from his Nomex combat uniform and carefully traced a route that led across the ford along Coral, moved north, and entered Objective Dragon from the north. "Let's call this Direction of Attack Asp."

Stonevitch studied the Coral-to-Asp approach. "It's risky. Crossing an underwater assault bridge will take plenty of time. I'd rather cross a fixed bridge. Maybe if we took Coral, we could attack west at the Gang and seize the concrete bridge on Viper. They won't expect us from the east."

A hurt expression flashed across Sergeant Jacobs's face, as if the lieutenant's caution would rob his bridge layers of playing a central role in the operation.

"Coral to Asp is very risky—too risky," Stonevitch replied, looking up at the stormy sky. "Can we gamble on being able to ford the Gang in this weather? What if we took Coral and took the Viper bridge from the east?"

Casey considered this option, tracing the direction of attack along Coral to Viper. After a few seconds of consideration he nodded, the gesture signifying that Coral to Asp was much too risky.

"It's up to you," Stonevitch announced, looking at his watch. "As far as I can see, it's either Cobra or—if you're feeling lucky—Coral to Viper. Either way, getting across the Gang is our biggest challenge. Either way we have to seize a bridge."

A clap of loud thunder roared in the heavens.

If Casey decides to attack along Cobra, go to Section 5.

If Casey decides to attack along Coral to Viper, go to Section 6.

Section 109

> *In a tank division there are no written orders!*
> —General von Mellenthin

"White One, keep moving! Don't stop. The bastards want us to slow down so they can hammer us with artillery. Plow through the mines! Keep going!"

"Roger, Steel Six," Scott's excited voice answered. "We're moving now!"

The 2d Platoon rolled again, leaving behind the M1A2 tank that had struck a mine. Casey checked the damaged tank for survivors.

The tank commander waved, signaling that he and his crew were okay. Casey waved back, knowing that First Sergeant Washington would pick up the survivors and try to get the tank back in service.

Casey looked away as *Cossack* rolled forward. Explosions and artillery flares created brilliant flashes of alternating dark and light. Casey adjusted his hatch to the open-protected position as Scott's three remaining tanks surged ahead.

Farther up Cobra, 155mm artillery shells exploded along the ridges in bright orange-red bursts. Flares lit up the night sky as machine-gun fire erupted at the front of the column. Tracers abruptly whizzed through the air, striking the tanks in brilliant sparkles.

"Contact, troops CS220440. Engaging," Scott reported over the radio. Scott's tanks didn't stop. Casey saw them blazing away at both sides of the road. With the tanks still on the move at twenty miles an hour, every machine gun in 2d Platoon was searing the high ground on the left and right side of the road with fire.

Enemy infantry squads in foxholes and shallow trenches returned fire, trying to stop the tanks. Casey saw the fleeting shadows of groups of enemy soldiers along the forward slope of the ridge, moving north. He quickly swung the turret to the left side of the road, eager for revenge.

"Troops!"

"Identified!" Graham screamed.

"Get the bastards!" Casey yelled. *Cossack* charged forward, its 7.62mm machine gun rattling a deadly song, plastering an enemy position to the right front. Casey watched through his thermal sight, the enemy soldiers plainly visible in the dark as white hot spots in his green-tinged thermal sight. He saw four or five enemy soldiers knocked backward by Graham's accurate fire.

Sergeant Sellers's Bradley Stinger fighting vehicle also got into the act. The air defense sergeant hosed the right side of the road with exploding 25mm HE rounds. Other vehicles in the column also engaged on the move, spraying both sides of the defile with fire at the slightest hint of opposition.

Just southwest of the village of Sori, a narrow cut, constructed of rock and concrete, constricted Highway 21 to a single lane. This rock drop had been part of the initial allied defense to block Highway 21 from enemy movement south. The enemy had cleared the rock drop in their advance south, but this choke point still presented a problem for Casey's attacking column.

Sergeant Scott, true to his hell-bent-for-leather reputation, did not hesitate. The enemy made an all-out effort to stop the American tanks in the cut. Illumination flares popped overhead as enemy antitank gunners, from the top of the steep embankments on both sides of the narrow cut, took aim at Scott's advancing tanks. Other enemy lined the gauntlet, firing small arms and throwing explosive satchel charges.

Scott's tank accelerated, pushing forward of the other tanks by fifty meters, ramming into the cut. *Cossack* followed 2d Platoon's tanks. Racing forward, the tanks sprayed the crests of the embankments with cannon and machine-gun fire.

An enemy RPG gunner fired at the lead tank as it entered the cut. Through his vision blocks Casey saw the grenade strike the top of the turret of Scott's tank. The top of the tank was consumed in a mushroom-shaped cloud of flames, but the tank kept moving. Buttoned up and protected by several inches of special armor, Scott's tank made it through the gauntlet of fire, gunning down the RPG team in the process. Without stopping, the second and third tanks machine-gunned the remaining enemy defenders.

Like a blessing from on high, artillery fell on the cut, bursting above the ground and showering the enemy infantry with shrapnel. The enemy fire ceased as the VT artillery shells nailed the defenders to the ground. Moving forward relentlessly, the tanks filed through the cut. Under intense machine-gun fire and artillery, the enemy seemed to disappear into the avalanche of Team Steel's advance.

The tank column smashed on, unstoppable, peppering the enemy with machine-gun and cannon fire, penetrating every enemy roadblock. The 2d Platoon raced past the intersection of Highway 21 and the road that led to Sori, then sprinted northwest toward the bridge.

As Casey turned the corner he saw the burning debris of five destroyed enemy APCs, the apparent victims of the MLRS rocket strike. He took silent satisfaction in his decision to fire the MLRS; the strike had landed right on an enemy defensive position at the exit of the defile.

"Steel Six, this is White One. I see the bridge. It's still intact. I say again, the bridge has not been destroyed!"

Casey's heart soared. This was the first good luck he'd had all night. If they could seize the bridge, he just might succeed.

"Get to the bridge! White One, keep moving. Don't let them blow it up!" Casey shouted over the radio.

"Engaging Vetts on the bridge now. Request artillery!" Sergeant Scott responded, the sound of machine-gun fire echoing in the background of his radio transmission.

More flares popped overhead. A mad fusillade of machine-gun fire erupted from the enemy defending the bridge.

"Working it. Vee Tee in effect," Keeley replied without cue. "Everybody better stay buttoned up. Danger close!"

The 2d Platoon fanned out into a jagged *V* formation, with Scott's tank in the lead and machine guns blazing.

Roll the dice.

If you roll 2-5, go to Section 86.

If you roll 6-12, go to Section 97.

Section 110

> *Nothing is more important in war than unity in command.*
> —Napoleon

The captain looked up at the heavens. The rain had stopped, which was a relief, but the night was still as black as pitch without a trace of the moon. The heavy clouds hung oppressively low in the sky.

Casey felt uneasy. He hoped he had done everything possible to set the stage for success.

Casey stood in the open hatch of his tank, nicknamed *Cossack* by the previous commander. The light of the IVIS display and other instruments in the tank commander's station gave the turret a soft green glow. He watched the battalion support platoon refuel his tank. In the thick fog he could see only the vehicles in front of and behind him.

Casey was worried about the mission as a hundred "what-ifs" played out in his head. What worried him most was the fog. It swept into the valley, wrapping the area in a thick, opaque blanket. The fog seemed to take turns with the rain, rolling in when the rain stopped and diminishing when the rain fell. He feared, in spite of his high-tech, IVIS-equipped M1A2 tanks, that the fog would play hell with his ability to control Team Steel.

Fifteen minutes after midnight, the lead platoon of Team Steel arrived at the planned refueling site, in a wooded valley three kilometers south of the line of departure (LD). Soldiers on the ground met the tanks and guided them forward. Waving small green chem lights, as would ground crews at an airport, the guides led the heavy armored vehicles into predesignated refueling positions next to the large fuel trucks. Twelve HEMMTs—huge, eight-wheeled, 2,500-gallon fuel trucks—lined the road. The trucks were spaced sixty meters apart.

The HEMMTs refueled two vehicles at a time from hoses extending from their back ends. Tank loaders jumped from hatches and stood on the flat back decks of their M1A2s as the men on the ground handed them metal-tipped fuel nozzles. Within minutes JP8 was flowing into the thirsty M1A2 tanks and Bradley fighting vehicles.

"Sir, visibility stinks. I can barely see three hundred meters with my driver's thermal viewer," Private Weaver, Casey's driver, announced over *Cossack*'s intercom.

"Tell me something I don't know," Casey announced sarcastically, unable to mask his concern. Casey's speech at the operations order had not pulled the team together as he had hoped. Relieving Lieutenant Stonevitch had been a traumatic event for Casey and Team

Steel. Casey felt that his officers resented him for Stonevitch's dismissal.

So be it, Casey thought. What else could he do? He felt absolutely certain that he had made the right decision. Time was the most important element in war. He couldn't waste a minute coddling an impertinent officer. He had no choice but to relieve Stonevitch.

Young Second Lieutenant Andrews, who had barely learned to lead a tank platoon, was now the executive officer. Casey had sent him to organize the refueling operation and coordinate the passage of lines. So far, everything was working according to plan. Still . . .

Casey took off his tanker's helmet and listened to the sound of a unit preparing to attack. The high-pitched whine of *Cossack*'s powerful 1,500-horsepower engine filled the night air. Casey's gunner, Sergeant Graham, and the loader, Specialist Kriel, crouched on the back deck of the tank and handled the fuel hoses extending from the huge HEMMT fuel truck. The entire company team was refueling. The operation was scheduled to take fifteen minutes.

Tense moments ticked by as the vehicles refueled. Each M1A2 tank had a five-hundred-gallon fuel tank, but each vehicle would need only a three-minute shot of JP8 to fill its fuel tank. At a consumption rate of about fifty gallons an hour, the M1A2 could run for only ten hours without refueling. Fuel, Casey knew, would be one of his principal worries.

"Captain Casey?" a voice shouted from *Cossack*'s side.

Casey looked down and saw the young face of his new XO. "Andrews, what are you doing here?"

"I coordinated the passage of lines on the radio," Andrews replied. "I was worried about the support platoon getting lost in this fog. I didn't want anything to go wrong at the refueling site."

Casey grimaced. He suddenly realized how complex this operation had become; refueling prior to crossing the line of departure, passing lines through a friendly allied infantry brigade just after the artillery preparation, penetrating the enemy's defenses, and then lining up with the 1-12th. "Are you sure they know we're coming up Viper?"

"Roger, Sir. I talked with their operations officer. He's a major who speaks perfect English. We're all set for 0045. The lane is marked by thermal and infrared chem lights. The tank drivers will be able to see the passage lane with their driver's thermal viewers. Everyone else can follow the route with their AN/PVS-7 night vision goggles. The major told me that his brigade laid several antitank minefields to the sides of the passage lanes. I'll pass a digital message to all platoon leaders with the minefield locations and the route markings."

"Good job, Andrews," Casey answered, realizing that in minutes Team Steel would leave the safety of friendly territory and cross into enemy lines. "Did you get anything else from this major?"

"Yes. He says he's heard tanks north of his position in the vicinity of Viper. They're worried that the enemy tanks may conduct an attack in this dense fog. He couldn't identify any exact locations. The fog is too thick and his unit doesn't have thermals."

"Okay, you'd better get back to your tank," Casey said, then paused. Enemy tanks. The sound of tank engines could indicate that the enemy was withdrawing, although that idea was probably too good to be true. The enemy might also be moving into fighting positions. Maybe the artillery will get them. "I want you to follow Sergeant Tremain's engineer platoon. If we run into any enemy antitank minefields, I'll need you to help move them up and conduct the breach."

"Wilco, Sir," Andrews replied eagerly. "I'll do my best!"

"I know you will," Casey replied with a smile. He glanced at his watch, pushed the battery light button, and noticed the time. "Now hurry up, we attack in fifteen minutes."

Andrews threw a quick salute to his commander and ran off into the darkness. Casey pensively checked his watch as the time passed. Then, on schedule, he heard the distinctive sound of the planned artillery preparation. Shells shrieked high overhead toward their predesignated targets. Allied artillery and mortars fell along the southern sections of Cobra and Coral to mask the point of penetration. At the same time, three 155mm howitzer battalions and an MLRS rocket battalion pulverized suspected enemy positions along Viper. Once the artillery firestorm stopped and a hole was created in the enemy's defenses, Casey's team would rush forward.

"Jesus," Sgt. Charlie Graham exclaimed as he stood on *Cossack*'s back deck and listened to the roar of the artillery strikes. The earth trembled with the blast of successive explosions. "The cannons are clobbering them. Maybe this won't be so hard after all. No one can withstand that much artillery fire."

Casey didn't answer. The artillery was firing "dumb" shells, not brilliant munitions. The new, special brilliant munitions—shells that could sense enemy armored vehicles automatically and detonate above them through the marvels of millimeter wave and acoustic detection technology—were being held back for tomorrow's offensive. In addition, this artillery targeted suspected enemy positions, not confirmed locations. There were no forward observers to see the effects of the fire. No one would know how effective the artillery preparation had been until his team went forward.

"Mount up, we're moving out," Casey ordered. He placed his CVC helmet back on his head. Graham handed the fuel hose to a soldier on the ground and climbed back into *Cossack* through the loader's hatch. Specialist Kriel followed.

The vehicles in front of Casey raced their engines. The 2d Platoon, composed of four M1A2 Abrams tanks led by Sergeant First Class Scott, moved off to the start point (SP). McDaniel's four M2 Bradleys followed the lead tank platoon.

"Steel Six, this is Steel Seven," First Sergeant Washington reported to Casey over Team Steel's command radio frequency.

"Steel Seven, this is Six. Send it," Casey replied.

"I'm with the M113 platoon," First Sergeant Washington announced. "We're all set here. The 1st Platoon is refueling now."

"Roger," Casey answered. "See you on Dragon. Out."

Cossack clanked forward at six miles an hour, moving carefully out of the refueling site, following the last Bradley fighting vehicle in Lieutenant McDaniel's 3d Platoon. The thick fog rolled back, hiding the column and reducing normal vision to less than a hundred meters.

Team Steel's command group consisted of the artillery officer, Lieutenant Keeley, in a FIST-V followed by a BSFV. Sergeant Sellers's Bradley Stinger fighting vehicle carried an air defense missile team in the back armed with Stinger missiles. The chances of engaging enemy aircraft seemed slim, but Casey was glad to have the Bradley's 25mm firepower added to his command group.

Casey turned around in his open turret and saw Lieutenant Keeley's FIST-V trailing close behind. Keeley, the company team FIST (fire support team leader), was a crucial part of the mission. Although each M1A2 could send digital calls for artillery fire automatically through their IVIS system, the complicated artillery coordination and control that Casey needed to smash his way through the valleys was best handled through Keeley. Casey worried that the FIST-V would have trouble keeping up with *Cossack*.

The fog, as thick as soup, forced the tank drivers to slow down to a snail's pace to avoid losing their way. But Casey's platoon leaders reported that all their vehicles were rolling forward as planned.

Casey ducked down inside the turret and checked his IVIS display. The IVIS reported the location of all his M1A2s automatically and graphically represented their locations on his map screen. From the screen he could monitor the movement of most of his vehicles. These locations were precisely accurate and automatically updated by each tank's POS/NAV satellite system.

Unfortunately, only twenty-one out of forty-five vehicles in Team Steel registered automatically on Casey's IVIS screen. The M1A2s, Wolverines, Bradleys, and the FIST-V had IVIS interface and POS/NAV systems. Every other vehicle had to determine its location in the old-fashioned way—with their vehicle-mounted GPS devices called PLGRs (pronounced "pluggers"), maps, and night vision devices.

Even worse was that Casey had not confirmed any enemy locations. He looked at his watch. It was 0045. He scanned his IVIS screen and saw that Scott's 2d Platoon was right on schedule, crossing the LD and moving north toward Tongak. Casey's plan was to bypass the town to the east, travel north, and get back on Highway 17. If Team Steel moved fast, Casey intended to race by the enemy before they knew he was there.

"Steel Six, this is White One. LD now. Zero and four. Visibility three hundred meters. No contact," Sergeant Scott reported.

"Roger, White One. Enemy tanks suspected in Tongak. If you see them, take them out but keep moving. Over," Casey ordered.

"Wilco," Sergeant Scott answered.

The steady crash of artillery pounded the ground north of the passage lane. As scheduled, the howitzers shifted their fire to targets along Viper, moving north in a wave of destruction.

Cossack moved carefully between the markers designating the passage lane. The lane followed a narrow dirt trail, marked on both sides by thermal and infrared chem lights. Some of the markers were very difficult to see, and Weaver was able to make them out only in his driver's thermal viewer. Casey closely followed *Cossack*'s movement on his POS/NAV system, directing Weaver through a predesignated course that he had programmed to help guide the way.

Finally, *Cossack* exited the passage lane and crossed the line of departure. Casey looked through the thermal eyes of his CITV and saw McDaniel's Bradley platoon to his front, moving northeast on Viper to bypass Tongak. Casey turned the viewer around to look behind him and saw the FIST-V and the Bradley Stinger fighting vehicle.

Casey scanned to the rear of the BSFV for the engineers. Through his CITV screen he could see the CEV (combat engineer vehicle) moving steadily through the passage lane. He couldn't make out anything behind the CEV. It appeared to be the last vehicle.

"Steel Six, this is Steel Five," Andrews's nervous voice radioed Casey. "We have a break in contact, sir. I don't think Sapper Six has all the engineers with him."

"Sapper Six, report your location," Casey ordered. There was an ominous silence on the command frequency. Casey waited nervously for a response while he switched to his IVIS screen.

A series of bright flashes, followed by three large explosions, echoed in the valley.

"Oh, my God," Sergeant Tremain answered weakly. "We've moved off the passage lane. I don't know where my CEV is. I can't see a thing in this fog!"

"Steel Six, this is Steel Five. The lead assault bridge and two APCs just hit antitank mines. Two M113s are burning. I'm right behind them with the CEV. We've got wounded men here. They all drove right into the middle of a goddamned minefield," Lieutenant Andrews shouted over the radio.

Casey's heart sank. Events were rapidly cascading out of control.

"Steel Six, this is Steel Five. What do you want me to do?"

Casey knew that he had to decide quickly, before the situation got worse. He had two options: order Lieutenant Andrews to sort out the mess in the passage lane and continue the attack with 2d and 3d Platoons, or hold 2d and 3d Platoons in place and return to assist Lieutenant Andrews to get his force out of the minefield.

If Casey decides to return to help Lieutenant Andrews, go to Section 49.

If Casey decides to continue the attack, go to Section 36.

Section 111

> *The revival of the night attack is due—overdue. Its moral ripples spread disorganization far beyond physical reach.*
> —B. H. Liddell Hart

A fine, misty rain blew into Casey's face, carried by the strong north wind. Occasionally thunder roared far above. The dark, foreboding sky seemed to hold the promise of a new, more brutal storm.

Casey looked at his watch. It was 0915. He knew that every second counted, especially for the infantrymen of the 1-12th, who were trapped and alone, surrounded by the enemy.

"We got everybody?" Casey asked.

"My first sergeant, First Sergeant Washington, is coordinating re-supply. He'll be back in an hour," the executive officer replied with a dourness that barely hid his contempt for the newcomer.

Casey eyed the officer who had just spoken. The company executive officer (XO) stood behind the other officers with his arms folded defiantly across his chest. Thin and tall, the man's most striking feature was his tired deep blue eyes. Regardless of the fatigue that registered on the man's face, Casey instantly recognized that the XO was someone to reckon with.

Casey stood in front of five officers and four NCOs who were waiting in a semicircle in front of an M1A2 tank. Several of the officers fidgeted nervously.

"We don't need this guy," Casey heard a red-headed lieutenant whisper to the infantry officer next to him.

"I'm going to give it to you straight because we don't have much time. I'm Captain Tom Casey. As of now, I'm in command of Team Steel."

"By whose order?" the executive officer interrupted. "I took command of this company this morning, when we were told that Captain Buford was killed. This company's been through a lot together. I've been with this unit in battle. We haven't heard anything about you taking command."

"I know," Casey replied, trying to force a smile. "The situation is changing very fast. You've done a great job—all of you have—but I have orders to take command."

"You haven't answered my question," said the XO. "The name's Stonevitch. First Lieutenant Sergei Stonevitch."

"Well, Lieutenant Stonevitch, the orders come directly from Major Cutter. I just left the TOC. We have a critical mission to conduct. Our new orders are to attack to rescue an infantry battalion that's in desperate need of help."

"When are we supposed to do this?" Stonevitch asked.

"Team Steel crosses the line of departure tonight at 0045," Casey replied, disregarding Stonevitch's insubordinate tone.

A few of the officers whispered their disbelief. The others registered their concern in scowls and looks of surprise.

"Whose brilliant idea is this?" Stonevitch complained.

"I'm not here to debate it," Casey replied, shooting a look at Stonevitch to counter the lieutenant's challenge. "It all boils down to this: we're the only unit that can break through to the infantry before they're overrun by the enemy. A bigger force would arrive too late, only to count the dead. If the 1-12th has any chance at all, it's if we can break through tonight."

Stonevitch glared at Casey in cold silence.

Casey knew that the first challenge to his command had arrived. How he handled this situation would determine the success or failure of his leadership. These officers, he knew, had fought together. They knew and trusted one another. They didn't know him. He was asking them to risk their lives on a desperate mission. He had to win them over, and he had to do it fast.

"Here's the situation," Casey explained as he unfolded his plastic-covered map on the front slope of the tank. He picked up two big rocks and fixed the map so that the officers could see the area of operations as he briefed them. He pointed to the map. "This is our area of operations. Our mission is to penetrate enemy lines and link up with the infantry on Objective Dragon. We have about fifteen hours to prepare."

"We're attacking tonight?" the red-haired second lieutenant sneered. "The enemy's all over the place. We had a hell of a fight yesterday. Why do we get all the good deals?"

"What's your name?" Casey questioned.

"Lieutenant Bill Pender. 3d Platoon, A Company, 2-9th Infantry."

"You'll be my 4th Platoon from now on, Pender. Your call sign will be Green," Casey ordered as he faced down the lieutenant's challenge. "Team Steel is the only team that can do this right now. That's just how it is. Every other unit is getting ready for the main attack on 3 October."

"How do you intend to do this?" another infantry lieutenant chided. The thin, cocky infantryman looked as if he had been a long-distance runner in his college days. He glanced at Lieutenant Stonevitch as if for support.

"This is how we'll do it," Casey answered. "We'll cross lines, attack north along one of these south-to-north corridors, link up with the 1-12th Infantry, and defend Objective Dragon until the task force arrives."

"Sir, I'm Sergeant First Class Scott, 2d Platoon leader," a short black NCO interjected. "How many men does the 1-12th have left right now?"

"A light infantry battalion has about six hundred men assigned. They've been fighting for four days now. The latest report says that the 1-12th is down to about two hundred and fifty."

The NCO shook his head in disbelief. "They're getting murdered."

"That's exactly what will happen if we don't break through to them," Casey answered, pointing to the map. "As you can see on the map, I've sketched out three possible directions of attack. The first thing we need to decide is the best way to get to the 1-12th."

"We went through that approach yesterday," McDaniel answered. "Highway Twenty-one is the only way. Highway Seventeen—what you've labeled Viper—is lousy with enemy. We took casualties there yesterday. We lost Lieutenant Shriver and six other men."

"Jim's right. The enemy's all over Viper," Stonevitch added. "We should attack up Cobra. We've trained along Highway Twenty-one a few times. McDaniel's infantry knows that ground like the back of their hand."

Casey nodded. "Major Cutter recommended Viper. The maps show it to be the widest avenue of approach. He thinks that Viper would allow us to maximize our firepower."

"Viper may be the Leavenworth solution," Stonevitch insisted. "But I'm telling you that Viper is a death trap. Besides, we don't even know if those bridges are still standing. Maybe they're blown by now."

Casey shook his head. "The division's UAV reports that both bridges are still up."

"Sure could have used those UAVs a few days ago." Stonevitch shook his head. The rest of the officers mumbled in agreement. "UAV or not, Viper is a gauntlet. There are keyhole shots all up that valley. You could hide a battalion in there. We're not going up there again."

"The UAVs have been busy. As you may know, the enemy found a way to sabotage our satellite systems. Some kind of computer virus. Our recon capability at theater level is just now getting back on line," Casey persisted, trying to change the tone of the discussion. "But let's get back to earth. Our mission is here, to rescue the 1-12th Infantry on Objective Dragon. What if we take Coral?"

"No bridge. The Gang is too wide and the water is too deep to ford," Stonevitch countered. "Anyone who can read a map can see that there are only two choices."

The officers talked in hushed tones among themselves. Most seemed to agree with the XO.

Casey's eyes locked with Stonevitch's. With a nod of his head, Casey motioned to the XO to step to the side. Stonevitch clearly understood the gesture. The two men walked to the rear of the tank while the other officers huddled closer to the map.

Stonevitch stopped next to Casey. Brazen and sure, Stonevitch tilted his head to the left and stared in defiance at Casey. The lieutenant's blue eyes openly challenged the captain.

"Okay, you've got one minute. What's your problem," Casey announced.

"Problem? I've been fighting with these men for the past week. You want me to hand over command of Team Steel to you. I don't know you. I don't know if you know anything about the enemy, the terrain, or how to fight a company team. If you want my help, you'd better listen to what I have to say. My life, and the lives of the soldiers I've been with, swing in the balance."

Casey didn't blink. He searched the eyes of the officer in front of him. In those eyes he saw pure defiance. Casey glanced at his watch. Somehow this isn't how he had pictured his first day in command.

"Well, what'll it be?" Stonevitch pressed.

Casey considered his options. He saw two possibilities: relieve Stonevitch immediately and replace him with the senior platoon leader, or agree with him.

**If Casey decides to relieve Stonevitch,
go to Section 3.**

**If Casey decides to agree with Stonevitch,
go to Section 4.**

Section 112

Study FRAGO (Fragmentary Order) Operation Cold Steel, shown below:

Copy 5 of 36 copies
1st Brigade
020209 OCT XX

FRAGO, Operation Cold Steel
Reference: Map, series: area of operations special (attached)
Time zone used throughout the order: local

Task Organization:

TM C (STEEL)
  M1A2 tank platoon
  M1A2 tank platoon
  Bradley infantry platoon
  Bradley infantry platoon
    Engineer platoon (+)
    2 HABs
  BSFV
  FIST
  Attached M113 APCs (13 M113s)
  1 HEMMT

1. Situation
  A. Enemy
    (1) Terrain
      a. Decisive terrain = hilltop at CS222463
      b. Key terrain
        Bridge Highway 21 at CS211446
        Bridge Highway 17 at CS237447
      c. This operation will be conducted in restricted to severely restricted terrain. "FM 34-130 Intelligence Preparation of the Battlefield" defines restrictive terrain as terrain that hinders movement

to some degree. Little effort is needed to enhance mobility, but units may have difficulty maintaining preferred speeds, moving in combat formations, or transitioning from one formation to another. Restricted terrain slows movement by requiring zigzagging or frequent detours. Restricted terrain for armored and mechanized forces typically consists of moderate to steep slopes or moderate to densely spaced obstacles such as trees, rocks, or buildings. Severely restricted terrain hinders or slows movement in combat formations unless some effort is made to enhance mobility. This could take the form of committing engineer assets to improving mobility or of deviating from doctrinal tactics, such as moving in columns instead of line formations or at speeds much lower than those preferred (pp. 2–15).

    (2) Weather

        a. 24-hour forecast (as of 2 October)

            Sky conditions: overcast

            Visibility: less than 300 meters during heavy fog

            Weather: heavy rains and fog

            Temperature: max. 56 degrees F; min. 40 degrees F; wind chill negligible

            Winds: 4–8 knots from the north

        b. 48-hour forecast (as of 2 October)

            Sky conditions: clearing

            Visibility: in excess of 2,000 meters

            Weather: light rain, sunshine

            Temperature: max. 70 degrees F; min. 55 degrees F; wind chill negligible

            Winds: 2–4 knots from the north

    (3) Light Data

        a. Lunar

Day	Moon Rise	Start NVG	Stop NVG	Moon Set	% Illum
02	0015	0045	0525	1315	0%
03	0018	0048	0528	1318	1%

        b. Solar

Day	BMNT	Sunrise	Sunset	EENT
02	0510	0600	1858	1925
03	0512	0602	1856	1923

(4) Enemy Composition

a. The 14th Truck Mobile Division (TMD) is the first defensive echelon of the 1 Infantry Corps defense. This infantry division is assessed at 45–50% strength. The 14th TMD is defending generally along Phase Line (PL) Audi, current line of departure (LD) from CS1940 to CS3040, and centered on the Gang River PL Cressida with the mission to destroy the 1-12th Infantry Battalion (U.S.) vic. CS2246. The 1st Armor Brigade (approximately 60 T-72 tanks, 70% strength) is located north of PL Datsun vic. CS2555, refitting and rearming while 14 TMD completes destruction of 1-12th Infantry located vic. CS2246. The 1st Armor Brigade expected use is as the corps's counterattack force to block any penetration of the main defensive zone. Estimated strength of divisional and regimental artillery units is 50–60%. The most probable course of action is to continue its defense in current positions for at least 32 hours.

(5) Locations: As shown on attached overlay.

(6) Movements: 1st Armor Brigade will most likely move south to counter any penetration of PL Cressida (Gang River). It is expected that they will take four hours to move two tank companies, five hours for a battalion, and eight hours for the entire brigade from their templated assembly areas vic. CS2555 to PL Cressida.

(7) Capabilities: 14th TMD consists of two infantry regiments (approximately 1,200 men per regiment at current strengths), a mechanized infantry battalion (approximately 20 VTT-323 APCs), a tank battalion (approximately 20 product-improved T-62 tanks), an artillery regiment (two 122mm and one 152mm self-propelled [SP] howitzer battalions).

(8) Most likely course of action: Defend in sector to block U.S. forces from moving north of PL Cressida while they complete the destruction of the 1-12th Infantry Battalion pocket vic. Objective Dragon.

B. Friendly

(1) 1st Brigade: The 1st Brigade attacks, 042000 Oct. in zone to destroy enemy forces vic. Objectives Manchu (CS2148) and Crusader (CS2548).

(2) Mission of unit to our west: 3d (allied) BDE, main effort, de-

fends in the west to defeat 13 ID. 051000 Oct. attack to destroy enemy forces south of PL Datsun.

(3) Mission of unit to our east: 6th (allied) BDE defends in the east to defeat 7th TMD. 040900 Oct. attack to destroy enemy forces south of PL Datsun.

(4) Mission of unit to our rear: None

(5) Mission of supporting units: None

(6) Mission of reinforcing units: None

C. Attachments and Detachments

(1) Attachments: None

(2) Detachments: None

2. Mission: TF 2-72 attacks 030045 Oct. with Team Steel to link up with 1-12th Infantry Battalion (Light) vic. Objective Dragon (CS2246) and defend Objective Dragon until linkup with TF 2-72 (-) twenty-four hours later.

3. Execution

A. Concept of operation: Annex A (operation overlay)

(1) Commander's intent:

Purpose: Link up with 1-12th Infantry Battalion (Light) and defend with 1-12th vic. Objective Dragon (CS2246).

Method: Conduct company team–sized armored raid to penetrate enemy lines in zone (CS2140 to CS2640 to CS2048 to CS2648), moving rapidly and bypassing enemy forces as required to link up with 1-12th Infantry Battalion (Light).

End state: Team Steel, attached to 1-12th Infantry Battalion (Light) after completion of linkup, defends until TF 2-72 conducts linkup NLT 040045.

(2) Maneuver: Team Steel will plan, prepare, and execute a company attack in zone to link up with 1-12th Infantry Battalion. Upon linkup with the infantry, Team Steel is attached to 1-12th Infantry Battalion (Light). TF 2-72 will attack in zone to penetrate enemy defenses and move rapidly to secure the decisive ground vic. Objective Dragon.

B. Coordinating Instructions:

(1) PIR (priority intelligence requirements):

a. Location of chemical munitions and delivery systems.

b. Location of enemy defensive positions and obstacles along Routes 17 and 21.

c. Enemy tank battalion reserve location and movement to conduct CATK.

d. Enemy OPs in TF Zone on critical observation sites.

e. Crossing sites over Gang River.

f. Locate enemy RAG (regimental artillery group) and DAG (division artillery group).

g. Report bypass of all end units.

h. Loss of momentum or speed of movement.

i. Enemy use of chemical or biological weapons.

(2) MOPP (mission-oriented protective posture) Level 2 upon LD.

(3) Recognition signals.

Day: Near—orange air recognition panel

Far—green smoke

Night: Near—blue-filtered flashlight

Far—thermal tape in triangular shape

4. Service support: See Brigade SOP.

5. Command and signal

A. Command: Brigade commander will collocate with TF 2-72 TOC during Team Steel's attack.

B. Signal

(1) Current SOI in effect.

(2) Alternate or emergency signals.

a. Purple smoke—breach lane (initial marking, maintained as vehicles pass through)

b. VS-17 panel on antenna—litter urgent casualty

c. Red smoke—emergency medevac signal

(3) Retrans locations: CS210390

Acknowledge

Pickett

Col

OFFICIAL:
Ward
S3

DISTRIBUTION: A
Critical Events Time Line

Time	Action
020100 Oct	Brigade OPORD issue
030001 Oct	Intelligence update
030015 Oct	Artillery preparation on selected targets
030045 Oct	Team Steel LD. Artillery moves, shift fires to designated targets
030700 Oct	Arrive at Objective Dragon
030715 Oct	Transition to the defense
032000 Oct	TF 2-72 (-) attacks in zone
040045 Oct	TF 2-72 linkup with Team Steel

**Study the maps on the next two pages,
then go to Section 2.**

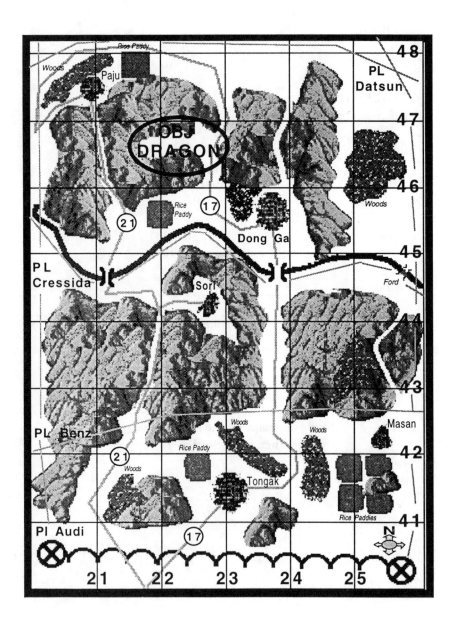

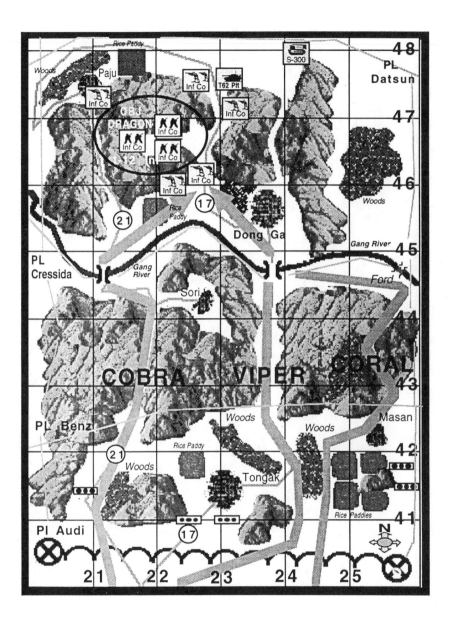

Appendix A

WEAPONS DATA

Weapon	M1A2 Tank	M2A2 Bradley
Weight (tons)	70	24
Height (inches)	118	118
Width (inches)	145	126
Length (inches)	387	258
Fuel (gallons)	505 (11.2 hr)	175 (9.7 hr)
Main gun/range	3,000 (120mm)	2,700 (25mm) (HEI-T)
Effective range	2,000m	2,000m
Crusing range	465kms	480kms
Main gun basic load	40 Rds	900 - 7 TOW
Armor type	Special	Normal
Crew	4	3 crewmen/6 infantrymen

Weapon	T-72 Tank	T-62 Tank	VTT-323
Weight (tons)	41	38	10
Height (inches)	91	94	75
Width (inches)	142	130	114
Length (inches)	363	366	213
Fuel (gallons)	263 (20 hr)	240 (18 hr)	129 (16 hr)
Main gun/range	2,400m (125mm)	1,600m (115mm)	2,000 (14.5mm)
Limited visibility range	800m	800m	800m
Crusing range	600kms	450kms	425kms
Main gun basic load	40 Rds	40 Rds	3 AT3 AT missiles
Armor type	Reactive	Normal	Normal-thin
Crew	3	4	4 crewmen 10 infantrymen

Maximum Effective Range of Weapons

Weapon	Range (meters)
M1A2 120mm cannon	3,000
M2HB .50-cal. MG	1,200–1,600
7.62mm co-ax MG	900
7.62mm loader MG	900
Smoke grenade launcher	30
Thermal sights (TIS)	2,000
M2 Bradley 25mm cannon	1,700 (APDS), 2,700 (HEI-T)
M2 Bradley TOW ATGM	65–3,750
7.62mm co-ax & 5.56mm M249 SAW MG	900
Javelin	65–2,000
AT-4 Carl Gustav 84mm	10–280
M16A2 rifle 5.56mm	300

Appendix B

The MIA2 Tank

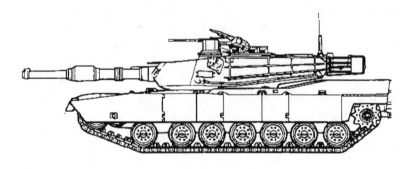

Weight: 69.54 tons
Turret Height: 93.5 inches
Length (gun forward): 387 inches
Width: 144 inches
Ground Clearance: 19 inches
Ground Pressure: 15.4 psi
Gas Turbine Engine: 1,500 HP
Speed: Max. 41 mph: cross-country, 30 mph; 10% slope, 16 mph; 60% slope, 3.9 mph
Acceleration (0–20 mph): 7.2 seconds
Main Armament: 120mm M256 smoothbore cannon
Coaxial Weapon: 7.62 M240 machine gun
Loader's Weapon: 7.62 M240 machine gun on skate mount
Commander's Weapon: .50-caliber M2 machine gun
Cruising Range: 270 miles
Fuel Capacity: 500 gallons
Vertical Obstacle: 42 inches
Trench Obstacle: 9 feet
NBC System: 200 SCFM clean cooled air
Crew: 4 men

The combination of effective protection and absolute lethality has been the soldier's dream since the dawn of warfare. Shields, chain mail, and suits of armor provided security against existing threats until improved weapons emerged to counter that armor. Above all, these new weapons had to enhance, not impede, the warriors' ability to fight. The longbow, the crossbow, and eventually gunpowder came forth, defeating once-impenetrable armor.

Leonardo Da Vinci, in the fifteenth century, provided the first concept of an armored vehicle: a device furnishing mobility in battle while enveloping the warrior in a protective shell.

It took more than four centuries for Da Vinci's concept to reach fruition. In 1915 the first British "tanks" appeared on the battlefields of France. These metal monsters, some weighing as much as thirty-four tons, with dual cannon, multiple machine guns, and a crew of eight men, brought a new dimension—firepower, shock, and maneuver—to the positional warfare of World War I. The combination of firepower, mobility, and protection led military leaders and theorists to rethink the strategies of warfare.

The Blitzkrieg of World War II suddenly, and with stunning success, thrust armored warfare to the forefront. The regrettable, lightning-fast conquests by the German Panzer Corps signaled a coming of age for the tank. Combined-arms forces, spearheaded by fast-moving tanks, became the dominant force on the battlefield.

As tank armor increased, the ability to penetrate it decreased. This technological clash between lethality and protection continued until a leap ahead in design occurred years after the war.

In 1979, the M1 Abrams series main battle tank was introduced, and a legend was born. This remarkable new weapon system, with its combination of speed and quickness, firepower, and advance armor, was the culmination of years of exhaustive research. The M1 could withstand a hit from any current antitank projectile, direct lethal firepower with pinpoint accuracy, and negotiate virtually any terrain with the quickness and agility of a vehicle a fraction its size. "Fightability" had now been elevated to new levels, another step closer to the warrior's dream—the ultimate fighting machine.

The legacy of armor continues today with the emergence of the M1A2 main battle tank, a weapon system offering dramatic improvements in system supportability, survivability, and fightability.

The M1A2 main battle tank is equipped with improved armor, increased lethality, high agility, and a low silhouette.

The armor protection of the M1A2 is superb. Experience from Operation Desert Storm and continued live-fire testing assures that armor protection is not an empty claim. Unlike all previous U.S. tanks, the M1 is built completely from armor plate (a sandwich of special Chobham armor and ceramic blocks, depleted-uranium mesh, and rolled homogenous armored plate) instead of a cast hull and turret. This armor protection, combined with outstanding quickness and mobility, nuclear-biological-chemical protection, automatic fire suppression, and ammunition compartmentalization, establishes the M1A2 as today's most formidable main battle tank. In addition, the M1A2 suite of advanced displays, controls, and survivability enhancements as well as the addition of data and power management systems elevates the fightability of the main battle tank to new levels.

The most innovative feature of the M1A2 system is the core vetronics system, which is to the close combat weapon system what avionics is to the jet fighter. Instead of separate, hard wiring components, all controls are lined through two electronic buses, one controlling power, the other data. In an integrated weapons system, all elements must be both tolerant and reliable, not only on their own but in concert with the system as a whole.

The M1A2's vetronic system not only improves combat operations through the integration of faster, more accurate target acquisition systems, it improves supportability through inherently reliable digital electronics and critical component redundancy. Integrated within the M1A2 are a number of exceptional subsystems that function together as a whole, enabling the soldier to perform much more effectively on the battlefield. In addition, the commander, gunner, and driver can analyze most problems through built-in testing embedded in the system.

One of the primary increases in combat effectiveness that the M1A2 offers is hunter-killer target acquisition. This capability is centered around a key M1A2 component, the commander's independent thermal viewer (CITV). The CITV enables the commander to view the entire battlefield, separate from the gunner, while still directing main gun firing. The hunter-killer capability provides the M1A2 main battle tank with a decisive advantage in the heat of close combat.

Because the M1A2 system is fully integrated, mutual position navigation on the battlefield is now a reality. Each commander is provided with position information on his tank, the tanks in his command network, and fixed enemy positions. This permits designated battlefield synchronization of all platoon and company assets.

The CITV image and position navigation information are depicted on the commander's integrated display. Position information can be instantaneously transmitted to other command elements through the SINCGARS radio system (single channel ground/air radio system). SINCGARS is a frequency-hopping radio system that is extremely difficult to jam or intercept.

Steer-to navigation data along with system status is transmitted to the driver through the driver's integrated display. This unit combines the operation of three panels into one line-replaceable unit.

The tank commander's view of the battlefield is enhanced through an entirely redesigned tank commander's weapon station (TCWS). The improved TCWS offers the tank commander a dramatic increase of his field of view.

The M1A2's primary sight employs a dual-axis stabilized head, enabling the gunner to effectively track evasive ground and air targets. Algorithms in the core system calculate target motion and permit the gunner to engage and destroy evasive targets.

The gunner's control and display panel has automated ballistic solutions of both ground and air targets. It also has the capability to accommodate smart munitions that are currently under development.

Today, fightability is the culmination of the weapon system's ability to help the soldier make the most effective, best-informed decision in the least amount of time. The performance of the M1A2 tanks, and the tankers that crew them, have defined that term.

Glossary

Agility: Mental and organizational ability to act faster than the enemy. Agility is as much a mental as a physical quality.

Alternate Position: Position given to a weapon, a unit, or an individual to be occupied when the primary position becomes untenable or unsuitable for carrying out its task. The alternate position is located so that the individual can continue to fulfill his original task.

AN/PVS-7 Night Vision Goggles: Lightweight, battery-powered, passive night vision device that allows the operator to see in low light (moonlight) levels. The goggles weigh 1.5 pounds and offer clear vision under normal after-dark conditions out to 150 meters.

Assembly Area: Area in which a force prepares or regroups for further action.

Attack: Offensive action characterized by movement supported by fire.

    Deliberate Attack: Attack planned and carefully coordinated with all concerned elements based on thorough reconnaissance, evaluation of all available intelligence and relative combat strength, analysis of various courses of action, and other factors affecting the situation. It generally is conducted against a well-organized defense when a hasty attack is not possible or has failed.

    Frontal Attack: Offensive maneuver in which the main action is directed against the front of the enemy forces and over the most direct approaches.

    Hasty Attack: Offensive operation for which a unit has not made extensive preparations. It is conducted with the resources immediately available in order to maintain momentum or to take advantage of the enemy situation.

    Main Attack: Principal attack or effort into which the commander places the bulk of the offensive capability at his disposal. An attack directed against the chief objective of the battle.

    Supporting Attack: Attack designed to hold the enemy in position, to deceive him as to where the main attack is being made, to prevent him from reinforcing the elements opposing the main ef-

Glossary

fort, and/or to cause him to commit his reserves prematurely at an indecisive location.

Attrition (Attrit): Reduction of the effectiveness of a force caused by the loss of personnel or materiel.

Avenue of Approach: Air or ground route of an attacking force of a given size leading to its objective or to key terrain in its path.

Axis of Advance: General route of advance, assigned for the purposes of control, which extends toward the enemy. An axis of advance symbol graphically portrays a commander's intention, such as avoidance of built-up areas or envelopment of an enemy force. It follows terrain for the size of the force assigned to the axis. A commander may maneuver his forces and supporting fires to either side of an axis of advance provided that the unit remains oriented on the axis and the objective.

Base of Fire: Fire placed on an enemy force or position to reduce or eliminate the enemy's capability to interfere by fire and/or movement of friendly maneuver elements. It may be provided by a single weapon or a grouping of weapon systems.

Block: To deny the enemy access to a given area or prevent enemy advance in a given direction. It may be for a specified time. Units may have to retain terrain and accept decisive engagement.

BMNT (Before Morning Nautical Twilight): Time between night and sunrise when there is sufficient light to navigate without night vision devices.

BMP: Russian-made infantry fighting vehicle armed with a 73mm cannon, a 7.62mm machine gun, and an AT-3, AT-4, or AT-5 anti-tank missile launcher.

BP (Battle Position): Defensive location oriented on the most likely enemy avenue of approach from which a unit may defend or attack. Such units can be as large as battalion task forces and as small as platoons. A unit assigned a BP is located within the general outline of the BP.

BRDM: Russian-designed armored car used for reconnaissance and command and control. It is usually armed with a 14.5mm machine gun.

Buttoned Up: When all protective hatches on a tank or an armored personnel carrier are closed.

Canalize: To restrict operations to a narrow zone by using existing or reinforcing obstacles that may interfere with subsequent operations.

CAS (Close Air Support): Air action against hostile targets that are in close proximity to friendly forces; this action requires detailed integration of each air mission with the fire and movement of those forces.

Checkpoint: Predetermined point on the ground used as a means of coordinating friendly movement. Checkpoints are not used as reference points in reporting enemy locations.

CITV: Commander's independent thermal viewer.

Clear: To destroy or force the withdrawal of all enemy forces and reduce any obstacles that may interfere with subsequent operations.

Coax: Machine gun mounted in the turret of a tank in a way that its line of fire is parallel (coaxial) to that of the cannon set on the same mounting. In the M1A1, an M240 7.62mm machine gun is mounted coaxially with the M256 120mm cannon. The co-ax is fired by either the tank gunner (primary) or tank commander (alternate). The co-ax is fed by a bin that contains 2,300 rounds of 7.62mm ammunition.

Coil: Arrangement of vehicles forming a circle.

Combat Multiplier: Supporting and subsidiary means that significantly increase the relative combat strength of a force while actual force ratios remain constant. Examples of combat multipliers are economizing in one area to mass in another, surprise, deception, camouflage, electronic warfare, psychological operations, and terrain reinforcement.

Commander's Guidance: Commander's tool to direct the planning process. It should consist of six elements: the restated mission, the initial concept of the operation, the scheme of maneuver, the time plan, the type of order to be prepared, and the rehearsal technique.

Commander's Intent: Commander's stated vision of the battle, which defines the purpose; the end state with respect to the relationship among the force, the enemy, and the terrain; and how the end state will be achieved by the force as a whole. The commander's intent can be explained in terms of the mission's object, reason, and importance.

Glossary

The object is the purpose of the action. The reason is the end state with respect to the relationship among the force, the enemy, and the terrain. The importance explains how the end state will be achieved by the force as a whole and how far to go to achieve that end state in terms of combat power.

The acid test of understanding the commander's intent is for the subordinate to act in concert with the commander's desires in a situation in which the circumstances are different from those foreseen at the time that the plan was issued and when the commander cannot be reached for a decision.

Company Team: Team formed by attachment of one or more nonorganic tank, mechanized infantry, or light infantry platoons to a tank, mechanized infantry, or light infantry company either in exchange for or in addition to organic platoons.

Concept of Operations: Graphic, verbal, or written statement in broad outline that gives an overall picture of a commander's assumptions or intent in regard to an operation or series of operations. It includes at a minimum the scheme of maneuver and the fire support plan, described in sufficient detail for the staff and subordinate commanders to understand what they are to do and how to fight the battle without further instructions.

Contain: To stop, hold, or surround the forces of the enemy or to cause the enemy to center activity on a given front and to prevent his withdrawing any part of his forces for use elsewhere.

Coordinating Point: Control measure that indicates a specific location for the coordination of fires and maneuver between adjacent units. Coordinating points are usually indicated whenever a boundary crosses the forward edge of the battle area (FEBA) and may be indicated when a boundary crosses phase lines (PLs) used to control security forces. In NATO, physical contact between adjacent units is required.

Counterattack: Attack by a part or all of a defending force against an enemy attacking force, for such specific purposes as regaining ground lost or cutting off or destroying enemy advance units, and with the general objective of regaining the initiative and denying to the enemy the attainment of his purpose in attacking. In sustained defensive operations, counterattack is undertaken to restore the battle position (BP) and is directed at limited objectives.

360

Cover: Natural or artificial protection from enemy observation.

Covered Approach: (1.) Any route that offers protection against enemy observation or fire. (2.) An approach made under the protection furnished by other forces or by natural cover.

Cross Attachment: Exchange of subordinate units between units for a temporary period; for example, a tank battalion detaches a tank company that is subsequently attached to a mechanized infantry battalion, and the mechanized infantry battalion detaches a mechanized company that is then attached to the tank battalion.

CVC Helmet: Crew vehicular communications helmet. Each CVC helmet has a microphone and earphones to allow intercom and radio communications. Vehicle crew members wear the CVC helmet on the vehicle to communicate with other crew members and to talk over the radio.

Dead Space: Area within the maximum effective range of a weapon, a surveillance device, or an observer that cannot be covered by fire and observation from a given position because of intervening obstacles, the nature of the ground, the characteristics of the trajectory, or the limitations of the pointing capabilities of the systems.

Decisive Engagement: Engagement in which a unit is considered fully committed and cannot maneuver or extricate itself. In the absence of outside assistance, the action must be fought to a conclusion and either won or lost with the forces at hand.

Decisive Terrain: Key terrain is decisive terrain if it has an extraordinary impact on the mission. Decisive terrain is rare and will not be present in every mission. To designate terrain as decisive is to recognize that the successful accomplishment of the mission, whether offensive or defensive, depends on seizing or retaining the terrain. The commander designates decisive terrain to communicate its importance in his concept of operations, first to his staff and later to subordinate commanders.

Defilade: Protection from hostile observation and fire provided by an obstacle such as a hill, ridge, or bank. To shield from enemy fire or observation by using natural or artificial obstacles.

Defile: Narrow passage that tends to constrict the movement of troops.

Delay: To trade space for time, inflict maximum damage on the enemy force, and preserve the force within the limits established by the issuing commander.

Depth: Extension of operations in space, time, and resources.

Destroy: To physically disable or capture an enemy force.

Direct Fire: Fire directed at a target that is visible to the gunner or firing unit.

Direction of Attack: Specific direction or route that the main attack or the main body of the force will follow. If used, it is normally at battalion and lower levels. Direction of attack is a more restrictive control measure than axis of advance, and units are not free to maneuver off the assigned route. Direction of attack is usually associated with infantry units conducting night attacks, or units involved in limited visibility operations, and in counterattacks. (In NATO, referred to as an attack route.)

Direction of Fire: Direction on which a cannon or missile is laid. It represents the direction to the most significant threat in the target area.

Displace: To leave one position and take another. Forces may be displaced laterally to concentrate combat power in threatened areas.

Dominant Terrain: Terrain that, because of its elevation, proportions, or location, commands a view of and may offer fields of fire over surrounding terrain.

DPICM (Dual Purpose Improved Conventional Munitions): Artillery shells that contain submunitions (bomblets) that can damage armored vehicles and devastate unprotected troops.

Economy of Force: Allocation of minimum essential combat capability or strength to secondary efforts, so that forces may be concentrated in the area where a decision is sought. A principle of war.

Engagement Area: Area in which the commander intends to trap and destroy an enemy force with the massed fire of all available weapons. Engagement areas are routinely identified by a target reference point in the center of the trap area or by prominent terrain features around the area. Although engagement areas may also be divided into sectors of fire, it is important to understand that defensive systems are not designed around engagement areas but rather around avenues of approach. Engagement areas and sectors of fire are not intended to restrict fires or cause operations to become static or fixed; they are used only as a tool to concentrate fires and to optimize their effects.

ETAC: Enlisted tactical air control team. In an armored task force, the ETAC consists of two air force personnel, usually sergeants, who operate out of a M113A2 APC equipped with both FM and high-frequency (HF) radios. The mission of the ETAC is to control close air support for the task force.

FASCAM (Field Artillery Scatterable Minefield): Scatterable minefield, composed of antitank or antipersonnel mines, delivered by artillery.

FEBA (Forward Edge of the Battle Area): Forward limit of the main battle area (MBA). Used in defense.

Field of Fire: Area that a weapon or a group of weapons may effectively cover with fire from a given location.

Fire and Movement: Simultaneous moving and firing by men and/or vehicles. This technique is used primarily during the assault of enemy positions.

Fire Support Plan: Plan on how fire support will be used in an operation. It should include a portion for each means of fire support involved.

FIST (Fire Support Team): In fire support operations, a team made up of a team chief (field artillery lieutenant) and the necessary additional personnel and equipment required to plan, request, coordinate, and direct fire support efforts for company-sized units.

Fix: Actions taken to prevent the enemy from moving any part of his forces from a specific location within a specific period of time by holding or surrounding them to prevent their withdrawal for use elsewhere.

FRAGO (Fragmentary Order): Abbreviated form of an operation order (OPORD) used to communicate mission changes to units and to inform them of changes in the tactical situation.

Front: Lateral space occupied by an element measured from the extremity of one flank to the extremity of the other flank. The unit may be extended in a combat formation or occupying a position, depending on the type of operation involved.

Frontage: Width of the front plus that distance beyond the flanks covered by observation and fire by a unit in combat.

Gap: Any break or breach in the continuity of tactical dispositions or formations beyond effective small-arms coverage. A weak spot in the enemy's defenses.

GLD (Ground Laser Designator): Handheld device that paints targets with invisible laser light to direct laser-guided munitions with pinpoint accuracy.

GPS Extension: Gunner's primary sight extension.

Grid Coordinates: Set of numbers designating the location of a point in respect to a grid. The first two letters represent grid area references to the correct map sheet. The numbered coordinates are expressed to the nearest 100, 10, or 1 meter in a single expression. Example: CS329378 (nearest 100 meters); CS32943785 (nearest 10 meters), or CS3294837853 (nearest 1 meter). Grid coordinates always consist of pairs of number groups: CS3945, for instance, is read 39 grid line to the right and 45 grid line up. Grid coordinates on a map are always read right, then up.

HMMWV (Highly Mobile Multipurpose Wheeled Vehicle): Acronym for the three-quarter-ton truck. Also known as a Hummer or Humvee.

IPB (Intelligence Preparation of the Battlefield): Systematic approach to analyzing the enemy, weather, and terrain in a specific geographical area. It integrates enemy doctrine with the weather and terrain as they relate to the mission and the specific battlefield environment. This is done to determine and evaluate enemy capabilities, vulnerabilities, and probable courses of action.

Initiative: Setting or changing the terms of battle by action. Initiative implies an offensive spirit in the conduct of all operations.

Interdict: To prevent or hinder by any means the enemy's use of any area or route.

Key Terrain: Any locality or area the seizure, retention, or control of which affords a marked advantage to either combatant.

LC (Line of Contact): General trace delineating the location where two opposing forces are engaged.

LD (Line of Departure): Line designated to coordinate the commitment of attacking units or scouting elements at a specified time. A start line.

LD/LC (Line of Departure is Line of Contact): Designation of forward friendly positions as the LD when opposing forces are in contact.

Limit of Advance: Easily recognized terrain feature beyond which attacking elements will not advance.

LZ: Landing zone.

Maneuver: Movement of forces supported by fire to achieve a position of advantage from which to destroy or threaten destruction of the enemy. A principle of war.

Mass: (1.) Concentration of combat power at the decisive time and place. A principle of war. (2.) To concentrate or bring together fires so as to mass fires of multiple weapons or units. (3.) Military formation in which units are spaced at less than normal distances and intervals.

METT-T (Mission, Enemy, Terrain, Troops, and Time available): Acronym used to describe the factors that must be considered during the planning and execution of a tactical operation. Example considerations are:

Mission: The who, what, when, where, and why of what is to be accomplished.

Enemy: Current information concerning the enemy's strength, location, disposition, activity, equipment, capability, and a determination as to his probable course of action.

Terrain (includes weather): Analysis of information about vegetation, soil type, hydrology, climatic conditions, and light data to determine their impact on current and future operations for both enemy and friendly operations.

Troops: Quantity, level of training, and psychological state of friendly forces, to include the availability of weapons systems and critical equipment.

Time available: Time available to plan, prepare, and execute operations for both enemy and friendly forces.

Minefield: Area of ground containing mines laid with or without a pattern.

MRLS (Multiple Rocket Launcher System): American multiple rocket launcher that is built on an M2 Bradley chassis. The MRLS carries twelve rockets per vehicle that can hit targets 30 kilometers away. The rockets carry DPICM (dual purpose improved conventional munitions) warheads. When the rockets detonate over their targets, the warheads explode and scatter hundreds of bomblets over a 700- by 100-meter area.

Neutralize: To render ineffective or unusable (Joint Chiefs of Staff Publication 1).

Objective: (1.) Physical object of the action taken (for example, a definite terrain feature, the seizure and/or holding of which is essential to the commander's plan, or the destruction of an enemy force without regard to terrain features). (2.) Principle of war that states that every military operation should be directed toward clearly defined, decisive, and attainable objectives.

Offense: Combat operation designed primarily to destroy the enemy. Offensive operations may be undertaken to secure key or decisive terrain, to deprive the enemy of resources or decisive terrain, to deceive and/or divert the enemy, to develop intelligence, and to hold the enemy in position. Offensive operations include deliberate attack, hasty attack, movement to contact, exploitation, pursuit, and other limited-objective operations. The offensive is undertaken to seize, retain, and exploit the initiative; as such, it is a principle of war.

Open-Protected Position (M1A2 Tank Commander's Hatch): Semi-open position of a tank commander's hatch that offers a seven-inch gap between the top of the hatch and the top of the turret. In this position the hatch protects the tank commander from objects falling from the top and allows him to see through the gap. Because the tank commander must help direct the driver when the tank is moving, the tank commander's ability to see the immediate area is critical. The open-protected position is the preferred position when enemy artillery or mortar fire is likely. When the tank commander is completely buttoned up, his vision is restricted to the narrow field of view offered by the periscopes that ring the tank commander's station.

Operation Overlay: Overlay showing the location, size, and scheme of maneuver/fires of friendly forces involved in an operation. As an exception, it may indicate predicted movements and locations of enemy forces.

OPORD (Operation Order): Directive issued by a commander to subordinate commanders for effecting the coordinated execution of an operation. Includes tactical movement orders.

Orders Group: Standing group of key personnel requested to be present when a commander at any level issues his concept of the operation and his order.

Overwatch: (1.) Tactical technique in which one element is positioned to support the movement of another element with immediate direct fire. (2.) Tactical role of an element positioned to support the movement of another element with immediate direct fire.

Passage of Lines: Passing one unit through the positions of another, as when elements of covering forces withdraw through the forward edge of the main battle area, or when an exploiting force moves through the elements of the force that conducted the initial attack. A passage may be designated as a forward or rearward passage of lines.

PL (Phase Line): Line used for control and coordination of military operations. It is usually a recognizable terrain feature extending across the zone of action. Units normally report crossing PLs but do not halt unless specifically directed. PLs often are used to prescribe the timing of delay operations.

Primary Position: Place for a weapon, a unit, or an individual to fight; it provides the best means to accomplish the assigned mission.

Priority of Fires: Direction to a fire support planner to organize and employ fire support means according to the importance of the supported unit's missions.

Priority Target: Target on which the delivery of fires takes precedence over all other fires for the designated firing unit/element. The firing unit/element will prepare, to the extent possible, for the engagement of such targets. A firing unit/element may be assigned only one priority target.

Retain: To occupy and hold a terrain feature to ensure that it is free of enemy occupation or use.

Reverse Slope: Position on the ground not exposed to direct fire or observation. It may be a slope that descends away from the enemy.

Reverse Slope Defense: Defense area organized on any ground not exposed to direct fire or observation. It may be on a slope that descends away from the enemy.

Glossary

RPG (Rocket-Propelled Grenade): Russian-designed, shoulder-fired antitank weapon. The RPG can destroy most APCs. It can penetrate an M1A1 tank only if the warhead strikes the rear of the tank or the track.

Sector: Area designated by boundaries within which a unit operates and for which it is responsible. Normally, sectors are used in defensive operations.

Secure: To gain possession of a position or terrain feature with or without force, and to deploy in a manner that prevents its destruction or loss to enemy action.

Seize: To gain physical possession of a terrain feature from an enemy force.

SOI (Signal Operating Instructions): Pamphlet issued by each unit that contains codes and frequencies for radio operations.

SP (Start Point): Clearly defined initial control point on a route at which specified elements of a column of ground vehicles or a flight of aircraft come under the control of the commander having responsibility for the movement.

Strongpoint: Key point in a defensive position, usually strongly fortified and heavily armed with automatic weapons, around which other positions are grouped for its protection.

Support Force: Units charged with providing intense direct overwatching fires to the assault force.

Suppression: Direct and indirect fires, electronic countermeasures (ECM), or smoke brought to bear on enemy personnel, weapons, or equipment to prevent effective fire on friendly forces.

Synchronization: Arrangement of battlefield activities in time, space, and purpose to produce maximum relative combat power at the decisive point. Synchronization is both a process and a result. It need not depend on explicit coordination if all forces involved fully understand the commander's intent and have developed and rehearsed well-conceived standard responses to anticipated contingencies.

TAC (Tactical Command Post): In an armored task force the TAC is usually represented by an M113A2 APC mounted with at least three FM radios.

Target Overlay: Overlay showing the locations of friendly artillery units, targets, boundaries, and fire support coordination measures.

Task Organization: Temporary grouping of forces designed to accomplish a particular mission. Task organization involves the distribution of available assets to subordinate control headquarters by attachment or by placing assets in direct support (DS) or under the operational control of the subordinate.

TC: Tank commander.

Terrain Analysis: Process of interpreting a geographical area to determine the effect of the natural and man-made features on military operations.

TOC (Tactical Operations Center): Element within the main command post (CP) consisting of those staff activities involved in sustaining current operations and in planning future operations. Staff activities are functionally grouped into elements or cells. Units at battalion level and above normally have a TOC.

Turret-Down: Position in which an entire vehicle is behind cover, but the commander can still observe to the front from the turret hatch or cupola.

T-55: Russian-made main battle tank that has a 100mm tank cannon.

T-62: Russian-made main battle tank that has a 115mm tank cannon.

T-72: Russian-made main battle tank that has improved armor protection, improved mobility, and improved firepower over the T-55 and T-62 tanks. The three-man-crewed T-72 (driver, gunner, and tank commander) has an automatic loader and a lethal 125mm cannon.

UAV: Unmanned air vehicle. A small robot plane with a sophisticated suite of cameras and sensors used for targeting and reconnaissance.

Vee: Arrangement of vehicles or personnel in the shape of a *V* with two elements up front to provide a heavy volume of fire on contact and one element in the rear to overwatch or maneuver. Also, the point of the *V* as the trail element. A *V* formation may be used when the leader requires firepower to the front and flanks.

VT (Pronounced Vee Tee): Variable time fuse for artillery shells that produces an airburst that showers the ground with fragments.

VTT-323: Armored personnel carrier used primarily by North Korea. The VTT-323 is a licensed copy of the Chinese YW 531 APC. This APC carries between four and ten infantrymen. It is armed with a 14.5mm machine gun in its turret and an AT-3 Sagger antitank missile or an AT-4 Spandrel antitank missile. The VTT is lightly armored; it has five road wheels and a small conical turret.

Glossary

Warning Order: Preliminary notice of an action or order that is to follow. Usually issued as a brief oral or written message, it is designed to give subordinates time to make necessary plans and preparations.

Wedge: Formation of vehicles or personnel with one element leading and two elements in the rear to overwatch or maneuver. It permits excellent fire to the front and good fire to each flank; facilitates control; permits sustained effort and provides flank security; lends itself readily to fire and movement; and is often used when the enemy situation is vague and contact is imminent.

Withdrawal: Retrograde operation in which a force in contact with the enemy frees itself for a new mission.

Zone: Area of responsibility for offensive operations assigned to a unit by the drawing of boundaries.